# Robert Altman and the Elaboration of Hollywood Storytelling

# Robert Altman and the Elaboration of Hollywood Storytelling

Mark Minett

OXFORD
UNIVERSITY PRESS

# OXFORD
## UNIVERSITY PRESS

Oxford University Press is a department of the University of Oxford. It furthers the University's objective of excellence in research, scholarship, and education by publishing worldwide. Oxford is a registered trade mark of Oxford University Press in the UK and certain other countries.

Published in the United States of America by Oxford University Press
198 Madison Avenue, New York, NY 10016, United States of America.

Library of Congress Cataloging-in-Publication Data
Names: Minett, Mark, author.
Title: Robert Altman and the elaboration of Hollywood
storytelling / Mark Minett.
Description: New York : Oxford University Press, [2021] |
Includes bibliographical references and index.
Identifiers: LCCN 2020018119 (print) | LCCN 2020018120 (ebook) |
ISBN 9780197523827 (hardback) | ISBN 9780197523834 (paperback) |
ISBN 9780197523858 (epub)
Subjects: LCSH: Altman, Robert, 1925–2006—Criticism and interpretation.
Classification: LCC PN1998.3.A48 M56 2021 (print) |
LCC PN1998.3.A48 (ebook) | DDC 791.4302/33092 [B]—dc23
LC record available at https://lccn.loc.gov/2020018119
LC ebook record available at https://lccn.loc.gov/2020018120

1 3 5 7 9 8 6 4 2

Paperback printed by LSC Communications, United States of America
Hardback printed by Bridgeport National Bindery, Inc., United States of America

# Contents

# Acknowledgments

At times, the path to the completion of this book has seemed long and meandering, replete with ultimately pointless digressions. I would compare it to an Altman film, but that would give you the wrong impression about Altman. Along my way, I have had the tremendous good fortune to be aided by a sprawling cast larger and arguably more colorful than that of *Nashville*.

At Oberlin College, I benefited from the encouragement of William Patrick Day, the late Daniel Goulding, John Hobbs, and Mike Reynolds. Their kindness and patience allowed me to believe I might have a place in academia. As a graduate student, I was supremely lucky to find myself in the University of Wisconsin–Madison's Film Studies program, where my advisor, Jeff Smith, provided a model of scholarship and mentoring that I can only aspire to. I am indebted to the entire Film Studies faculty—Ben Brewster, Kelley Conway, Lea Jacobs, Vance Kepley, JJ Murphy, and Ben Singer—for training me as a thinker, scholar, and teacher. Thanks are due to UW's Media and Cultural Studies faculty—Michelle Hilmes, who oversaw my initial work on Altman's television career, Michael Curtin, and Julie D'Acci—for broadening my perspective on and deepening my understanding of media studies. I owe a profound debt to David Bordwell and Kristin Thompson, whose scholarship, personal and professional generosity, and passion have shaped and enabled my trajectory as a scholar.

I am also grateful for the community of colleagues and friends I found in Madison. Maria Belodubrovskaya, Colin Burnett, Casey Coleman, John Powers, Dave Resha, Brad Schauer, and Jake Smith have been faithful and trusted allies and advisors. Vincent Bohlinger, Andrea Comiskey, Eric Crosby, Kait Fyfe, Jonah Horwitz, Pearl Latteier, Charlie Michael, Katherine Spring, Tom Yoshikami, and the late Rebecca Swender provided much-appreciated and much-needed support. Comm Arts staffers Linda Henzl, Linda Lucey, Sandy Rizzo, and Mary Rossa indulged my difficulty with forms, processes, and deadlines, and allowed me to succeed.

This manuscript would have been impossible to produce without access to the archival resources at the Wisconsin Center for Film and Theater Research and the University of Michigan's Altman Archive. I would like to thank Maxine Ducey, Dorinda Hartmann, Emil Hoelter, and Mary Huelsbeck for their generosity and assistance. At the University of Michigan, Peggy Daub,

Kate Hutchens, and Philip Hallman went out of their way to ensure my visits to Ann Arbor were productive. I could not have asked for a better research experience. Many thanks to Jim Healy, for giving me the opportunity to meet with several of Altman's most important collaborators. Stephen Altman and the late Kathryn Reed Altman went out of their way to offer their support for this project. Michael Murphy, Keith Carradine, and Matthew Seig kindly shared their valuable time, knowledge, and experience.

I am very fortunate to have found a place at the University of South Carolina. I owe a special thanks to my colleagues Mark Cooper and Susan Courtney for their selfless mentoring and robust feedback, and I am indebted to the faculty of the Film and Media Studies Program—Heidi Cooley, Sue Felleman, Julie Hubbert, Laura Kissel, Evren Ozselcuk, Lauren Steimer, and Kelly Wolf—for their friendship and support. The Department of English has proven to be a lovely home for my research and teaching. Nina Levine, Sam Amadon, Liz Countryman, Eli Jelly-Schapiro, Qiana Whitted, Hannah Rule, and Kevin Brock deserve particular thanks for their assistance and indulgence. I am also grateful for grants from the Office of the Provost and the College of Arts & Sciences that aided in the completion of this book. Finally, I am incredibly grateful to my editor at Oxford University Press, Norman Hirschy, and assistant editor Lauralee Yeary for their confidence and guidance and to the two anonymous readers who offered invaluable feedback.

My father, William Minett, fostered my love of film and supported me without reservation. Thank you. Heather Heckman has been the wise and highly competent Miller to my mumbling McCabe. She's helped me with my figures, improved my operations, and been a much better partner than I deserve. This book is dedicated to my late mother, Sandra Minett, and to two Jo's—my late grandmother, Jo Hawkins, and my daughter, Jo Heckman Minett—for inspiring me.

# About the Companion Website

ww.oup.com/us/robertaltmanhollywoodstorytelling

Oxford has created a website to accompany *Robert Altman and the Elaboration of Hollywood Storytelling*. Materials that cannot be made available in a book, namely illustrative video clips, are provided here. The reader is encouraged to consult this resource in conjunction with each chapter. Examples available online are indicated in the text with Oxford's symbol ⊚.

# Introduction

Robert Altman's death in 2006 brought an end to a remarkable filmmaking journey that spanned six decades. Several months prior, he received an honorary award from the Academy of Motion Picture Arts and Sciences. Altman had been nominated for best director five times by the Academy, first for *M*A*S*H* in 1970 and finally for the 2001 film *Gosford Park*. He had, though, never won, a fact that would seem to confirm his status as a maverick—both part of and apart from Hollywood. The academy's announcement of the award framed it as a "recognition of a career that has repeatedly reinvented the art form and inspired filmmakers and audiences alike."[1] Anodyne as it may seem, this plaudit suggests an important perspective frequently absent from the extant critical literature on the filmmaker. The dominant critical position presents Altman's oeuvre as rejection, a modernist movement away from Hollywood practice and toward a democratization of the screen, upending the inherently conservative ideological work of Hollywood storytelling.[2] A minority position, less concerned with Altman per se than with the Hollywood mode of filmmaking within which he worked, proposes that Altman, along with his Hollywood Renaissance peers, assimilated art cinema techniques, harnessing the innovations of European auteurs, but doing so largely in service to the standard aims of the Hollywood cinema.[3]

Both positions, though to different extents, overstate the stakes and underestimate Hollywood's capacity for meaningfully accommodating innovation. Both accounts, furthermore, misapprehend Altman's formal strategies and, to varying degrees, fail to consider what the Academy acknowledges—that Altman's long career involved repeated reinvention. Altman did not reject Hollywood. This is a plot that is best understood as serving the purposes of the auteurism industry, which thrives on career-encompassing accounts focused on uncovering a filmmaker's core expressive preoccupations and assessing the ideological implications of any novel uses of cinematic form. Altman's work, though, is also not wholly assimilable to classical Hollywood. He did not tell the same old stories in the same ways for the same old purposes, simply adding an arty gloss appropriated from European art cinema.

*Robert Altman and the Elaboration of Hollywood Storytelling.* Mark Minett, Oxford University Press (2021).
© Oxford University Press. DOI: 10.1093/oso/9780197523827.001.0001.

In contrast to sweeping generalizations, this book aims to describe the filmmaker's day job, that is, the concrete and contingent configurations and modulations of aims and strategies that characterize filmmaking practice, both within and across films. In doing so, it reveals an Altman barely glimpsed in previous critical accounts. This re-examination of his seminal work during the Hollywood Renaissance period of the early 1970s sheds new light on both the films and the filmmaker, reframing Altman as a complex, pragmatic innovator whose work exceeds, but is also grounded in, the norms of Hollywood storytelling. His films of the early 1970s display a classical-plus relationship with Hollywood tradition, in which Altman works within and from key Hollywood storytelling norms while elaborating on and around them in order to also fulfill extraclassical or nonclassical aims. Additionally, Altman's aims were not just or even primarily product-oriented. That is, he was not exclusively focused on producing perfectly polished Hollywood films, or even refined embodiments of his cinematic philosophy and overarching worldview. Instead, his objectives were significantly practice-oriented. Altman was focused on achieving and sustaining a particular kind of filmmaking experience that might provide greater opportunities for creative encounters with circumstance.

The approach presented here holds significant implications for the study of cinematic authorship and of Hollywood's formal norms, calling into question long-standing assumptions about the subjects and methodology of auteurist criticism and the nature and dynamics of the Hollywood cinema. Displacing the ahistorical thematic exegesis and impressionistic misdescription that have dominated accounts of Altman's films, this book strives to employ rigorous description, robust analytic frameworks, archival research, and, in places, statistical methods to demystify what are widely agreed to be the defining aspects of Altman's filmmaking. This book's findings require that we rethink the supposition that "Hollywood" names a cramped and rigid set of norms that Altman defied in the spirit of politically modernist art cinema. In demonstrating that this opposition has been overdrawn, the book provides a clear example of how a filmmaker might work collaboratively and pragmatically within media institutions to elaborate and expand on their sanctioned practices and aims. We misunderstand Altman's work, and the creative work of Hollywood filmmakers in general, when we insist on describing innovation as opposition to institutional norms. We do the same when we describe those norms as assimilating Altman's innovations instead of acknowledging the more complex range of possible relationships between filmmaking aims and strategies and institutional constraints and opportunities.

In many ways, the imperative to manufacture a comprehensive study of a filmmaking career works against comprehension of filmmaking complexity. To insist on that complexity, this study takes a historically bounded approach, focusing on an iconic six-year and eight-film period ranging from *M\*A\*S\*H* (1970) to *Nashville* (1975). This period has been deemed essential to understanding both the Hollywood Renaissance as a broader movement and Altman's overall authorial profile. A careful reexamination and recharacterization of Altman's body of work in this crucial period provides a critical perspective on assertions about Altman's career both before and after. Such a reexamination also suggests a new model for understanding innovative filmmaking within and across institutions.

Reframing Altman as an elaborative filmmaker revitalizing Hollywood cinema, this book's chapters isolate for analysis the aspects of his authorial profile typically held to define his work and to defy mainstream norms. In each case, careful reexamination discovers Altman to be working situationally to expand the customary aims and capacities of Hollywood style by desanctifying some of its mustier standards and practices. His films' alleged narrative lack, for instance, turns out to be a perversely efficient approach to conventional Hollywood storytelling that integrates and alters rather than assimilates or approximates aspects of art cinema narration. In mathematical terms, Altman's narrative approach is additive rather than subtractive or simply equivalent to Hollywood's standard storytelling. Likewise, the subliminal, wandering zooms that supposedly characterize Altman's films during this period prove to be critical mirages. Altman's actual practice is dominated by highly intentional and narratively significant, though also frequently ornamental, uses of the zoom. Similarly, Altman's novel employment of overlapping dialogue is not designed in service to either liberatory or democratic chaos. Rather, Altman and his collaborators' development of this technique consists of technological innovation driven by an elaborative logic: the multiplication of recording tracks expanded the domain of sound design and encouraged more meticulous audio hierarchies rather than more democratic, unplanned uses of sounds. The standard assumptions of expansive on-set improvisation and willful rejection of the screenplay are tested against the archival record to demonstrate that Altman's actual practice involved strategic elaboration. The book's capstone chapter makes use of the redrawn "Early Altman" established in the previous chapters to upend critical deployments of "Earlier Altman's" time in industrial filmmaking and filmed television. These media forms have frequently been mischaracterized, most often via a reduction to simple training grounds that Altman suffered or subverted before escaping, or graduating, into the unfettered auteurism of the Hollywood

Renaissance. By carefully establishing institutional contexts and re-examining key works in light of the book's revised account of Altman's later practices, the chapter both illuminates significant continuities of practice and reframes Hollywood's regularly denigrated media siblings as complex creative venues worthy of careful study.

## Rejection, Assimilation, and Elaboration

Unlike the majority of book-length work on Altman, then, this is not an "authorship study" in the traditional sense of grand-scale thematic exegesis and ideological assessment.[4] Instead, it is best understood as aligned with what Stephen Crofts has termed the "author in production institutions" mode of historical authorship study. This mode is most prominently represented by the work of Kristin Thompson and David Bordwell in, for instance, Thompson's *Herr Lubitsch Goes to Hollywood*, and Bordwell's book-length studies of Ozu, Dreyer, and Eisenstein.[5] As Crofts describes it, under this model, the filmmaker is understood as having "of necessity to work within existing industrial and institutional frameworks and dominant aesthetic conventions."[6] Such an approach is particularly pertinent given the core question of this book—how are we to understand the formal design of Robert Altman's work in the context of the early 1970s Hollywood Renaissance period's contested relationship with the frameworks and conventions provided by Hollywood storytelling practice?[7] Answering that question requires a reconsideration of the boundaries of and the creative possibilities within institutions such as Hollywood.

Because my focus is on Altman's approach to storytelling rather than, say, the interdependent but profitably separable question of how Altman negotiated the budgeting and financing of his films during his career, the general framework applied here is that of "poetics."[8] Bordwell, a key figure in introducing the poetics approach to media studies, distinguishes it from methods-based approaches by articulating a general domain of inquiry (rather than a master theory)—the "inquiry into the fundamental principles by which artifacts in any representational medium are constructed, and the effects that flow from those principles." This book synthesizes what Bordwell terms analytical poetics, which studies "particular devices across a range of works or in a single work," and historical poetics, which asks about "how artworks assume certain forms within a period or across periods,"[9] or, "how and why [fundamental] principles [have] arisen and changed in particular empirical circumstances."[10] These principles, more often than not, "will be in the nature of norms, those explicit or implicit guidelines that shape creative action," and "govern conventions." Norms, then, can be described as a delineation and hierarchization of aims as well as a paradigmatic set of more or less favored options for filmmakers.[11]

Bordwell argues that the study of filmmakers and filmmaking practices is usefully guided by two key ideas, proposing that, "we should assume that the stylistic organization we detect is the result of filmmakers' choices among the alternatives available to them," and that such choices are both enabled and constrained by institutional contexts. Filmmakers are historically situated intentional agents guided by a "problem/solution model," in which "stylistic strategies" are best understood as "solutions to problems." These problems, or goals, may be of the filmmakers' own making or institutionally determined.[12] This "institutional dimension" plays a role in setting the agendas of filmmakers and in forming "the horizon of what is permitted and encouraged at particular moments. The filmmaker works, most proximately, within a social and economic system of production, and this involves tacit aesthetic assumptions, some division of labor, and standard ways of using technology." These constitute a "mode of filmmaking practice," which both constrains and enables the filmmaker's choices.[13]

It is easy to imagine objections to the utility of the institutionally constrained intentional agent model for the study of Robert Altman. To some extent the rejectionist account depends on the notion of an unshackled, improvisatory Altman whose films operate, as Robert T. Self puts it, to depict a "subliminal reality" that "recognizes the unspoken, and unspeakable, dimensions in human interactions," and whose approach "resides in lyrical fictions, in metaphoric discourse, and in inexplicable human associations." Yet Self presents Altman as goal-oriented, describing the depiction of "subliminal reality" as "the goal of his movies."[14]

Skeptics of the problem/solution model might be persuaded by Altman himself, speaking at a 1975 American Film Institute seminar:

> The whole business, as one of my cohorts pointed out to me, of what this art is is just solving problems. You start out and you say, "Okay, we're going to do a picture about Buffalo Bill and Sitting Bull." "Well, shit, how can you do that?" You say, "Well, you could do it in a Wild West show." One problem solved. Whack! Now you've got the basis for the thing. From this point on until the last day, you're solving a bunch of problems. You set up a goal and then you start cutting your way through the underbrush to get to it.[15]

Indeed, the thrill of on-set problem-solving was one of Altman's major motivators, a key reason why he persisted in filmmaking and why his output was so prodigious. Stephen Altman (who, beginning with *McCabe & Mrs. Miller*, regularly worked on his father's films and has had a significant career as a production designer) reported that his father was motivated by "the excitement of going to set and dealing with what he's going to get—the 'battlefield of problem-solving.'"[16]

Bordwell's evocation of "empirical circumstances," cited earlier, signals a foundational tenet of poetics—that scholars and critics should "invoke concrete evidence that allows [others] to appraise [their] claims," whether in relation to historical contexts or the design of creative works.[17] This book's emphasis on close and careful description, then, is not just a corrective to the rampant underdescription in previous scholarship on Altman; it is founded on the principle that evidence should be an essential component of critical activity, both to the formulation of theories and the presentation of arguments. Bordwell conceives of poetics as a domain in which analysis is "driven by data and midrange concepts rather than by abstract or absolute doctrines."[18] It is arguably the adherence to these kinds of absolute doctrines rather than a commitment to a more dynamic and targeted process of theorizing, testing, and revision that has led to the overclaiming found in standard explanations of the novel aspects of Altman's storytelling. These accounts tend to apply a formulation in which a novel device is assumed to serve a disruptive function—where overlapping intelligible dialogue automatically undermines narrative clarity, where a zoom's perspectival distortions necessarily dissolve narrative space. The contextualizing evidence of a particular zoom's configuration and coordination with other aspects of style and narrative situation, or of the careful design of any particular passage of overlapping dialogue, can only get in the way of these kinds of predetermined functional claims.

This book instead starts from something approximating what Meir Sternberg has referred to as "the Proteus Principle," which holds that, "any effect can be produced by an infinite number of forms, and any form can produce an infinite number of effects."[19] This serves as the basis for Sternberg's functionalist approach, which lends itself to poetics in its deliberate avoidance of predetermined analytic outcomes. Bordwell has incorporated Sternberg's functionalist approach in his own work—arguing that analysts are best served by assuming that identifiable formal features and techniques "are not necessarily ends in themselves. They are most fruitfully considered a byproduct of a holistic strategy, an effort after effect."[20] This perspective complements consideration of the role of practice-oriented preferences like those indicated by this book's account of Altman.

It is also usefully supplemented by psychologist J. J. Gibson's concept of "affordances," a term that recurs throughout this book. As adopted by media scholars, "affordance" refers to the notion that, while formal features, works, and contexts (like institutions) are not determinate, they are also not wholly neutral in that their contours present to those engaged with them both constraints and opportunities for effects and actions.[21] Creative agents like Altman might recognize and capitalize on the full range of affordances provided by institutional frameworks or filmmaking technologies, or they may perceive and act on only a few. Similarly, these creative agents design works whose features present a range of affordances to audiences, who may or may not recognize and capitalize on these opportunities. A key point of this revised account of Altman's work is that he recognized how common structures, features, and techniques might be elaborated on and around to create affordances for a greater range of experiences than standard Hollywood storytelling. Likewise, Altman managed to negotiate the affordances offered by the technologies and institutions of Hollywood filmmaking so as to accumulate the authority to fashion both these novel works and the novel production environments he preferred.

A historical poetics of Altman's early 1970s oeuvre requires, then, redescribing Altman's formal strategies, reassessing their functions in light of his films' complex design and through robust functionalist frameworks, and more carefully contextualizing them by situating them in relation to specified institutional norms of aims and practices, both aesthetic and technological. In my discussion of Altman's use of the zoom, I use a qualitative/quantitative approach to construct an account of the immediate context of zoom practices in the work of Altman's early-1970s contemporaries. However, to a large extent, this book relies on established scholarship to constitute the bases for claims about the key underlying "modes of film practice." Here, the work of David Bordwell and Kristin Thompson, particularly their work with Janet Staiger in *The Classical Hollywood Cinema: Film Style and Mode of Production to 1960*, has been extremely useful. Bordwell, Thompson, and Staiger define a mode of film practice as "an integral system, including persons and groups, but also rules, films, machinery, documents, institutions, work processes, and theoretical concepts." The authors rely on extensive primary source research and the employment of a large context set of 100 films to provide a carefully argued description of classical Hollywood cinema. In their subsequent work, Thompson and Bordwell develop what have become the standard accounts of classical Hollywood narrative structure and narration, and Bordwell's account of the art cinema as a mode of film practice, though not uncontested, is broadly regarded as authoritative. Their names, then, appear frequently in this book not just because Bordwell and Thompson are progenitors of the poetics approach to cinematic form, though Thompson frames her particular approach as neoformalism, but because of the extent, rigor, and influence of their work in relation to the particular modes of film practice relevant to understanding Altman's filmmaking.

Indeed, tensions in the literature on Altman, with accounts unevenly split between what I label rejectionist and assimilationist, are based largely in a disagreement about how to place Altman in relation to classical Hollywood storytelling and European art cinema. As previously noted, assessments of Altman's goals and practices tend to cluster at one end of this spectrum of classificatory possibilities, situating Altman as a modernist art cinema auteur and a radical rejectionist of Hollywood practices. Self's seminal work on Altman frames his feature films as a break from a "Classical Narrative Past," embodied in his pivot away from the Warner Brothers B film *Countdown* (1967).[22] After he was removed from that film during the editing process, "Altman," according to Self, "renounced authorship of its conventional narrative work."[23] In doing so, Self implies, Altman rejected not just *Countdown*'s studio-directed revisions to his work, but Hollywood storytelling itself, turning instead to the norms of art cinema narration. To define art cinema, Self cites the narrational parameters described by Bordwell's "The Art Cinema as a Mode of Film Practice"—authorial expressivity, objective and subjective realism, and ambiguity—while emphasizing art cinema's tendency to "liberate the spatial and temporal systems from subservience to narrative cause and effect."[24] Along these lines, Self claims that Altman's next film, *That Cold Day in the Park* (1969), "for the first time . . . displays the expressionistic style of art cinema that subverts this subordination."[25] For Self, Altman's follow-up, *M\*A\*S\*H*, confirms his transition "from journeyman television director in the classical storytelling tradition to director as auteur in the art cinema" and progenitor of a "new American cinema" that was "modernist" in its orientation.[26]

Robert Kolker's similarly influential work also labels Altman a "modernist" filmmaker, emphasizes Altman's rejection of classical Hollywood storytelling, and describes *M\*A\*S\*H* and the films in its wake as radical experiments in "decentralization." According to Kolker, "what Altman creates is not the conventional structure of a whole analyzed into its parts, but a simultaneity of the whole *and* its parts, a simultaneity the viewer must always attend to."[27] Altman's films, Kolker proposes, present spectators with an expansive diegetic world that they are then left to sort through on their own.

This purported radical openness and freedom, this revolutionarily unstructured depiction of space and time, accomplished through spurning classical Hollywood storytelling in favor of modernist art cinema practices, is central to the rejectionist account of Altman. Its influence is pervasive, disfiguring otherwise invaluable scholarship. Take, for instance, the characterization by Nick Hall, relying on John Belton for poetic support, of Altman's overall approach to the zoom in *McCabe & Mrs. Miller* as "preoccupied with depth, and with making direct transitions into the depth of the mise-en-scène, via the zoom. Here, Belton suggests, 'Altman's zooms function like jazz improvisations superimposed on a fixed melody: whether motivated or not, they signal his presence as a narrator.'"[28] We should, of course, be skeptical of the claim that all zooms function to signal the overt presence of a narrator, though, as chapter 2 relates, there is, within the film, a significant internal patterning of certain kinds of zooms, coordinated with key narrative moments, which like much formal patterning works both expressively and as a sign of the filmmakers' formal virtuosity. I would agree, though, that a significant number of *McCabe & Mrs. Miller*'s zoom shots are preoccupied with depth, a preoccupation that extends, as chapter 5 illustrates, at least as far back as Altman's largely zoom-free work in filmed television on *Combat!*.

Hall offers the following example to support and develop his (and Belton's) claim about the film ⊚ (see the companion website for a video clip):

> In *McCabe*, the zoom towards a banjo [*sic*] player strumming in a gambling parlor is a particularly strong example of the film's many zooms through cluttered and dimly-lit interiors. The soundtrack is as confusing as the image: the low, overlapping chattering of the gamblers vies for attention with the banjo [*sic*]. The zoom advances slowly and uncertainly. It finally picks out the banjo [*sic*] player, but, like virtuoso single-take Steadicam shots often found in later films, part of the visual pleasure of the mobile frame lies in this uncertainty of the final destination. Zooms like these, Belton suggests, create "a very flat, dimensionless space which enhances the enclosed, claustrophobic nature of the film."[29]

While it seems self-defeating to assert without explanation that a zoom into a cluttered mise-en-scène through multiple planes of depth, including a figure who walks across the foreground in medium shot during the zoom in, suggests a "very flat, dimensionless space," there are more substantial problems to be found in the analysis and misdescription of this particular zoom shot. These errors repeat and rely on the rejectionist account's misapprehension of Altman in each of the three dimensions that, respectively, constitute the subjects of the first three chapters of the book—narrative design, the zoom, and overlapping dialogue.

The narrative situation developed by the shot is more focused than Hall acknowledges. McCabe returns to the improvised gambling parlor from a brief upstairs tour of the overnight accommodations at Sheehan's, which he finds entirely, and understandably, unsatisfactory. His initial one-word response to Sheehan's offerings, "shit," punctuates the transition back to a shot of the first floor of the establishment, where two side-characters have been discussing personal grooming at the bar. Their conversation is accompanied by the introduction of the diegetic pizzicato fiddle to the soundtrack, which continues to be heard across the cut into the next shot—the one addressed by Hall. Over the cut to that shot, McCabe's offscreen voice returns to the soundtrack, as he colorfully elaborates on his previously stated opinion of Sheehan's establishment while descending the stairs. The camera tilts down and then pans left to follow McCabe, trailed by Sheehan, as he moves into the parlor. The murmur of the men is audible but clearly de-hierarchized on the soundtrack. At some moments, the fiddle becomes inaudible under McCabe's dialogue, the conversing men, and footstep sound effects. The camera comes to a rest as McCabe sits down at his seat at the table, which another man gives up without being asked, and McCabe is now framed in the lower half of the screen on the right rule-of-thirds line. He cracks a joke, the men all laugh, and they begin playing cards.

This redescription establishes that the scene has a clear narrative center—McCabe's move back to the table and his confident, charismatic assertion of dominance in this new milieu. The camera movement up until this point maintains McCabe's compositional dominance in the shot, and even as McCabe sits at the crowded table audience attention is likely to remain primarily tethered to McCabe. The soundtrack similarly prioritizes McCabe's dialogue. While there are some intelligible bits of the miners' conversations, the general sense provided by the dialogue, intelligible or not, is of amused, excited anticipation for the card game—just what McCabe wants. I find it hard to accept that this mise-en-scène or narrative situation deserves to be called confusing, even though the frame is full of men. I suppose the feeling could be described as claustrophobic, though extending this characterization to the entire film, as Belton does, is flatly wrong. More likely, Sheehan's establishment is presented as a counterpoint to the more spacious accommodations for gambling and prostitution developed by McCabe and Mrs. Miller's entrepreneurial endeavors. This kind of close and careful consideration of narrative situation, though, seems less important to Belton's account than the modernist logics of expressive technological essentialism by which optics necessarily smoosh diegetic space and subvert storytelling.

It is when McCabe proposes the men make this "a quarter game" that the zoom in begins, and while it is true that it has its terminus at the fiddler, and that its route undergoes alteration, characterizing its trajectory as uncertain seems flatly wrong. Before getting to the zoom itself, though, given that Hall's claim is one of surprising attentional trajectories, it is important to robustly describe the shot's blocking—a key cinematic technique for directing attentional focus. At the beginning of the zoom, McCabe, as described earlier, is in the lower right middle-ground. The majority of the men are seated around the table, and while McCabe is seated at the table's far side, the men on the near side are lower in the composition than McCabe, ensuring that his face is visible as he leans in to deal (Figure I.1). Moreover, while the shot could be described as dimly lit—the backs of the men on the near side of the table are in shadow—a lantern hung overhead and slightly left of center motivates the golden glow that illuminates the faces of the men on McCabe's side of the table as well as, significantly, the face of the fiddler, sitting apart in the near background. Not only is the fiddler well lit in the shot, he is also compositionally prominent. He is only slightly right of the absolute center of the composition, and his head is just above those of the men on the far side of the table. Moreover, he is positioned directly adjacent to McCabe, occupying the compositional gap between McCabe and the man seated to McCabe's right. In short, even before the zoom in on the fiddler, he is already well lit and positioned as close to the center of attention as possible. That he is also the source of diegetic music makes the notion that a zoom discovers him for the audience even less likely.

What the zoom does instead is emphasize and juxtapose the fiddler with McCabe's satisfied grin. The initial trajectory of the zoom is actually a straight line toward the fiddler, and the magnification of the character is matched by an increase in the volume of the fiddle. The shift in the zoom's direction characterized by Hall as displaying uncertainty is actually a slight pan right toward McCabe as he turns to ask Sheehan to "give these boys a bottle on me," an ingratiating request given prominence by the sound mix. McCabe is in focus

**Figure I.1** *McCabe & Mrs. Miller*

during the request, but as he turns back to the table and the zoom continues, the fiddler, glancing up at McCabe and now the only remaining character in the shot, comes into focus. A very slight pan left pulls the framing to rest finally on the magnification of his hands, strumming away. Essentially, the move here connects McCabe's seduction of the men with the pizzicato fiddle music and the fiddler, who seems aware of McCabe's maneuvering and serves as its playful, commentative accompanist. The zoom also allows Altman the opportunity to virtuosically orchestrate a shot that both elaborates and then moves through a densely packed depth staging.

The functions afforded by the shot's use of the zoom are obviously more robust than the rejectionist account allows for. It provides an aperture framing, surpasses obstacles (the table and men), and connects McCabe directly to the fiddle. It certainly plays a role in directing attention, but this should be understood not as a journey of space-flattening uncertainty but as focusing the audience on aspects of the mise-en-scène and soundtrack that provide commentary on the story events. Here, thanks in part to the coordination of the zoom with the design of the mise-en-scène and soundtrack, the attention-calling is more plausibly explained as an act of emphasis than discovery.

This extended example illustrates the dangers and limitations of the rejectionist account, but it also suggests a problem with its opposite—the "assimilationist" view of Altman that places his work, particularly his early 1970s oeuvre, squarely within the tradition of Hollywood filmmaking, albeit with the caveat that this tradition was undergoing significant revision during the late 1960s and 1970s. While the prioritization of narratively significant sound and the careful direction of attention using framing and blocking are standards of Hollywood storytelling, the employment of indirect narrational commentary is more evocative of the authorial expressivity associated with the European art cinema. Self makes a point of describing Altman as part of a "New American Cinema" rather than New Hollywood, probably in order to further mark what he sees as the distance between Altman's art cinema practice and classical Hollywood storytelling. But other scholars have consistently framed Altman within the big tent of the New Hollywood concept or, as I do, frame Altman's work within this period as part of the Hollywood Renaissance. Labeling this period in Hollywood filmmaking has proven a tricky task for film scholars, and, before elaborating more fully on what I label the assimilationist position, it is worth reviewing the ways in which "New Hollywood" has been deployed and how Altman has been situated in relation to these groupings.

Perhaps the most cited statement on the disputed meaning of New Hollywood comes from a footnote in Jon Lewis's 1995 book on Francis

Ford Coppola, *Whom God Wishes to Destroy . . .*, in which Lewis remarks, "there have been, I know, a lot of new Hollywoods."[30] Murray Smith has observed, "since the 1960s, there has been a proliferation of terms designating more-or-less fundamental shifts in the nature—and thus the appropriate periodization—of Hollywood," of which he names "New Hollywood, the New New Hollywood, post-classicism," and "post-Fordism and postmodernism."[31]

In much of the literature on New Hollywood, this shifting nomenclature has consistently been linked to groups of directors. This is not to say that accounts of New Hollywood have ignored economic or technological factors, but that groups of directors and their films have served as a primary focal point of the scholarship and as a justification for labels attached to certain groups, and what some term group styles, that during this period either arose or whose arising has been asserted by critics and scholars.

For instance, Diane Jacobs, writing in 1977, popularized the term "Hollywood Renaissance" to describe filmmakers whose "major works" were made after 1970. She includes on her list Altman, as well as Ashby, Cassavetes, Coppola, Mazursky, Ritchie, and Scorsese.[32] Jacobs usefully characterizes her grouping as a shared response to a particular industrial formation:

> What distinguishes certain films of the Seventies is neither artistic superiority nor administrative autonomy—but a happy combination of the two, a fusion of ability, accessibility, and yes, inspiration, at a fortuitous juncture in time. Someone got it into his head that an amorphous under-30 audience did exist out there, that it was tired of the costume drama and the safe situation comedy, and that with business so bad anything new was worth a try. The phenomenon that resulted was not a matter of one or two outstanding individuals . . . but of a conglomeration of talent descending upon Hollywood and insisting on having a say in the future of movies.

Using Altman as her example, Jacobs describes how even though his films during the period were made for different distributors, "each is an 'Altman' film with an Altman crew and cast and look." Citing Jerzy Toeplitz's *Hollywood and After*, she attributes this development to "permutations in the role of the producer" resulting from the dissolution of the studio system and changes in the organization of production aligning the producer with director rather than studio.[33] Steve Neale takes up Jacobs's "Hollywood Renaissance" term and similarly applies it to "a window of opportunity" constituted by "a brief moment of aesthetic adventure that happened between the mid-1960s and the mid to late 1970s and then vanished." He defines New Hollywood around a second group of films and filmmakers "generally exemplified by *Jaws* and *Star Wars*."[34]

Although scholars have frequently disagreed about how and whether to define or subdivide New Hollywood, they seem to have reached a consensus about the major influences on New Hollywood filmmakers. David Cook describes how, in the late 1960s, Hollywood faced a serious recession and struggled to capture and retain audiences. One strategy was based on a 1968 survey commissioned by the MPAA, which found that, "being young and single is the overriding demographic pre-condition for being a frequent and enthusiastic movie-goer." Hollywood's response was to target a younger, hipper, and more educated demographic. By appealing to "tuned-in youth" the industry believed it could ride out the recession. The industry's solution was to encourage and promote domestic "auteurs" who might produce Hollywood's version of art cinema.[35]

Logically enough, then, for most film scholars the unity of the New Hollywood designation relies not just on a historical period but also on the consistent employment of filmmaking techniques characteristic of art cinema within Hollywood filmmaking. Paul Ramaeker takes the influence of art cinema to be the key influence on New Hollywood, creating first a wave of what he terms "Hollywood Art Cinema" from 1965 to 1971 and then a cycle of "Hollywood Art-Genre Films" from 1971 to 1978.[36] Similarly, Mark Shiel argues, "as widespread acclaim was achieved by European art cinema masterpieces . . . particular European auteurs, including Truffaut, Godard, Rohmer, Fellini, Antonioni, and Bergman, were celebrated in the United States as part of a pan-European New Wave which an emerging generation of filmmakers . . . began to emulate."[37]

As Neale points out, the claim of influence by European auteurs has sometimes been conflated with a second influence, and a second kind of auteurism—that practiced by the critics of *Cahiers du Cinema* and imported and modified by Andrew Sarris. According to Neale, this second auteurism valorized "hitherto undervalued Hollywood directors" rather than European art cinema filmmakers, and it is this veneration of "Old Hollywood" directors that influenced "younger Movie Brats like Martin Scorsese, Brian De Palma, Steven Spielberg, and Francis Ford Coppola." Neale argues that Hollywood Renaissance directors like Altman, Arthur Penn, and Mike Nichols, "most of whom began their directorial careers in film or television in the 1950s and the early 1960s, were much more influenced not by older Hollywood directors and the critical culture that valued their work, but by ideas of film art associated with European directors."[38] Schatz similarly argues that it was on the Movie Brats, the film-school generation whose university training provided them with a "conceptual handle on film history and theory," that American auteur theory had its impact.[39] In a real sense, they *were* the "tuned-in youth" to whom the industry was so eager to appeal. James Bernardoni has also cited auteurist conceptions of Hitchcock and Hawks as major influences on New Hollywood filmmakers, and has gone so far as to claim that *M\*A\*S\*H* and *Jaws* (1975) were attempts at following in the tradition of Hawks, though as misdescribed by auteurist critics.[40]

Bernardoni's basic premise—that *M\*A\*S\*H* contains elements of Hawksian screwball comedy—may be valid, but given Altman's lack of a film school education and consistent placement in the earlier of the two groups of New Hollywood filmmakers, it is also problematic for the distinction that Neale, Schatz, and others wish to make within New Hollywood. While Neale is likely generally correct in affirming Sarris's influence, his generational thesis argu- ably presents a false choice. Dividing New Hollywood cleanly into two cadres based on their age and "educations" elides the probability that the two groups shared, to a significant extent, in an American film culture that was not lim- ited to university classrooms. There seems to be little evidence for the notion that art cinema was located outside universities while Hollywood auteurism was located inside them. The influence of art cinema and auteurism, the major foci of American film culture, can be indexed according to a number of factors that extend well beyond film schools, including box office success, industry and critical awards, popular press coverage, and publications like *Movie*.[41]

Given the fairly concentrated genre-revisionist nature of Altman's early 1970s output, it seems particularly important that even if we accept the validity of distinguishing between the Hollywood Renaissance and the movie brat– dominated New Hollywood we also acknowledge that Altman straddled both domains. His work during the period we might designate as "New Hollywood proper" refers to the filmmakers and genres of classical Hollywood, while also showing the influence of the techniques and innovations of the art cinema, particularly their foregrounded authorial expressivity.

Self's work wisely acknowledges both of these influences but incorporates them into an argument for Altman's rejection of Hollywood norms. He does so partly by framing Altman's genre work as more reflexive than revisionist. While he acknowledges that, "Within the industry, Altman's constant manipu- lation of various genres during the transitional 1970s amounted to an ongoing research and development effort on behalf of one of Hollywood's most suc- cessful commodities," he also labels these films, "a subcode of the Hollywood fringe."[42] Altman's genre films, according to Self, "lay bare the terms of generic readability" and "call attention to themselves as products made by the enter- tainment industry."[43] These may be qualifiedly accurate claims, but focusing exclusively on these functions would seem to disregard the ways in which they participate in an ongoing tradition of revisionism and self-consciousness in Hollywood filmmaking. Self incorporates into his account of Altman the influence of auteurism and art cinema aims, but he does so in a way that disregards how these influences might be integrated with Hollywood practice.

The assimilationist take on these questions can be found in *The Classical Hollywood Cinema*. In a subsection titled "Since 1960: The Persistence of a Mode of Film Practice," Bordwell and Staiger argue that, in the same way that "the 'old' Hollywood had incorporated and refunctionalized devices from German Expressionism and Soviet montage, the 'New' Hollywood has selectively borrowed from the international art cinema."[44] While acknowledging that New Hollywood filmmakers "sometimes flaunt the act of narration" and "[imitate] the look of European art films," the authors propose that this has not constituted "simple copying" of art cinema. Instead, Bordwell and Staiger claim that New Hollywood has "absorbed" art cinema practices such as the jump-cut, the sound bridge, the elimination of the dissolve, and the freeze-frame, and, importantly, that they have "merged [them] with certain conventions of the classical style." For Bordwell and Staiger, the inclusion of art cinema conventions does not necessarily constitute a wholly distinct form of American filmmaking but instead represents the assimilation of art cinema practice by Hollywood. As they put it, "the New Hollywood has absorbed narrational strategies of the art cinema while controlling them."

This assimilation is ensured, and control is maintained, through two means—maintaining "a coherent genre framework" and "the almost complete conservatism of style." Bordwell and Staiger claim that, "No recent American director has produced an idiosyncratic style comparable to even Truffaut's or Bergman's, let alone to that of Antonioni or Bresson." Even Robert Altman, whom they identify as "probably the most interesting stylist to emerge in the New Hollywood," does not escape "the classical paradigm" in his "use of technique." Specifically, in what is essentially a direct rebuttal of the rejectionist position, the authors claim that, "the classical," narratively oriented, "premises of time and space remain powerfully in force," in Altman's films and the films of the New Hollywood.[45]

Because of the broad focus of *The Classical Hollywood Cinema*, Bordwell and Staiger do not support their specific assimilationist claims about Altman's filmmaking practice during the 1970s. Instead, they rely on an analysis of *The Conversation* (1974) to show how that film's generic and narrative structures constrain the implications and impulses of its use of art cinema techniques to portray its protagonist's damaged subjectivity. Indeed, while I am generally sympathetic to the absorptive account of Altman, I am not aware of any sustained study of Altman's films that demonstrates how and to what extent they conform to the larger assimilationist case for New Hollywood. I am also not entirely satisfied with the tendency of the either/or, on/off nature of the assimilationist account to, like the rejectionist account, lead to overclaiming for and mis- and underdescription of the features and functions, novel or not, of Altman's filmmaking.

Instead, I propose a third option—an elaborative account of Altman's work that allows for a more dynamic range of possibilities within Hollywood storytelling than permitted by the assimilationist position. Specifically, it allows for the possibility that innovations may work in ways that are expansive and additive, rather than contrary or assimilable, in relation to the standards and formulae of Hollywood filmmaking.[46] Bordwell's *On the History of Film Style* traces the history and development of depth staging in cinema, concluding with the following observation:

> My research questions, focusing on the elaboration of norms, have led me to stress continuity. The lesson of this is quite general. Modernism's promoters asked us to expect constant turnover, virtually seasonal breakthroughs in style. In most artworks, however, novel devices of style or structure or theme stand out against a backdrop of norm-abiding processes. Most films will be bound to tradition in more ways than not; we should find many more stylistic replications and revisions than rejections. Especially in a mass medium, we ought to expect replication and minor modifications, not thoroughgoing repudiation. We must always be alert for innovation, but students of style will more often encounter stability and gradual change.[47]

While this description of the innovation of norms is not far off from the assimilationist account of New Hollywood in *The Classical Hollywood Cinema*, it does seem slightly more open to more meaningful change. The key term in the "replication/revision/rejection" triad is, of course, "revision."

Bordwell equates norms to the "principles underlying" creative action and "govern[ing] conventions."[48] To that extent, a norm consists not just of a craft practice but also of the guidelines for when and how, or toward what end, to employ that practice or technique. Thus, norms are constituted not just by practices but by purposes. While the assimilationist account appears to allow for the revision of techniques, it also seems to severely constrain the possibility of revised purposes. Bordwell describes the relationships between purposes in classical Hollywood cinema as one in which a system of narrative logic "subordinates" other stylistic systems.[49] In other words, it seems that narrative purposes dominate all others, even if, as Bordwell acknowledges, the "integrity of the structure" secured by the narratively oriented system is "a dynamic one, with the subordinated factors constantly pulling against the sway of the dominant."[50] I would follow Rick Altman in suggesting this language of dominance may overdetermine assessments of the relationships between functions in the classical Hollywood cinema.[51] Meanwhile, the rejectionist account, even if one were to entertain the incorrect notion that it accurately describes the specific purposes of Altman's departures from particular institutional norms, tends to overreach in categorizing such departures as wholesale rejections of the overall system of principles, purposes, and techniques. The elaborative account, on the other hand, expands the range of possibilities by suggesting a dynamic in which classical Hollywood's narrative purposes might not dominate but instead provide an enabling foundation neither departed from nor even necessarily pulled against but instead elaborated on and around in ways that negotiate and reformulate standard experiential affordances.

I would propose, then, that Robert Altman's approach to filmmaking—his use of technique, his aims, and his relation to the presiding norms of Hollywood and art cinema filmmaking—is best framed as elaborative. During what has been described as the Hollywood Renaissance period, Altman functioned not just as part of the Hollywood filmmaking industry but also largely within the norms of Hollywood filmmaking practice. That said, he also elaborated on and around those norms and practices, incorporating into his films art cinema techniques and aims in piecemeal fashion, while largely relying on and maintaining classical Hollywood's storytelling priorities and functions. Sometimes, this elaboration required the rejection of what Altman viewed as Hollywood's fustier rules—the supremacy of the shooting script, the prohibition against overlapping dialogue—but these rejections were attended by frequently virtuosic compensations that are, perhaps, best captured by the term used by the Academy of Motion Picture Arts and Sciences—"reinventions."

As a result, what Altman was able to offer Hollywood's under-thirty, film-literate target audience was not a radical, modernist art cinema that rejected Hollywood storytelling, but it was, nevertheless, and as the promotional material for *Brewster McCloud* puts it, "something else" (Figure I.2). That something else, though, is best understood as something more. Altman's filmmaking offered audiences more than just a Hollywood film repackaged with art cinema techniques, more than just the standard story. The account produced here may seem deflating, as it backs away from depictions of Altman as fomenting—and his work as embodying—a radical shift from Hollywood norms and their ideological implications. But in an institution like Hollywood, even the "New" Hollywood of the late 1960s and early 1970s, radical opposition to contextual norms would likely prove to be a dead end; not only for a filmmaker's career but also as a means by which to meaningfully and enduringly change the paradigms of filmmaking practice and audience

**Figure I.2** Wisconsin Center for Film and Theater Research

expectations. Instead, Altman's strategy of elaboration displays the kind of consistent intentional and incremental experimentation that was perhaps more likely to have a sustained influence on filmmakers and their audiences.

## Reconstructing Early Altman

Given the impressive breadth of Robert Altman's career it would be impractical to attempt to meet the goals of this book—understanding the essential aspects of Altman's authorial profile and his place in relation to the Hollywood storytelling tradition—and at the same time account for six decades of filmmaking. This is especially true given one of the major problems with Altman scholarship—the tendency to overclaim while underdescribing his work.

Instead, this book focuses primarily on Altman's films from 1970 to 1975, a period that sits at the heart of the Hollywood Renaissance, and then moves backward to his time in industrial films and filmed television, building on and affirming the previous chapters' insights about Altman's approach to negotiating industrial norms.

The early 1970s saw the release of eight films directed by Altman— *M\*A\*S\*H* (1970), *Brewster McCloud* (1970), *McCabe & Mrs. Miller* (1971), *Images* (1972), *The Long Goodbye* (1973), *Thieves Like Us* (1974), *California Split* (1974), and *Nashville* (1975). This era is regarded by scholars and critics as formative in relation to Altman's reputation. As Graham Fuller puts it, "[Altman's] place among the elders of American *auteurism* had already been assured by his work between 1970 and 1975 . . . the period when Altman developed his style of mock documentary realism, characterized by overlapping dialogue, improvisation, offhand irony, and those floaty zooms into dead space and the quick of life."[52] Altman is widely regarded as being at the height of his filmmaking prowess during this period, with *Nashville* seen as the culmination of his developing approach to cinematic storytelling. More important than the veracity of this view of Altman's early 1970s oeuvre is the fact that it is held by so many. It therefore serves as a prime reference point from which to begin a reevaluation of Altman's work and key aspects of his "biographical legend."[53]

Chapter 1 initiates this project by correcting common misunderstandings about Altman's approach to narrative form during the early 1970s. Goaded by the filmmaker's own assertions about the insignificance of plot and his desire to diminish its role in his films, many critics and scholars in the oppositional camp present Altman's films as antinarrative and, therefore, anti-Hollywood. This characterization, though, relies on an underdeveloped conceptualization of "narrative" that conflates narrative structure, narration, and storyworld.

Once we apply these fundamental distinctions to analysis of Altman's early 1970s films, it becomes clear that they largely fit within the norms of classical Hollywood storytelling structure. Even *M\*A\*S\*H* and *Nashville*, with arguably nonstandard narrative structures, are organized around key classical strategies. Rather than "anti-Hollywood" or "anticlassical," Altman's narrative strategies are best regarded as perversely classical. That is, Altman employs principles and techniques associated with the classical Hollywood cinema's preoccupation with efficient storytelling not for the sake of narrative economy as an end in and of itself but as the means with which to make room for his elaborative expansion of the aims of Hollywood storytelling. Moreover, meeting Altman's elaborative aims requires the integration rather than substitution or assimilation of art cinema narrational strategies. Altman drapes on his classically structured narrative "clotheslines" an overt and reflexive narrational voice that selectively ironizes its subjects and primes audiences for interpretation. This grounded approach simultaneously enables a "closure without comprehension" strategy that resolves his narratives' causal structures while also leaving their affective and thematic implications ambiguous. The robust account of Altman's approach to narrative and his commitment to the classical narrative "clothesline" in chapter 1 provides a foundational revision that subsequent chapters draw on in their reconsideration of the other key aspects of Altman's authorial profile.

Chapter 2 demystifies Altman's use of the zoom, his hallmark visual technique. Critics, preferring to treat the technology metaphorically or metaphysically rather than pragmatically, have substantially mischaracterized Altman's approach as either rejecting or transcending Hollywood cinema's typical employment of mobile framing in service to narrative drama. David Thompson has claimed that Altman's zooms "roam free, drifting around a scene like a bloodhound following the scent, zooming almost casually on to significant details or simply making surprising connections."[54] Robin Wood has gone further, arguing that Altman has "grasped [the zoom's] potential for dissolving space and undermining our sense of physical reality."[55]

The systematic, comprehensive, and contextualized qualitative/quantitative approach taken in chapter 2 suggests otherwise. The chapter first concretizes the zoom, isolating the describable features and plausible functions of Altman's early 1970s zooming. It then applies those parameters to a statistical comparison of individual Altman films with one another and, as a group, with a context set of over seventy contemporaneous films by eighteen directors. Doing so provides insight into early 1970s Hollywood zoom style and the nature and distinctiveness of Altman's approach. Rather than serving an overarching interest in narrative disruption, Altman's preference for the zoom reflected the technique's utility for a broad range of purposes. Zooms were contingently employed in response to the specific problems presented by individual films. In the main, Altman's zooms further comprehension of and strengthen engagement with dramatic action. Perhaps most surprising, the roving, "searching and revealing," approach so often taken as a given by critical accounts is largely absent during this period. The zoom serves not as a maverick director's rogue eye, penetrating existential assumptions, but as a pragmatic tool. It proved useful for solving the regular problems of Hollywood filmmaking and also allowed elaborative and frequently aestheticizing flourishes whose qualities cut against the standard account of an improvisatory zoom style. For Altman, the zoom was an authorial signature, not an act of political modernism. Chapter 2 firmly establishes that during the early 1970s this signature aspect of Altman's authorial profile is aimed at the vitalization rather than the dissolution of Hollywood storytelling.

Where chapter 2 uses statistical analysis to supplement formal description, chapter 3 presents a history of formal elaboration intertwined with technological innovation, demonstrating that standard accounts mischaracterize Altman's signature sound technique, his use of overlapping dialogue. Scholars have been intent on reading overlapping dialogue as a radical break from classical Hollywood's insistence on clarity. Much like the anecdotal studio executives who were constantly firing Altman for his employment of the technique during his early career, these critics have underestimated the multidimensionality and capaciousness of Altman's practice and of the Hollywood cinema. Once again treating pragmatically executed innovation as a counterideology, these accounts both mis- and underestimate Altman's elaborative approach. The critical reception of *M\*A\*S\*H* in 1970 established the key critical tropes that would prime future scholarly overreach. Andrew Sarris's description of Altman's use of overlapping dialogue as "anarchic" provides a kernel that eventually grows into Self's conclusion that the film's "chaotic" sound design subverts the entirety of its narrative logic.[56]

The analysis offered in chapter 3 demonstrates that *M\*A\*S\*H*'s sound design is, in fact, both highly manipulated and highly conscious of narrative aims. The chapter supplements careful redescription of the employment of overlapping dialogue across key films of the period with archival evidence and firsthand accounts to reveal how Altman and his collaborators innovated solutions allowing them to record and mix dialogue so as to simultaneously convey the impression of naturalism, provide a vehicle for overt narrational commentary, and ensure the intelligibility of essential narrative premises. I track this innovative problem-setting and pragmatic problem-solving from *M\*A\*S\*H* to the more difficult productions of *Brewster McCloud* and *McCabe & Mrs. Miller*, and through the introduction of the Lions Gate 8-Track system on *California Split*. This trajectory demonstrates the consistently multifaceted nature of Altman's aims. Indeed, even with the move to 24-track recording technology on *Nashville*, Altman continued to prioritize the intelligibility of narratively essential dialogue, working with his collaborators to carefully manipulate the soundtrack and direct audience attention. This finding provides a stark contrast to Rick Altman's canonical account of the film as wholly liberating auditors from the dictatorship of the narrativized Hollywood soundscape (until an alleged shift in the sound strategy at the film's climax betrays Altman's entire political project).[57] Instead of ideologically virtuous chaos, what we actually find is functionally virtuosic orchestration that represents not a rejection of Hollywood but its opening-up to, among other effects, increased auditor agency.

Chapter 4 demonstrates that Altman's on-set improvisations were both constrained and motivated by the storytelling approaches and practice-oriented preferences established in the book's first three chapters. In doing so, it jettisons the standard account in which Altman is said to have casually discarded the script, the key management tool in the Hollywood production system, in favor of the anarchic possibilities of communal filmmaking—what one critic has described as something more akin to "an improvisational encounter group than a showcase . . . for plot."[58] In place of this subtractive, rejectionist account, chapter 4 employs archival research and close analysis to argue for an additive, elaborative account of what I term Altman's "transpositional" script-to-screen strategies.[59] Comparing preproduction scripts drawn from multiple archives with the final films, this chapter clearly establishes the "improvisatory ceilings" for key early 1970s Altman films, revealing the extent to which Altman's approach during the period depends on retaining rather than rejecting most of his scripts' scenic and narrative structures. It is around rather than in place of these causal chains that Altman economizes in the manner described in chapter 1, rejecting redundancy and thematic and dramatic cliché in order to make room for multiple forms of elaboration.

These elaborations include constrained versions of the improvisatory flourishes and reimagining of character traits that provide the basis of his reputation, but they also involve the improvisation of thematic motifs, the multiplication of "middleground" characters, and the creation of affordances to exercise favored techniques like the zoom and overlapping dialogue. In place of the romantic and anecdotal image of Altman as having liberated himself, his cast, and his audiences from the shackles of Hollywood scriptwriters, this chapter traces the history of a comprehensive suite of elaborative strategies that depend on retaining substantial aspects of Hollywood tradition—including the script as a management tool.

There is an overarching methodological trajectory across the book's first four chapters from analysis based primarily on the features of the films to an intensified integration of archival documents and the reconstruction of production practices. These methodologies are fully synthesized in the book's final chapter, which focuses on redressing the standard accounts of what we might call "Earlier Altman," the director of industrial films and filmed television. As we shall see, these accounts have shaped understanding of Early Altman, but they have also been deformed by misperceptions about what that Early Altman constituted. Beyond methodology, then, chapter 5 synthesizes the previous chapters' reappraisal of the canonical Altman to reframe his earlier work and to more accurately assess its relationship to his early 1970s oeuvre.

Just as standard accounts have tended to formulate their vision of Early Altman around historically reductive binaries—rejection versus assimilation, art cinema versus Hollywood—so, too, have accounts of Altman's career trajectory tended to efface dynamic intra- and intermedial relationships in favor of tracing the constraint and emergence of norm-breaking expressivity. Chapter 5, in contrast, depicts a professional film worker who developed his talent through a series of context-contingent experiments. The standard account has glancingly suggested that Altman's time at the Kansas City–based Calvin Company making industrial, or "sponsored," documentaries—twenty-minute promotional films for products and institutional agendas—trained him to be an observational filmmaker capturing, on the fly, the details of life. While educating him in this outsider posture, Calvin somehow also managed to train Altman in Hollywood's illusionist norms. This paradox is typically left unexplored. Similarly, Altman's time in filmed television is taken to be more work camp than training ground, a forum in which his agency as director was shackled to the writer/producer-dominated medium's "zero degree" version of Hollywood style.[60] By this account, the budding auteur's only avenue for true expression was the occasional, carefully concealed, subversion of convention. Filmed television, then, is said to have inadvertently schooled Altman in the art of opposition and fueled his desire to reject Hollywood's norms by forcing him to reproduce them. Critical commentary in this vein does not pause to consider that television might have afforded Altman opportunities to innovate. Rather, the received accounts embark on a search for continuities with the 1970s work of the auteur they celebrate. Because that figure is largely a critical invention, this search is frequently frustrated.

Chapter 5 relies on archival research and systematic analysis of Altman's earliest professional work to show how these phases of Altman's career are actually related. Industrial filmmaking and filmed television contributed much more to Altman's development than rote "training" in the base-level competencies of zero-degree Hollywood style. Instead, they steered Altman toward novel production practices that he would later employ in his feature films. At the same time, these institutions were dynamic enough to afford Altman the opportunity to experiment, to push beyond their minimum, and sometimes minimal, expectations, and to embellish his work with the kinds of formal flourishes recognizable in his early 1970s oeuvre. Indeed, the elaborative attitude toward institutional norms described in the previous chapters proves to be a compelling framework linking "Earlier Altman" with "Early Altman" and, in the process, challenging hierarchizing assumptions about the nature and direction of institutional influence on filmmakers whose careers span media forms.

This book, then, firmly establishes Altman as an innovative filmmaker within the Hollywood tradition who pushed to expand Hollywood story-telling practice by elaborating around its classical narrative core. Given the distinct institutional context of early 1970s Hollywood, it should come as no surprise that his particular elaborative aims often resembled those of art cinema. In service to these elaborations, Altman developed a set of innovative techniques and practices, many of which can be traced to earlier stages of his career that have heretofore been viewed as semioppressive training ground institutions rather than domains that provided their own affordances for cre-ative filmmaking. In applying and expanding on these approaches in his fea-ture filmmaking, Altman is best understood not as rejecting Hollywood film practice but as broadening the repertoire of options available to Hollywood's filmmakers and the range of experiences available to audiences who might be in search of "something else" and "something more."

# 1

# Perverse Clotheslines

## Altman and Narrative Elaboration

"Nobody has ever made a good movie. Someday someone will make
half a good one . . . [by] taking the narrative out, taking the story out
of it."

—Robert Altman

The key plank in oppositional accounts of Altman tends to be the filmmaker's
strained relationship with narrative—embodied in pronouncements like the
one just quoted and echoed in the criticism and scholarship that followed
from them.[1] How could a filmmaker with this attitude ever be understood as
anything but radically separate from classical Hollywood storytelling practice? But critical and scholarly accounts of Altman's relationship with narrative tend to rely on overgeneralization and underdescription, in relation both
to Altman's films and to the conceptual framework necessary for robust narrative analysis. Understanding the elaborate and elaborative narrative strategies
on display in Altman's early 1970s films requires a multidimensional conceptualization of narrative.

David Bordwell has suggested distinguishing between three aspects of narrative: story world, plot structure, and narration. Story world, for Bordwell,
encompasses premises relating to "agents, circumstances, and surround-
ings," though we should also include premises relating to events. Structure
addresses "the arrangement of the parts of the narrative," and narration
describes "the moment-by-moment flow" of storytelling.[2] While these
aspects are interdependent, they are not indistinguishable. Conflating them
risks effacing the complexity of design and effects that narrative form affords
filmmakers and filmmaking modes. Examining Altman's early 1970s oeuvre
while maintaining a conceptual distinction between these three dimensions
yields a fuller portrait of Altman and his collaborators' narrative methods,
while also demonstrating the need to resituate these films in relation to the

*Robert Altman and the Elaboration of Hollywood Storytelling*. Mark Minett, Oxford University Press (2021). © Oxford University Press. DOI: 10.1093/oso/9780197523827.001.0001.

norms of both classical Hollywood and art cinema. As Bordwell points out, "artworks constantly cross theoretical categories," and Altman's elaborative expansion of Hollywood storytelling's capacities and purposes involves the multidimensional integration of disparate narrative norms.[3]

Characterizations of Altman's storytelling practices as non- or anticlassical, underwritten by analyses that focus on the nonstandard narrational aspects of these early 1970s films, tend to elide the nuanced problem-set that the context of Hollywood filmmaking in this era presented filmmakers. Altman, whose films required Hollywood distribution, formulated his aims and practices in relation to an institution that demanded a degree of narrative standardization but that, due to its shrinking and irregular audience, was also willing to make room for and to reward financially successful stabs at innovation. Altman's approach aimed at appealing to Hollywood's temporary target audience of young, cine-literate filmgoers who wanted more than the standard story. His multidimensional narrative strategy is best understood as innovation through elaboration, augmenting Hollywood classicism's potential appeals by integrating the techniques and the attendant aims of some forms of art cinema.[4] This is not, then, the rejection of classical norms in favor of an oppositional cinema. It is also, though, not the straightforward "incorporat[ion] and refunctionaliz[ation]" of art cinema's "technical tics" suggested by the assimilationist account.[5]

Crucially, Altman's strategy was built on a foundation of classical Hollywood narrative structure. Bracketing off *M\*A\*S\*H* and *Nashville*, the structurally experimental films that bookend the period, clarifies how the majority of Altman's films adhere to the general structuring principles described in Kristin Thompson's scholarship on Hollywood storytelling. The narratives of these films are organized around goal-oriented protagonists, move forward along a discernible causal chain, and display four relatively equivalent large-scale parts connected by turning points. This structural classicism is made evident in qualitative/quantitative analyses of each film's act structure as well as through close analysis of both the comparably straightforward *McCabe & Mrs. Miller* and the Bergman-inspired *Images*. Moreover, while *M\*A\*S\*H* and *Nashville* undeniably feature structural innovation, focused analysis of these films reveals the coordination of novelty with classical structuring strategies.

Altman's films synthesize classical structuring strategies with a suite of narrational approaches that are elaborative perversions of classicism. These approaches couple many of the key techniques and affordances of classical narration with nonclassical practices in the service of goals that invert or redirect their conventional purposes.[6] Thus, both the wide-ranging *Nashville* and the more protagonist-oriented *McCabe & Mrs. Miller* can be understood simultaneously as exercises in elaborating a digressively uneconomic milieu and as forums for virtuosically efficient expositional design. *Brewster McCloud*, arguably the most self-consciously experimental film of this period, displays narrative devices that are both "far out" and narratively purposeful. Moving from the broader scope of narrative structure to a narrower, moment-by-moment focus on the narrational analysis of individual scenes and sequences makes it possible to see how Altman's early 1970s films twist Hollywood norms, expanding the range of classical storytelling through the incorporation of narratively excessive and overt narrational techniques. It is clear that, in spite of these films' classical or quasi-classical structures, it would be inadequate to describe them as simply classical. Indeed, Altman and his collaborators' storytelling strategies assimilate classical principles and techniques rather than being assimilated by those principles.

Moreover, these films straightforwardly display several tendencies of art cinema narratives. The nonclassical qualities of Altman's early 1970s narratives are evident in three overlapping narrational strategies—the use of "punctuational" devices, the foregrounding of narrational voice, and the overt priming of the audience to interpret rather than merely comprehend. Finally, these films also display significant, if limited, resemblances to art cinema in their novel complication of the classical emphasis on closure. In pairing thematic and emotional ambiguity with the often-ignored resolutions of their climaxes and epilogues, these films enact an elaborative narrative strategy best described as "closure without comprehension."

## Free from the Prison of Narrative: Altman as Escape Artist

A shared sense of a narrative difference or depletion in Altman's films has provided a more-or-less stable ground for the dominant oppositional strain in Altman scholarship. It has been fed by Altman's assertions of hostility to narrative form, and it is largely founded on claims about narrative structure. Self has frequently claimed that Altman's films hold narratively radical power. According to Self, "cues for constructing the story in every one of Altman's films challenge the dominant narrative schema of Hollywood movies."[7] Focusing almost exclusively on the narration in Altman's films, Self allows this analysis to lead him to conclude, mistakenly, that "narration structures the films without the discursive order, the continuity of story that is the cornerstone of the Hollywood model."[8] Altman's films are experiments in "meandering, unfocused, ambiguous narrative forms."[9] They are "characterized by a loosening of cause-effect logic, a blurring of story problems, a shortage of deadlines, a tenuous linking of actions and scenes, and an open-ended and episodic chronology of events."[10] However, these career-spanning claims about the narrative structure of Altman's films, embedded in a discussion of their display of the conventions of art cinema narration, are plainly inaccurate in relation to Altman's early 1970s films. In fact, the majority of these films display a classical narrative structure.

Critics who reviewed Altman's films during the early 1970s frequently made similarly bold assertions about their lack of narrative structure. While many of the films received mixed reviews, most reviewers agreed that the films' narratives were somehow lacking—that these were certainly not classical Hollywood narratives, and were, sometimes, barely even narratives. Pauline Kael asserted that *Brewster McCloud*, instead of displaying the tight, economic structure characteristic of classical Hollywood narratives in which each scene links to the next in a chain of cause and effect, was "disconnected" and made up of "individual sequences" that "don't reveal what they're for."[11] The *Variety* review of *McCabe & Mrs. Miller* complained that it contained a "diffused comedy-drama plotline which is repeatedly shoved aside in favor of bawdiness," and that, "fully a quarter or more of the film's 121 sluggish minutes pass before the story begins to move."[12] An anonymous reviewer in *Media and Methods* concludes, "*McCabe* is a collection of semi-dramatic episodes rather than a clear-cut plot."[13] Kael explains the failings of *Images* thus: "When he has a dramatic framework, Altman can do so much to affect us emotionally by his virtuosity with visual images that he may at times think that words don't matter, that images do it all, and 'Images' seems to have been made in that conviction."[14] Here, "words," the opposite of "images," seems to be Kael's poetic substitution for "dramatic framework" or narrative structure. Of *The Long Goodbye*, John Coleman, writing for *The New Statesman*, claims, "the plot, if one may be so bold [as to call it a plot], is elliptical and confused in the extreme."[15] Coleman later describes *California Split* as "the first truly aleatory movie,"[16] and *Variety* agrees with Coleman's assessment, describing the film as, "an aimless, strung-out series of vignettes."[17]

*Newsweek*'s Paul D. Zimmerman even crafted a critical narrative framed around Altman's ongoing attempts to escape from the institutional custody of classical narrative. For Zimmerman, Altman's experimentation involves "going behind the central action to create a third and fourth dimension to moviegoing," thereby "enlarg[ing] the screen."[18] He writes of *Images* that its "loosely structured story offers no formal restraints" to Altman and has "taken him down the path of self-indulgence, which, after all, is the risk of freedom."[19] To Zimmerman, *The Long Goodbye*'s plot "is a prison from which [Altman] continually escapes, only to find himself caught again. It is a measure of his inventiveness that he can fascinate us even as his search for new forms falls short of its goal."[20] In Zimmerman's eyes, Altman finally reaches this goal in *Thieves Like Us*, where "for the first time, Altman frees himself entirely from the strictures of conventional storytelling. His robbers seem to drift from episode to episode in the rhythms of life itself."[21]

There is probably no more important contribution to the creation of this aspect of Altman's biographical legend than Aljean Harmetz's 1971 *New York Times Magazine* profile. Harmetz interviewed Altman during a visit to the set of *McCabe & Mrs. Miller*, and the piece, titled "The 15th Man Who Was Asked to Direct *M\*A\*S\*H* (and Did) Makes a Peculiar Western," is the first lengthy profile of Altman after his "out-of-nowhere" success on *M\*A\*S\*H*. Harmetz, supplemented by quotes from Altman, claims to summarize the director's filmmaking philosophy in the following passage:

> He wants to catch the accidents of life and fling them on the screen hard enough to knock the breath out of the audience. He wants to weight the screen down with vulgarity, pleasure, pain, ugliness, and unexpected beauty. He wants, magically, to change two dimensions into three. Altman is, of course, doomed to failure—which he admits in his rare morose moments: "Nobody has ever made a good movie. Someday someone will make half a good one." To Altman, a "good movie" is "taking the narrative out, taking the story out of it."[22]

Zimmerman's declaration that Altman's work consisted of "going behind the central action to create a third and fourth dimension to moviegoing," thereby "enlarg[ing] the screen," effectively echoes the language used by Harmetz, likely derived from the director's own statements.[23] This multiplication of dimensions is connected to a devotion to realism, a filling-out of the subject beyond what is suggested to be the two-dimensional treatment of the world offered by conventional Hollywood narratives. Standard narrative is opposed to realism, and plot is opposed to accident. Yet this is a false choice. Zimmerman is right to describe Altman's project as adding dimensionality to cinema during the early 1970s, but wrong about the extent to which this requires escaping from classical narrative structure. Instead, as we shall see, Altman's innovative solution is based on elaboration rather than rejection.

Altman, in later interviews, returns to the idea of a spare narrative, but seems to drop the idea of entirely eliminating narrative. Instead, he refers to narrative structure as a thin framework on which to hang his true concerns. In a retrospective interview with Graham Fuller, Altman states, "A plot, to me, is a clothesline. For example, as I read *The Long Goodbye*, it occurred to me that

Raymond Chandler's story was merely a clothesline on which to hang a bunch of thumbnail essays, little commentaries—because that's what he was most interested in. I thought, 'This is exactly my interest in it.'"[24] Referring to *McCabe & Mrs. Miller*, Altman says, "The story became an easy clothesline for me to hang my own essays on. The audience recognized those traditional things— the whore, the killers—so I did not have to dwell on them. Instead I was able to say, 'You think you know this story, but you don't know this story, because the most interesting part of it is all these little sidebars.'"[25]

Implicit in these statements is that the films' narrative structures are actually fairly conventional. How else could Altman feel secure that audiences would immediately "recognize" and "not have to dwell" on the narrative, freeing a portion of attention that he could redirect to the novel aspects of his storytelling? Instead of assuming that Altman's personal filmmaking philosophy necessitated a radical break from or dissolution of narrative structure, it makes more sense to view the need for conventional narrative structure as a key part of Altman's strategy for delivering his mini-essays. This is not to say that Altman's films of the early 1970s were, on the whole, entirely conventional. Altman's storytelling was atypical both in the ways he used stylistic techniques, which I discuss in more detail in the two chapters that follow, and in the distinct narrative strategies he elaborated on and around conventional narrational and structural techniques. Altman and his collaborators devised a suite of solutions that allowed him to provide both conventional narrative and something else. Indeed, Altman cans be said to have relayed his narratives in a way that was perversely classical, providing a classically structured story but doing so in a manner that also served his nonclassical aims.

The first step, then, in reassessing Altman's early 1970s storytelling is illuminating the films' classical narrative structures. Altman's post-*M\*A\*S\*H* films of the first half of the 1970s, with the arguable exception of *Nashville*, are essentially classical in their narrative structure. That is, they all feature goal-oriented protagonists struggling to overcome obstacles in order to reach their goals. Moreover, the character psychologies at the core of these structures are not as diffuse or troubling as some scholars believe. What drives these characters, even in the *Persona*-inspired psychodrama *Images*, is not that difficult to ascertain. Saying that character comprehension is "not that difficult" might lead to objections. Given classical Hollywood's goals of immediate clarity and ease of comprehension, how can a narrative be classical if there is any difficulty at all? One response might be that introducing a level of difficulty on top of a narrative structure does not necessarily entail the sort of radical break from, attack on, or subversion of Hollywood that scholars like Self have argued exists. Instead, it displays and takes advantage of the range and flexibility afforded by the classical Hollywood system, which has frequently depended on and lent itself to imaginative and innovative filmmakers with multifaceted objectives. Particularly during the late 1960s and early 1970s, a time when Hollywood was struggling to appeal to a younger, hipper, more cine-literate audience, Altman's capacity to augment Hollywood story-telling with art cinema techniques and aims seems like a significant means of survival.

## Altman's Classically Structured Storytelling

What did the classical clothesline consist of? Thompson's *Storytelling in the New Hollywood* provides the most persuasive account of the norms of Hollywood storytelling structure, based on close and careful analyses of a broad swath of Hollywood films as well as craft discourses. Building on the findings of *The Classical Hollywood Cinema*, Thompson's book is oriented around the question of whether the narratives of New Hollywood mark a sig-nificant departure from past practice. She first firmly establishes the norms of classical Hollywood storytelling structure and then systematically shows how "post-classical" films, including blockbusters like *Back to the Future* (1985) and auteurist Hollywood films such as Woody Allen's *Hannah and Her Sisters* (1986), fit within and elaborate on the classical model. An appendix details how scores of films correspond with the descriptive and analytic model she proposes.

Thompson argues that Hollywood films have largely adhered to a struc-ture that consists of four large-scale parts of relatively equal length, typically around 20–30 minutes, which she describes as the setup, complicating action, development, and climax. Hollywood's narratives are organized around goal-oriented protagonists in pursuit of their objectives, and each large-scale part plays a characteristic role in structuring this pursuit. Turning points provide the hinges between large-scale parts, setting the stage for the next chunk of action and often spinning it in a new direction. They can do so in a range of ways, but most commonly by clearly articulating a character's goals or tactics or by shifting those goals or tactics. Finally, Hollywood's narratives frequently consist of two lines of action, one of which will almost always be romantic, and turning points and act structure are usually coordinated with both of these lines.[26] With this explicit, albeit condensed, account of classical Hollywood narrative structure in place, we can productively ask to what degree Altman's early 1970s films reflect these concrete norms.

Under close inspection, the six films between *M*A*S*H* and *Nashville* display many of the typical features of classical Hollywood narrative structures. They have goal-oriented protagonists. Turning points, usually connected to character goals and strategies, separate four relatively equal large-scale parts, with a brief epilogue at each film's end. Many of them have the sort of dual storylines that Thompson describes as characteristic of Hollywood, with a romantic plotline supplementing the major storyline. The exact formal features of the narrative structure of each film varies, but this is, of course, to be expected since the classical Hollywood cinema consists not of strict rules but of a set of norms allowing for a range of options.

Table 1.1 describes the proportional distribution of the films' narrative structures. Thompson's findings suggest that Hollywood narratives' large-scale parts are relatively proportional, and here it is clear that the individual parts of Altman's early 1970s films tend to make up around 20%–30% of the total running time of each film, with some exceptions. Climaxes, for instance, tend to be somewhat abbreviated.

Instead of detailing the narrative structures of all six of these films individually, I provide extended description of only two—*McCabe & Mrs. Miller* and *Images*. It is useful, though, to summarize the goal-orientation of the six films' protagonists:

- *Brewster McCloud* actually has two protagonists. The titular major protagonist seeks to construct a pair of wings that will allow him to "fly away"

**Table 1.1** Narrative Structures

| Title | Setup (%) | Complicating Action (%) | Development (%) | Climax (%) | Epilogue (%) |
|---|---|---|---|---|---|
| *Brewster McCloud* | 21 | 24 | 35 | 18 | 2 |
| *McCabe and Mrs. Miller* | 21 | 32 | 27 | 16 | 2 |
| *Images* | 26 | 35 | 18 | 18 | 5 |
| *The Long Goodbye* | 23 | 26 | 32 | 17 | 1 |
| *Thieves Like Us* | 24 | 20 | 29 | 24 | 3 |
| *California Split* | 23 | 23 | 28 | 20 | 7 |
| Mean | 23 | 27 | 28 | 19 | 3 |

to freedom. Meanwhile, Frank Shaft, a San Francisco "supercop," seeks to solve a series of strangulation murders that have taken place in Houston.

- McCabe, in *McCabe & Mrs. Miller*, is a businessman who seeks to establish and profit from the saloon and whorehouse he establishes in Presbyterian Church. He also pursues a romantic relationship with his business partner, Mrs. Miller.
- Catherine, in *Images*, is a schizophrenic who hallucinates dead lovers and a doppelganger and seeks to resolve this condition.
- Elliott Gould's Philip Marlowe, in *The Long Goodbye*, is out to clear the name of his best friend, Terry Lennox, by solving the murder of Lennox's wife.
- Bowie, in *Thieves Like Us*, is a small-time bank robber whose goal shifts to stealing enough money to escape to Mexico with his new girl, Keechie.
- Bill, in *California Split*, is a divorced gambling addict and magazine writer who befriends the inconstant Charlie in the hopes of finding some adventure and then must win big at a high-stakes poker game in Reno in order to pay off his bookie.

As should be expected, the specific goals and strategies of these individual characters modulate over the course of each film, but the previous summary stands as an accurate overview. These are not the sort of sketchy, meandering protagonists one might expect to find in art cinema. Instead, while certainly quirky, they are fairly conventionally motivated.

I would contrast this description of Altman's early 1970s protagonists to the description of Altman's typical protagonists offered by Self, who argues that Altman's "nondirected plot[s]," are, "a function of questioning, uncertain, alienated, sometimes crazy central characters." The implicit analytic principles here—that form necessarily follows subject matter and that characters with these designated traits cannot pursue goals—predetermine and distort the description of the film's narrative features. Self's account of Altman seems to draw on Elsaesser's influential work on American film in the 1970s, where he posits that the shift in prospective audience led to ideological refashioning of films to "reflect stances of dissent typical among minority groups." According to Elsaesser, identifying progressive filmmaking in this context requires "looking for signs that the director had thematized in the very structure of the narrative an awareness of the problem [the noncommitted protagonist] is facing."[27] Elsaesser, then, refocuses thematic exegesis and ideological assessment away from subject matter and onto form, providing encouragement to later seekers of oppositional filmmaking as well as a causal explanation for shifts in formal strategies.

Whether or not we accept this interpretive logic, the evidence suggests that it is not applicable to Altman. Interestingly, Elsaesser actually singles Altman out as "one of the few modern directors who still occasionally employ a symbolic language that clearly belongs to the epoch of the classical *mise-en-scène*: the symbolization of objects through thematic use in the narrative. One would have thought that it belongs too obviously to a cinema of purposive development and positive meanings to be of use in any other form than as quotations."[28]

Nevertheless, to illustrate his case Self claims, "The meandering quality of plot in *McCabe & Mrs. Miller* aptly follows from the indecisive personality of McCabe," but this assertion is at odds with the film's evidently classical narrative structure.[29] The film's setup actually makes it clear that McCabe seeks to be a successful businessman, or a "purveyor of paradise" as the film's promotional material states. McCabe is a cocksure gambler who arrives in the mining town of Presbyterian Church looking to buy land on which to open his own saloon, out of which he plans to run some whores. He takes a trip to Bear Paw to acquire three low-rent prostitutes, and during his negotiations we are afforded a glimpse of Mrs. Miller in a pimp's room. When McCabe returns to Presbyterian Church we learn that he is paying the local miners to build his saloon during their off-hours. By the end of the setup, it is clear that McCabe has no idea how to manage the prostitutes, one of whom stabs a miner. Immediately preceding this, McCabe rejects an invitation from the town's other major business-owner, the scuzzy store-owner, hotelier, and saloon-keeper Sheehan, to work together to keep other entrepreneurs out of Presbyterian Church. Rather than a meanderer, then, McCabe is goal-oriented. And while he may be in over his head when it comes to running prostitutes, the comparison between McCabe and Sheehan clearly displays McCabe's entrepreneurial (and hygienic) superiority.

The film's first turning point comes with the arrival of Mrs. Miller in Presbyterian Church. She proposes a business partnership based on her expertise in whoring and McCabe's evident ignorance, and McCabe reluctantly accepts. Mrs. Miller's arrival also initiates the romantic storyline of the film. As is typical of the complicating action in classical Hollywood narrative structure, McCabe's plans undergo a shift, as he yields to Mrs. Miller's advice to build a proper whorehouse and a bathhouse, and McCabe's saloon is relatively unsuccessful while the whorehouse generates an impressive profit. Meanwhile, Mrs. Miller treats McCabe like any other john, stymieing his pathetic overtures. Whereas originally McCabe was the dominant male who rejected partnership, after Mrs. Miller's arrival he is now both partnered up with and clearly marked as inferior to Mrs. Miller. She not only brushes aside his romantic advances by making him pay for sex but also reproaches his business stratagems and bookkeeping skills. The complicating action, then, in reversing key premises established in the setup, has functioned in some ways as the sort of counter setup that Thompson describes as typical.[30]

The film's second turning point comes with the arrival of the Mining Company's representatives, as they purchase Sheehan's businesses and attempt to negotiate a buyout with McCabe. When a drunken McCabe fails to recognize the limits of the men's patience, suggesting a selling price well above what they offer, the pair give up on making a deal and leave town, sending a trio of killers to dispatch with McCabe. The film's development follows McCabe's belated recognition of his mistake and unsuccessful attempts to rectify his error—first by bargaining with the unresponsive killers and then by trying to find the company men before they leave the region. The development, then, progresses in a way that is typical of classical Hollywood narrative structure. McCabe's attempts to negotiate serve as delays, putting off a final confrontation with the killers, while at the same time creating moments of suspense. When these attempts fail, McCabe contacts a lawyer in Bear Paw, whose vainglorious speechifying convinces McCabe to stand his ground. A delaying subplot featuring an innocent young cowboy whom McCabe initially mistakes for an assassin and who enjoys the whorehouse before being murdered by one of the actual hired killers serves to provide suspense and clarify the stakes. During the development, the romantic relationship between Mrs. Miller and McCabe is also advanced. Mrs. Miller's concern for McCabe's well-being—she offers to sneak him out of town—suggests that her concern for her partner may be about more than business. McCabe makes his feelings for Mrs. Miller clear in a sideways take on a classical device for conveying exposition—a monologue—as he prepares for his trip to Bear Paw while mumbling disjointedly to himself.

In a scene that, in coordination with the scene with the lawyer which immediately precedes it, serves as the film's third turning point, McCabe returns to Presbyterian Church and clearly states his goal, informing Mrs. Miller that he will stay to protect his rights as a businessman. This sets the stage for a conventional climax, where the hero will move in a straightforward manner toward resolving this goal. McCabe either will or will not successfully defend himself from the trio of killers who hunt him down. In a game of cat and mouse played out during a heavy snowfall, during which the lead assassin accidentally lights the town's church on fire, McCabe does manage to kill the hired guns. He is, though, shot twice in the process, and he bleeds-out in a snow drift. The townspeople successfully fight off the blaze, and their endeavors are directed by Sheehan, who seems to have been elevated to a position of leadership in the town. A brief epilogue reveals that Mrs. Miller, who is with McCabe during his final night and then abandons him before dawn, has retreated to an opium den. There is an openness to this final state of affairs—what will Mrs. Miller do next? But the film's major narrative lines have been closed off with McCabe's death. Even though he has killed the killers, they have also killed him, providing what is, for Altman, a typically ironic closure to the question of whether McCabe will maintain his grasp on his holdings. And his romance with Mrs. Miller is similarly quashed, with the audience left to consider whether her current state is the result of disappointment over business or romantic losses. *McCabe & Mrs. Miller*, then, does not display the meandering plotlessness commonly attributed to it. Instead, it is classically structured. McCabe's actions are consistently directed toward achieving his goals, even if his tactics and strategies are only inconsistently or qualifiedly successful.

Altman's next film, *Images*, is understood by critics as an early example of his semiregular forays into Bergman-esque psychodrama, and it serves as a companion piece to 1977's *Three Women*. Indeed, Altman has told at least one interviewer that, "*Images*, I think, was an imitation of Bergman's *Persona*, which I was very impressed with."[31] Yet *Images*, while challenging, in no way presents the same challenges to comprehension or the same rejection of Hollywood storytelling norms that can be found in Bergman's melding of modernism and art cinema. In fact, even when compared to Roman Polanski's *Repulsion* (1965), a more popular, more conventional art cinema psychodrama that, like *Images*, features a homicidally disturbed female lead, the film's narrative structure is clearly far more orthodox. As with *Images*' protagonist, Catherine, *Repulsion*'s lead character, Carol, undergoes a complete mental breakdown over the course of the film. Carol, though, has no goals or strategy to speak of, apart from barricading herself away from imagined attackers. *Repulsion* is essentially structured around repetition and intensification—each day, Carol yields a bit more to her paranoia and fear. Altman's *Images*, on the other hand, is structured around the protagonist's strategic attempts to defeat her schizophrenia.

What is often viewed as Altman's most direct foray into art cinema should instead be seen as his revision of the psychological thriller or, perhaps, female gothic. The fact that *Images*' Catherine is mentally disturbed complicates understanding of the film's narrative threads, but the film is, indeed, organized around the story of a woman pursuing her goals. Here, the goal is mental health, and so the film's setup establishes that Catherine's mental illness manifests in hallucinatory episodes in which she hears her own voice on the telephone and imagines her husband, Hugh, suddenly transformed into another man. The setup takes place over the course of one evening, with

Hugh off at work, and with the voice of Catherine's doppelganger harassing Catherine with allegations that Hugh is actually with another woman. When Hugh returns home and Catherine suddenly sees him as another man, she decides to seek relief in a fairly conventional manner—via a therapeutic retreat to the countryside.

The film's turn into the complicating action comes as Catherine and Hugh arrive at their country house where, rather than finding relief, Catherine experiences an intensification of her visions. She first sees, from a distance, her doppelganger waiting for her at the house, and she then once again imagines seeing the man. This time, though, Catherine both sees Hugh as the man and also sees him apart from Hugh, introducing what will prove to be a dangerous flexibility to her imaginings. Her conversation with this imagined man reveals to the audience that he is her deceased former lover, Rene, complicating the established infidelity-related premise by suggesting that it is Catherine who has been unfaithful to Hugh. Catherine eventually attacks Rene and wounds him, introducing another important premise—that she can injure the figments haunting her. Another complication arises when a second former lover, Marcel, arrives with Hugh as he returns from shopping. Marcel, unlike Rene, is still alive, and he brings his daughter, Susannah, with him. He is, though, equally threatening to Catherine since he is extremely sexually aggressive, constantly groping Catherine. Meanwhile, Catherine has been seeing images of herself outside her windows. Later that night, yet another complication arises as Catherine sees Hugh as Marcel and Marcel as Hugh. Catherine has to fight off a sexual attack by Marcel, and afterward she experiences a lengthy hallucination/flashback in which she makes love to Hugh, Marcel, and Rene. This sequence, while nominally one of the most art cinema-esque of the film, also serves to reveal a great deal of backstory, fleshing out Catherine's affairs with Rene and Marcel and suggesting that Catherine conducted these affairs because she wished to become pregnant in spite of Hugh's sterility. The sequence culminates with Catherine now hallucinating her doppelganger in the place of Hugh. By the end of the complicating action we have another counter-setup. The premise that Catherine has retreated to the country house in order to get better has been turned on its head. Instead of getting better, she now seems significantly worse-off than before—her hallucinations have intensified dramatically. Additionally, whereas during the setup it seemed that Catherine's hallucinations were prompted by fears of Hugh's infidelity, it is now clear that it is Catherine who has had at least two affairs.

Catherine's initial strategy for escaping her mental illness has failed, and in the development portion of the film she acquires another. The turning point comes the morning after the dream sequence, when Catherine once again sees

Rene. This time, though, Catherine shoots Rene in the chest with a shotgun, which puts an end to his appearances, killing his "ghost." Catherine's belief that she can stop her hallucinations if she "murders" them becomes key to how she will "get better." Before she can follow through with this strategy, though, she must overcome the delays and obstacles the development presents. When Marcel appears in Catherine's bedroom and mentions the sex they had the previous night—during Catherine's dream sequence—she decides he must be an apparition and finds a pair of scissors to stab him with. But before she can impale Marcel, Hugh bursts into the room. When Catherine talks to Hugh, she learns that Marcel returned to the house before him, raising the possibility that it was in fact the real Marcel whom she almost stabbed. The uncertainty about whether Marcel was or was not real is resolved when his daughter tells Catherine he had been downstairs with her, but the premise that Catherine may attack the real person rather than the hallucination calls her strategy into question and presents her with an obstacle.

It is worth pausing here to emphasize how different *Images'* hallucinating Catherine is from *Repulsion's* hallucinating Carol. In Polanski's film, Carol's hallucinations externalize her paranoid fantasies, giving the audience access to the subjectivity of someone who is mentally disturbed in a way that is typical of art cinema. It is her *experience* of mental illness that is the subject matter of the film. In *Images*, Catherine's hallucinations, while also externalized for the audience to view, become the subject of the protagonist's goal-oriented strategizing and, therefore, of narrative movement. Our access to Catherine's subjectivity is, then, conventionally narrativized, while our access to Carol's subjectivity is descriptive and provocative, illustrating the inner turmoil of one woman's mental breakdown rather than advancing a classical story structure.

When Hugh is called into the city for work his presence is removed as an obstacle in the way of Catherine reaching her goal—she need no longer be concerned that she is mistaking Hugh for a hallucination—and his departure marks the turn to the climax, where Catherine is free to pursue her strategy to its conclusion. After dropping Hugh off at the train station, Catherine smiles when she sees Marcel in town flirting with a woman, providing an indication of her belief that, because the real Marcel is in town, any Marcel she might encounter on her return home will be a hallucination. Marcel does, in fact, appear on Catherine's return, and she happily stabs him and goes to bed, leaving his bloodied body on the floor. The next morning, Marcel's body remains on the floor when Catherine answers the door for her neighbor. When the neighbor's dog seems overly curious about smells coming from within, Catherine worries that she may have killed the real Marcel. Her fears are augmented when

Susannah arrives looking for her father, but Catherine quickly learns from her that Marcel did, in fact, safely return home the previous night. After Catherine drives Susannah back to her home, she encounters her doppelganger once again, this time walking down the road. Catherine's plan is fully realized, and the climax comes to an end, when she runs this final hallucinatory figure off the road and over a cliff with her car. The epilogue delivers a conventional last-minute twist, however, as Catherine returns to her empty home in the city, expecting to find Hugh. Instead, her imagined double appears as she is showering, and Catherine realizes she has actually driven an early-returning Hugh off the cliff. The film confirms this by replaying the scene, now showing Hugh falling to a gruesome death. Her doppelganger, who during the setup had made imaginary phone calls to Catherine accusing Hugh of infidelity, has fooled Catherine and extracted her revenge.

While *Images*' subject matter and exteriorizing of subjective experience are more closely associated with the European art film, Altman has harnessed these features to a protagonist's goal-oriented strategizing and a clear four-part structure. Even the early 1970s film considered a straightforward example of Altman's art cinema approach to narrative is actually quite classical in terms of its narrative structure. Likewise, close analysis of *McCabe & Mrs. Miller*, whose production and release generated the foundational accounts of Altman's rejection of narrative, provides evidence undermining oppositional accounts of Altman's storytelling practice. Of course, it is more difficult to make the case for Altman's employment of conventional narrative structure in relation to the films that bookend this period—*M\*A\*S\*H* and *Nashville*. I have set aside an examination of these two films since they seem to be the exceptions to Altman and his collaborators' standard approach to narrative structures during this period. Even so, these films are not as divergent as standard accounts suppose. Their episodic, sprawling, and more open narratives are still constrained and shaped by classical principles.

While neither of these films' narratives are structured around a conventional goal-oriented protagonist in an entirely orthodox manner, they are not therefore necessarily incoherent, nor do they lack a character hierarchy that gives shape to plot structure. *M\*A\*S\*H*, for instance, does not roam freely among the camp's medical professionals. Instead, scenes focus on Hawkeye Pierce and Trapper John, played by the film's two major stars. Moreover, it is a lone character, Hawkeye, whose presence truly serves to structure the film. After an opening featuring the unit's commanding officer, Colonel Blake, hoping aloud that the new surgeons he requested will arrive soon, the film cuts to Hawkeye's arrival in Korea, clearly marking him as the film's central figure. Hawkeye then drives himself and the other new surgeon, Duke, to the base in a stolen jeep. The film ends with Hawkeye and Duke receiving their discharge orders and then departing in the same stolen jeep. Trapper, who does not arrive until late in the film's setup, remains behind and inherits Hawkeye's dog. The fact that the film begins with discussion of Hawkeye's arrival and ends with his departure makes evident that $M^*A^*S^*H$ is not a wholly free-wheeling, narratively decentered film "about the ensemble" but instead is structured, at least in part, around a protagonist singled out by the narrative design in order to provide a sense of coherence.

$M^*A^*S^*H$'s narrative structure is most commonly described as episodic, but this is only qualifiedly true. In fact, the film displays an overarching quasi-classical narrative structure, with four large-scale parts that function more or less conventionally in relation to Hawkeye's pursuit of his overarching if somewhat abstract objective—bending the Army, or at least his $M^*A^*S^*H$ unit, to his liking. The setup builds the essential situation at the $M^*A^*S^*H$ camp, introducing all of the main characters and culminating with the arrival of Hot Lips, which serves as the turning point into the complicating action. The core conflict established in the setup is between Hawkeye and misguided or sanctimonious allegiance to social convention—embodied in Frank Burns's overt religiosity and Hot Lips's unreflexive adherence to "regular army" protocols. Hot Lips is immediately aligned with conservatism during her introductory tour of the base when she sees Trapper sucker punch Burns for mistreating a private and sides with Burns. The complicating action, then, largely focuses on the conflict between this pair and the rest of the camp, led by Hawkeye, Trapper, and Duke. Crucially, even though it is Trapper who ratchets up the conflict by punching Burns, it is Hawkeye who eventually ensures that Burns is removed from camp by provoking him into a violent nervous breakdown via lewd questions about his sexual encounter with Hot Lips.

It is only with the removal of Burns as an obstacle that $M^*A^*S^*H$ becomes episodic. Its extended third part essentially consists of four episodes: treating Painless's impotence through a travesty of religion that thematically reinforces Hawkeye's triumph over Burns, resolving the question of Hot Lips's natural hair color, attempting to prevent the camp's "houseboy" Ho-Jon from being inducted into the Korean Army, and Hawkeye and Trapper's surgical golf outing to Japan. While this large-scale part of $M^*A^*S^*H$ is unusually episodic, it is important to also note that not all of the third act's episodes are narratively disjointed from the rest of the film. Even with Burns's removal at the end of the complicating action, Hot Lips remains in the camp, and over the course of $M^*A^*S^*H$'s quasi-development she begins to be brought into the fold. First, she is "brought low" and humiliated as almost the entire camp gathers to see the color of her pubic hair, after which she futilely warns the entirely unsympathetic Blake that she will resign her commission if nothing is done to restore order. Then, after Hawkeye and Trapper return from Japan they discover Hot Lips and Duke fornicating in their tent. The third act ends, then, with Hot Lips apparently having given-in to Hawkeye's faction.

Even so, a dangling cause from Hot Lips and Burns's active campaign against Hawkeye and his allies remains from the complicating action, when the pair sent a formal letter of complaint to Blake's superior, General Hammond. In the film's final large-scale part, Hammond follows up on the complaint but is distracted from the enforcement of military order when Hawkeye mentions that Hot Lips won't even let the camp play football. Hammond immediately becomes interested in setting up a high-stakes game between his own team and the overmatched M*A*S*H unit. Importantly, it is Hawkeye who comes up with the "ringer" strategy that will allow the unit to defeat Hammond's forces and win the bet, and as part of the game Hot Lips leads a team of cheerleaders composed of the unit's nurses. While the climax can hardly be seen as the sort of clear and straightforward movement toward the protagonist's goals common in Hollywood, it does conclude with the entire unit brought together in celebration of their victory, as two troop transport trucks return to the M*A*S*H camp with the drunken revelers. That the reshaping of the community, rather than returning home, has been Hawkeye's true goal becomes clear in the film's epilogue, as he and Duke respond rather solemnly when notified their time with the M*A*S*H unit has come to an end.

While not entirely classical in its structure (which may actually be sanctioned by Hollywood genre norms, given the film's status as a military comedy), M*A*S*H still displays remarkable similarities to the norms of Hollywood storytelling practice. Table 1.2 revises the previous table, incorporating a breakdown of M*A*S*H's narrative structure. With its slightly long development and slightly truncated epilogue, M*A*S*H's division into large-scale parts more or less conforms both to Altman's overall practice during the period and to the norms of classical narrative structure.

Table 1.2 also incorporates structural statistics for *Nashville*, and it is worth noting how this revision barely shifts Altman's recalculated means. Of course, the table's clean "four-part plus epilogue" breakdown of *Nashville*, a narratively sprawling film with a famously sprawling ensemble of twenty-four major characters, might lead one to wonder whether the terms of Thompson's model are being applied arbitrarily. Given what has been convincingly described by David Bordwell as the "network narrative" structure of *Nashville*, is it plausible to posit for it a classical structure? This characterization of *Nashville* is, of course, a provocative move, and it is not meant to be taken as an assertion that the film's narrative structure is unremarkable or totally normative. For

**Table 1.2** Narrative Structures (complete)

| Title | Setup (%) | Complicating Action (%) | Development (%) | Climax (%) | Epilogue (%) |
|---|---|---|---|---|---|
| M*A*S*H | 23 | 20 | 35 | 18 | 4 |
| Brewster McCloud | 21 | 24 | 35 | 18 | 2 |
| McCabe and Mrs. Miller | 21 | 32 | 27 | 16 | 2 |
| Images | 26 | 35 | 18 | 18 | 5 |
| The Long Goodbye | 23 | 26 | 32 | 17 | 1 |
| Thieves Like Us | 24 | 20 | 29 | 24 | 3 |
| California Split | 23 | 23 | 28 | 20 | 7 |
| Nashville | 28 | 25 | 21 | 23 | 3 |
| New Mean (change) | 24 (1%) | 26 (−1%) | 28 (0%) | 19 (0%) | 3 (0%) |

instance, Thompson's model suggests that the large-scale parts in Hollywood films tend to consist of twenty-to-thirty-minute chunks, with developments or complicating actions doubled in films with long running times. The percentage-based approach employed in the charts presented here thus elides the fact that the large-scale parts I posit for the 160-minute *Nashville* are much longer than the classical norm. Altman and his collaborators seem to have puffed-up the narrative's large-scale parts rather than taking what Thompson describes as the more common route of doubling individual acts.[32] Rather than being fully assimilable, then, I would argue that the film instead uses classical structuring strategies in order to give more shape than is usually acknowledged to an otherwise sprawling epic. Even Bordwell, while acknowledging the "haphazard," "gappy," and "inconclusive" nature of the film, recognizes that it displays a clear setup and at least one turning point.[33]

I would propose, though, that evidence suggests an account of the narrative structure—or, more accurately, the narrative structuring—of *Nashville*, should avoid terms such as "haphazard." The film's major structuring strategy employs Hal Philip Walker's political emissary, John Triplette, as a kind of "clothesline" protagonist, to appropriate a term from Altman's own pronouncements on narrative form. Triplette is the most prominently and determinedly goal-oriented of the film's characters. Moreover, his goal—to raise support for Walker by enlisting Nashville's musical talent—impinges on the less classical storylines of the majority of the film's remaining characters. This is evident in the collection of the entirety of the film's major characters, save for Connie White, on and around the stage at the Parthenon rally for Walker at the climax of the film—their presence due to the narrative work accomplished by Triplette.

Just as *M\*A\*S\*H* opens, more or less, with Hawkeye's arrival, *Nashville* opens with Walker/Triplette's virtual arrival, as a Walker van pulls out of a garage and begins its promotional drive around Nashville, blasting his colloquial political "wisdom" from its speakers. Triplette is a less regular presence in *Nashville*'s sprawling narrative than Hawkeye is in *M\*A\*S\*H*, but Walker's campaign—its vans and its cowgirl foot soldiers—seem to be everywhere. Triplette's major objective is to recruit Barbara Jean, Nashville's biggest female star, as well as the preening patriarch of Nashville's music scene, Haven Hamilton, to sing at the Parthenon campaign event. But Haven's careful tending of his reputation and Barbara Jean's mental fragility and overbearing husband/manager, Barnett, present Triplette with significant obstacles. Triplette is also assigned the minor connected goal of putting on a fundraising "smoker" for the campaign.

Triplette is employed as more than a generally unifying force—his narrative is dispersed and developed across the film in a way that suggests the employment of a four-part structure with turning points. Bordwell describes how scenes featuring musical performance tend to provide moments of "convergence," where multiple characters gather together so that narrative development may take place. A novel use of crosscutting augments these convergences by creating sequences that cut back and forth to separate spaces within and across venues, multiplying the number of characters a given segment might feature. In doing so, the filmmakers amplify a practice that Warren Buckland, following Steven D. Katz, labels zone staging, in which characters are established in separate zones within a scenic space.[34] The setup concludes with one such sequence as Altman cuts between performances at the Old Time Picking Parlor and The Deemen's Den, as well as Triplette's temporary base of operations—the home of Delbert and Linnea Reese. On a phone call with the bartender at Deemen's Den, Triplette and Reese arrange for the pathos-inspiring Sueleen Gay to perform at Walker's smoker, and this for the first time makes explicit Triplette's larger strategy and purpose in Nashville. This moment, when, to quote Thompson, a "protagonist's goal jells and he or she articulates it," arguably provides the film with its first turning point.[35]

The Triplette-centered transition between *Nashville*'s first two large-scale parts is also marked by the first transition from day-to-day. Arguably, the day-to-day transitions serve as the more prominent structuring principle in the film, and this principle's abstract, non-character-centered nature conforms more to the looseness of prototypical art cinema structure. But with the exception of the turn into the climax portion of the film, Altman pairs this nonclassical structuring principle with the classical structuring technique afforded by Triplette. Thus, the film's second turning point, into the development, accompanies the conclusion of another day's activities. After a series of large-scale performances at the Grand Ole Opry, many of the film's characters gather at another, smaller, performance venue. Here, Altman cuts between tables within the same space and also assembles several major players at the main table—seating Triplette with Delbert, Haven Hamilton, Connie White (and husband), and Barnett. *Nashville*'s, or at least Triplette's, second turning point is provided when Haven conditions his appearance at the Parthenon on Barbara Jean's participation. Triplette looks over at the loudly complaining Barnett and resignedly agrees to Haven's terms, clarifying the shift in strategy and reinforcing Barnett's role as obstacle.

The film's third Triplette-oriented turning point, into the climax, comes, as Bordwell notes, at Barbara Jean's performance at the Opry Belle the following day.[36] Before her performance, Barnett refuses Reese and Triplette's entreaties, but after Barbara Jean breaks down during her performance, Barnett placates the unruly crowd by promising an appearance at the Parthenon. Triplette can now move directly toward his minor and major goals—Walker's smoker, followed by the disastrous Parthenon performance where Barbara Jean is assassinated. After the assassination, Walker rushes away in his limo, and a bewildered Triplette walks off the stage, effectively washing his hands of Nashville. He managed to achieve his goals, but with disastrous consequences. The presumed crackpot wannabe country star Albuquerque takes the microphone amid the chaos and leads the crowd in a strangely effective rendition of "It Don't Worry Me," providing the film with the kind of decidedly ambiguous epilogue discussed in this chapter's final section.

Tracking Triplette's narrative movement in relation to his goals provides indications of a four-part structure, with relatively equivalent portions that fit within Thompson's model. That said, there is a great deal of elaboration around this structure, though the organization of this elaboration is itself not entirely haphazard. Indeed, other character trajectories are coordinated around the underlying four-part structure. The same sequence in which Triplette sets up his smoker also explicitly establishes that Bill and Mary's marriage is souring, as Bill asks a hostile Mary why she is not color-coordinating her outfit with his. This sequence also introduces the premise that Delbert's wife, Linnea, is being pursued by Tom (the third member of the musical trio Bill, Mary, and Tom), when he calls her and proposes they meet up. Likewise, Triplette's complicating action also features Tom intensifying his phone campaign for Linnea, and at a separate table during the previously discussed post–Grand Ole Opry club scene, Bill tells his driver/friend Norman that he thinks Mary is having an affair. The film then cuts to Mary in bed with a sleeping Tom. In Triplette's development section, Linnea is absent, but after a scene in which Triplette attempts to recruit the sparring Bill and Mary for the Parthenon performance, Tom is shown making a phone call looking for another romantic hook-up. In a scene at the No Exit Inn in the film's climax section, Bill watches gleefully as Mary learns Tom has slept with the faux–BBC reporter Opal while they have been in Nashville, and Linnea succumbs to Tom's rendition of "I'm Easy." Later, Linnea calmly leaves Tom in bed, treating him like a child and resolving their plot line. At the Parthenon, Bill seems to have participated in an elliptical pattern in which the film's men "hook-up" with L.A. Joan, whom he arrives with, but he reunites with Mary after the shooting, climbing onstage and dragging her away. Linnea is similarly reunited with Delbert, who accompanies her offstage.

Thompson actually cites *Nashville* as an example of one form of what she terms multiple-protagonist narratives, and her model accounts for different permutations of this narrative form, noting, for instance, that different characters' pursuits tend to be structured in parallel—as this analysis suggests is the case in *Nashville*.[37] Of course, *Nashville* is extreme in its sprawl and less precise in the coordination of its structure than other multiple-protagonist narratives Thompson tends to. But as the preceding analysis has hopefully established, it is also a far cry from chaos. Triplette's goal-oriented pursuit of musical talent provides a coherent and fully integrated support for the structured proliferation of narrative premises and the elaboration of a dense, thematically resonant milieu.

## Altman's Perverse Classicism

To the extent that Triplette's classical narrative journey underwrites *Nashville*'s nonclassical excess, the film—in spite of its novelty within Altman's early 1970s oeuvre—may be regarded as exemplary of the virtuosically perverse approach to narrative classicism on display in these films. Getting at this virtuosity and perversion, though, requires carefully considering how the parameters of narration are coordinated with story world and narrative structure. Bordwell's summary of classical Hollywood's approach to narration around narrational knowledgeability, communicativeness, and self-consciousness provides a useful starting point. He describes the mode's general norm as, "omniscient, highly communicative, and only moderately self-conscious. That is, the narration knows more than all the characters, conceals relatively little . . . and seldom acknowledges its own address to the audience."[38] As we shall see, Altman's narrative strategies sometimes involve the qualified rejection of aspects of these norms, but most often involve their revision and repurposing toward his own ends.

At its most conventional, classical Hollywood employs its narrational strategies in service to storytelling that is usually described as highly efficient and economic in its relentless focusing of audience attention and interest on forward movement along a causal chain. This would seem to present an obvious contrast with Altman's films, which are replete with digressive scenarios and foregrounded background characters. However, instead of assuming that this kind of sprawl necessarily leads to aimless large-scale narrative structures and meandering moment-to-moment narration, we might closely examine how, in *Nashville*, viewed as Altman's ode to narrative dispersion, and *Brewster McCloud*, Altman's self-declared "something else," he and his collaborators actually tackle this challenge of elaboration. One key strategy is best described as perverse economy. That is, these films make exceptionally skillful use of the affordances offered by the expansive range and high degree of communicativeness common in Hollywood narration to achieve efficiency in the moment-to-moment delivery of narrative premises, though in the service of unconventional aims.

Clarifying this aspect of Altman's elaborative strategy requires distinguishing between efficiency and economy, terms that underwrite descriptions of classical Hollywood's storytelling principles but are often treated as interchangeable. For our purposes, I would suggest narrowly defining efficiency as generating maximal outputs through minimal inputs, with screen time probably serving as the most important input in moving image media storytelling. Economy, on the other hand, involves purposefully harnessing those inputs toward a profitable aim, and by most accounts classical Hollywood cinema's normal aim is the clear presentation of narrative action organized around a goal-oriented protagonist. Altman's films often display highly conventional narrational techniques that are, arguably, incredibly efficient but that are not, strictly speaking, economic by Hollywood norms. That is, their efficiencies are not necessarily employed "profitably"—to engage audiences in the advancement of a classical narrative causal chain. Instead, they are employed for a more diverse set of purposes, many of which are likely to be seen as wasteful in relation to Hollywood's norms. Moreover, there is sometimes an ironizing reflexive function built into their use that would seem to counter the kind of narrative immersion that Hollywood tends to aim for, at least in its dramas.

This characterization of Altman's strategy should, of course, not be taken as a claim that Altman's films fail to tell a coherent, classically structured story—a canard I hope to have convincingly overturned. Again, Altman's approach to storytelling is best understood as classical-plus.

At an American Film Institute seminar held at the same time that *Nashville* was being assembled in the editing room, Altman described how crucial his team felt it was to provide the proper introduction to the film's characters given that there would be "probably twelve" storylines running concurrently in the film. But, he states, "the interesting thing is that when the audience starts to know that, and if we can ever get our introduction properly in the thing, I think people pick up on all of these stories. It seems almost like the less you give them, the more they seem to understand it."[39] This suggests an intriguing principle—efficiency is not just a compromise but the most effective expository strategy for ensuring the comprehension of multiple interwoven narrative threads. This perhaps results from the need to signal the film's break from the classical norm of a single goal-oriented protagonist who would usually be identified, in part, through a high degree of expositional attention. When no one character is singled out through an extra portion of expositional material, the audience is left to find another way to understand the film's series of introductions. This principle also recognizes the capacity of an individual film to train the audience to engage with it according to its intrinsic norms. For *Nashville*, this would involve displacing the extrinsic norm of narrative economy with the perverse intrinsic norm of efficient excess.

Altman's statement at the AFI seminar also clearly signals that editing *Nashville*'s "introduction" provided a particularly significant challenge for the filmmakers—how to effectively introduce twelve storylines and twenty-four major characters? Five characters are quickly established in the film's second sequence, set in Haven Hamilton's recording studio, but it is the sequence that follows, set in the Nashville airport, that reveals Altman and his collaborators at their problem-solving best, and at their most perversely economic. Here, they establish nearly a score of characters while initiating many of their conflicts and storylines in what must be record time. This is a remarkable feat that is commonly overlooked in the oppositional account's celebratory characterization of Altman's filmmaking as narratively lax, elliptical, and meandering.

To accomplish this perverse wonder of concentrated and preliminary exposition—central to classical Hollywood communicativeness—the film makes intensified use of the kind of zone staging discussed earlier.[40] In effect, it deploys an omniscient narration—the kind of unrestricted narrational range characteristic of classical Hollywood—but in service here to an atypically expansive number of narrative zones. The sequence establishes and then alternates between multiple major zones and, in some cases, embeds within them minor zones of expositionally efficient overlapping character interaction. The film establishes four key zones in and around the airport: the exterior on the runway side of the airport where Barbara Jean's arrival is celebrated, the parking lot, the airport restaurant, and the airport corridors. The exposition and the sprawling cast of characters eventually converge around the primary hub of Barbara Jean before shifting to the secondary hub of the parking lot, from which the characters and audience embark on their journey into Nashville proper.

It is worth examining this surprising narrational virtuosity (as opposed to haphazardness) at length. The sequence begins by alternating between each of the four zones, starting on the runway, and employing an entirely conventional device for efficiently providing exposition—the television news report. The reporter informs his viewers, and the film's audience, that the gathering crowd is awaiting the arrival of Barbara Jean, returning to Nashville after receiving treatment at a burn center. The report quickly cues the audience to understand that Barbara Jean is an extremely popular singer, with "three thousand fans" awaiting her arrival, and that she is likely in a fragile state. The film then cuts to the second key zone, the airport's main corridor, and to a shot of a music stand which prominently displays posters featuring the face of Karen Black, who will portray country singer Connie White. This shot also introduces Private Kelly, who eagerly asks the shop girl about Barbara Jean's arrival, raising a curiosity question about his interest in Barbara Jean that will be intensified throughout the film's first half. We then move to the parking lot, where another featured actor, Jeff Goldblum, whose unnamed character is identified in the end credits as "Tricycle Man," arrives at the carport on his three-wheeled motorcycle, followed by Walker's campaign van. Tricycle Man performs a magic trick for a chauffeur as he walks into the airport, establishing his major trait as a magician and providing a chance to characterize the chauffeur, later identified as Norman, who is slow to recognize the trick, as a bit dim.

Tricycle Man provides the vehicle for a shift to the final zone of the airport restaurant, where four more major characters are efficiently established across overlapping embedded zones ⊛ (see the companion website for a video clip). At the restaurant's bar, Mr. Green, dressed in a brown suit, asks the waitress, Sueleen Gay, for a sundae while a cook, Wade, watches as Tricycle Man performs another trick. Critics often overstate the role of Tricycle Man's movement through Nashville as a vehicle for the integration of Nashville's disparate narrative lines, but here his movement and his magic provide the basis

for concrete expositional strategies. Indeed, when Wade calls Sueleen's attention to the trick, she doesn't reply to Wade but instead establishes the tone of
their relationship by walking past him and flirting with Tricycle Man. As with
the television report, the film employs a conventional expositional device as
an unnamed diner tries to make small talk with Mr. Green by asking him what
brings him to Nashville—essentially a request for backstory. His pestering
interjections during Green's attempts to order a series of unavailable sundae
flavors prompt Green's explanation that he lives in Nashville, and that his
niece is coming to see his sick wife—the two key premises needed to understand the character. This last bit of information is overlapped with Sueleen's
flirtations with Tricycle Man, as she tells him that she wrote "a real hot song"
and asks if he wants to hear it. When he does not object, Sueleen proceeds to
sing off-key. Wade's shouted declaration that, "there are some freaks out here,
let me tell you," signals the rude boisterousness that becomes his most narratively salient trait, along with his unrequited interest in Sueleen. And as she
continues her song, the film cuts to another zone of space in the restaurant, in
which Delbert Reese licks his lips, wipes his mouth, and then gets up all while
intensely gazing at Sueleen with evident sexual interest. This shot instantly
characterizes Delbert while also marking his impending departure from the
restaurant. Moreover, this moment efficiently integrates its characterization
of Delbert with its establishment of the key premises that will drive Sueleen's
tragic storyline—her sexual allure, coupled with a lack of talent and abundance of ambition. Indeed, the song that she sings, "I'll Never Get Enough," is
reprised in the film's final act to jeers from ogling men expecting a striptease
at Walker's smoker. Delbert's characterization here will have its payoff in the
aftermath of that performance as he hits on the traumatized Sueleen in a moment that somehow inspires both pathos and intense disgust.

After a short exterior scene in which Barbara Jean's plane finishes taxiing,
the film returns to the interior of the airport and introduces another quartet of
characters, beginning with L.A. Joan. The scantily clad Joan is ironically positioned next to a sign that warns passengers that they will be searched for concealed weapons, with an arrow on the sign pointing directly at her body. Joan's
sexual circulation serves as one half of the character's major line of action
throughout the film, and this diegetically coincidental emphasis on her body
and attire provides its prelude. Delbert stares at Joan from across the corridor,
silently reinforcing his established character trait. When Delbert misidentifies a passing man as "John Triplette," his purpose in the airport, to pick up
Triplette, becomes clear. This also signals to the audience that Delbert is un-
familiar with Triplette, marking Triplette as a Nashville outsider. The actual
Triplette eventually introduces himself to Delbert, and while they greet one

another two more new characters, Mary and Bill, pass by. Delbert, now predictably, ogles Mary to the point of distraction. Triplette reclaims his attention by asking his name, and Delbert introduces himself as "Del Reese," naming the character for the audience. When Triplette comments admiringly on the young women in patriotic uniforms handing out political fliers it playfully indicates his character's political rather than sexual preoccupation, marking a contrast with Del that underlines the pair's divergent character traits.

Outside the airport, Haven Hamilton, introduced in the film's second sequence as a vainglorious country singer, arrives with Lady Pearl and his son Buddy, also introduced earlier. The television reporter narrates their arrival, reinforcing the character premises established earlier in the film and marking Haven as a friend of Barbara Jean—a connection crucial to Triplette's plot line.

Meanwhile, inside the airport, intra-zone overlap is employed to introduce another new character and to efficiently set in motion Mr. Green and L.A. Joan's storyline. Green greets Joan, calling her Martha, and cueing the audience to understand that this woman is Green's niece. "Martha" quickly lets her uncle know that she has changed her name to L.A. Joan. While she does so, another major character, Tom, passes by, surrounded by a group of flight attendants. This immediately introduces Tom's most salient characteristic— his strong interest in and popularity with women. When Joan interrupts her uncle to get Tom's autograph she both establishes the central dynamic in her relationship with her uncle, disregarding him in favor of any available man, and attaches two more key traits to Tom, identifying him as "a rock star," and part of "Tom, Bill, and Mary." The interaction also allows Tom's response to Joan, advising her to "stop that diet before you ruin yourself," to hint at the character's complex, partly misogynist relationship to women. While the camera focuses on Tom and the flight attendants, the soundtrack features Green telling Joan that her Aunt Esther wants to see her, extending the earlier premise that Green's wife is sick by also informing Joan and the audience that she is in the hospital. Here, Green is given a goal—getting Joan in to see Esther—and is stymied for the first time, as Joan is distracted by the first in a string of men, which establishes a dynamic that makes up the bulk of Green and Joan's storyline.

From this, the film returns to the music stand earlier frequented by Private Kelly in order to introduce Bill and Mary. Bill is excited that the stand is selling their album, and in expressing his excitement he identifies himself and Mary to the shop girl and to the audience as the other members of the "Bill, Mary, and Tom" trio, rearranging the names in a way that indicates tensions within the group. Mary's indifference to Bill's excitement indicates a chill in their relationship, and Bill's self-deprecating reference to himself as the "handsome one" on the album cover suggests a charm that marks the character as sympathetic. When Bill sees the poster of Karen Black, which has a Hal Phillip Walker for President sticker plastered to it, and remarks, "Hal Phillip Walker looks exactly like Connie White," he both reinforces one of his major character traits, a good-natured sense of humor, and names Karen Black's character for the audience, while also playfully developing a key theme—the conflation of politics and music.

This indirect presentation of theme coupled with efficient, if similarly indirect, exposition continues in the zone outside the airport, where the majority of the characters converge around the spectacle of Barbara Jean's arrival. First, Triplette and Delbert emerge past a security guard blocking the path of a crowd of Walker campaigners. The mixture of Barbara Jean fans and Walker supporters both extends the thematic framework of the film and foreshadows Barbara Jean's interaction with the campaign. Triplette tells Delbert that he likes "the idea of bands," suggesting that Triplette is planning some sort of event. The voice of the television reporter returns, informing his audience that Barbara Jean was burned in a tragic accident involving a fire baton while Lady Pearl tells the uninterested Haven at length about the hours of preparation the junior baton twirlers put in for Barbara Jean's arrival. A cut to Private Kelley as the reporter discusses the fire baton foreshadows Kelley's concern for Barbara Jean's well-being, while also foreshadowing the subsequent revelation that Kelley's mother once rescued the singer from a fire. Delbert approaches Barnett, who immediately shouts at Delbert that he has no time, quickly establishing that character's central trait of harried hostility. Delbert names Barnett for the audience when he calls out to him, and Barnett's earlier presence in the window of Barbara Jean's plane is likely sufficient to cue the audience that he is her manager. Barnett's immediate response to Delbert suggests both Delbert's second-class role in the hierarchy of Nashville and his position as someone who asks for favors. The interaction also raises an important question, introducing a line of action that will be central to Nashville's storyline—what does Delbert want from Barnett? When the film returns to Kelley looking out at Barbara Jean's arrival, Tom walks up to look at him, and upon seeing his uniform aggressively asks him if he has killed anybody this week, providing a clear signal of Tom's difficult, unsympathetic nature, even in the context of the mid-1970s liberal audiences Altman made his films for. Tom also tells a Walker volunteer that he doesn't "vote for nobody for president," a stance that contrasts with or complements his hostility toward the private, depending on one's political perspective, and is suggestive in relation to the film's political/musical thematics.

More character exposition ensues as Haven introduces Buddy to the crowd, thereby providing exposition about his son's time at Harvard Law School, and inappropriately suggests that when the twirlers grow up they might want to date him. As Barbara Jean disembarks in her white dress, she is accompanied by Barnett, who wards off a reporter. Bill and Mary now also look on from inside the airport, where they are greeted by the chauffeur, Norman, who is named in their conversation. Norman asks after the absent Tom, calling attention to a dynamic that will be key to the musical trio's storylines in Nashville. Barbara Jean, immediately marked as fragile by references to her return from a hospital stay, graciously greets the twirlers, and her smiling face and gratitude for a bouquet of flowers delivered by a small child mark her as genuine and sympathetic, unlike Haven. The film then cuts back to yet another set of characters looking out at Barbara Jean—Wade and Sueleen. The optimistic Sueleen tells Wade that she is waiting for Barbara Jean, but the cynical Wade reprimands her for her naiveté, telling her that Barbara Jean will not sing unless she is getting paid, quickly establishing the dominant pattern in their character relationship.

From this, the film moves on to more direct narrative work, as Barbara Jean tells the crowd that she will be performing at the Grand Ole Opry later that week, establishing an appointment. When Barbara Jean asks Barnett if the people she can see inside the airport are her fans, Barnett tells her that they are just airport security, extending a pattern first indicated by his hostile reaction to Delbert in which Barnett tries to limit her exposure to others. When Barbara Jean ignores his answer and tells Barnett that she wants to go greet the fans, she establishes the couple's key character conflict and reinforces her positive, sympathetic character traits. Her ensuing collapse on the way to greet her fans provides the film with its first major causal incident. A shot of an intensely concerned Private Kelley gazing at the collapsed Barbara Jean while others rush around him reinforces the question of what motivates Kelley's interest in the singer.

Up to this point, the segment of the film set in and around the airport and culminating in Barbara Jean's arrival and collapse has taken slightly less than ten minutes of the film's extensive runtime. Yet in that time, *Nashville* has introduced fourteen of the film's twenty-four major characters. Each has been given at least one identifiable trait that will play a central role in that character's storyline, and most have been assigned multiple traits and engaged in first instances of the patterned activity that will make up their storylines. With the setup still incomplete, Altman has already done a great deal of highly efficient storytelling. Barbara Jean's arrival at the airport provides a hub from which the narration can range into and across multiple zones, thereby introducing the sprawling cast of characters in a manner that also creates affordances for establishing the film's thematic dynamics.

Even so, this opening sequence fails to establish a focus on a strong central protagonist. Altman, then, might be highly efficient, and *Nashville*'s narration is arguably both classically communicative and omniscient, but the economy on display in *Nashville* is fundamentally perverse. These classical narrational strategies are heightened and then employed in relation to an at best quasi-classical narrative structure designed to support digression and elaboration rather than to enhance causal momentum. We can imagine a single protagonist film that focuses on Triplette's ruthless attempts to put together a concert for Walker. Or we can imagine a film where Triplette relentlessly pursues the political exploitation of Barbara Jean, who attempts to establish control over her own life in spite of the obstacles presented by her overbearing husband and the Nashville music industry. *Nashville* is neither of these—even though, as we have seen, Triplette's agenda does provide the major structuring element of the film. Instead, we see Altman skillfully applying one of the major lessons of classical Hollywood narration—concentrated exposition—in service to his classical-plus aims—the elaboration of an expansive and thematically resonant story world.

In *Narration in the Fiction Film*, Bordwell relies on the term "fabula," a Russian Formalist concept describing "the story's state of affairs and events," and one that more or less neatly aligns with the narrative dimension of story world. A key parameter of a film's narration, Bordwell suggests, is the "quantity of fabula information" a given film offers in relation to a "hypostatized ideal." This ideal is based on the "conventions of genre or mode," which help determine what amount of information is "the 'correct' amount to permit coherent and steady construction of the fabula." A given film's narration may be "rarefied" in that it "supplies too little information about the story," or it may be "overloaded" in that it "supplies too much."[41] The perverse economy on display in many of Altman's early 1970s films displays a dynamically unconventional relationship to this narrational parameter. It is easy to see how *Nashville* might be categorized as overloaded, conveying an excessive amount of story world information in relation to classical norms. But the efficient redundancy of the film's expositional strategies suggests that the narration is better characterized as *excessive* in that it conveys just the right amount of information given its excessively prolific story world. At the same time, *McCabe & Mrs. Miller*'s narration might be regarded as sparse, given the amount of time spent on establishing a milieu of relatively incidental characters. That film's filling out of milieu is not accomplished at the cost of narrative structure but through the efficient, indirect presentation of information about its male protagonist.

Here, too, I would suggest that the narration is better characterized as excessive, that story world premises are parceled out so as to meet demands including but also going beyond those of classical narrative storytelling.

In general, there is a wide range of possible non-narrative functions that an excessive narration can be employed in service of, as well as a wide range of forms that this sort of narration may take. For instance, when we describe a film or a scene as digressive, we might attribute this to its consistent display of excessive narration. Such digression may be motivated by generic aims, as in slapstick comedies where narrative movement may sometimes seem to come to a halt in favor of noncausal events such as comedic routines. This kind of "pie and chase" alternation, discussed by Donald Crafton, involves the interweaving of the narrative and the comedic. Even so, scholars have sometimes misestimated the narrative content and underpinnings of some comedies, describing their narration as overloaded rather than excessive.[42] In a different vein, art cinema narration is often sparse *or* overloaded due to its common aim of providing an exceptionally high degree of realism—fleshing out milieu and character beyond straightforwardly narrative requirements. Narration becomes sparse when the film's narrative momentum stops to let a digressive, realism-oriented moment play out, or may be wholly sparse, as the provision of sufficient story world information to achieve a coherent overall comprehension of the film's narrative is generally set aside in favor of filling out a realistic world. There may also simply be, as in neorealist films shot on location, an overabundance of background detail that the narration makes available for the viewer, resulting in an overloaded narration to the extent that fascination with this information interferes with the uptake of embedded premises necessary to comprehend the storyline. Daniel Barratt has employed the concept of "informational load" to describe how some films "interrupt the generation of certain inferences and hypotheses" for strategic ends. According to Barratt, "in experimental situations, psychologists sometimes prevent the subject from entertaining certain propositions by simultaneously giving them a 'distracting task' such as counting backward or performing simple arithmetic."[43]

It is possible that the overabundance of non-narrative detail in Altman's films serves a similar function, distracting audience members from actively considering narrative questions in a way that results in a minimization of narrative substance in their remembered experience of the films. However, as we have seen, bountiful narrative information is made available. Excessive narrational strategies like those on display in Altman's early 1970s films strive to have their cake and eat it too. That is, they aim for narrative uptake and something extra. This is, obviously, a difficult task to set oneself, and Altman's tendency to employ excessive narration might explain the difficulty some critics and scholars have found in identifying the classical narrative strategies providing affordances for his innovations.

Kristin Thompson has defined "excess" as the presence of devices that "no amount of narrative or other types of motivation can completely contain." According to Thompson, "classical Hollywood-style narrative cinema attempts to minimize our concentration on excess by subordinating the material aspects of the film to the narrative flow." Other films, though:

> may deflect our attention from an exclusive concentration on narrative, toward style and unstructured material. The simplest, most traditional way of doing this involves the presentation of the picturesque composition. . . . Such excess can exist primarily because it does not interfere with our understanding of the narrative to any great extent. Classical narrative films are usually highly redundant; the fact that attractive compositions draw our eye does not mean our attention drifts entirely away from the significant elements of the causal chain.[44]

Thompson's example holds resonance with my discussion of Altman's ornamental zoom practice in the next chapter, and the suggestion of an aesthetic motivation for excess complements the realist and comedic motivations discussed earlier. It also, though, seems to contradict Thompson's own definition of excess as something that neither narrative nor "other types of motivation" can account for. Excessive narration would seem to be similar to but also more than Thompson's narrower starting point. It may be explicable in terms of realist, aesthetic, generic, or other motivations, and it may be typical of narration in certain genres, like comedies.

Moreover, as Thompson's account implies, classical Hollywood storytelling incorporates strategies that make excessive narration compatible with its other norms. Thompson points to classical storytelling's narrational redundancy as compensating for moments of distraction. Similarly, narrational efficiency might free up time for the multiply motivated distractions of excess.

It is useful here to return to Bordwell's description of classical narration as "omniscient, highly communicative, and only moderately self-conscious." The perverse economy on display in *Nashville* depends on the virtuosic enactment of these first two narrational norms in the service of story world excess, but the narration in Altman's early 1970s films often departs from classical norms when it comes to self-consciousness—the degree to which the narration is more or less overt, foregrounding its address. In art cinema this often, but not always, takes the form of a reflexivity that calls attention to the conventions and traditions of storytelling. As Bordwell puts it, "self-conscious art cinema narration often signals that the profilmic event is . . . a construct."[45]

Overt narration in art cinema also, and perhaps more commonly, provides cues that promote an engagement with authorial expressivity, as the narration emphasizes themes and gestures toward preferred interpretative responses that we take to be intended by the filmmaker. This expressivity sometimes entails articulating overlapping or complementary "judgmental factors" promoting an "attitude with respect to the [story world] or perceiver," which Bordwell acknowledges is often called "tone."[46]

Altman's films from the early 1970s are atypical in the context of classical norms in terms of the degree to which their narration is overt. However, and as we shall see in our examination of *Brewster McCloud*, the purpose of this overt narration is not always, or even not most commonly, the kind of scathing reflexive criticism of pernicious, illusionistic Hollywood conventions that standard accounts foreground.[47] Instead, overt employment of these conventions often provides affordances for more diverse aims.

In many ways, *Brewster McCloud*, marketed as, "something else from the director of *M\*A\*S\*H*," lives up to its publicity. It features, among other things: a nondiegetic ornithologist lecturer, a reflexively parodic San Francisco "supercop" who loses a baby-blue colored contact lens before committing suicide, a cartoonish contraction of time in which a couple goes on their first date and are formally wed the same day, an angel who bathes nude in a public fountain and winks into the camera, and an epilogue in which the cast—dressed as circus performers—take their bows over the dead body of the film's eponymous character.

In spite of all of this, the film's narrative structure is essentially classical. While *Brewster McCloud*'s central figure is indeed its title character, the film follows in a tradition of Hollywood films featuring parallel protagonists—two characters "who pursue distinctly different, sometimes conflicting goals and who are often spatially separated during much of the action," according to Thompson. These protagonists "are usually strikingly different in their traits, and their lives initially have little or no connection. Yet early on in the action, one develops a fascination with the other and often even spies on him or her."[48] Thompson acknowledges that parallel protagonists offer distinct challenges to Hollywood filmmakers who, "face the problem of moving between the two and still maintaining a clear, redundant, linear classical narrative progression."[49] *Brewster McCloud* actually resolves this dilemma relatively easily since both lines are organized around Brewster's actions. Brewster is a likely killer, and Shaft investigates the killings. Indeed, Shaft's investigation into the murders that accompany Brewster's movements through the narrative closely resembles Thompson's observation that it is typical for one protagonist to be fixated on the other.

It is on the parallel classical clotheslines of Brewster's quest for wings and Shaft's quest for a killer who is probably Brewster that Altman hangs the digressive comic antics, political satire, and faux-sociological/ornithological insights of the film. But the narrative structure does more than provide a hanger for disconnected authorial expressivity. Instead, Altman integrates his repertoire of novel storytelling aims and techniques with classical structuring and narrational devices in innovative and elaborative ways. It is perhaps due to this characteristic mixing that critics so often find it easy to overlook his films' more classically narrative qualities.

As in *Nashville*, Altman incorporates a great deal of concentrated exposition into *Brewster McCloud*'s setup, although in this earlier film the narration is arguably much more perverse in its aims. Whereas *Nashville*'s efficient narration strives to account for the proliferation of narrative around an expansive milieu, *Brewster McCloud*'s narration is aimed at overt ironization of its narrative subject and of conventional narrative strategies. After an introduction by the film's ornithologist lecturer that is directly addressed to the camera and a short opening sequence in the Astrodome in which the credits start, stop, and begin again, the third segment of the film consists of Brewster chauffeuring Wright, a grotesque old miser in a wheelchair, as he collects from the four nursing homes that he owns.

The sequence serves several narrative functions key to the setup's establishment of the initial situation. It develops audience knowledge of Brewster, informing the audience, when Wright comments that he never should have hired Brewster that morning, that he is new to the job. The audience is prompted to ask how this relates to a previous scene where Brewster was shown designing wings and why he would take a job with this horrible man. Brewster is named here for the first time, as Wright berates him. The audience also becomes familiar with Brewster's deportment. Throughout, his face is relatively expressionless—a lack of affect at odds with the implication, by the sequence's end, that Brewster is guilty of three strangulations and sending the wheelchair-bound Wright, in the sequence's climax, rolling down the highway to his death. The initiation of Wright's descent is elided, and Brewster is an obvious suspect except for his consistent indifference.

The sequence's depicted narrative action is coupled with highly conventional expositional techniques on the soundtrack, though the implementation of these techniques is functionally perverse. The lecture is removed from the soundtrack at the beginning of the sequence—replaced with the diegetic sound of the car radio, which provides important exposition about the initial situation ⊙ (see the companion website for a video clip). The radio initially provides the zany antics of AM disc jockeys "Hudson and Harrigan," but their morning show is repeatedly interrupted by news bulletins. The first breaks the news that prominent local resident Daphne Heap—seen in the film's second segment murdering the national anthem and then berating a black marching band—has been murdered. The audience has not been directly informed that the singer in that scene was Heap, but when she is described as "the soprano who sings the national anthem at the Astrodome before every ball game," the connection is made fairly clear. The next update informs the audience of a trio of related murders and that local politician Haskell Weeks has called in a detective from San Francisco, "a man identified only as Frank Shaft," to investigate. The next update reports that Heap's "prized pigeons" were released by the killer, providing a clue to the killer's motives while also elaborating on the film's bird motif and recalling a point raised earlier by the ornithologist's lecture about caged birds and freedom. The montage's final update informs the audience that Shaft is being flown into Houston at Weeks's expense and that his arrival is imminent.

Altman's use of a radio news bulletin, like his use of the television reporter in *Nashville*'s setup, participates in a classical Hollywood tradition, described by Bordwell, where:

> The narration reinforces the homogeneity of the fictional world by means of a non-theatrical device: the use of public and impersonal sources of information that can be realistically or generically motivated within the film. The most common instrument is the newspaper. . . . Other public transmitters of information include radio, television, bulletin boards, posters, ticker tape, tour guides, and reference books. . . . These impersonal sources of story information also prove invaluable in toning down the self-consciousness of montage sequences.[50]

*Brewster McCloud*'s use of media to provide exposition is remarkable, though, for how its design and placement actually mark it as overt and reflexive, effectively perverting a key function of the technique. The film's overall narrative design seems to have no interest in either "reinforc[ing] the homogeneity of the fictional world" or "toning down the self-consciousness" of its narration. Indeed, the film opens with a nondiegetic lecture about ornithology that lays out the film's thematics and then goes on to replay its opening credits in coordination with the aforementioned marching band's second stab at the national anthem. Several absurdly conventionalized elements of the presentation of the radio bulletins serve to extend the film's reflexive momentum, directing attention not only to narrative premises but also to narrational mechanics. Placed behind the announcements' prototypical authoritative "newsvoice" is an equally conventional beeping sound and the clicking of a printer. The bulletins include stiff lines like "Here's an important bulletin just handed me," and the description of Weeks as, "a long-time friend of the city." The denaturalization of the bulletins' exposition is reinforced through the juxtaposition of this staid and self-serious reporting style with the contents of the morning show, including an "amateur minute" during which one guest lets out a rebel yell followed by the sound of a splat and either Hudson or Harrigan inquiring, "Who threw that tomato?" Here, the vulgarity of the exposition-free morning show does more to ensure "diegetic homogeneity" than the classical device. After all, the diegesis that *Brewster McCloud* presents is full of grotesques and bird shit, and as any "morning zoologist" could confirm, Hudson and Harrigan's show is more realistic than the news bulletins that interrupt it. The digressive vulgarity seems more natural than the conventional approach to naturalizing narratively essential exposition.

This novel situation is suggestive of a pattern that cuts across Altman's early 1970s films, although *Brewster McCloud* provides an admittedly extreme example. Narrative work is often handled in a way that is reflexive and self-conscious—undermotivated by realism or plausibility and overmotivated by transtextual justifications like genre convention or cliché. The worlds in which the narratives take place, on the other hand, are often abundantly and excessively detailed and "realistic," whether in their complex multidimensionality, as in *Nashville*, or their vulgarity, as in *Brewster McCloud*. The use of media as an overtly corny expositional device is repeated in other Altman films from this era. In *The Long Goodbye*, Marlowe is given a ride home from police lockup by a newspaper reporter who summarizes the narrative situation and is never heard from again. In *California Split*, Elliott Gould's character presses a button to activate a video tutorial on high-low poker available in a poker hall. An inveterate gambler, he certainly has no need for such a tutorial. The enthusiastic tone of the video is contrasted with the rather depressing milieu of the poker hall, heightening the film's pervasive aura of irony, but the video does narrative work—providing the audience with important information about a key aspect of the film's narrative milieu.

Altman, then, perversely couples classical narrative functionality with moments of ironizing reflexivity, and it seems as though critics have generally overlooked the narrative work in favor of tending to this authorially expressive narrational voice. Arguably, this has contributed to the perception of Altman's films as narratively lax. But difference does not mean absence. That is, simply because Altman's films are reflexive or ironic does not mean that they are not also, on a moment-by-moment basis, simultaneously engaged in narrative work. Indeed, considering Altman's target audience—the young, hip, and cine-literate frequent filmgoer—Altman's strategy seems to be particularly shrewd. It appeals to and rewards their awareness of cinematic convention while still making use of conventionalized narrative devices to move them through the film's plot. Altman is having it both ways, achieving a perverse version of the multifunctionality that Hollywood filmmakers typically aim for, where one of the aimed-for functions is not narrative immersion but ironizing reflexivity. Moreover, Altman and his collaborators seem to have convinced a significant portion of his critical audience that he was also never telling them a story, achieving a kind of miracle of movie mesmerism in which narrative work is hidden by reflexive excess and elaboration.

A second example from *Brewster McCloud*, though one where a more directly nonclassical, authorially expressive narrational strategy is mobilized in a manner that also efficiently achieves expositional ends, serves to illustrate a variation on this perversely multifunctional approach. It would be easy to reduce the function of the film's recurring nondiegetic ornithological lectures to the provision of a layer of arch, ironic commentary—a judgmental narrational voice. Indeed, one of the obvious functions of the lectures is the cueing of distanced interpretation of diegetic elements rather than direct narrative engagement. However, what may seem to be instances of rarefied narration, or at least a layer of narratively inert commentary, prove to also be engaged in focusing and refining the audience's narrative inferences and hypotheses.

This is certainly true of the lecturer's employment during the film's complicating action, as Shaft begins his investigations of the serial murders and Brewster, having stolen an expensive camera, goes to the zoo to take pictures of the birds as reference for his wing-designs. At the zoo, the grotesquely abusive off-duty police officer Breen sees Brewster and covets his camera. At the same time, Louise—a blonde woman in a trench coat who has appeared in earlier sequences and seems to literally be Brewster's guardian angel—looks on. As the film cuts to her, the lecturer returns to the film's soundtrack, discussing the Brazilian green macaw, a bird "as beautiful as it is rare." As Louise watches Breen approach Brewster, the lecturer asserts that the macaw, "soon becomes familiar with persons who it sees frequently, but it has an aversion to strangers and sometimes attacks them with great fury. . . . Parental behavior—when an intruder disturbs or endangers the nest or young, some birds slip away quietly and unobtrusively. Some may attack the intruder." The placement of the ornithologist's lecture over the shots of Louise watching Breen cues the audience to infer that Louise has a protective, parental relationship with Brewster, and this hypothesis is supported by the look of concern on Louise's face. At the same time, the lecturer's discussion of furious attacks cues the audience to formulate one possible answer to the film's overarching mystery—the identity of the serial strangler. By positioning Louise in relation to this characterization of the green macaw, the narration encourages us to consider whether she may have killed Heap, Wright, and the others in order to defend Brewster.

However, the narrative work accomplished by the lecture is complicated by the presence of Breen in a green jacket. Indeed, it is initially somewhat unclear who the audience is meant to take as the metaphoric object of the lecture, particularly given the violent rage Breen breaks into when dealing with his family and his disgusted, envious reaction to Brewster—a stranger. Because Breen is certainly not beautiful, and because the framings more often favor Louise, the audience likely quickly discards this hypothesis as the lecture develops, but the lecture clearly takes advantage of the looseness of metaphor in order to carry ironizing weight—Breen's violence and racism (and his appearance) are certainly not beautiful, nor are these traits rare, given what the film has already shown us. The lecture, then, is multifunctional—overt and excessive but also narratively useful. Its digressions ironize but also advance important narrative questions.

Indeed, Altman seems to be particularly skilled at presenting narrative information that is disguised as excessive digression, that only *seems* to be the sort of chaos his biographical legend narrowly focuses on—the illusion of escape from narrative as an appealing feint. In another instance, later in *Brewster McCloud*, Brewster steals the car of Suzanne, a quirky Astrodome security guard, so he can pick up the developed zoo photos. Suzanne, though, interrupts his theft and volunteers to accompany him to the lab. In the moment, their conversation during the ride to Brewster's next goal seems entirely digressive—rarefied narration that contributes nothing to narrative development beyond compounding Suzanne's eccentricity. But almost all of the dialogue serves as dangling causes that will be put to use as part of the film's narrative structure. Suzanne reveals that she is a racecar driver, and that she stole her car from another driver who had tried to rape her a few weeks earlier. Later in the film, Suzanne drives the car in a comic chase sequence during which she successfully evades Shaft, and the man she stole the car from reappears outside her apartment, confronts Brewster, and becomes another victim of the serial strangler. The only part of their conversation that does not serve a narrative purpose is Suzanne's digression on the subject of diarrhea and Mexican food. This, though, contributes to a thoroughgoing motivic pattern around bird shit.

Of course, not all of the digressive moments in Altman's early 1970s films are secretly instances of highly communicative narration, but it is clear that one of Altman's talents is making the narrative seem chaotic, or, perhaps, integrating his chaotic conceits with his narrative concerns. In the early 1970s,

Altman regularly employed a robustly classical narrative structure and the classical storytelling norms of highly communicative and omniscient narration as the often-perverse underpinning of, or complement to, the novel aims and features of his work. *Nashville*'s airport sequence demonstrates how Altman enables and enacts an unconventionally wide-ranging, though still somewhat classical, narrative structure through the virtuosically efficient employment of concentrated and preliminary exposition. And even in *Brewster McCloud*, when Altman is arguably at his most undeniably experimental, he finds ways to merge the ironic and the chaotic with the narratively purposeful, disguising storytelling in narrationally rarefied moments of digression and delivering premises through norm-bending narrational self-consciousness. Framing Altman's approach simply as rejectionist or assimilationist in relation to Hollywood's storytelling norms misses the perverse ways in which Altman's elaborative approach masterfully confuses and compounds the narrative with the excessive in order to expand the possibilities of Hollywood practice.

## Altman's Nonstandard Narration

Altman's early 1970s films incorporate classical Hollywood narrative structure and the perverse integration of classical narrational aims and strategies with nonclassical means and ends. This does not, though, capture the whole story. The remainder of this chapter focuses on the novel ways in which Altman's approach to narration and narrative exhibits nonclassical features more akin to art cinema. Art cinema's narrational norms are typically organized around a threefold focus on realism, authorial expressivity, and ambiguity. Realism here involves both the external realism of social context conveyed through "excessive" narration and the subjective realism of internal character psychology contemplated by excessively lingering on character behavior or disclosed by subjectively deep narration providing relatively direct access to a character's perceptual and/or mental experiences (an approach to narrational omniscience conceptually distinct from the wide-ranging narration discussed in the chapter's previous section). Authorial expressivity is articulated through overt and frequently reflexive narration, and ambiguity is typically expressed through suppressive, rather than highly communicative, narration. Apart from narration per se, art cinema also displays characteristic approaches to other aspects of narrative form. Some, like the art cinema's episodic plots and loose causal structure, have already been shown here to fail to capture the narrative structure of Altman's early 1970s cinema. On the other hand, art cinema's ambiguity-motivated tendency toward open endings proves to be more relevant to Altman's storytelling.[51] In general, Altman's early 1970s films employ resolutions and epilogues that close major narrative lines but also fail to establish a new stable state of affairs. These endings trouble character comprehension and audience sympathy, and they leave significant thematic elements open to interpretation. The overall strategy is described here as "closure without comprehension."

Given the history of claims that Altman worked in the mode of art cinema storytelling, it might come as a surprise that the subjective depth of his films' narration during the early 1970s is actually consistently shallow. Whereas much of art cinema explores subjectivity by granting access to characters' mental states through dreams, visions, skewed perceptions, and so forth, Altman's films generally avoid this sort of narrational depth. In *Brewster McCloud* there is a short dream sequence from Brewster's point of view in which he soars above the clouds. In *Images*, the narration is frequently filtered through the mentally disturbed protagonist's subjectivity as she has visions of her former lovers as well as the embodiment of her dark side. The film's soundtrack frequently features Catherine's voice racing through recitations of the children's book she is writing. This subjective depth, though, seems more plausibly motivated by generic concerns in line with the female gothic or psychodrama than by an inherent interest in subjective realism. The narration reliably reports on these distorted perceptions to cue audience curiosity and suspense around Catherine's attempts to understand and then strategize escape routes from her suffering. Instead of direct access to mental subjectivity, Altman's early 1970s films more often provide narrational depth through the conventional device of the monologuing protagonist—revised in these films as the mumbling monologue. Both the titular McCabe and *The Long Goodbye*'s Philip Marlowe participate in this approach to the revelation of subjectivity, and they might be connected to the eponymous protagonist of *Popeye* (1980) to conjure a Blessed Trinity of Altmanian Mumblers.[52] This novel innovation synthesizes subjective depth with what is essentially excessive narration—rambling self-talk that often seems more digressive than it actually is.

The narrational aspect in which Altman does more closely approach the conventions of art cinema filmmaking is the previously discussed overt narrational voice that can be found in his films. Just as art cinema tends to prioritize authorial expressivity so, too, do Altman's films frequently feature a shaping narrational voice. While it is unclear that these features call attention to Altman per se—cueing audiences to think, "*Altman* feels this way about that abstract idea"—they do stand out from the norms of classical narration. Bordwell and Thompson allow that classical narration can

be intermittently overt, but Altman's methods go beyond the normal reservation of conspicuous storytelling for beginnings and endings—of films
and scenes—or for the targeted purposes of specific genres.[53] Rather than
gauging the relative overtness of Altman's narrational voice against the classical norm, though, it might be better to offer a description of the significant
features of that voice. Altman's early 1970s films display three major overlapping strategies: punctuative devices, ironizing juxtapositions, and the
priming of interpretative frameworks. Taken together, these strategies constitute the authorially expressive narrational "voice" elaborated on the classical
foundations of Altman's films.

In interviews, Altman has consistently identified "punctuation" as a key
storytelling device, and it is generally recognized as such by critics. Fuller,
for instance, asks Altman about, "the intention behind [devices like the loud-
speaker in *M\*A\*S\*H*, the ornithological lectures in *Brewster McCloud*, the
musical theme in *The Long Goodbye*, radio programs in *Thieves Like Us*, and
the Hal Philip Walker campaign in *Nashville*?]" We could add to Fuller's list
the Leonard Cohen song score in *McCabe & Mrs. Miller*, the children's story
in *Images*, and the Phyllis Shotwell songs in *California Split*. These devices are
often referred to as connective tissue, ways of unifying what are considered
to be the disparate elements of Altman's stories. Describing these devices as
simply connective fits with the rejectionist view of Altman's work as extremely
digressive—its fragmented and elliptical storytelling requiring a unifying or
audience-orienting device. But as this chapter has demonstrated, such an account of Altman's storytelling structure is misleading.

Instead of reducing the role of these devices to the provision of amusing
and urgently needed connective tissues, it is worth considering the extent to
which they function as authorial intrusion—overt commentary on the subject matter. After laying out his question, Fuller proposes that the enumer-
ated devices are oriented around providing "ironic commentary." Altman
responds that, "It's punctuation to me. . . . I still look for punctuation or commentary, and I find it very helpful. . . . Layering a movie in this way gives me
more options. If something doesn't work, I can cover an awful lot of sins by
using these devices."[54] Significantly, Altman equates punctuation with both
the kind of problem-solving implied, in part, by the connective tissue justification and with commentary. In fact, he seems to conflate the two. Discussing
the visual puns in *The Player* (1992), Altman states that they are, "all punctuation. Commas, pauses, and dashes that also comment on what you're seeing
at the time."[55] Referring to *Brewster McCloud*, Altman tells an interviewer, "I
wanted a form of punctuation . . . and I had the idea of a guy giving a lecture on
birds and then gradually becoming one himself."[56] Whether it is in setting the

tone or providing the sort of ironic commentary that Fuller identifies in his question to Altman, these devices frequently go beyond merely providing an after-the-fact formal unity.

Further examination of *Brewster McCloud* helps make this clear. As was discussed earlier, the nondiegetic ornithologist whose lecture is intercut with the story of Brewster and Frank Shaft offers an opportunity for Altman to ironize and satirize his subject matter. He also primes the audience to understand the film as employing a certain tone and as potentially responsive to a certain line of interpretation. The first proper sequence of the film features this disheveled ornithologist in a travesty of a college classroom where he looks directly into the camera and, while providing no exposition about the narrative's settings, characters, or its action, introduces several of the film's motivic and thematic elements. He begins by laying out his lecture's subject matter, and the film's thematic concerns, "The flight of birds, the flight of man. Man's similarity to birds, birds' similarity to man . . . we will deal with them for the next hour or so and hope that we draw no conclusions elsewise the subject shall cease to fascinate us and alas another dream would be lost." The reference to "the next hour or so" establishes a congruence between the lecture and the film, cueing audience members to interrogate his words for double meaning. The lecturer's stated hope that no conclusion will be drawn provides further guidance to the audience, priming them to value the ambiguity associated with art cinema.

Moving in front of his desk, the ornithologist continues to provide guidance to the viewer, proposing the salient questions that should occupy their thoughts:

> Man, incontestably the most advanced creature, has only to observe the flight of birds to realize the weight of the earth's imprisonment. And so, the desire to fly has been ever present in the mind of man but the reality has been long in coming. Has man truly realized his dream? To answer that we must isolate the dream. Was the dream to attain the ability to fly or was the dream the freedom that true flight seemed to offer man?

Cueing the audience to formulate questions is standard practice for Hollywood films. Noël Carroll has argued persuasively that much of popular entertainment is underwritten by an erotetic structure focused on raising and answering questions about what is happening and what will happen.[57] What is unusual here, though, is that *Brewster McCloud*'s initial scene provides only very indirect cues with which to formulate questions about narrative action. Instead, the opening moments privilege thematic questions.

The opening lecture also foregrounds narrational tone, or voice. The disheveled appearance of the lecturer and the classroom combine to create a comically ironic tone. Before the lecture begins, a shiny tin foil bird flutters onto then falls off of a desk. The ornithologist calls the bird "Hobbes" as if the audience should take it to be a real bird, but its appearance undercuts this inference, while its name suggests philosopher Thomas Hobbes—adding a factor for viewers to weigh in their construction of the film's thematic import. After bumping into an ostrich skeleton, the lecturer waits for its jiggling to conclude before continuing. The commentative functions of the lecture are extended when the image track cuts away to the Houston skyline and then reframes on the Astrodome just as the lecturer opines on, "the mortal damage man is doing to man's environment in comparison to the piddling nuisance birds cause man. It may someday be necessary to build enormous environmental enclosures to protect both man and birds, but if so it is questionable whether man will allow birds in or out as the case may be." This ironizing juxtaposition is closely orchestrated. The image track cuts from an exterior shot of the Astrodome to an interior shot just as the lecturer says, "in or out," comically reversing the spatial relations put forward by the soundtrack.

The opening sequence of *Brewster McCloud* has, then, established the narrative's thematic elements, cuing the audience to view the narrative according to an interpretive framework privileging openness over conclusive meaning. It also establishes a reflexive, ironizing tone suggesting audience members not take seriously what they see, that they welcome comic accidents and that they may be expected to accept unconvincing narrative elements (the corollaries of the tinfoil bird) even if they fall short of the norms of plausibility. Essentially, Altman has provided a tutorial in how to engage with his distinct, elaborative brand of storytelling.

Hal Philip Walker's presidential campaign serves a similar role in *Nashville*. Even though Altman has claimed that there is no particular political message he sought to convey, the prominence of the Walker campaign encourages the audience to think about politics and the notion of America. Indeed, the campaign provides the entry-point into *Nashville*'s story world, as the title card is matched precisely with the word "Nashville" on a banner reading "Tennessee State Headquarters. Nashville" hung across the garage door of Walker's campaign headquarters. As the door slides open the campaign's sound van pulls out of the garage, blaring Walker's appeal to voters. As previously discussed, Walker's campaign serves as both the background to and the driving narrative force behind *Nashville*, and by opening on the red, white, and blue campaign van the film signals its narrative importance. It does so, of course, while also establishing the film's core motifs of politics and Americana. Walker's speech, emphasizing the insidiousness of politics, immediately provides a thematic frame for the film's viewers:

> I've discussed the Replacement Party with people all over this country. And I'm often confronted with the statement, "I don't want to get mixed up in politics," or, "I'm tired of politics," or, "I'm not interested." Almost as often someone says I can't do anything about it anyway. Let me point out two things. Number one, all of us are deeply involved with politics whether we know it or not and whether we like it or not. And number two, we can do something about it. When you pay more for an automobile than it cost Columbus to make his first voyage to America, that's politics.

As with *Brewster McCloud*, Altman primes a reading strategy at the beginning of his film, highlighting the notion that politics is inescapably integrated with American life. At the same time, the inherently dishonest—unadjusted for inflation—illustration of this point by Walker satirizes political agents.

Walker's folksy evocation of Americana provides a thematic bridge to the next scene, set in a recording studio where Haven Hamilton, a diminutive man in a rhinestone jumpsuit, sings a bicentennial-themed song with the refrain, "We must be doin' something right to last two-hundred years." The confusion between politics and show business is reiterated throughout the film, not just in the narrative action of putting on a show for the candidate but also in the way Walker's supporters—essentially political doppelgangers of rabid country music fans—invade the airport during Barbara Jean's arrival. If their t-shirts and signs were changed to read, "we love you Barbara Jean," their presence and behavior would seem perfectly normal.

This initial priming attended by commentative punctuation can also be found in *Thieves Like Us* and *The Long Goodbye*. For instance, the opening sequence of *The Long Goodbye* begins with "Hooray for Hollywood" playing over the distributor's logo and a fade in on a Hollywood placard hung inside Marlowe's shabby apartment. This signals the reflexive, ironic tone of the film—although it is important to qualify a characterization of this particular film's reflexivity since it is too often taken as a scabrous attack on Hollywood. Instead, Altman describes the thinking behind the reflexivity in *The Long Goodbye* as follows:

> So I read Leigh Brackett's script, and in her version, in the last scene, Marlowe pulled out his gun and killed his best friend, Terry Lennox. It was so out of character for Marlowe, I said, "I'll do the picture, but you cannot change that ending! It must be in the contract." . . . It said, "This is just a movie." After that, we had him do his

funny little dance down the road and you hear "Hooray for Hollywood," and that's what it's really about. . . . It even looked like a road made in a Hollywood studio. And with Eileen Wade driving past, it's *The Third Man*![58]

This "just a movie" explanation of the film's reflexivity lacks a critique of Hollywood storytelling's insidious audience manipulation and instead suggests an attempt to deflate the unreflexive self-seriousness with which Hollywood and its fans, particularly fans of the Marlowe character, view its iconography.

Indeed, one could argue that *The Long Goodbye* is more about the culture of contemporary Hollywood as a geographical region or community than it is about Hollywood as a filmmaking tradition or economic institution. I referred earlier to Altman's stated desire to hang ethnographic essays on his narrative clotheslines, and much of the work the film does is concerned with showing how Marlowe's reliance on old-fashioned but not necessarily unadmirable values, like trusting one's friend, can lead to disappointing results and "loser" status in the 1970s Hollywood/L.A. milieu. In that sense the opening juxtaposition of "Hooray for Hollywood" with "Hollywood" as shabby decor can be seen as not simply part of the "just a movie" reflexivity but also a priming of the audience to think about the ironic distance between the celebration of Hollywood values and the values of contemporary Hollywood.

This contrast is furthered by the latter part of the opening sequence, as Marlowe, having failed to satiate his cat, leaves his apartment for the all-night grocery store at the same time that Terry Lennox leaves the Malibu Colony on his way to Marlowe's ⊛ (see the companion website for a video clip). This sequence, which features several of the multiple renditions of the title song that serve as the punctuational complement to the film's reflexive references, displays another example of ironic juxtaposition. Here, the juxtaposition comes via crosscutting as Altman cuts between two lines of action that offer multiple points of comparison. Both men have been "clawed"—Marlowe by his cat and Lennox by his wife—and both men are driving somewhere. However, while the shabbily dressed Marlowe travels in his antiquated car to the grocery store to buy cat food, Lennox, zooming away from the gated Malibu Colony in a modern sports car photographed to emphasize its beauty, drives away from the woman he has just killed (or, from the perspective of the first-time viewer, at least punched repeatedly, since Lennox pauses to put driving gloves on to cover the bruises on his hands). The renditions of the title song are also contrasted, as Marlowe enters the grocery store to the sounds of a Muzak version of "The Long Goodbye," while Lennox is accompanied by a jazzy rendition sung by Jack Sheldon. The systematic use of ironizing juxtaposition primes the audience to view Marlowe as a comparative loser in the Hollywood milieu, a point made by the film's critics who use this loser frame to condemn Altman for "encourag[ing] audiences to laugh smugly."[59] But such critics miss the sympathy that Altman seems to have for losers. Perhaps they have never owned a cat and simply cannot empathize, but the juxtaposition of a wife-beater with a man who goes to a late-night grocery store to satisfy his cat hardly seems consistent with a project bent on the malicious humiliation of Marlowe. Instead, the sequence presents the moral universe and the narrative trajectory of *The Long Goodbye* in microcosm.

A similar use of ironic juxtaposition through crosscutting can be found at the end of another of Altman's films—*McCabe & Mrs. Miller*. There, Altman cuts between McCabe's attempts to evade the trio of hired killers and the townspeople's attempts to extinguish a church fire. This juxtaposition is particularly ironic given that the true heart of the town has been McCabe and Mrs. Miller's whorehouse, and that the church has largely been abandoned to the dour outsider minister who seems to have built it without assistance. That the church is burning because one of the killers mistook the parson for McCabe after he self-righteously seized McCabe's shotgun minutes earlier compounds the irony. So, too, does the fact that the impromptu firefighting brigade is led by Sheehan, who sold his interests to the mining company who hired the killers. So, as McCabe, in spite of somehow having managed to dispatch the hired killers, slowly bleeds out in the snow, Sheehan is victorious, and the church is saved. The tragedy of McCabe's inglorious death, juxtaposed with the comic antics of the rallied townsfolk's firefighting, creates an irony that is funny, sad, and political.

Whereas many critics describe Altman's ironies as simply mean and sneering, there is a tragicomic strain to his commentary that they often overlook. For instance, Keechie and Bowie's love scene in *Thieves Like Us* is ironized through juxtaposition with an overblown "American School of the Air" adaptation of *Romeo and Juliet* that plays on the soundtrack. The irony created here can be interpreted as a heavy-handed undercutting of Keechie and Bowie's newfound love, or it might be taken as an attack on popular media, which fantasizes rather than confronts reality—in this case, the reality of Depression-era America. But the irony is also tragic, since these young lovers, like Romeo and Juliet, will find their love dissolved by death by the end of the film. Indeed, over the course of the film Altman consistently uses Depression-era radio as a punctuational device to emphasize the tragi-comic relationship between popular media and the popular dilemma of the Depression. Altman employs here a key strategy of art cinema narration, an overt authorially expressive voice, but expands its aims toward also achieving the common classical objectives of sentiment and sympathy through irony—a canny strategy given that his hip, cine-literate target audience was likely to resist conventional appeals.

Altman's narration, then, can be said to be distinctly overt, characterized by the use of punctuational devices, incorporated into a strategy that primes the audience for certain reading strategies and that makes consistent use of ironic juxtaposition for authorially expressive and affective purposes. This narrational voice, and its congruence with authorial expressivity, marks Altman's major departure from the norms of classical Hollywood storytelling. There is, though, at least one other important way in which Altman's early 1970s narrative practices differ from classical Hollywood norms—the means by which they handle closure. Altman's endings tend to be unhappy, and while, as previously demonstrated, they do offer resolutions to their major lines of action, they also tend to emphasize openness and that hallmark of art cinema—ambiguity. This novel strategy elaborates on classical norms with an art cinema inspired move toward ambiguity, providing "closure without comprehension."

This strategy synthesizes aspects of narrative structure, story world, and narration, providing climaxes with resolutions, but those resolutions are often a mixed bag of success and failure that perversely open up questions of causality and proper affective and interpretive response. In this sense, Altman's resolutions fall within the realm of the perversely classical discussed in the previous section rather than being more straightforwardly art cinematic in their function. More concretely in the realm of art cinema ambiguity, though, is that while Altman's films do incorporate epilogues, these epilogues fail to follow classical Hollywood norms by establishing new stable states of affairs that reinforce closure. Instead, they tend to open up and complicate thematic and character-oriented questions so that they resonate well after the credits end. The differences here with the structuring features and functions of classical closure are largely in the narrational details—the withholding of clarifying premises, a targeted refusal of redundancy, an avoidance of narrational judgment oddly coupled with an overt narrational voice—but the overarching unease that Altman's films often gift their audiences is highly indebted to art cinema.

While Hollywood norms permit the occasional unhappy ending, Altman's protagonists have an impressively, or depressingly, high fail rate. Of his eight early 1970s films only two feature a protagonist who achieves his goal—M*A*S*H's Hawkeye and California Split's Bill (who wins more than enough money to pay his bookie). Brewster McCloud falls to his death in the AstroTurf-lined cage of the Astrodome. McCabe bleeds out in a snowdrift. Catherine kills her husband rather than curing her schizophrenia. Marlowe is proven wrong about Terry Lennox and then kills his best friend. Bowie is shot to death by the authorities, and Triplette's political rally becomes the scene of an assassination. The consistency of failure and disappointment in Altman's films is remarkable, and it certainly intimates an authorial worldview, or at least a view of his target audience's worldview. Perhaps one or two films where the protagonist fails to achieve his or her goals would be unremarkable, but the consistent lack of success in Altman's work does seem to complicate his classicism.

Altman's endings, though, present more than simple failure. They tend to mix failure with success. For instance, Brewster's wings do work, and he manages to fly, just not away. McCabe achieves unlikely success in killing the three gunmen. Catherine initially does seem to have killed/cured her schizo-phrenia. Marlowe solves the mystery of Terry Lennox's death, even if doing so overturns his motivation for investigating that death as well as the murder of Lennox's wife. The two successful resolutions are tinged strongly with sadness, as *California Split*'s Bill finds no satisfaction in his winnings but instead wishes only to go home, leaving his friend Charlie sitting alone and angry in the casino. Likewise, Hawkeye seems shaken by his release from the military, perhaps because it forces him to abandon the community he has refashioned to his liking. The mixed emotions that give way to sadness embody the complex and ambiguous emotional valence of Altman's films. In that sense, Altman seems to perversely expand the emotional range of the "happy Hollywood ending," compounding it with his own novel brand of art cinema's signature ennui. Stable emotional comprehension seems unattainable.

Many of these resolutions also tend to open up questions rather than provide the audience with satisfactory answers to every thematic and narrative question—they not only fail to fill narrational gaps, they create new ones at the very last moment. While the narrative line of the goal-oriented protagonist is closed off—in each case the protagonist clearly either does or does not reach his or her goal—there remain smaller questions left unanswered or perhaps even opened-up by the very act of resolving the plot's major question. In some cases, these open questions have to do with character motivation. For instance, why does the previously passive Marlowe shoot Terry Lennox? Altman acknowledges that this is designed to be shocking and confesses that he believes its arbitrariness forces the audience to realize *The Long Goodbye* is "just a movie," thereby serving a reflexive aim common to art cinema. It also is likely to lead audiences to rethink Marlowe's character traits. Has this violence been bubbling under the surface of the character throughout the film? If it has, behind every "It's OK by me" that Marlowe mumbles like a mantra may have been another step toward moral outrage–driven homicide. The issue, in this case, seems irresolvable. In another departure from classical norms, the ambiguity around character motivation also makes it difficult to understand the narration's attitude, its narrational judgment, toward Marlowe.

The epilogues to Altman's films often contribute to this irresolvability by providing a twist that creates further puzzlement and forces rethinking. *Images'* epilogue does this in a fairly conventional manner, revealing that Catherine mistakenly murdered her husband when her doppelganger appears in the doorway to her bathroom. Even without this epilogue, the resolution of *Images'* climax, in which Catherine drives her double off a cliff, is difficult for the audience to comprehend. For instance, who is Catherine's doppelganger? What does she represent? Altman does drop hints throughout the film, as in Catherine's final conversation with Susannah where she confesses to her own loneliness as a child and asks the girl what she would do if Catherine were no longer around and she felt lonely. "[I'd] tell myself stories, play in the woods. I'd make up a friend," Susannah tells her, suggesting through movie-psychology the avenue through which Catherine's schizophrenia may have manifested. Because of the complexity of the narrative and the narrational reliance on Catherine's troubled subjectivity, the audience's first encounter with the resolution and its even more unsettling epilogue are likely to require a further, back-tracking engagement with the details of the film in order to achieve fuller comprehension and a sense of true resolution. As my discussion of *Images'* narrative structure suggests, these details are in place (at least in terms of large-scale structure), and comprehension is attainable, but the fact that it is likely delayed and that it requires re-watching the film arguably tilts *Images'* closure toward the nonclassical. We might imagine a more redundant, and more communicative, classical alternative ending with an extensive flashback montage sequence that bundles these premises together. But *Images* seems more interested in extending ambiguity.

*McCabe & Mrs. Miller's* epilogue—its closing shot of a small vase as seen through the opium-altered POV of Mrs. Miller—is also fairly open and also difficult to understand unless the viewer considers it in relation to a digressive storyline featuring a laborer and his mail-order bride. Toward the end of the film's complicating action, the ill-tempered Bart Coyle receives a fatal head-injury while brawling with a man who misidentifies Bart's wife as one of Mrs. Miller's prostitutes. *McCabe & Mrs. Miller's* development features the widowed Ida entering into Mrs. Miller's service. As Miller prepares Ida (whom she dresses in her own clothing and whose hair matches Mrs. Miller's) for her new vocation, she tells her doppelganger that if she finds her work unpleasant she should "Think of something else. . . . Look at the wall. Count the roses in the wallpaper." The film's conclusion, then, seems to show Mrs. Miller tragically following her own advice, though understanding this requires recollection of what might conventionally be viewed as narrative sprawl. As with *Images*, there is a backing away from heightened narrational communicativeness, a withholding of redundancy in service of lingering ambiguity.

The *Long Goodbye*'s brief epilogue, with Marlowe walking away from Lennox's bungalow down a long street, creates a very strange moment when Marlowe begins playing his tiny harmonica and breaks into a jig. How are we to reconcile this behavior with the serious act of killing his friend? To what extent does this dance represent some underlying aspect of Marlowe's character, a regression into the total embrace of his "It's OK by me" mantra, or, perhaps, an acknowledgement that the film is "just a movie"? The ambiguous narrational attitude toward Marlowe discussed earlier is extended here at the same time that the narrational voice becomes otherwise overt. The accompanying nondiegetic reprise of "Hooray for Hollywood" on the soundtrack overtly foregrounds a connection to the film's opening interpretive priming, essentially soliciting the audience to mobilize that thematic material to help resolve this ambiguity.

The epilogue of *California Split* is particularly baffling ⊙ (see the companion website for a video clip). Bill reveals to Charlie that he never actually had the special feeling that he claimed was his motivation for betting big in a high stakes poker game and for embarking on his historic winning streak at the craps table. Charlie responds by telling Bill a joke and then saying angrily, "Don't mean a fucking thing, does it?" Here, the "it" can stand for the nonsensical joke, gambling, their lives and friendship, and so on. Charlie, and the film's narration, fail to specify. It is up to the viewer to try to understand. Again, there is closure—Bill has won, and he is ending his friendship with Charlie—but there is only troubled, incomplete comprehension of the film's thematic and character-driven questions. Charlie's assertion of meaninglessness can be understood as a relatively overt narrational gesture toward an analogous art cinema ambiguity or as an expansive authorially expressive answer to whichever or all of the questions Charlie may have been asking. The evocative final image of a spinning gaming wheel focuses the audience on uncertainty as a key framework for their interpretive work.

As we saw with *The Long Goodbye*, these endings, both puzzling and unifying, at times call back to the reading strategies that the films' openings overtly primed. The epilogue of *Brewster McCloud* is perhaps even more puzzling than the previous examples. After Brewster falls to his death, the nondiegetic shares space with the diegetic as the cast of the film, dressed like circus performers, are brought out to take their bows on the Astrodome turf while Brewster/Bud Cort's dead body lies motionless on the ground. What is the audience to do with this highly reflexive moment? The quasi-diegetic status of the film's epilogue engages with the narrational stance that its opening took in relation to the diegesis. The narration has consistently cued the audience to interpret the film's events thematically and ironically rather than to simply invest fully in sympathetic emotions. The emotional poignancy of Brewster's death is arguably permitted, and somehow possibly heightened, by the complication of its reflexive framing.

The relatively open ending of *Nashville* similarly summons forth the film's first sequences. Not only has the political been thoroughly integrated with the nonpolitical at the musical event, but the relationship between assassination and the political and the musical has also been mixed up. The assassination of Barbara Jean resolves both the political question of whether Triplette will pull off the Walker rally and the musical career questions of whether Barbara Jean will attain mental health, as well as how (rather than whether) Sueleen Gay's aspirations will be crushed. It is, of course, a shocking and discomfiting resolution, particularly since the assassin's motivation is left unclear. When, in the epilogue, the audience is led by the eccentric Albuquerque, singing under a giant American flag and a Hal Phillip Walker banner, in a chorus of "It Don't Worry Me," the film has returned to the interpretive priming of its opening sequences and offers an answer to Haven Hamilton's earlier number—perhaps specifying that the "something right" that America has done to last two hundred years consists of being able to not care too much. But in spite of the narrationally overt juxtapositions presented by the epilogue's evocative imagery and soundtrack, this disturbing answer is more likely presented to be pondered rather than to be taken as a definitive statement of political history or philosophy. The simultaneous and exhilarating revelation of the previously withheld vocal talents of Albuquerque, singing plaintively though not necessarily earnestly, adds another element whose import the audience is left to contemplate. Even as her singing eventually unifies the crowd, narrational judgment—for instance, a condemnation of complacency—is made ambiguous. The feelings and interpretive frameworks offered seem too contradictory and complex.

Through their peculiar openness, a closure without comprehension that repurposes art cinema tropes and values by elaborating them alongside and on top of classical narrative closure, Altman's early 1970s films display a distinct orchestration of the ambiguity of art cinema narration with the structural norms of Hollywood storytelling. This, when added to Altman's overt narrational voice and his ability to achieve a kind of perverse economy in his nominally sprawling and digressive storytelling, marks Altman's innovations as impossible to assimilate within any one set of filmmaking norms. The majority of Altman's films during this period clearly employ classical Hollywood narrative structures, and even those films that are more difficult to completely reconcile with Hollywood's large-scale structures still display significant classical features. Thus, while Altman publicly professed a desire to eliminate narrative, his early 1970s films display neither its evacuation nor straightforward opposition to conventional narrative form. Instead, these films provide an elaborative expansion of the potential of Hollywood story-telling, exhibiting novel narrative designs that augment the possibilities for what could be supported by the classical Hollywood clothesline.

# 2
# Quantifying the Subliminal

## Altman and the Elaborative Zoom

The heavy reliance on the zoom in Robert Altman's films has rightly served as a cornerstone for accounts of Altman's innovative visual style, but scholars and critics have tended to misdescribe his strategy, often in service of claims for Altman as disruptive, oppositional auteur. There is an important distinction to be made, of course, between the zoom lens, a lens with variable focal distance that, among other advantages, allows a filmmaker a great deal of flexibility in the placement of the camera, and the zoom in or out as a means of varying the framing within the shot. While both the zoom lens itself and the zoom are important and obviously interconnected components of Altman's visual style, it is the act of zooming that has been the dominant focus of the critical literature on Altman, whether from the rejectionist or assimilationist perspective. Not only has this zoom usage been tethered to accounts of on-set improvisation (accounts that are tested in chapter 4) but also it has been integrated with the more general insistence that Altman's films interrogate and reject the norms guiding classical Hollywood storytelling.

In the specific case of the zoom, it is the technology's characteristic presentation of space—its creation of mobile framing without actual camera movement, its potential to traverse great distances quite rapidly, and its lack of perspectival parallax, the shifting of foreground and background relations produced by actual movement through space—that has proven to be particularly fertile ground. That is, Altman's use of the zoom is part of a larger strategy presenting diegetic space not as a coherent, narrativized given, but, as Kolker puts it, "as a place of inquiry" into which the zoom serves as "a narrative probe . . . a means to discover" and "connect."[1] Rather than simply accepting this widespread notion, though, this chapter treats Altman's early 1970s oeuvre as a place of inquiry, and, by systematically probing the films themselves, seeks to rediscover and resituate Altman's problem-solving strategies in relation to the aims and techniques of Hollywood storytelling.

*Robert Altman and the Elaboration of Hollywood Storytelling.* Mark Minett, Oxford University Press (2021). © Oxford University Press. DOI: 10.1093/oso/9780197523827.001.0001.

The approach undertaken here lies in direct opposition to accounts like Kolker's, which tend to be impressionistic and overgeneralized, in that it is based on both close and careful description of particular zooms and an overarching qualitative/quantitative analysis of the use of the zoom from *M\*A\*S\*H* to *Nashville*. In employing quantitative methods, I am participating in a tradition of scholarship, commonly referred to as Cinemetrics, that uses statistical methods to pursue questions about the history of style in moving image media. These methods, as Yuri Tsivian has put it, enable scholars to "not only intuit but also demonstrate" assumed stylistic practices, and to illuminate practices that had been unseen or, perhaps, obscured by longstanding assumptions.[2] My analysis here is developed around an inventory of functional purposes of the zoom, based on observable traits but requiring some analytic judgment, and it is complemented in places by the quantitative analysis of a broader set of descriptive factors, such as the ratio of inward-directed zooms to outward-directed zooms. This systematic analysis provides the groundwork for consideration of Altman's films in relation to one another and also for a comparison between Altman's early 1970s oeuvre with the general functional norms of classical Hollywood cinema and art cinema. The description and analysis offered here goes even further, though, by also examining the zooms of seventy-nine other films released between 1970 and 1975. Developing this set of contextualizing data provides evidence with which to refine claims about the novelty of Altman's work and to develop informed responses to broader questions pursued by scholars about the influence of a filmmaker's background and "training" on their employment of stylistic techniques.

This contextualized close analysis makes plain that the use of the zoom in Altman's films cannot be fully assimilated within the normal zoom practice of his immediate contemporaries, either in quantity or type. As a general conclusion, this is likely unsurprising. However, the redescription offered here also clearly establishes that the zooming in these films is neither completely irreconcilable with classical Hollywood norms nor best described through the kind of mystificatory characterizations commonly employed by critics. Instead, it seems likely that Altman's distinct practice-oriented preferences (e.g., for operating on a low budget, shooting on location, shooting simultaneously with multiple cameras, and developing a shooting strategy on-set) led him to rely on the zoom as a preferred solution to the general problem of achieving mobile framing. Furthermore, the zooms in Altman's films are neither as spatially subversive nor as aimless as the standard story would have us believe. Not only do they seem, on average, to be carefully considered but also there is little evidence to support assertions of a characteristic roving exploratory effect common in critical discourse. Instead, Altman and his collaborators seem to have capitalized on the affordances of the zoom in a way that elaborates on conventional storytelling aims, intensifying engagement with characters and burnishing the image with the kind of aestheticizing depth compositions associated with a quality look.

If this finding sounds rather mundane, it is not because the zoom work in Altman's films is not frequently complex and virtuosic but because the heuristics and agendas of scholars and critics have primed us to favor the discovery, or revelation, of certain kinds of "significance." Practitioner discourse around the zoom's disruptive potential, as articulated by Hollywood's guardians of quality cinematography, generated a set of premises that could be employed by critics to identify and articulate sites of reflexive resistance to the dominant mode. What the evidence suggests, though, is that Altman discounted these same premises, adopting a more flexible notion of the effects of the zoom, the psychology of the spectator, and the potential of Hollywood storytelling.

What's more, while it is accurate to broadly describe Altman's visual strategy during this period as heavily reliant on the zoom, it is important to avoid relying solely on summary accounts, whether of a half-decade, a decade, or a multiple-decade career, when characterizing Altman's approach. A film-by-film analysis of the zoom strategies on display within the relatively narrow domain of Altman's early-1970s oeuvre reveals significant fluctuations between projects. Moreover, close analysis makes clear that it would be inaccurate to describe the shifts in zoom strategy across this period in terms of a straightforward development that involves, say, steadily accruing intensification and sophistication. Instead, individual films display Altman and his collaborators setting and solving problems in a manner responsive to the contingencies of subject matter, technology, and personnel. The fluctuating zoom strategies evident in these early 1970s films serve conventional purposes while also reflecting an overarching goal of functional elaboration, experimentation, and expansion whose precise instantiation may be modulated from film to film or from scene to scene. Altman and his collaborators seem never to have been content with just employing the standard techniques in order to meet the standard storytelling aims, and the zoom provides a flexible ally in surmounting not just spatial but also standardized limitations on what Hollywood filmmaking might achieve.

## Roving and Creeping: The Standard Account of Altman's Zooms

Critics and scholars have largely followed two descriptive lines when discussing Altman's use of the zoom. They have characterized his zooms as a central part of what Michael Dempsey labels Altman's "roving" approach to mobile framing,[3] and they have described the zooms' sometimes slow forward and backward movements as "creeping" or "subliminal." The description of Altman's camerawork as roving seems to be intended to draw a contrast with a narrowly functional mobile framing in which the camerawork is more obviously narratively purposeful. The roving label also serves to imply the looseness and freedom associated with Altman's approach to filmmaking. The clearest characterization of Altman's roving predilections comes from Bordwell, who also suggests that Altman is participating in a broader development in film practice:

> From a wide-angle view of the setting the filmmaker might zoom in and pan with the actors as they played out the scene. Still tighter zooms would be reserved for moments of crucial drama. This "searching and revealing" approach, allowing the camera to scan the action and overtly pick out key details, became a significant norm of the 1960s and 1970s. It was elaborated by such newcomers as Petrovic (*I Even Met Gypsies*, 1967) and Robert Altman (*M*A*S*H*, 1970) as well as by veterans like Visconti, Fellini, Bergman, and most notably, Rossellini.[4]

Here Bordwell uses "searching and revealing" rather than "roving," but the meaning, at least for the first stage in the process he describes, is largely similar. The director, in response to the unfolding performances, uses the pan and zoom as a kind of participant in the ongoing revelation of salient narrative information. In this way, the pan and the zoom might be thought of as replicating an individual's attentional processes when responding to action within a wide field of visual information. The pan scans the field, and the zoom focuses on pertinent or interesting information. Significantly, the use of "roving" and/or "revealing" indicates, first, that the content or arrangement of the shot's mise-en-scène and/or the audience's narratively oriented interest are not sufficient to have already directed attention to that which is "revealed" by the zoom, and, consequently, that there is a move from a nondirected scanning of the image to a directed approach, with the direction provided by the zoom-in.

The second aspect of the couplet designated by Bordwell, the use of "tighter zooms" for "moments of crucial drama," suggests a different kind of searching and revelation, with a zoom in to a close up encouraging the audience to search, or contemplate, an actor's features with the expectation that their internal mental state will be revealed. This seems obviously different in function from the first meaning, particularly since at "moments of crucial drama" we can expect audiences to already be primed to focus their attention on expressive faces. As we will see, this kind of zoom, one form of what I will shortly describe as an "intensifying" zoom, is a significant and fairly widespread aspect of zoom practice.

We should also note the cohort with which Bordwell places Altman—alongside art cinema filmmakers. This makes a certain amount of sense given the nontraditional, overt function Bordwell attributes to this kind of zoom. In classical Hollywood cinematic practice, audience attention is primed to be more narratively focused and is more consistently being directed through the narrative via multiple levels of storytelling convention, so that there is no real need to search. As we shall see, though, whether this approach is one that can only be associated with art cinema is, for our purposes, largely irrelevant because in actuality Altman rarely, if ever, undertakes it during the early 1970s.

The second common characterization of Altman's zooms, as "subliminal," focuses on what Bordwell has described as their frequently slow, "creeping" quality.[5] Unlike the "searching and revealing" zoom, Bordwell does not explicitly associate this form of the zoom with art cinema. And although Bordwell has pointed out that these creeping zooms are often rather abruptly intercut, some critics and scholars have focused on their slow, sometimes almost imperceptible, movement, in service of larger claims about the quasi-meditative function of the zoom in Altman's films. John Belton and Lyle Tector have written that when Altman zooms "in the interest of 'guiding the audience's consciousness' or intensifying a mood—the effect is usually next-to-subliminal."[6] While the strictly descriptive aspect of "subliminal"—that the zooms are barely noticeable—is sometimes, and only sometimes, true of Altman's zooms, the connotations of the term seem to be more important to many critics, who often seek to credit them with special, almost metaphysical power that goes beyond the simple avoidance of conscious notice—a low bar for techniques in popular storytelling media. For instance, Belton and Tector approvingly cite Robin Wood's claim that Altman has "grasped [the zoom's] potential for dissolving space and undermining our sense of physical reality."[7] Likewise, while the pair acknowledge that one result of the zoom's selection of details for the audience may be the foregrounding of a narrating presence, they claim that, "especially in later Altman [based on the context they seem to mean Altman's films after *McCabe & Mrs. Miller*], zoom methodology is so consecrated to exploring the essential life-and-energy system of the world under scrutiny that the notion of a discrete narrator virtually recedes."[8]

As with the descriptions of Altman's approach to narrative, we can see a tendency to describe Altman's practice in a way that connects him strongly to the kinds of abstract high purposes most commonly attributed to art cinema, thereby justifying claims for Altman as a new form of auteur, a practitioner of American art cinema. For some, though not for Bordwell, this similarity has served as part of a larger argument linking Altman with a broader oppositional approach to classical norms. As with the claims about the narrative design of Altman's films, one important problem with both the roving and subliminal characterizations is that they depend on misdescriptions of the actual features of the films and their functions.

Looking more closely at the zooms in Altman's films reveals a nuanced and shifting approach that is, importantly, partly based in practical concerns. Altman and his collaborators are best seen as problem solvers, and they often set for themselves problems that exceed or elaborate on those typical of Hollywood cinema. Furthermore, those problems can be set, and the realm of possible solutions constrained or expanded, by what we might describe as practice-oriented preferences—filmmakers' preferred ways of working. Obviously, these preferences are responsive to institutional norms, budgetary requirements, and the state of technology. While the use of the zoom in Altman's films has often been framed around a kind of distanced visual and spatial exploration, to a large extent these zooms can be seen as a consequence of Altman's practice-oriented preferences engaging with his institutional context.

If we acknowledge that Altman preferred a looser on-set experience in which actorly improvisation was encouraged then we can see why using a zoom lens that would allow his camera operator to respond to that improvisation more flexibly and, moreover, provide the actors with more space in which to improvise, would be seen as advantageous. This is especially true given Altman's preference for location shooting, as nonstudio interiors can often be particularly cramped. Furthermore, if we recognize that Altman preferred to keep his options open on the day of shooting, we can understand how a zoom, with its variable focal length, might become a favored solution. By most accounts Altman loved the day-to-day problem-solving process of filmmaking, to the extent that he once told an interviewer that he would continue making films even if it meant losing his wife and children.[9] For the reasons cited earlier, the zoom allowed Altman to stay engaged in this process more thoroughly. In doing so, it also presented other affordances, further opportunities to elaborate on the standard functions of shots with mobile framing. The results of the analysis offered below support a plausible case that starts from this framework, in which Altman used the zoom first to meet the standard aims of Hollywood storytelling and then also to exceed them in distinctive and contingent ways that we can describe with some precision.

## Contexts for Elaboration: Key Premises and Principles for Understanding Altman and the Zoom

The zoom, of course, has its own history—one that precedes and exceeds the contributions of Altman or, indeed, of any filmmaker or filmmaking tradition. Central to understanding the nature and distinction of the use of the zoom in Altman's films, then, is the historical context in which those zooms were employed. Nick Hall's excellent history, *The Zoom: Drama at the Touch of a Lever*, as well as Jonah Horwitz's unpublished research on the zoom in American cinema from 1958 to 1969, offer substantial insight into the technique's use up to and during the Hollywood Renaissance period in which the zoom became the visual signature of Altman's filmmaking. Both accounts emphasize an attempt by Hollywood practitioners to come to terms with the expressive and pragmatic affordances of the developing zoom technology and at the same time to constrain the zoom's perceived "difference" from established Hollywood practice, both by warning against "overuse" and by positing an opposition between "good" zooms, those that were concealed and restrained, and "bad" zooms that were obvious and emphatic.

Horwitz distinguishes between two periods in the run-up to the early 1970s based on their contrasting approaches to the use of the zoom. The first period, running from 1958 to 1966, he characterizes as employing "The Parsimonious Approach," with zooms "typically used only a few times during a given feature," and usually for not more than three out of a set of five functions that Horwitz has identified: POV shots in which the zoom replicates the mental focusing and attention of a character; calling attention to a detail of the mise-en-scène that was previously unemphasized; suggesting proximity or part/whole relations; intensifying an emotional moment, typically through a zoom in on a human face; and for reframings or following shots that are motivated by figure movement. Because the zoom is used so sparingly during this period, Horwitz posits that each use is likely to be treated as a "capital-E 'effect': an overtly stylized gesture."[10] The late 1960s brought in a second approach to zoom usage, which Horwitz describes as a period of "Hypertrophy." It is marked by a multiplication of functions for the zoom and practically exponential growth in the number of zooms that can be found in American

films—upward of hundreds, according to Horwitz. In addition to technological innovations, Horwitz suggests other factors that may have motivated this
shift, including the widespread use of the zoom in the influential realms of
European art cinema and observational documentary, and a developing taste
for the softer look produced by zoom lenses, particularly at their longest and
most telephoto settings.[11]

Horwitz argues that even during the period of "Hypertrophy," the
zoom was controversial. Discussion of zooming in the pages of *American
Cinematographer* was marked by distaste for the technique, with a "general
trend toward increasing, indeed decadent, numbers of zooms [being] frowned
upon, without any specific culprits being named."[12] According to Horwitz, "a
few directors responded to the overuse of zooms . . . by forbidding it altogether."[13] Hall points out, though, that for Hollywood cinematographers, the
real culprits from which they were "attempting to wrest control of the zoom"
were their "colleagues in television, news filming, and industrial production.
Mainstream feature film cinematographers, speaking through the trade's
mouthpiece publication, *American Cinematographer*, began to "define what
might be described as a 'quality' or 'Hollywood' zoom," a kind of concealed
zoom that "would not be used as a shock effect, but as a tool of efficiency
and convenience, justified by the professionalism, restraint, and finesse with
which it was used." However, many prominent films showed "very different
applications of the zoom to those described by their chief cameramen: more
obtrusive, and less adeptly concealed." The result, says Hall, was that in the
1960s the zoom shot was "a technique fraught with contradictions."[14]

Even so, Hall asserts that, because of both their "ability to create a unique
visual impression," and their "time and money saving" flexibility, during the
1970s, "zoom lenses were used more and more in feature films and television series," becoming "embedded in film style." Another key factor in their
burgeoning popularity, and one that holds particular interest in terms of
zoom style in Altman's films, was the innovation of "programmable electronic
zoom controls," which enabled a more quality look, making "changes of focal
length smoother and more consistent."[15]

We can find in these attempts by the guardians of Hollywood's cinemat-
ographic standards to discursively guard against the shock of the new, as
well as in the contradictions Hall notes between discourse and practice, the
possible origins of the misapprehension of Altman's own zooming by critics
from what I've termed the "oppositional" camp. In some ways, by framing
Altman's zooms as radically disruptive, these critics were simply restating
the claims of Hollywood's old guard while reversing their evaluative valence.
Altman's capacity for elaborative innovation, though, rests in his ability to

move outside of these binaries. That is, Altman seems to qualifiedly reject the standard-bearing practitioner perspective as overdetermined by the concerns of specialists and detached from audience capacities, if not tendencies. Would audiences really find the zoom's perspectival shift—the difference between magnification and "actual" movement—as salient and as disturbing as Hollywood cinematographers did, with their trained eyes and territorialism? And if not, why should he feel compelled to circumscribe the use, and uses, of a technique that offered so many pragmatic and elaborative affordances?

Hall rightly criticizes standard accounts of the technique's use in filmmaking for focusing too narrowly on Altman and a handful of other designated feature film auteurs rather than considering a broader set of filmmakers, "working in [what is characterized as] an otherwise barren wasteland of run-of-the-mill studio productions." They also ignore what Hall accurately describes as, "the porous border between television and features." Hall goes on to claim that, while "there is no doubt that Robert Altman was innovative and unusual in his use of zooms . . . a serious examination of many other uses of the zoom in film and television during the 1970s suggests that Altman's approach to the zoom may not be quite as exceptional as has been traditionally argued."[16] He then provides an illuminating account of television cinematographer Walter Strenge's employment of the technique, followed by brisk analysis of the use of the zoom in several Altman films.

There are a few significant problems, though, with Hall's approach and his methodology. First, what Hall seems to be claiming here is not that the functions of Altman's zoom usage are more "normal" in relation to classical Hollywood norms, but that other filmmakers also made use of the "novel," authorially expressive aspects of Altman's zoom approach that, Hall implies, rely on the antinaturalistic, medium-specific visual qualities of the zoom. In his earlier discussion of the use of the zoom in Frankenheimer's *The Train* (1964) to slowly zoom in on a wristwatch in anticipation of an air-raid siren, Hall notes how the zoom in some places "overlaps and intermingles with established modes of classical narration," while also providing something else, a visual magnification that is "smoother and more controlled than physical movement, one that is editorial and evokes an authorial choice about what action to pay attention to, rather than . . . seeming to follow the flow of the action."[17] This contrast between physical camera movement and the use of the zoom may be structured into *The Train*, but a significant amount of skepticism should be applied both to Hall's implicit claim that even the smoothest, most recognizably "zoomy," zoom necessarily evokes recognition of an overt authorial intervention, and to the related notion that a physical camera movement could not also readily signal such an intervention. Likewise, it seems wrong to suggest that the integration of moments of overt narration is anti-thetical to the established norms of classical narration. Indeed, according to Bordwell, Thompson, and Staiger's account, the degree of self-consciousness in classical narration fluctuates within and across sequences.[18] In some ways, these assumptions risk reintegrating the oppositional account's claim about the diegetically disruptive function of the zoom while extending its import to a broader set of filmmakers. On the other hand, I view Hall's underlying notion that the use of a new technique could be integrated with, while also exceeding the aims of, "established modes of classical narration" to be com-plementary with the notion of elaborative authorship and the innovation of classical Hollywood storytelling. Indeed, the "established modes" that Hall nods to here were, themselves, the result of an ongoing process of innovation and elaboration.

The second issue I would take with Hall's account is the notion that we actu-ally know what Altman's zoom usage was like during this period, let alone the ways in which it was "exceptional." As this chapter's introduction indicates, a precise, robust account of the features and functions of the use of the zoom in any one of Altman's films, let alone how Altman's strategies might shift contin-gently from film to film, has been neglected by standard accounts in favor of impressionistic characterization and overgeneralization.

The final, interconnected, issue is one of methodology and evidence. It is debatable whether the question of what might be novel, or not, about even a known "Altman" is best addressed through a comparative case study with a television cinematographer, or any single filmmaker. There is a burden to show that any case study is representative of a broader set of practices and norms. Hall's insightful account of Strenge's formal strategies nicely troubles the snobbish notion that filmed television is somehow inherently unsophis-ticated, unartful, or dissimilar from what any given feature filmmaker might employ. At the same time, it is insufficient as a convincing representation of the relative novelty of Altman's approach. For instance, there is nothing in Hall's account to establish that both are not similarly unrepresentative in re-lation to a broader set of zoom practices, whether in feature filmmaking or filmed television. The methodology employed in this chapter seeks to address this issue in four key ways.

First, while I, like Hall, think the question of zoom practice in television is crucial to understanding the full context and causes of zoom practice in moving image media in any given historical period, I also think a narrower project of delineating zoom practice in feature filmmaking during the early 1970s is useful, particularly when understanding how the zooms in Altman's films may or may not stand out in relation to the most proximate set of practices and norms.

Second, I tackle this narrower project through the construction of a relatively broad context set that surveys the films made between 1970 and 1975 by twenty filmmakers, from a variety of feature filmmaking cohorts or backgrounds. To do so, I rely in part on Peter Krämer's work on New Hollywood from 1967 to 1976. Krämer provides a useful inventory of directors who made top-ten hit films during the period and places them in several cohorts based mainly on their filmmaking backgrounds: established "Old Hollywood" directors, European directors, film school generation directors, and directors who made their reputation largely in television.[19] I refine this categorization by distinguishing, based on their distinct modes of production, between directors with backgrounds in live and filmed television, and by adding another grouping of particular interest to film historians—those filmmakers who have been described as "Hollywood Renaissance" filmmakers by Diane Jacobs in her influential book.[20]

I then select a survey set of seventy-nine films made up of the available work of eighteen total filmmakers, three filmmakers from each of the six groups of "hitmakers." First, I chose three filmmakers who had previously served, like Altman, as directors of filmed television: Burt Kennedy, Sam Peckinpah, and Joseph Sargent. I then chose three directors who made live television: John Frankenheimer, Arthur Hiller, and Sidney Lumet. I also selected three members of the "film school generation": Francis Ford Coppola, George Lucas, and Steven Spielberg (who also got his start in filmed television, though later than the directors in that group), and three directors who had persisted from "Old Hollywood": Richard Fleischer, Don Siegel, and Robert Stevenson. I selected three "Hollywood Renaissance" filmmakers: Hal Ashby, Michael Ritchie, and Martin Scorsese.[21] Scorsese, of course, should also be considered a member of the film school generation, given his training at New York University. In the same way, Coppola is included by Jacobs as a contributor to the Hollywood Renaissance. Finally, I include the American work of three European directors: John Boorman, Milos Forman, and Roman Polanski. A complete list of the films analyzed is provided in the appendix.

Obviously, because the films on this list were not randomly selected there is no way to test for their representativeness of early 1970s feature filmmaking as a whole. But the diversity of the filmmakers represented here, as well as their relative, if, for some, inconsistent financial success provides other benefits. In no way does this set constitute the kind of list of established auteurs that Hall warns against. Instead, it delivers a set of filmmakers from a variety of backgrounds and for a variety of audiences. For instance, Robert

Stevenson made films exclusively for Disney during this period. At the same time, the set does include many contemporaneously and historically influential filmmakers and films that have been the subject of a good deal of critical and scholarly interest. Finally, constructing the set largely around filmmakers' institutional backgrounds provides data related to questions about how and whether such backgrounds might influence filmmaking. While it is not the project of this book to fully explore these questions in relation to this data, the results presented here do suggest some tentative hypotheses.

Third, working from this context set, I conduct a quantitative/qualitative analysis of the use of the zoom along a more robust and more clearly articulated set of parameters than has previously been the case. The data collected is both descriptive and analytic. For the context set, I track both the quantity of zooms and some key features, and I also attribute one or more of a set of specified functions to each zoom. I will elaborate on these features and functions shortly, but in establishing a set of parameters I hope to move beyond the tendency toward impressionistic description and analysis that often evades the precision necessary for closely comparing practices and the supporting argumentation useful for understanding, refining, or rejecting claims.

Finally, in presenting this data and analysis, I rely on medians and boxplots to describe what might be considered normal and exceptional practices. These descriptive methods are likely less familiar to general readers than the more common statistical descriptors of means and standard deviations.[22] In order to reduce the impact of outliers in skewing the understanding of typical practice, the boxplot makes use of the median rather than mean number to anchor the interpretation of typicality within a set of data. Moreover, whereas standard deviations sometimes misleadingly imply a symmetrical distribution of data around the mean, the boxplot clearly depicts skewed distributions. That is, in data sets in which the spread of instances does not form a symmetrical bell curve, describing the data through medians and quartiles and representing it as a "whiskered" box plot provides a better understanding of representativeness, novelty, and distribution. For example, shot length, one of the well-established quantitative variables in film history, will tend to be skewed right (or high). This is because shots cannot be shorter than zero seconds, but can, in some extreme cases (particularly in the digital era), last for dozens of minutes or even hours. The result is an asymmetrical distribution that has many observations grouped on the low end (to the left of the x-axis) and a few observations at the very high end (to the right of the x-axis).[23]

The "box-and-whiskers" form of the boxplot shows both the center and the spread of the data represented. It consists of a box drawn "between the lower and upper quartiles," encompassing the median, or middle instance, of the lower half of values and the median of the upper half of values, from the 25th to 75th percentiles, "with a solid line drawn across the box indicating the [overall] median." The box, then, encloses what is known as the interquartile range (IQR). Straight lines, or whiskers, extend from the top and bottom of the box, typically to the largest and smallest values, respectively. In data sets including extreme values, though, these lines extend only to what are known as the upper and lower adjacent values, the largest and smallest values that are not outliers. Outliers in the box-and-whiskers plot are determined in relation to the IQR. Mild outliers, represented by an open circle, fall outside what are known as the upper and lower inner fences, at distances of 1.5 times the IQR above and below the box top and bottom. Extreme outliers, represented by a closed, or blackened circle, fall beyond the upper and lower outer fences, which are more than three times the IQR above or below the box top and bottom.[24]

The box-and-whiskers plot not only provides an intuitive picture of center and spread but also excels at comparing samples or groups to one another. It is thus well-suited to the identification of norms and deviations from those norms.[25] Boxplots comparing Altman's use of the zoom to that of the filmmakers in the context set point to what is likely to be novel (or not) about Altman's zoom practice. These graphical displays are useful in developing hypotheses and moderating claims about the extent to which filmmakers' backgrounds may be narrowly predictive of their zoom usage.

At the basic level of how often the zoom is employed by filmmakers, or zoom frequency, measured here as zooms per minute, the box-and-whiskers plot depicted in Figure 2.1 immediately makes clear that Altman's films are exceptional, to say the least. Altman's zoom rate is not merely at the high end of normative 1970s zoom practice as established in the context set—it sits entirely outside of the rates observed in the context set. Each of Altman's early 1970s films is an extreme outlier, ranging from *Thieves Like Us* with 1.01 zooms per minute to 2.57 zooms per minute in Altman's next film, *California Split*. Indeed, Altman's *minimum* zoom frequency exceeds the maximum among his peers. The highest number of zooms per minute outside of Altman can be found in Sam Peckinpah's *Junior Bonner* (1972), the sole other extreme outlier in Figure 2.1, at 0.88. This is the peak of Peckinpah's zoom usage in the early 1970s. At the low end, Peckinpah employs only 0.16 zooms per minute in 1971's *Straw Dogs*, evidence that the zoom was a much less integral aspect of Peckinpah's visual strategies from film to film than it was for Altman.

Figure 2.2 provides a comparison of box-and-whiskers plots for zoom frequency by cohort. Taken by itself, the comparison suggests that both the Hollywood Renaissance and filmed television cohorts were remarkably more

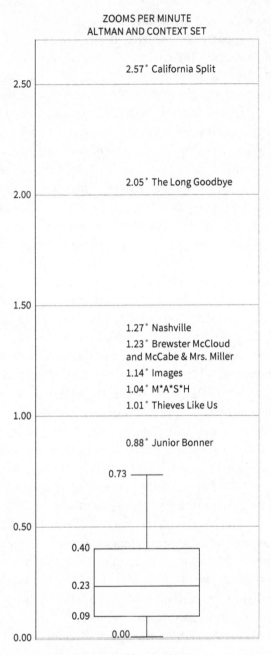

**Figure 2.1** Zooms per Minute Altman and Context Set

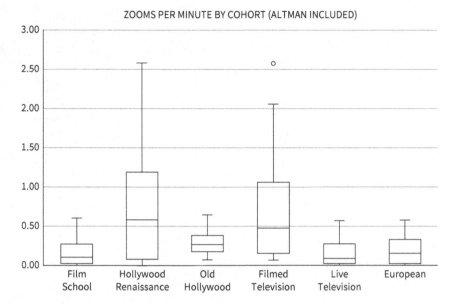

**Figure 2.2** Zooms per Minute by Cohort (Altman Included)

likely to make use of the zoom, with medians of 0.55 and 0.47 zooms per minute and upper quartiles at 1.19 and 1.07, a little less than double the highest data points in the other cohorts. The implications here for filmed television are particularly significant due to the persistence of a critical commonplace—the notion that filmed television veterans are more likely to rely on technological gimmickry in their work. For instance, James Bernardoni has claimed that, "television aesthetics' affinity for a visually bold style at the service of thematically uncomplicated content," has been emulated by New Hollywood filmmakers who worked in or grew up watching the medium.[26] The zoom, as Hall notes, is often seen as emblematic of television aesthetics during this period. Similarly, it seems right that the Hollywood Renaissance, a group of filmmakers who do not share a training ground but are viewed by critics as sharing a renegade, oppositional approach to Hollywood, would be more willing to use the zoom, a device disdained by the mainstream.

The representation of zoom frequency in Figure 2.2 would, then, seem to confirm these suppositions. However, Figure 2.3, a comparison that separates Altman from his Hollywood Renaissance and filmed television cohorts, suggests the need to qualify support for these positions. Once Altman is removed, the appearance of an overall heightened preference for the zoom in the Hollywood Renaissance cohort is greatly minimized, with a median of 0.15 that is still above the medians for the film school and European cohorts

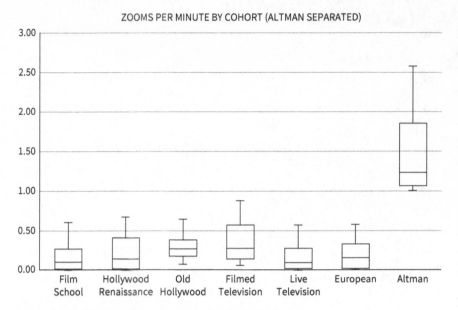

ZOOMS PER MINUTE BY COHORT (ALTMAN SEPARATED)

**Figure 2.3** Zooms per Minute by Cohort (Altman Separated)

but that now falls below Old Hollywood filmmakers' median of 0.27 zooms per minute. That said, the modestly larger size of the upper half of the inter-quartile range for the Hollywood Renaissance displays more skew in the data toward higher zooms per minute than in all other cohorts but filmed television. Likewise, the filmed television boxplot now displays a preference for zooming that seems less stark. Even so, Figure 2.3 provides significant evidence of a heightened use of the zoom on the part of these filmmakers. The filmed television group median of 0.28 zooms per minute is still higher than the medians of all of the other cohorts. Its upper quartile is significantly higher than that in all of the other groups.

Even if we accept the modest evidence here that feature filmmakers with a background in filmed television were more likely to make regular use of the zoom in this period, we do not need to accept Bernardoni's explanation of this increased use as the desire on the part of these directors for a visually bold style, especially at the cost of thematic complexity. It seems at least equally plausible that one would be more likely to find filmmakers with a particular appreciation of the benefits of the zoom and who are more skeptical about its claimed downsides among those who spent time in a medium with tight schedules and low budgets. Perhaps after seeing that television audiences were not left spatially and ontologically disoriented, directors with experience in filmed television felt it was safe to employ the device toward narrative and expressive ends.

It is interesting in this context that Old Hollywood filmmakers do not seem to have been less interested in using the zoom than imported European directors, the film school trained "New Hollywood" proper types likely to have grown up watching television that Bernardoni lumps in with the makers of filmed television, and directors who spent time in the culturally prestigious, thematically weighty realm of live television. The median zoom frequency for Old Hollywood filmmakers, at 0.27, is higher than for all these other groups, as is the upper quartile of 0.38. Moreover, the lower quartile, at 0.18, and lowest data point, at 0.08, are higher than the same markers for all other cohorts, including filmed television and Hollywood Renaissance filmmakers. This, along with the relative tightness of the interquartile range—at 0.2 the tightest of any cohort—suggests more conformity and regularity (as distinct from frequency per se) in the employment of the device. Perhaps this is due to an increased willingness on the part of Old Hollywood filmmakers to adhere to general industrial norms rather than to operate according to the kind of strident preferences for or against individual techniques on display by the arbiters of quality quoted in *American Cinematographer*. Arguably, their principles were equally dissimilar to the auteur-minded filmmakers in those other two cohorts, who likely viewed strong stylistic stances as marketplace advantages. In each of these groups, we find filmmakers who make very little to no use of the zoom.

The discussion thus far, while useful for complicating preconceptions and generalizations about the influence of background or the conceptualization of filmmaker group style, is necessarily highly speculative, working as it does from just 3–4 directors per cohort. There are several other key issues obscured by the previous discussion, and it is worth briefly examining each because their implications likewise argue for a less summary approach to describing the history of film style and formal norms.

First, each cohort has been more or less personified in the previous discussion, treated to some extent as a coherent and unified body. However, separating out individual directors within cohorts, as was done with Altman above, reveals that overreliance on summary representations obscures disparate tendencies within groups. Figure 2.4 makes this plain. For instance, the zoom frequencies of filmed television directors Peckinpah and Sargent's early 1970s oeuvres, with IQRs extending from 0.71/0.72 to 0.32/0.13, are similar to each other but fairly dissimilar from filmed television director Kennedy's tightly packed IQR, which extends only from 0.19 to 0.13. Kennedy's zoom frequency is much closer to that of Old Hollywood filmmaker Don Siegel,

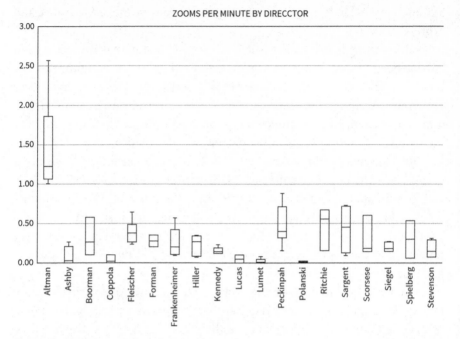

Figure 2.4  Zooms per Minute by Director

who has an IQR extending from 0.27 to 0.15. Likewise, Old Hollywood film-maker and 1970s Disney stalwart Robert Stevenson's IQR, from 0.29 to 0.08, most closely resembles that of former live television director Arthur Hiller, which extends from 0.35 to 0.09.

The relatively large spread within Peckinpah and Sargent's bodies of work indicates at least two other issues common to the discussion of filmmaking style. First, there is a tendency to reify or essentialize a filmmaker's formal practices in a kind of binary yes/no, high/low manner; yet there is ample evidence here that the work of many directors is less consistent, at least in their handling of the zoom. While filmmakers like Coppola, Lumet, Lucas, and Polanski seem to have decided to use the zoom only very sparingly, if at all, others have comparatively robust IQRs, indicating a film-by-film approach.

Second, the design of the context set around directors rather than cinematographers risks overemphasizing the role of the director in setting a film's visual style. To some extent, this is justifiable since many directors, particularly in the auteur-driven early 1970s, operated not just as gatekeepers or collaborators for choices about visual style but also as originators. However, standard accounts of filmmaking tend to privilege directors to an extent that is difficult to defend. The design of the context set is partly a response to the kinds of questions that have been asked about the influence of directors and their backgrounds on the use of the zoom. Moreover, the results already discussed complicate general accounts framing the director as the default source for all creative decisions. Just as a robust IQR raises the possibility of dynamism in a director's approach from film to film, it also raises the question of whether it is the director's approach that changes and whether the visual style, in part or total, should be taken as a reflection of the vision or choices of the director per se. It seems likely, for instance, that for Steven Spielberg's two feature films of the period, which have wildly divergent zoom usage, the cinematographer was a major determinant. *Sugarland Express* (1974), shot by Vilmos Zsigmond, has 0.54 zooms per minute while *Jaws* (1975), shot by Bill Butler, has only 0.06 zooms per minute. The other, non-Altman helmed, film of the early 1970s shot by Zsigmond that is included as part of my survey, Boorman's *Deliverance* (1972), has a similarly high 0.58 zooms per minute, while Butler's other film, Coppola's *The Conversation* (1974), for which he receives co-credit with Haskell Wexler, has a relatively low 0.11 zooms per minute. This suggests, perhaps unsurprisingly, that cinematographers had distinct zoom preferences that might determine or coincide with a given director's preferences on a project. What to make, though, of cinematographer Gerry Fisher's 90–95th percentile 0.65 zooms per minute on Fleisher's *See No Evil* in 1971 and his 0 zooms in 1973 on Lumet's *The Offence*? Here, Fisher seems willing to adjust zoom usage to the preferences of the director. Or, perhaps, as with directors, a cinematographer's preferences are more dynamic than typically thought. Of course, one of the drawbacks of developing a context set around directors is that it does not offer, or only coincidentally offers, a complete account of any cinematographer's work with the zoom during this period.

What all of this adds up to, of course, is that the causality behind zoom usage is multifactorial. For instance, even Zsigmond's high zoom frequency might be explained by the subject matter of *Sugarland Express* and *Deliverance*—two films that depict a surplus of vehicles (cars in the former and canoes in the latter) in motion. My survey of early 1970s American cinema makes clear that this is a particular sweet spot for the zoom, with several of the films surveyed concentrating their zoom usage disproportionately around vehicles in motion. When those cars (or canoes) are in action sequences, the rate of cutting typically increases, thereby increasing the incidence of shots with zooms. Moreover, Spielberg (and Zsigmond) may have been going for a quasi-vérité aesthetic on *Sugarland Express*, which was loosely based on the true story of accidentally antiestablishment young lovers on a cross-country road trip. A similar aesthetic would not be an obvious choice for a film about a beach town menaced by a giant shark.

Perhaps what is most interesting about the data developed here, though, is that while the causes and patterns of zoom frequency are difficult to parse for the majority of films and filmmakers in the context set this is emphatically not the case for Robert Altman. While Zsigmond, a consistently high zoomer in his other films of the period, served as a cinematographer on three of Altman's early 1970s films, the zoom frequencies of his three films with Altman (1.23 on *McCabe & Mrs. Miller*, 1.14 on *Images*, and 2.05 on *The Long Goodbye*) were 2–4 times as high as those of his non-Altman helmed films. All of Altman's films, regardless of cinematographer, are extreme outliers in zoom frequency. This is not to say that the cinematographer had no impact on how the zoom was used in these films, but it does seem unusually clear that Altman set the regular employment of the zoom as a precondition and preference for decision-making about his films' visual strategies.

Frequency, though, is not the only way in which Altman's zoom usage can be distinguished from that of his cohort. Norms encompass not just the rate of usage of techniques but also their descriptive and functional parameters—the range of features they display and the aims toward which they are applied. Though not comprehensive, the context set employed for this chapter provides the most robust measurement yet of zoom practices in early 1970s American cinema. As such, it serves as the substantial evidentiary basis for both a preliminary description of the likely functional norms for zoom usage during the period and for a comparative analysis that might establish the specific ways in which Altman's zoom purposes resemble or depart from those norms.

Given the flexibility of the zoom, and its use by a diverse group of filmmakers in multiple filmmaking contexts, it would be impossible to produce an inventory of the zoom that captures every possible purpose. Therefore, the following list is not intended to be all-inclusive but is instead intended to serve as a useful starting point, and it should be judged on the basis of whether it adequately and plausibly captures the features and functions of the zooms on display in Altman's oeuvre and in the context films. This inventory is largely inductive rather than deductive. That is, it was generated by closely examining the use of individual zooms and then articulating and revising categories. Each zoom provided a test and an opportunity to fine-tune this inventory, and while I believe that in its present form it convincingly captures the great majority of zooms on display in American cinema of the period it is, of course, open to further revision.

There are at least eleven zoom-types that are particularly salient to understanding the functional norms of zoom usage in American cinema during the early 1970s: reframing, revealing, attentional, POV, intensifying, emphatic, connective, aperture, aesthetic, zoom past, and refreshing. To give some shape to this inventory, these zoom-types may be conditionally grouped under four larger functional categories that follow the distinction between narrative, expressive, symbolic, decorative, and mimetic functions employed by Bordwell and other scholars of film style (see Table 2.1).[27] Reframing, revealing, attentional, and POV zooms, for instance, predominantly seem to be focused on narrative comprehension, while intensifying and emphatic zooms are more likely to focus on engaging the viewer affectively. The connective zoom is most likely to serve the symbolic function. The aperture zoom, enabled by the zoom past and serving as the vanguard incarnation of the broader category of the aesthetic zoom, is unsurprisingly largely decorative in function, though an argument could be made that by providing a sense of depth to the image aperture zooms also serve a mimetic function.[28] The final zoom type, the refreshing zoom, is essentially defined by the difficulty with which it may be placed within any of the functional categories, even given a fairly generous approach to categorization. It seems to serve the principle that movement maintains the perceptual interest of the audience, though certainly not by appealing to classical Hollywood standards of quality formal design in relation to mobile framing that demand the integration of narrative or expressive motivations. Even so, I qualifiedly place the refreshing zoom in the decorative category. As Altman's innovative early 1970s' oeuvre so clearly demonstrates, while the industry may articulate standards for achieving desired functions there may also be a more robust set of unsanctioned techniques for achieving those same functions.

This categorization should be taken as representative and instructive rather than comprehensive or determinant. In any given film one might find significant variation or complexity that troubles the straightforward functional equivalence implied by the convenient groupings here. For instance, we might compare an attentional POV zoom that replicates a character's subjectivity and fits well within the norms of Hollywood storytelling with the kind of seeking and revealing attentional zoom described above by Bordwell, and whose qualities seem to place it within the realm of art cinema. Such an

**Table 2.1** Zoom-Types Grouped by Common Functional Category

| Narrative | Expressive | Symbolic | Decorative | Mimetic |
|---|---|---|---|---|
| Reframing | Intensifying | Connective | Aperture | Aperture* |
| Revealing | Emphatic | | Aesthetic | |
| Attentional | | | Zoom Past* | |
| POV | | | (*often enables | |
| | | | Aperture zoom) | |
| | | | Refreshing* | |

attentional zoom might direct attention to an aspect of the narrative world, but instead of furthering narrative comprehension it might function purely descriptively, calling attention to a detail for the sake of filling out a realistic milieu or making a symbolic point. Or, it might overtly indicate material necessary for thematic interpretation significant to narrational judgment and in doing so advance authorial expressivity.

It is also important to note here that the fulfillment of the attributed functions should not be seen as exclusively within the realm of the zoom. The mystification of the zoom is partly the result of a tendency to exaggerate the significance of its unique visual properties and to downplay both those visual features it might share with a moving camera and the zoom's capacity for functional overlap with camera movement. Not every zoom is about disintegrating space, and the zoom often serves aims just as mundane as those served by a mobile camera. There are, though, several purposes for which the zoom is particularly useful, and the inventory here attempts to capture them. Finally, although these zoom-types were largely generated inductively, this list overlaps with and was refined by considering Horwitz's useful description of typical zoom functions in his history of the zoom. That said, there are some important divergences. This conditional categorization of zoom-types will hopefully be further clarified by the following, more extensive, discussion of each in turn.

The first of the predominantly narrative zoom-types, and probably the most common kind of zoom (as well as the most common type of mobile framing in general), is the *reframing* zoom. While some definitions of reframing limit its scope to very slight movements that maintain a figure's position within the frame, my use of the term here is a little broader. For my purposes, reframing involves using the zoom to manage the placement of salient figures, either by maintaining the figure's place in the composition or by handing-off compositional primacy from one figure to another. This includes minor zooms as well as fairly major zooms typically accompanied by camera movements like tilts and pans that follow a figure's trajectory through space. These zooms in and out are not closely or primarily coordinated with the affective development of the dramatic action but rather are used in the service of compositional conventions for following the dramatic action in a spatial sense. Its function, then, is most commonly narrative in that the reframing is usually in service of ensuring the dramatic focus of a given scene or sequence is in a prominent compositional position and therefore marked and available for the viewer's attention.

The *revealing* function of the zoom is limited to zooms out which reveal significant or interesting aspects of the narrative world, such as figures or objects that appear as a result of the expanding view. It is important to note that my use of the term "revealing" here, associated as it is with the zoom out, is different from the way the term is used by Bordwell, where a zoom in reveals a previously visible but overlooked part of the image by bringing it to the audience's attention. Often the revealing zoom is used as an entry point into a scene, beginning on a detail and then zooming back from it to reveal the scenic space. In this case its function fits within a fairly conventional pattern for scenic elaboration, described in *The Classical Hollywood Cinema*, which involves beginning a scene "by framing a detail and then by means of various devices (dissolve, cut, iris, or tracking shot) [revealing] the totality of the space."[29] So, for instance, a shot might begin with a close-up of a hand on a ringing telephone and the revealing zoom out that follows will reveal the scenic space and the character who is answering the phone.

The *attentional* function of the zoom is perhaps the function most closely linked with Altman's approach by critics and scholars. When Bordwell talks about the "searching and revealing" approach he is largely talking about using the zoom to pick out details of the image and directing the audience's attention to those details through a zoom in. Here, the narrational function of mobile framing is overt, especially in those "revealing" cases where the zoom in seems to discover an aspect of the mise-en-scène that the audience's attention was not previously directed toward. Importantly, a similar degree of self-consciousness could be achieved by use of a mobile camera; there is nothing intrinsic to the zoom technology in and of itself that marks it as particularly overt. That said, what is for critics the essential novel characteristic of zoom technology, its magnification of part of the image without the parallax-inducing movement through space of a dolly or track, arguably creates an effective impression of the subjective attentional processes of an individual, and so the zoom is particularly well-suited for the kind of POV-inflected attentional zoom to be discussed shortly. In those cases, though, the notion of an immobile subjective presence is established in the viewer's mind by convention. In any event, attentional zooms are typically disconnected from "natural" narrative interest in that they discover the point of interest for a focused viewer who is either looking elsewhere (at the compositionally or narratively established center of attention) or an unmoored viewer looking everywhere, as in the strong version of a Bazinian-neorealist long take. Along these same lines, attentional zooms are likely to be detached from the kind of affective underlining or enhancement of emotional engagement that is key to the function of the intensifying zoom described in what follows.

Essentially combinatory and frequently a modifier of a zoom's main intent, *POV* zooms are employed not just to prompt or parallel audience members' mental and perceptual engagement with the image but also to represent the visual and mental subjectivity of a character within the diegesis. So, if a character's attention is directed at a detail within his or her visual field, the POV zoom will function as an attentional zoom while at the same time signaling the audience that it is witnessing that character's subjective processes. Likewise, if a character's feelings toward a narrative figure grow, a POV zoom in might both intensify the audience's emotions and signal an understanding of the intensity of the character's mental state, thereby modifying the kind of intensifying zooms that will be discussed next. Of course, this kind of POV zoom in might simply provide information about a character's mental state without cueing a parallel affective response in the audience, particularly if the audience has not been primed to engage sympathetically with the character whose POV they momentarily share. In that case, the POV zoom, regardless of the inferred emotions of the aligned character, would be narrative rather than expressive in function.

Of the zooms most likely to be associated with expressive functions, the *intensifying* zoom is the most typical within the context set. Here, the zoom is usually closely coordinated with the development of dramatic action or with the emotional intensity of the narrative. Intensifying zooms in to close-ups of emoting characters are far and away the more commonly employed type, but zooms out can at times intensify the emotion of a narrative moment, particularly when used to underline a character's isolation or loneliness. For instance, the opening title montage of Sam Peckinpah's *The Ballad of Cable Hogue* (1970) features a series of intensifying zooms out from the title character as he wanders through various desert landscapes, searching futilely for water. Typically, though, intensifying zooms move inward, and they usually end in a close-up or extreme close-up of an actor's expressively emotional face. The trajectory of the mobile framing combines with the magnification of the element of the mise-en-scène that, hypothetically at least, contains the most affective potential in order to shape the arc of the audience's emotional reaction. Less affectively charged intensifying zooms in may simply serve to echo, through forward movement, the forward development of a narrative situation, so that when that situation is fully elaborated, the framing is at its tightest. Here, it is audience interest in the situation rather than sympathetic emotion per se that is augmented. It seems likely that innovations in zoom technology, particularly the development of electronic zoom control, which allowed for smoother and more precise manipulation of the zoom, made intensifying zooms a more common and more effective option during the early 1970s.

The other commonly expressive zoom is the *emphatic* zoom. This is perhaps the most well-known and conventionalized zoom, such that contemporary films often employ the emphatic zoom as a reflexive pastiche rather than as a straightforwardly expressive device. The emphatic zoom in is distinguished from the strictly attentional or intensifying zoom by its high velocity, and it serves as the narrational equivalent of an exclamation point. We might imagine a stock example derived from a spaghetti western in which the zoom quickly snaps in from a long shot of a gunfighter to the gun simultaneously drawn from its holster. Because of its punctuative potential it most closely resembles the POV zoom in that it seems to always be combined with other zoom functions. The emphatic zoom is employed in a way that takes advantage of the zoom's unique technology, as the velocity of the mobile framing is most often unmatchable by a moving camera. One might surmise that it is because of the distinct nature of the emphatic function that it became the signature function of the zoom in its heyday.

The *connective* zoom functions to link two details or figures within the narrative world in order to generate an idea or understanding. In its most common, symbolic, incarnation, we might expect a zoom out from a first detail ending with the prominent display of a second detail, where the linking of the two raises questions of shared significance and prompts an interpretive, theme-seeking, response. Sometimes, though, the connective zoom might simply reinforce or articulate an aspect of the narrative situation by traversing the distance from, say, a worried man patting his pockets in the foreground to another man removing cash from a wallet in the background of the original framing. Because the likely more common, symbolic, version of this sort of zoom operates in the realm of the abstract and the associational, one might expect connective zooms to be more common in art cinema than in Hollywood storytelling. Not only are connective zooms, like attentional zooms, overt, but they overtly cue associative interpretations, signaling authorial expressivity. My analysis of the films for this study shows that connective zooms do, indeed, seem to be fairly rare. They constitute just 1% of all of the purposes toward which the zooms were put, the lowest incidence in the context set. But when they are employed, they often serve to reiterate or underline important thematic and narrative ideas, rather than to lightly suggest.

We need to depart briefly from the functional categories described thus far to get at the distinct, practice-oriented nature of the *zoom past*. As with the emphatic zoom, an aspect of the zoom's distinct technological characteristics is employed. Because the zoom involves a magnification of the image rather than a traversal of space, its "movements" in and out can continue on trajectories that might otherwise be hindered by obstacles within the shooting environment. Zooms can extend mobile framings beyond barriers like furniture, panes of glass, screens, and ledges that would halt tracks and dollies, and which even cranes might not be able to overcome. Moreover, even if a crane were a technologically feasible solution, the zoom past would likely offer a less expensive and more efficient solution to the problem, appealing to a filmmaker's pragmatic preferences. The zoom past's function is essentially practical and enabling, and so the classification of any zoom as a zoom past provides only part of the story. To fully capture any zoom past's functionality the analyst must also ask what the filmmaker seeks to achieve through the mobile framing that zoom technology makes if not possible then at least easier to accomplish. The zoom past is, therefore, almost necessarily paired with one or more other zoom types.

Partly because of their ability to zoom past objects in the foreground that are spatially but not visibly insurmountable, zooms are often employed to begin from or reveal interesting compositions in which a foreground object or objects create a kind of aperture, or frame, for the action taking place in the middleground or background. These *aperture* zooms most often function as decorative touches, ornamenting the beginning or ending, or sometimes the entirety of a shot. The framing of the shot's nominal subject may be more or less complete, and is sometimes only very partial, but the key feature here is an elaboration of the composition, whether the result is largely two-dimensional and graphic or, more often, a heightening of the sense of depth in the shot through placement of an object or objects in the near foreground. This kind of depth effect might be considered mimetic, lending an enhanced sense of three-dimensional space to an image projected on the two-dimensional surface of the screen, and by Altman's own account of his use of aperture framing in television, to be discussed in chapter 5, this was a functional affordance of which he was keenly aware.[30] But in practice the mimetic effect seems secondary or attendant to the creation of a "quality" image and to appealing to aesthetic conventions oriented around enhancing visual interest. It is the rare instance in which aperture framing provides the only depth cue, or even the only overlap or perspectival diminution in a shot. Its addition to other standard pictorial depth cues in the composition is so gratuitous as to make strictly mimetic motivation implausible.

Essentially serving a decorative function, then, the aperture zoom is here considered as the most frequently employed of a larger set of *aesthetic* functions served by the zoom. The overall category of the aesthetic is meant to encompass salient uses of the zoom to create or reveal interesting formal design, largely in ways that appeal to established aesthetic standards. For instance, one zoom out in Hal Ashby's *Harold and Maude* (1971) begins with an extreme long shot of the titular couple in a cemetery surrounded by headstones and ends with a composition in which the cemetery headstones form a regular, graphic pattern of dots in which Harold and Maude are swallowed up (Figures 2.5 and 2.6). Other aesthetic zooms might take advantage of the tendencies of the telephoto lens to blur foregrounded objects, beginning with an appealing or interesting unrecognizable abstract form and then zooming out to reveal the identity of what was previously a colorful blur. We shall see this kind of aesthetic zoom employed by Altman and his collaborators in *M*A*S*H*.

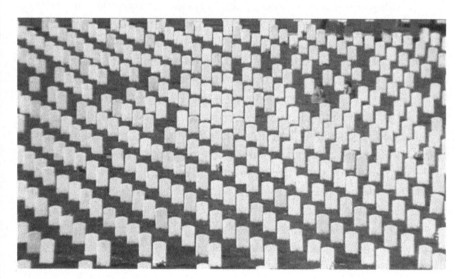

**Figure 2.5**  *Harold and Maude*

**Figure 2.6**  *Harold and Maude*

As was briefly discussed earlier, the final zoom type, the *refreshing* zoom, is disconnected from coordination with the elaboration of the narrative or with the rise and fall of dramatic action and any consequential emotional or intellectual engagement. Exploiting perceptual biases in favor of noticing and tending to movement, the refreshing zoom in or out seems to be used purely to refresh the image, to create a changing visual field so as to retain the attention of any audience member prone to boredom or distraction. In some ways, the refreshing zoom seems to cut against at least one conventional aesthetic standard of quality and economy—that all mobile framing should be motivated. On the other hand, it seems to reflect a base level assumption that has become more and more popular in contemporary Hollywood cinema—that keeping the camera moving adds visual interest and energy.[31] In that sense, Altman's use of the refreshing zoom in the early 1970s represents a sort of vanguard for visceral stimulation and for redefining aesthetic standards of what a quality look might entail. That any shot with mobile framing might be more visually appealing because it contains movement represents a comparatively vulgar principle unlikely to appeal to arbiters of quality, but it is an aesthetic principle, nonetheless. Given this difficult relationship to aesthetic standards it makes sense to separate it from the larger category of aesthetic zooms while preserving this understanding of the refreshing zoom's function.

Each identified zoom in the context set, and in Altman's films, is describable according to one or more of these zoom types. I say one or more because the zoom is no less versatile than any other cinematic technique, not just in the range of functions it might accomplish, but in the capacity of a carefully crafted zoom shot to serve multiple ends. It should come as no surprise that filmmakers aim for economy in the choice of technique. Ideally, they would prefer to choose a device that allows for multifunctionality. The previously touched on *Harold and Maude* example, with its zoom out from odd-couple courtship to the formal geometry of a vast cemetery, provides one example of the frequent multifunctionality of zoom usage. As discussed earlier, the zoom is aestheticizing, creating an interesting formal display, but it also provides a rare sighting of the symbolic connective zoom, suggesting a thematic statement about the regularity of death and foreshadowing Maude's own death. As this example illustrates, and as my above description of the zoom types has indicated, there is a great deal of opportunity for overlap in the zoom's functional affordances. Not only is the aesthetic-embedded aperture function largely, but not entirely, a subcategory of a broader functional category—the aesthetic zoom—others, like the emphatic zoom or the POV zoom, essentially serve as modifiers.

The data collected in this study provides some insight into how, and how often, the zoom was used multifunctionally in early 1970s American cinema. The context set has an absolute ratio of functions to zooms of 1.22:1, suggesting that there is a slight overall tendency toward multifunctionality—every fourth or fifth zoom use would likely be multifunctional.[32] This does not seem to be a strong inclination, though it would be interesting to compare it to multifunctionality in the use of similar techniques, particularly for tracks in and out. Even so, that ratio does help to contextualize Altman's zoom practice. The ratio of functions to zooms on Altman-helmed films is higher, at 1.44:1, which indicates that Altman may have been at the high end of multifunctional zoom usage during this period. When Altman's film-by-film multifunctionality ratios are combined with the film-by-film multifunctionality ratios for the context set, the functions to zoom ratio ticks up to 1.31:1, a not insignificant movement. Again, though, a boxplot comparison, with its more robust presentation of data, helps to clarify where Altman may lie in relation to broader norms. Figure 2.7 demonstrates that while the multifunctionality in Altman's films is not as exceptional as the difference in zoom frequency when compared to the context set—none of his films' multifunctionality is an outlier—the multifunctionality of all of his films sits

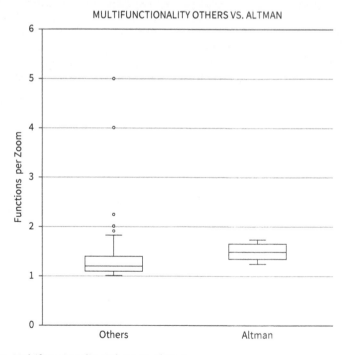

**Figure 2.7** Multifunctionality Others vs. Altman

above the context set's median, and Altman's median is above the upper quartile of the context set.

This visualization may be a bit misleading, though, because of the top 10 instances of multifunctionality, the top 5 all have very few zooms—fewer than 0.10 zooms per minute (Table 2.2). Two others have just eleven zooms each, with zooms per minute of 0.03 and 0.02. The next two films are Altman's *Images* and *M\*A\*S\*H*, with zooms per minute of 1.14 and 1.04, and the list is rounded out by Fleischer's *The Spikes Gang*, with .47 zooms per minute. At least two significant inferences can be drawn from this. The first is that extreme multifunctionality is more likely when the zoom is a relatively novel tool for the film or filmmakers. Perhaps because each instance is a departure from a film's internal norms there is a higher degree of conscious and focused motivation required to justify its use. The second implication is that Altman's multifunctionality is more exceptional in the context of more regular "zoomers." That is, his zooms are more likely to be elaborate, to modify or integrate one function or feature with one or more other functions or features, than are those of other filmmakers who also use the zoom as a more or less regular part of their filmmaking toolkit.

Looking beyond multifunctionality, the data here provide us with a clear descriptive profile of Altman's use of each zoom type, and it allows us to explore how Altman's zoom type usage may or may not be distinct within the

**Table 2.2** Multifunctionality Top Ten

| Multifunctionality Ranking | Title | Director | Functions per Zoom | Zooms per Minute | Total Zooms |
|---|---|---|---|---|---|
| 1 | *Macbeth* | Polanski | 5 | .01 | 1 |
| 2 | *Serpico* | Lumet | 4 | .01 | 1 |
| 3 | *Chinatown* | Polanski | 2.25 | .03 | 4 |
| 4 | *What?* | Polanski | 2 | .02 | 2 |
| 5 | *The Last of the Mobile Hot Shots* | Lumet | 2 | .06 | 6 |
| 6 | *Support Your Local Gunfighter* | Kennedy | 1.91 | .12 | 11 |
| 7 | *Leo the Last* | Boorman | 1.82 | .11 | 11 |
| 8 | *Images* | Altman | 1.73 | 1.14 | 114 |
| 9 | *M\*A\*S\*H* | Altman | 1.68 | 1.04 | 121 |
| 10 | *The Spikes Gang* | Fleischer | 1.58 | .47 | 45 |

broader context of early 1970s American cinema. Doing so overturns some commonplace assumptions about Altman's use of the zoom. For instance, the searching and revealing account of Altman's zooming, where Altman's zoom style is largely defined by the employment of the zoom in service of the attentional function, has dominated analyses of Altman's use of the zoom. For Altman critics, this use of the zoom, which Helene Keyssar has framed as a "democratic" approach, is predicated on providing the audience with wide views that de-emphasize the individual protagonist before overtly picking out details that may be narratively or narrationally excessive.[33] An examination of the data, though, makes clear that this characterization of Altman's zooms, at least during this period, is misleading.

First, it seems wrong to place so much focus on attentional zooming given that it serves a relatively minor role in these films' functional repertoire. As Figure 2.8 clearly shows, the attentional function accounts for only 5.2% of the functions served by Altman's zooming during this period. This is actually a smaller percentage than the context set's 6.4%. This is true even though the conceptualization of the attentional zoom in my framework is comparatively broad, and in adding labels like "democratic," "improvisational," "probing," or "aimless," to describe their purposes and trajectories, critics and scholars have actually squeezed Altman's attentional zooming into much narrower

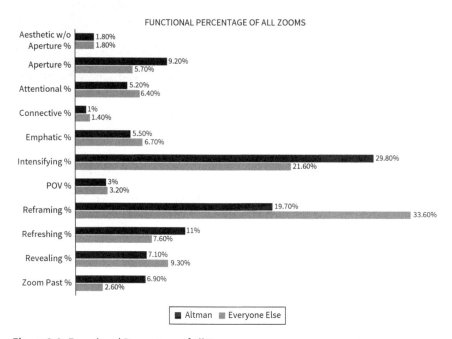

**Figure 2.8** Functional Percentage of All Zooms

concept sets than captured in my statistical analysis. Hypothetically, even if, as a percentage of his overall zoom usage or overall zoom type usage, Altman is no more of an attentional zoomer than his cohort, it is possible that his attentional zooms are, in fact, accurately characterized in a quasi-oppositional manner—democratic and aimless rather than controlled and focused. The attentional zoom might, therefore, warrant such outsized attention in spite of its scarcity. However, these characterizations, at least for the films of this period, largely misdescribe and, in doing so, mystify the films' evident zoom practices.[34] Indeed, it seems important to note not just that the representativeness of Altman's attentional zooming conforms to that found in the context set, but also that seven other zoom types are more likely.

Of the eleven categories of zoom type noted in my analysis, only three: connective (1.0%), nonaperture aesthetic (1.8%), and POV (3.0%), are used in Altman's films less frequently than the attentional zoom. As was discussed in chapter 1, in spite of Altman's categorization as a quasi-modernist art cinema filmmaker, the narration in his films (with the exception of *Images*) actually tends to be subjectively shallow. The finding here with regard to Altman's limited use of the POV zoom is, then, perhaps partly explained by his preference for objective narration. Given the overt, expressive qualities of the connective zoom, its paucity also undermines attempts to describe Altman as an art cinema filmmaker, especially given the context set's slightly higher (1.4%) proportional use of the connective zoom. The relative scarcity, within Altman's early 1970s oeuvre, of nonaperture aestheticizing zooms is actually identical to the zoom type's representation within the context set, suggesting that Altman's approach to decorative touches was largely focused on the creation of a "quality" look through compositions that emphasized depth. This also seems to be the case with the context set, although Altman appears to favor aperture zooms significantly more (9.7% vs. 5.7%) than the select group of peers whose work is examined here.

The emphatic zoom (5.5%) is used at a frequency comparable to the attentional zoom, and of the remaining zoom types the most frequently employed in Altman's films is the intensifying zoom, with a remarkable 29.8% of Altman's zooms serving this purpose. For the context group, though, the intensifying zoom (21.6%) is the second most frequent of the zoom types. Instead, the reframing zoom, in which the zoom is motivated by establishing or maintaining the proper placement of the figure within the composition, is much more common (33.6%). Altman's use of the reframing zoom (19.7%) is significantly lower than that of the larger group, but this still represents the second most frequent zoom type in his films, almost doubling the next closest zoom type, the refreshing zoom (11.0%).

The similarity between Altman and the context group in terms of the prominence and regularity of the reframing zoom within their zoom strategies again suggests that characterizing Altman's approach to the zoom as radically different is misguided. The quasi-metaphysical claims about Altman's zooming that often follow from this initial characterization, then, are similarly likely to be flawed. Take, for instance, Richard T. Jameson's assertion about *Nashville*'s zoom strategies in relation to Tricycle Man:

> His thoughtless mobility is sufficient to glide us into terrain we identify as our next scene, or up to a character we've been wondering about since he/she last passed through the frame. Altman pans and zooms not only with the man and his vehicle but also along the vectors so forcefully described and anticipated by the motion and the very shape of the machine.[35]

If one looks past the mystificatory invocation of "thoughtless mobility," of "vectors" and machinery, we find an assertion that basically maintains that Altman combines a pan with a zoom in order to maintain the compositional prominence of Tricycle Man. This is more or less the definition of a reframing zoom, the employment of craft toward a fairly straightforward end.

Altman's use of the reframing zoom at so high a proportional rate during this period suggests that his work largely conforms to institutional norms regarding composition and its role in the narratively naturalized maintenance of attention. His frequent use of the intensifying zoom, the second most common end for the context group, is a reminder or confirmation of the narrative orientation of both Hollywood and Altman's filmmaking. Since the intensifying zoom is coordinated with narrative elements and is most commonly employed to reinforce emotional engagement with characters, it is hard to argue that Altman is uninterested in engaging audiences through his storytelling—that he, as many standard accounts presume, largely or uniformly favors the oppositional distancing effects that are also presumed to go hand-in-hand with zoom technology. Altman's prioritization of engagement actually might surpass the standard for Hollywood practice, though to get a fuller picture of this we would need to examine the use of similarly employed forward tracks or dollies in the context set and Altman's films.

Another explanation for Altman's preference for the intensifying zoom, and one that offers a more minor revision to standard accounts while also explaining the lack of a more amped-up feeling from Altman's zooms in, is that the intensifying zoom was a strategy necessitated by the confusing, unconventional emotional resonances of his films' narrative situations. By using the intensifying zoom, Altman could push his audience into engagement with the characters. Whereas many such push-ins in Hollywood films are affectively redundant, merely adding emphasis to intensify already sympathetic reactions, Altman's intensifying zooms may have been employed as part of a strategy for encouraging affective engagement in a reluctant or affectively bewildered audience.

Altman also made greater proportional use of the arguably undermotivated refreshing zoom than did the majority of his peers in the context set, at a ratio of 1.7:1. Altman, then, might be understood as part of the vanguard of the movement towards the revised norms of contemporary Hollywood style, described by Bordwell as "intensified continuity," in which "traditional continuity," has been, "amped up, raised to a higher-pitch of emphasis."[36] While "amped up" seems inapt for Altman's work, we might see a connection to intensified continuity in the prioritized employment of mobile framing in service of intensified engagement. Indeed, Bordwell writes that Altman's "creeping zooms" were intercut "with an abruptness that anticipates the interrupted push-ins of today's movies."[37] That said, the specific features of Altman's intensifying zooms vary from film to film, and these "creeping zooms," are not as consistently integrated into Altman's approach as their prominence in his reputation might suggest. Refreshing zooms are used more often in Altman's films than in the majority of films in the context set. However, individual films within Altman's early 1970s oeuvre differ a great deal in their use of the zoom type. Only 2.8% of the zoom functions found in *Thieves Like Us* can be said to serve the refreshing function, whereas for Altman's previous film, *The Long Goodbye*, that proportion is 26.2%.

Apart from the intensifying and refreshing zooms, there are three categories of zoom-type that are more prominent options in Altman's zoom norms than in the broader norms suggested by the context set. Interestingly, these categories are significantly related in function. Altman's proportional use of the zoom past, the aperture zoom, and the nonaperture aesthetic zoom exceed the use in the context set at ratios of 3.1:1, 1.9:1, and 1.2:1 respectively. It is reasonable to suppose that the salience of the zoom past to Altman's technique is at least partly connected to his high use of the aperture zoom, with Altman routinely zooming past foreground objects that create an aperture effect. We should not, though, expect every aperture zoom to necessarily also be a zoom past, helping to explain why only 6.9% of Altman's zoom functions are zooms past while 9.2% are aperture zooms. Likewise, each zoom past is not necessarily also an aperture zoom, since some zooms past can also overcome obstacles that are offscreen. A significant portion of Altman's zooms past might be explained by his preference for shooting on location, including, perhaps, relatively cramped locations.

Earlier, I discussed the two major components of Altman's critical and scholarly "zoom profile." But, as some of this chapter's earlier discussion implies, the legend of Altman's zooms might best be understood as threefold. First, there are his penetrating and creeping, allegedly subliminal, zooms in on subjects. There is good evidence to support this claim, although as I stated earlier and as I will argue shortly, this description needs to be qualified and nuanced. Second, there is Altman's pan and zoom approach, a "searching and revealing" that essentially serves the attentional function. The salience of this technique to the distinctiveness of Altman's zoom profile is, I have shown, surprisingly overstated. Perhaps at least some of the popularity of this description of Altman can be attributed to the way it supports and is supported by the third element of Altman's zoom legend—his employment of improvisatory zooms. That is, the zoom allowed his camera operators to improvise by zooming in on the similarly improvised performances of actors as they caught their interest, essentially recording the camera operator's attentional processes.

Yet the evidence provided by the films does not support this aspect of Altman's zoom legend. Altman's proportional use of the attentional zoom both resembles that of the context set and falls below the majority of zoom types within Altman's own films. Moreover, what this analysis has shown to be truly distinctive in Altman's approach is that his zooms are frequently structured to create aesthetic effects and encourage dramatic engagement. This structuring cuts against a notion of zooming based on an improvised reaction. These films' aperture zooms frequently rely on the careful placement of the camera in relation to aspects of mise-en-scène so as to create interesting compositional effects that accentuate depth. Intensifying zooms display careful coordination with the development of the dramatic action so that each reaches its climax simultaneously with the other. Such evident construction severely qualifies what might be called the "responsive" account of Altman's zooming, contextualizing it as, at most, one aspect of a larger suite of strategies more regularly focused on emotional intensification and decorative elaboration.

Of course, there are elements of Altman's biographical legend that might be mobilized to support the view that his zooms are frequently loose improvisations in response to surprising points of dramatic interest. For instance, he tells Michael Wilmington that, "I say [to my camera operators], 'If you find something interesting, shoot it.' I know what I need to cut to make the movie, what I need to have. But when he's shooting, if he sees an actor doing something or something's happened, he can go for that."[38] He initially says something similar to Gavin Smith and Richard T. Jameson:

My camera style is very simple. I try to place the camera and allow the cameraman to shoot the scene that is happening in front of him, so that he goes to what is most interesting or what it is he wants to look at or what it is I want to look at, which is what I want the audience to look at. But I don't plan for any effect. We set the scene up, the arena, and we let the event happen and then we just film.[39]

But later in the interview, Smith and Jameson follow up, pointing out, "Your scenes are very composed, somehow. I'm struck how often you begin from a detail, and pan or tilt up into the action, and then you somehow end on another detail, and there's a form implied." Altman responds that, "I like scenes to be whole. I'll shoot a scene six ways, and every one of [these master shots] has a beginning and an end. I don't know which one I'll end up using."[40]

This suggests a negotiation between improvisation and structure that is often glossed over. In the same way that a given aperture or foregrounded object will provide an initial frame for the scenic space where the dramatic action will play out, Altman's depth-oriented touches provide a frame within which the relative dramatic looseness (whether actual or effectual) expected of Altman could take place, balancing the overall approach. Given the difficulty of reconstructing on-set improvisation, discussed in chapter 4, this is difficult to determine with certainty. In any event, it seems clear that the overall strategy is one that favors formal elaboration on narrative action, whether or not that narrative action truly was improvised.

## A Film-by-Film Approach: Accounting for Altman's Early 1970s Zooms

Altman's early 1970s oeuvre consists of eight films, and while they do share some prominent tendencies, such as zoom frequencies that lie well outside the context norm, each also displays an approach to the zoom that is significantly distinct in relation to the others. Whether based on evidence or impression, scholarly and critical work on filmmakers can tend to oversimplify and overunify a body of work. A scholar can reify a filmmaker, freezing the filmmaker's profile in place as if tendencies are unchanging and practices permanent. It is also easy to conflate chronological sequence with a teleological evolutionary progress in which the filmmaker's early work leads in a step-by-step manner to the accumulation of traits and purposes that eventually make up the reified profile. Later work is frequently discussed in terms of growth, deterioration, or departure. While these approaches may be fairly accurate for any given filmmaker, my assumption here is that change is more irregular and contingent, and that there is more work to be done in order to convincingly sketch out the range of developmental pathways both above- and below-the-line filmmakers might take. Since Altman's early 1970s work is viewed by most as canonical and defining, the temptation to unify that body, and in doing so to smooth out the irregularities in Altman's profile, is fairly strong. However, when one looks carefully at the use of the zoom within and across Altman's films it is hard to divine a wholly unified narrative beyond the fact of the zoom's consistent and exceptional prominence.

The previous section spoke to tendencies across Altman's early 1970s oeuvre. What I seek to do now, taking each film more or less in turn, is to complicate this picture and, in doing so, to move away from Altman as a unified, mysticized auteur guided by a coherent expressive vision and toward Altman as a problem-solving filmmaker, dealing with the challenges of unique situations, with ideas and practices that develop in multiple directions. In some ways, this goal is counterproductive in relation to the goals of conventional director studies. A more precise description of Altman makes it harder to simply say who he is as a filmmaker. My complicating account of Altman relies on the film-specific statistics of the number and types of zooms employed as well as closer situational looks at individual zooms and zoom patterns within the films themselves. A chart comparing each of Altman's film's distinct zoom profile with Altman's overall proportional use of the zoom type during the period accompanies the analysis of each film.

Altman's first film of the period, *M*A*S*H* (Figure 2.9), for which he handpicked director of cinematography Harold E. Stine, largely sets the tone for what was to come by employing a zoom frequency of 1.04 zooms per minute, an extreme outlier when compared to the context set. At the same time, it displays several tendencies that distinguish it from Altman's other films. Specifically, *M*A*S*H* makes the highest proportional use of aperture zooms (16.7%) and zooms past (13.3%), as well as revealing zooms (17.2%). While the fact that Altman elaborates on his zoom shots with depth-heightening compositions presents a key revision to the standard account of Altman's early 1970s zooming, his use of the aperture zoom in *M*A*S*H* is truly exceptional. Importantly, its use is frequently integrated with the revealing zoom and the zoom past. Finally, *M*A*S*H* displays the lowest proportional use of the intensifying zoom, at just 8.4% compared with an overall use of 29.8% for his films of the period.

In interviews, Tom Skerritt, who plays Duke and had earlier worked with Altman in television, has recounted how he warned his fellow actors to stay on their game since Altman's camera operators could and would zoom in on them at any time.[41] This has become a key part of the zoom legend of the film and, as discussed earlier, Altman's broader reputation. But what one actually

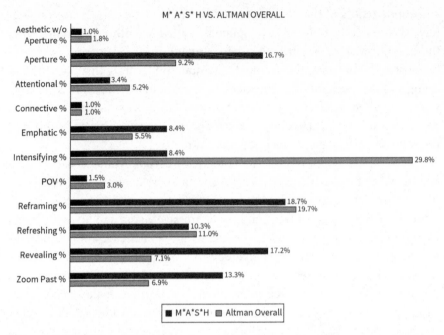

**Figure 2.9** *M\*A\*S\*H* vs. Altman Overall

finds on closer inspection is an approach to the zoom that is highly structured rather than strictly or even mostly improvisational. Indeed, Altman's zooming is arguably much more contingent on setting and production design than on his large cast of actors. The majority of the film takes place within the M\*A\*S\*H unit's encampment—a fairly tight cluster of tents that, with the move to interiors, provides relatively cramped quarters within which the surgeons must operate. It is tempting to surmise that the tents of the M\*A\*S\*H unit also provided cramped quarters for the makers of *M\*A\*S\*H* to operate, but since the film was shot on a Fox lot rather than on location, the filmmakers likely had a great deal of control.

Instead of using the zoom to respond to a cramped location shooting situation, Altman and Stine may have employed the technique partly to create the sense of cramped quarters, in combination with more aesthetically oriented purposes. Thus, many of Altman and Stine's exterior zooms are framed by ropes or other aspects of tenting in the foreground. For instance, when Hawkeye receives the news that he and Duke will be going home, Altman begins with a high angle extreme long shot of a compositionally centered Hawkeye sitting outside, framed in the foreground by elements of the canopies of various tents (Figure 2.10). The camera pans and cranes left and zooms out along with Hawkeye as he crosses the encampment's road to deliver the

Figure 2.10  *M\*A\*S\*H*

Figure 2.11  *M\*A\*S\*H*

news to Duke. An earlier high angle shot combining an aperture zoom with a reframing function similarly starts above the canopies of the tents and follows General Hammond's jeep as it arrives at the camp. The shot begins with the camera zooming out in tandem with the approach of Hammond's jeep, and this zoom out allows for the framing to retreat from its apparent position overtop the canopies without actually having to extend a crane over the tops of the tents. Instead, after the zoom out, the camera can simply be lowered to its final position in the shot, a view of Hammond's jeep coming to a stop framed by multiple foreground tent-related elements (Figure 2.11). While one could argue that this sort of use of the zoom past is necessary to negotiate, or literally overcome, the maze-like arrangement of tents, it is important to re-member that these obstacles are choices. A zoom vector that seems to surpass them and that emphasizes their presence in the image works, by design, to reinforce an overall sense of the camp as tightly packed while at the same time providing for aesthetic embellishment.

The same is true of many of the interior zooms found in the film. Take, for instance, Altman and Stine's handling of the arrival in the mess hall of the drunken parade celebrating Trapper's promotion to chief surgeon ⊚ (see the companion website for a video clip). The shot, perhaps the most virtuosic in the film, begins with an aperture framing—a view of the mess's window, in which Radar appears, peering in (Figure 2.12). On the left side of the frame a blurry vertical strip of light is visible, adding a further aestheticizing touch. This sort of "interior looking-out," or its complementary "exterior looking-in" framing is quite common in *M\*A\*S\*H*, and it constitutes a good deal of the aperture zooms and zooms past in the film, often in combination with foregrounded texture effects produced by the tents' mesh screens. The camera pans left with Radar as he moves to the mess's doorway and enters, followed by the parade of celebrants (Figure 2.13). Once again, this set-up is framed by out of focus foreground objects, and as the celebrants continue to enter, the camera zooms out, revealing that these blurry objects were, in fact, Hot Lips and Burns in the mess line on the left, and gleaming coffee dispensers on the right (Figures 2.14 and 2.15). Altman and Stine use their zoom strategy to emphasize the close quarters—a significant factor here, given the state of conflict between Hot Lips and Burns and Trapper et al.

In one shot, then, Altman and Stine underline a narrative premise and provide a zoom past, an aperture framing, a revealing zoom, and an aestheticization of the image based on the shifts in focus made possible by beginning the shot at a telephoto setting. Bordwell has discussed this last effect, the transformation of foreground elements into "misty blobs of colors" as

Figure 2.12  *M\*A\*S\*H*

Figure 2.13  *M\*A\*S\*H*

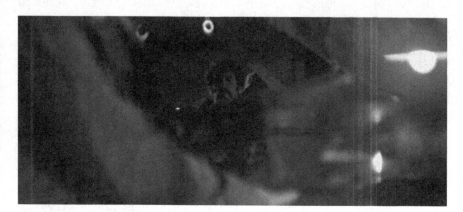

Figure 2.14  *M\*A\*S\*H*

Figure 2.15  *M\*A\*S\*H*

a result of the telephoto lens exploited by filmmakers such as Andrejz Wajda and Antonioni. Following Wajda, Bordwell describes them as "lelouches" after Claude LeLouche, who is believed to have popularized the effect, at least with European art cinema filmmakers.[42] The fact that we find evidence of this sort of aesthetic elaboration in Altman's films suggests one way in which he and his collaborators coupled art cinema characteristics with narrative aims.

Similar instances can be found in the milieu's other packed, chaotic zone—the operating room, where sequences consistently make use of zooms past, accompanied by foregrounded doctors, nurses, and surgical equipment, often as part of revealing zooms out beginning on a character or detail. Perhaps the most sophisticated of these zooms captures Hawkeye and Trapper's return from their surgical golf outing to Japan, dressed in antiquated golfing regalia ⊚ (see the companion website for a video clip). The pair is first shown arriving at the helicopter landing pad, surrounded by a sudden influx of wounded soldiers (Figure 2.16). Altman and Stine use an attentional zoom combined with a pan left and tilt down to zoom past a foreground helicopter and to pick out Hawkeye and Trapper's brightly colored legs and feet, following them past a badly burnt body in the foreground (Figure 2.17) to a waiting jeep. The film then cuts into the operating room, maintaining its emphasis on Hawkeye's red socks in a low height shot of his feet through blurry foregrounded elements (Figure 2.18). From here, the camera zooms out, revealing pails filled with bloody red gauze matching the color of Hawkeye's socks (Figure 2.19), and, on the right of the frame, Trapper's checked bloomers and yellow socks (Figure 2.20). This also serves as a connective zoom, emphasizing through juxtaposition the absurdity of the apparel and the relationship between Hawkeye and Trapper's need for frivolity and the grim nature of their vocation. Rather than

**Figure 2.16** *M\*A\*S\*H*

**Figure 2.17** *M\*A\*S\*H*

**Figure 2.18** *M\*A\*S\*H*

**Figure 2.19** *M\*A\*S\*H*

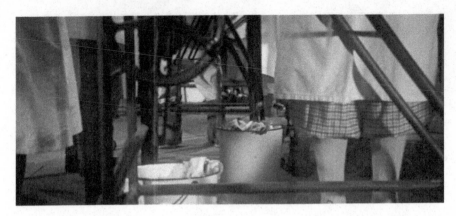

**Figure 2.20**  *M*A*S*H*

as a tool with which to pick out improvised moments amid a packed milieu, Altman and Stine here use the zoom in a structured manner to elaborate on the subject matter with decorative and ironizing touches.

An earlier sequence in the operating room substitutes a more straight-forwardly intensificatory use of the zoom for the conceptual deployment described previously. At the same time, it maintains the use of aperture framing and the zoom past. Here, Altman and Stine frame Hawkeye in the middleground center, between two surgeons positioned in the foreground on the left and right of the frame (Figure 2.21). The waist-high framing, angled slightly upward, leaves the faces of the surgeons offscreen, ensuring that they serve only as framing elements, while also initially keeping their bloody hands and the top of the patient they are operating upon visible in the bottom of the frame. From this position, the camera intensifies the drama of the moment—blood spurts from a patient's neck—as it zooms past the foreground elements and in on Hawkeye, calling out orders while a nurse affixes his surgical mask (Figure 2.22).

Setting aside the ornamental aspects of the zoom here, its use to intensify the dramatic action marks it as relatively unusual in the overall film (although the intensifying zoom is still more common in *M*A*S*H* than the majority of the context films). There are just seventeen intensifying zooms to be found in *M*A*S*H*. In this sense, it is similar to the film that immediately follows it, *Brewster McCloud* (Figure 2.23), which also has relatively few intensifying zooms—just nineteen, representing 10.9% of all the film's zoom functions, the second lowest of the period. Before we succumb to the temptation to move toward a broad, "early" early 1970s explanation to account for, or to assume, similarities between the two films, it is worth noting that, in contrast to *M*A*S*H*,

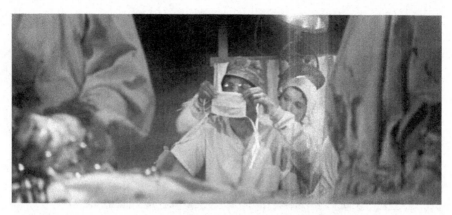

Figure 2.21 *M\*A\*S\*H*

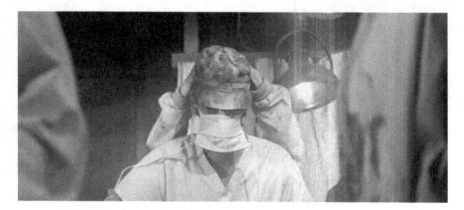

Figure 2.22 *M\*A\*S\*H*

*Brewster McCloud* displays the period's lowest proportional use of aperture zooms (3.4%), a fifth of that found in its predecessor. It also employs the emphatic zoom at a relatively high rate of 19.4%, more than twice *M\*A\*S\*H*'s 8.4%, although both films are above Altman's overall use during the period of 5.5%. Rather than a unified and straightforward evolutionary account, the use of the zoom in *Brewster McCloud* by Altman and the film's cinematographers, Jordan Cronenweth and his replacement Lamar Bowen (Cronenweth was supposedly too precious and slow for Altman's taste),[43] suggests a degree of experimentation with a device that was already a key technique in Altman's filmmaking toolbox, in addition to a broader tendency toward situational exploitation of the zoom's potentials.

One gets the sense that Altman and his collaborators' use of the intensifying zoom in *Brewster McCloud* is tentative since many of these zooms are

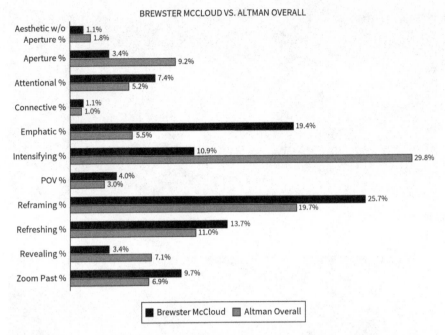

**Figure 2.23** *Brewster McCloud* vs. Altman Overall

unpolished. A significant example comes as part of a sequence in which Brewster, having lost his virginity to Suzanne, reveals first that he has invented a pair of wings that he plans to use to fly away and then that he is "responsible" for a series of strangulations ⊛ (see the companion website for a video clip). This consequential pillow talk is intercut with a flash-forward to Brewster in his workshop, where he reveals to his guardian angel that he has, against her prohibition, had sex and no longer wants her help. One of Altman and his collaborators' great strengths in subsequent films from this period is their ability to precisely and impactfully coordinate zooms with the narrative action, ending a zoom in a tight close-up just as a scene reaches its emotional climax. Here, Altman and company use the zoom toward the intensifying function, but without the precision typical of later films.

Two consecutive shots of Brewster and Suzanne in bed employ an intensifying zoom. The first (Figure 2.24) moves from a two-shot to an extreme close-up of Brewster's eye (Figure 2.25) as Brewster smiles in response to Suzanne telling him that since she took his virginity she is now responsible for him. Interestingly, by the time Suzanne delivers her line about responsibility the zoom has cut off all but the corner of Brewster's mouth, which can be seen curling slightly upward, subtly cueing Brewster's elation. Ending the zoom on Brewster's eye develops a motif of eyes that works its way throughout the film. The shot begins with the zoom underway, and there are barely two seconds left at the end of the shot after the zoom's completion, creating a relatively tight fit between technique and narrative development. The move to the following shot is a jarring axial cut out to a medium close-up of Brewster and Suzanne (Figure 2.26) that conforms to the discontinuous, experimental nature of the sequence. This shot constitutes a seventy-seven-second-long take of Brewster and Suzanne talking, but the intensifying zoom constitutes only six seconds of the shot and seems disconnected from its narrative development. As with the previous shot, the zoom is underway as the shot begins, but here it concludes in only a loose close-up of Brewster and Suzanne (Figure 2.27) during a moment of awkward shifting in the bed rather than the more impactful moment when Brewster asserts that he wants to "fly away" with

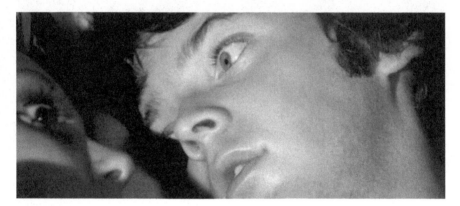

**Figure 2.24**  *Brewster McCloud*

**Figure 2.25**  *Brewster McCloud*

**Figure 2.26** *Brewster McCloud*

**Figure 2.27** *Brewster McCloud*

Suzanne. It presents, then, striking contrasts to the closely timed creeping zooms evident in later films.

This sequence concludes with Louise's departure from Brewster's workshop, and in its final shot Brewster has turned away from his work, realizing that with the loss of his guardian he is now relatively alone. This new state of affairs is reinforced by a relatively rare intensifying zoom out, in which a figure's isolation is emphasized through the expansion of the surrounding empty space—here emphasizing Brewster's solitude in the cluttered workroom (Figure 2.28). This zoom out also serves as an aperture zoom and a zoom past. The planks of wood that form an "x" in the center of the workshop provide a foreground frame for Brewster's solitude and at the same time serve to foreshadow Brewster's fate. Earlier in the film, Brewster had leaned on

**Figure 2.28** *Brewster McCloud*

**Figure 2.29** *Brewster McCloud*

the beams in a pose suggestive of the Passion of the Christ (Figure 2.29). The
shot's trajectory and its depth are enabled by the zoom's power to surmount
the physical obstacle of the crossbeams. This particularly interesting use of an
aperture zoom is one of the few such zooms in the film, which has in total only
six—the lowest proportional rate (3.4%) of any of Altman's films during this
period.

The relative underrepresentation of the aperture zoom might be explained
by the nature of the subject matter and overall approach. *Brewster McCloud* is
perhaps the most distinct of Altman's early 1970s films in its tone, attempting
a loose, often slapstick, humor and sending up the popular "supercop" genre.
The frequently vulgar and over-the-top sensibility may be responsible not just
for the decision to minimize the zoom's capacity to aestheticize but also the
high degree of reliance on the emphatic zoom, which often serves to shove

jokes into the faces of audience members. With thirty-four emphatic zooms, accounting for roughly one-fifth of the zoom functions in the film, *Brewster McCloud* outstrips all other Altman films and at the same time almost triples the median proportional use in the context group (6.7%). Several of the film's emphatic zooms are employed to emphasize bird-droppings landing on their target, a recurring motif in the film. The film's first emphatic zoom, in fact, zooms in on bird shit as it drops on a newspaper headline quoting Spiro Agnew's infamous claim that, "Society Should Discard Some U.S. People" (Figures 2.30 and 2.31). Other emphatic zooms point out puns, such as the license plate on Louise's car, "BRD-SHT" (Figures 2.32 and 2.33).

One other possible explanation for the relatively high number of emphatic zooms in *Brewster McCloud* is context based. In general, Altman's use of emphatic zooms dropped over the course of the early 1970s, with *California Split* and *Nashville* having only zero and four emphatic zooms respectively. This

Figure 2.30  *Brewster McCloud*

Figure 2.31  *Brewster McCloud*

**Figure 2.32** *Brewster McCloud*

**Figure 2.33** *Brewster McCloud*

tendency toward fewer emphatic zooms seems to be reflected in several of the context directors' bodies of work. Don Siegel began the half-decade with eight emphatic zooms in *Two Mules for Sister Sara* (1970), but by *Charley Varrick* (1973) employed none. Michael Ritchie used seven emphatic zooms in *Prime Cut* (1972) but zero in *Smile* (1975). Richard Fleischer used ten in *See No Evil* (1971) and only one in *Mr. Majestyk* (1974). Horwitz surmises that with the development of new reflex camera technology in the late 1960s filmmakers were able to move away from the " 'punctuating' zooms of the earlier period."[44] Filmmakers were, "discover[ing] ways to use the zoom that were less flagrant" and less likely to offend the powerful proponents of nonobtrusive cinematography cited by Horwitz and Hall.[45] It would not be surprising, then, if the emphatic zoom was gradually set aside as part of this movement and that Altman, while retaining some of the more esteemed functions of the zoom associated with European art cinema,[46] was increasingly willing to dispense with it.

The zooming on display in *Brewster McCloud*, while at a much higher frequency than was normal during the period, does not seem to have been highly systematic. On the other hand, *McCabe & Mrs. Miller* (Figure 2.34), shot by Vilmos Zsigmond, makes use of the zoom in a manner that is systematically punctuative. As was discussed in the previous chapter, Altman has frequently mentioned the importance of providing his films with "punctuation" that connects and emphasizes narrative and theme. In *McCabe & Mrs. Miller*, intensifying zooms, typically placed at the ends of scenes and featuring McCabe—the confident gambler turned hapless, lovelorn entrepreneur—serve as one such punctuating device, marking the salient moments in McCabe's fall. This punctuative patterning is the most distinctive aspect of the film's deployment of the zoom.

The first instance comes as McCabe establishes his initial poker game at Sheehan's saloon. Here, McCabe deals a hand of poker and tells the man holding the high card, a Jack, that he should begin the betting by saying, "jack off." The miners respond to McCabe's vulgar pun with a hearty round of laughter and McCabe's expression is one of crafty self-satisfaction. Altman

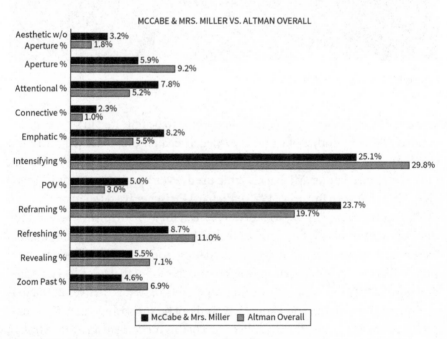

Figure 2.34 *McCabe & Mrs. Miller* vs. Altman Overall

emphasizes McCabe's reaction through the use of an intensifying and emphatic zoom in that moves from a loose close-up (Figure 2.35) to an extreme close-up (Figure 2.36) that frames him at the eyebrow and lower lip as he fingers his cigar. The quickness of the zoom as well as the tightness of the final framing mark its importance, its emphatic nature perhaps holding more significance given that there are half as many emphatic zooms in this film as there were in Altman's previous effort.

This is followed by a second instance, discussed in the book's introduction, which shifts from a fiddler to a similarly self-satisfied McCabe and then back to the fiddle. These zooms create a background against which to judge the next instance in the pattern, underlining the start of McCabe's descent. After McCabe returns from the nearby town of Bear Paw with three overpriced and inadequate prostitutes, they immediately get into a brawl with the miners.

**Figure 2.35** *McCabe & Mrs. Miller*

**Figure 2.36** *McCabe & Mrs. Miller*

When the childlike prostitute who will eventually stab a miner tells McCabe that she "has to go to the pot" and doesn't think she can "hold it." McCabe, who fingers a flask while nervously surveying his acquisitions, examining their own scraped knees, looks confused and somewhat defeated. An intensifying, emphatic zoom in (Figures 2.37 and 2.38) reinforces McCabe's dismay, providing a clear contrast to the previous instances and signaling that McCabe is now in over his head.

Shortly after one of McCabe's prostitutes stabs a miner, Mrs. Miller arrives in Presbyterian Church and over a hearty meal at Sheehan's proposes a partnership with McCabe, pointing out his unfamiliarity with the business of running a bordello. This undermines McCabe's identity as the most competent person in town, clearly established in an earlier scene that featured McCabe dismissing a proposal of partnership from Sheehan. McCabe stares, dismayed,

**Figure 2.37**  *McCabe & Mrs. Miller*

**Figure 2.38**  *McCabe & Mrs. Miller*

at his usual drink—a glass of whiskey and raw egg that he seems to order as a display of potency—while Mrs. Miller throws back a bar glass filled with coffee and demands his decision. At this key turning point we might expect another intensifying zoom in on McCabe, but Altman delays it momentarily. Instead, he provides the two drink-related shots (Figures 2.39 and 2.40), and then cuts to what appears to be an empty cup of coffee with an empty whiskey glass to its left and a deck of cards to its right (Figure 2.41). This tableau provides Mrs. Miller's choice of drink bracketed by the signs of McCabe's potency, and the slow zoom out from the cup gradually reveals McCabe sitting behind the low table on which the cup rests, drunk and muttering to himself. His first action is to roughly shove the coffee cup away ⊙ (see the companion website for a video clip). Here we have an intensifying zoom out and an implicit answer to Mrs.

**Figure 2.39**  *McCabe & Mrs. Miller*

**Figure 2.40**  *McCabe & Mrs. Miller*

**Figure 2.41** *McCabe & Mrs. Miller*

**Figure 2.42** *McCabe & Mrs. Miller*

Miller's question. Clearly, McCabe has been unhappily compromised, and the zoom finishes with a belching, solitary McCabe in a medium long shot, playing with his watch and pouring himself a shot of whisky (Figure 2.42).

This pattern of punctuative intensifying zooms broadens to include a zoom in on the money box where the love-struck McCabe is forced to deposit his payment to Mrs. Miller before he joins her in bed, fitting nicely as a variation on the narrower pattern that tracks McCabe's degradation. Importantly, this pattern—initiated at the end of the first proper scene in the film—reaches its ultimate expression at the film's end. Again, there is a variation on the core repetition of the intensifying zoom and McCabe (or a symbolic stand-in). This time, two intensifying zooms-in are intercut ⊙ (see the companion website for a video clip). The first is of Mrs. Miller, escaping from the tragedy of McCabe's refusal to avoid assassination into an opium den. After providing a static framing of snow beginning to cover McCabe's dying body, the film delivers an ostentatious long take beginning with a pan left, surveying the streets of Presbyterian Church's Chinese neighborhood and then swinging across the exterior of the den, whose door opens to reveal Mrs. Miller (Figure 2.43). The shot slowly zooms in on Mrs. Miller, moving from exterior to interior and from medium long shot to close-up (Figure 2.44). The film then cuts back to McCabe in the snow, but now an intensifying zoom in accompanies the shot, providing a remarkable parallel to the shot of Mrs. Miller in its speed, its change in shot scale, and in the placement and positioning of the figures (Figures 2.45 and 2.46). These are no improvised zooms, performed at the whims of a camera operator, but are instead carefully designed shots participating in a clear formal strategy.

**Figure 2.43**  *McCabe & Mrs. Miller*

**Figure 2.44**  *McCabe & Mrs. Miller*

**Figure 2.45**  *McCabe & Mrs. Miller*

**Figure 2.46**  *McCabe & Mrs. Miller*

The film's final four shots center on Mrs. Miller. As she picks up a tiny vase (Figure 2.47) and examines it we get what seems to be a POV shot (Figure 2.48), followed by a final intensifying zoom in on Mrs. Miller staring at the vase. As with the previous zooms, this one spans an impressive distance, moving from a tight close-up of her face to just part of an eye, which goes out of focus at the end of the shot (Figures 2.49 and 2.50). Another POV shot follows but seems to see the vase through the altered state of Mrs. Miller's opium high (Figure 2.51). As discussed in chapter 1, Mrs. Miller had previously advised a young prostitute to stare at the wall to take her mind off the pain of sex, a conversation that foreshadows Mrs. Miller's final state. McCabe's transition from cocky entrepreneur to lovelorn and befuddled businessman reluctantly partnered with the ultracompetent Mrs. Miller was marked by

**Figure 2.47** *McCabe & Mrs. Miller*

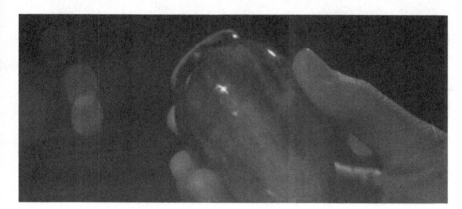

**Figure 2.48** *McCabe & Mrs. Miller*

**Figure 2.49** *McCabe & Mrs. Miller*

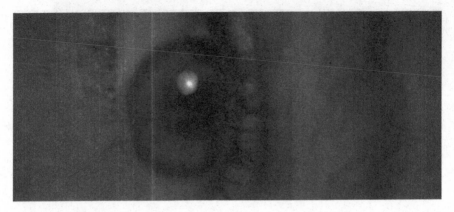

**Figure 2.50**  *McCabe & Mrs. Miller*

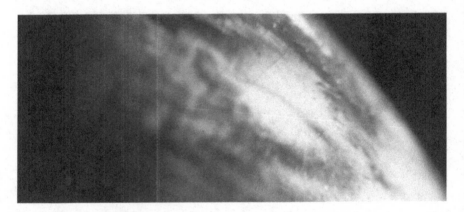

**Figure 2.51**  *McCabe & Mrs. Miller*

a cut to an intensifying zoom, and Mrs. Miller's potential transformation is similarly marked. It seems unlikely that Mrs. Miller's professed technique for dealing with pain will help her much this time, and it seems clear that her own entrepreneurial dreams have been undercut by McCabe's misplaced bravado. Altman and Zsigmond's systematic use of the zoom underscores these points, and the punctuative design marks a shift from the more haphazard use of the intensifying zoom in *Brewster McCloud*. While the zoom use here is expressive and overt, it calls attention not just to itself but to key characters in dramatic situations. The basis for Altman's patterned elaboration is narrative as, largely, are his aims.

*Images* (Figure 2.52), also shot by Zsigmond, similarly makes use of the zoom as part of formal patterning that supports the film's narrative design.

Here, though, the zoom is used more regularly, as a key strategy in the depiction of the protagonist's schizophrenia. Surprisingly, it is in *Images*, essentially a chamber piece with just five featured actors, that Altman makes greatest proportional use of the zoom for attentional purposes (8.6%). In *Nashville*, by comparison, only 5.4% of the zoom functions served are attentional. Moreover, close analysis of the attentional zooms in *Images* reveals that they rarely are of the "searching and revealing" sort. Instead, they tend to be directed and emphatic. This cuts against expectations established by standard accounts of Altman's use of the technique—to pick figures out of crowds. *Images*, after *Brewster McCloud*, has the highest proportional representation of the emphatic zoom function (though at 9.1% it is still less than half of *Brewster McCloud*'s 19.4%). More importantly, the film's attentional and emphatic zooms tend to be teamed with the POV function—at 7.1%, more than twice Altman's overall proportional rate of 3.0%. This makes perfect sense for a film with a hallucinating, frequently startled, schizophrenic protagonist, and which employs highly subjective narration.

*Images* is also remarkable among Altman's early 1970s oeuvre for its high usage of the nonaperture aesthetic zoom (6.6% when compared to an overall usage of 1.8%). Altman's use of aperture zooms tends to outstrip his use of nonaperture aesthetic zooms. Here, though, aperture zooms constitute only

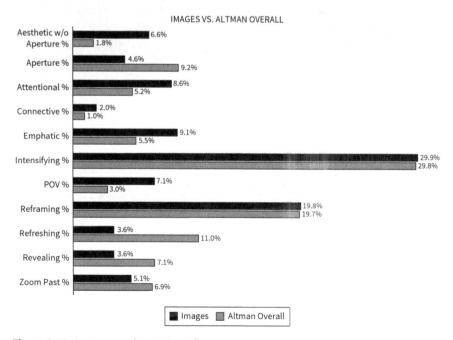

**Figure 2.52** *Images* vs. Altman Overall

4.6% of all zoom functions. This suggests a subjectively motivated extension of the lelouche strategy discussed earlier. Many of *Images'* aesthetic zooms rely on the zoom's power to throw an image into or out of focus. They often function as decorative touches to the beginnings and endings of shots, but they also expressively add to the sense of mental disturbance, of reality made fuzzy. Moreover, given that the discourse around *Images* framed it as an attempt at European art cinema inspired by Bergman, it makes sense that Altman and his collaborators provided the film with aesthetic flourishes intended to please an audience primed for interesting formal gestures. Several of these aesthetic zooms also seem to be POV shots, but many that are not marked as such zoom in on omnipresent crystals that always seem to be chiming, and which serve as a metonym for the protagonist's schizophrenia. Their support for the narrative can be understood as excuse or as complementary motivation for their largely decorative presence.

Lelouches aside, the film's first act is replete with examples that illustrate Altman and Zsigmond's approach to the zoom in the film. As the film transitions from its opening montage of Catherine at work on her children's book to the first proper scene, she receives a phone call from a friend. Catherine, though, hears her "doppelganger" cut in on the call, taunting her by suggesting her husband is cheating. After Catherine's friend promises to call right back, the next call she receives is directly from her cackling doppelganger. In response, Catherine slams the phone down and sits on her bed ⊙ (see the companion website for a video clip). This is depicted in a long take, with a reframing zoom out and a pan right and tilt down following Catherine as she moves from the bathroom, where she answered the call, to her bed. Once Catherine is seated on her bed, an intensifying zoom in begins (Figures 2.53 and 2.54), and as she turns her head there is a cut to a POV shot containing an emphatic zoom in initially showing Catherine's cluttered vanity and then picking out Catherine's glasses, whose lenses distort the objects behind them (Figures 2.55 and 2.56). Here we get the prototypical combination for the film—the emphatic, attentional, POV zoom in. This is followed by another intensifying zoom in on Catherine as she turns her head to look at her desk (Figures 2.57 and 2.58) and another emphatic, attentional POV zoom in on an object in the frame—crystals dangling over the desk (Figures 2.59 and 2.60). The sequence of shots concludes with a final slight intensifying zoom in on Catherine as she sits and thinks for a moment (Figures 2.61 and 2.62).

Both attentional zooms here are accompanied by reframing movements, slight pans and tilts, that allow them to locate and center their terminus while giving the impression, since the endpoint was either small or off-center in the original framing, that there is a searching quality to the shot. This searching

**Figure 2.53** *Images*

**Figure 2.54** *Images*

**Figure 2.55** *Images*

**Figure 2.56** *Images*

**Figure 2.57** *Images*

**Figure 2.58** *Images*

**Figure 2.59** *Images*

**Figure 2.60** *Images*

**Figure 2.61** *Images*

**Figure 2.62** *Images*

function is quite often, though, no more than a charade, with the object to which attention is directed fairly obvious from the beginning. Even so, my analysis attributes the attentional function to zooms with these sorts of reframings, which seems justifiable given the shots' POV status and their subject—a character's visual search and discovery.

A particular pattern appears in *Images* around these kinds of POV attentional zooms, wherein they accompany the majority of Catherine's sightings of her doppelganger. For instance, in one strange sequence a freshly arrived Catherine looks down from a ridgeline at her country house and notices a car arriving, from which she, or her doppelganger, exits. When the film cuts to this Catherine, she then looks up and sees the other Catherine standing on the ridgeline. The first sighting is a quasi-POV shot that zooms past Catherine, more or less assuming her eyeline. The second seems to be a full-blown POV shot. Both are also attentional zooms. In the first (Figures 2.63 and 2.64), the arriving car is initially small enough and far enough away that the idea that the zoom is required to pick the object out is plausible. In the second, the upper Catherine's figure is minute, and a tilt and pan that seem to survey the ridgeline inflects the zoom in so that it appears as though the figure has caught the lower Catherine's attention (Figures 2.65 and 2.66).

What is distinctive, then, about the use of the zoom in *Images*, seems to have been specially tailored to the goals of that particular film. This fits a general pattern in which each film of Altman's films has its own distinct zoom strategy, elaborated on a general approach that is exceptionally heavily reliant on the technology, generally favoring the reframing and intensifying zoom-types, and featuring an unusual proportion of aperture zooms and zooms past objects or screens. *Images* might be described as employing a particularly

**Figure 2.63** *Images*

**Figure 2.64** *Images*

**Figure 2.65** *Images*

**Figure 2.66** *Images*

subjective strategy, whereas *McCabe & Mrs. Miller*'s distinctiveness is both subtler—featuring a limited but extremely salient zoom pattern—and more "overt" in the sense that it functions, at least partly, as nondiegetic, authorial commentary. Both of these aims—expressing subjectivity and providing authorial commentary—could be said to be consistent with those of art cinema. But they do not dominate so much as punctuate or elaborate on Altman's fundamental zoom strategies. Moreover, both seem to be organized around character engagement, a central aim of classical storytelling.

*The Long Goodbye* (Figure 2.67), also lensed by Zsigmond, likewise features a distinctive zoom strategy, integrating the zoom with an approach to actual camera movement that Altman describes as follows:

> I decided that the camera [in The Long Goodbye] should never stop moving. It was arbitrary. We would just put the camera on a dolly, and everything would move or pan, but it didn't match the action; usually it was counter to it. It gave me that feeling that when the audience sees the film, they're kind of a voyeur. You're looking at something you shouldn't be looking at. Not that what you're seeing is off limits; just that you're not supposed to be there. You had to see over someone's shoulder or peer round someone's back.[47]

Altman compounds this unusual approach to moving the camera with his approach to the zoom, which Zsigmond explains:

> On *Images*, when we wanted to have something strange going on, because the woman is crazy, we decided to do this thing—zooming and moving sideways. And zooming and dollying sideways. Or zooming forward. What is missing? Up and

down! So we had to be able to go up and down, dolly sideways, back and forth, and zoom in and out. Then we made *The Long Goodbye* and Robert said, "Remember that scene we shot in *Images?* Let's shoot this movie all that way." And I said, "Robert, you are kidding? The people are going to get dizzy, people are not going to like it." He said, "Don't worry about it."[48]

As described by the filmmakers, the approach is based on constant arbitrary movement that forces the audience to cope with the shifting and sometimes unfavorable perspective on the action. Given the film's protagonist—an intrusive private investigator trying to understand all of the angles—Altman may have been interested in setting up playful formal parallels between subject and style. In any event, this emphasis on seemingly arbitrary mobile framing is reflected in the high proportion of refreshing zooms in *The Long Goodbye*—described above as, at least in part, zooms for the sake of zooming, although this categorization does not fully capture Altman's more elusive aims. At 17.9%, *The Long Goodbye* has the proportionally highest representation of refreshing zooms in Altman's early 1970s oeuvre, well above the overall of 11.0%.

*The Long Goodbye*'s particular approach to integrating the zoom with camera movement frequently functions to lend shots a drifting quality. Even

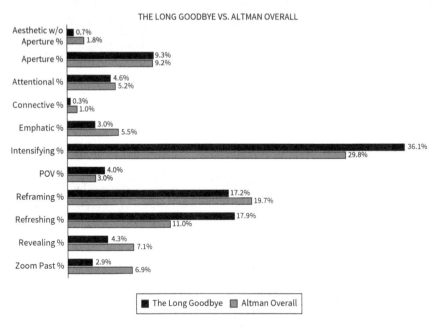

Figure 2.67  *The Long Goodbye* vs. Altman Overall

intensifying zooms in sometimes slide slightly to the left or right, presumably the result of a lateral or arcing dolly combined with a slight pan. This not only suggests a parallel between similarly off-kilter perspective and action but also adds a sense of volume and depth to the image. The sense of a dimensional space that is usually provided by an inward or outward camera movement's revealing and concealing of space behind the foreground figure (as opposed to the zoom's magnification or reduction of already visible background space) is accomplished here by the lateral movement. As established earlier, parallax was seen as an advantage actual camera movement held over zooms, and in *The Long Goodbye* the mimetic quasi-parallax effected by the zoom strategy might be understood as intermittently and novelly compensating for the zoom's perceived lack. Bolstering this effect, it seems as though several zooms transition into dollies in or out, creating confusion for the analyst, though probably not for otherwise occupied audience members, about where zooms and dollies begin and end.

The film's mobile framings tend to be executed in what might be called a drift-and-bounce fashion, in which the camera drifts laterally, reaches a predetermined boundary, and then drifts in the opposite direction. The majority of shots with mobile framings do not contain the moment of the "bounce" in them, but there is at least one shot with this bounce effect in many scenes. Even without a visible in-shot bounce, it is easy to reconstruct the "long take" practice of the filmmaking in which large chunks of scenes were shot in a single take by a particular camera and then cut up by the editor. This approach seems to guide the zooms in and out in the film, and many scenes display an arbitrary reversal in direction. Even so, there is still a high proportion of intensifying zooms—36.1%, compared to Altman's overall of 29.8%. The integration of a zoom function that depends on coordination with the narrative design and a seemingly arbitrary approach to mobile framing presents an interesting encapsulation of the frequently sneaky functional dynamics of Altman's filmmaking strategies. In conversation scenes, framings drift in and out, but they sometimes do so in a manner that seems to follow the flow of the conversation. When Marlowe locates Roger Wade at Dr. Verringer's clinic, he watches an argument between the two men over Verringer's unpaid fee ⊚ (see the companion website for a video clip). The sequence alternates between intensifying zooms in on each of the men, beginning and finishing with Verringer (Figures 2.68–2.73). As the conflict reaches its first peak, the intensifying strategy reverses, and there is a drifting zoom out from a single of Wade to a two shot of the pair of men (Figures 2.74 and 2.75).

Even if we acknowledge that the zoom in is designed to be intensificatory, it might be tempting to attribute this change in direction to the arbitrariness that

**Figure 2.68** *The Long Goodbye*

**Figure 2.69** *The Long Goodbye*

**Figure 2.70** *The Long Goodbye*

**Figure 2.71** *The Long Goodbye*

**Figure 2.72** *The Long Goodbye*

**Figure 2.73** *The Long Goodbye*

**Figure 2.74**  *The Long Goodbye*

**Figure 2.75**  *The Long Goodbye*

seemed to be Altman's goal; yet there is also a practical reason for the zoom out. Wade, played by Sterling Hayden, is a towering, physically imposing presence, and here the zoom makes way for staging that exploits this physicality, as he stands up and looms over the diminutive Verringer. At the same time, the conflict between the two men is not over, so the zoom out marks a pause before the conflict resumes. The zoom out from Wade is followed by a semiparallel shot that begins on Verringer and then zooms out to include Wade (Figures 2.76 and 2.77). After a cutaway to Marlowe watching the men, the conversation reaches another climax as Verringer pushes Wade to sign a check while another intensifying zoom reinforces the sense of mounting pressure on Wade (Figures 2.78 and 2.79). So, within a generalized attitude of seeming arbitrariness there are significant moments of structure, with the

**Figure 2.76** *The Long Goodbye*

**Figure 2.77** *The Long Goodbye*

**Figure 2.78** *The Long Goodbye*

**Figure 2.79**  *The Long Goodbye*

former acting as a sort of camouflage for the latter. When placed within a broader drift-and-bounce context, mobile framings in scenes like these are likely to feel relatively organic to audience members, even as they experience the enhanced engagement resulting from careful coordination.

This scene is also illustrative of Altman's structured approach to the zoom in *The Long Goodbye* in that the shots discussed here all look through a screen that serves as a variably detectable foreground filter for the action and a barrier to be zoomed past. While *The Long Goodbye* has the smallest proportion of zooms past of any of Altman's films, their novel features make them more salient to the visual design of the film than in Altman's other films. Here, they not only tend to surpass the boundary of a window or screen in order to achieve closer framings; they simultaneously create a dynamic relationship between planes of depth, elaborating a kind of marked screen that provides a variation on the aperture function. Including the scene discussed previously, there are three other significant moments in which the zoom past is used for aesthetic effect. A one-way mirror smeared with Marlowe's palm print frames his interrogation (Figure 2.80). Marlowe's walk on the beach is reflected in a window as the Wades argue (Figure 2.81). Finally, in a long take, Altman provides a connective zoom through a window and past Marlowe and Eileen Wade, linking their conversation—Marlowe is confronting her about her husband's possible complicity in a murder—with the image of Roger Wade committing suicide by drunkenly staggering into the surf (Figures 2.82 and 2.83). These all arguably reinforce the dynamic that Altman articulated previously, forcing the viewer to look past foreground objects and complicating their perception. At the same time, the zooms guide the audience's attention, underline emotion, and make ironizing connections. Again, the use of the

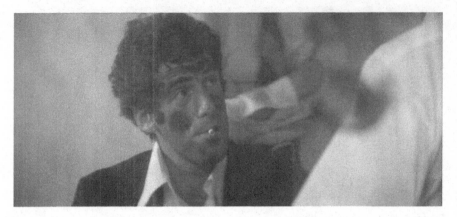

**Figure 2.80** *The Long Goodbye*

**Figure 2.81** *The Long Goodbye*

**Figure 2.82** *The Long Goodbye*

**Figure 2.83** *The Long Goodbye*

zoom in Altman's films is more multifunctional, more elaborate and elaborative, than the discourse around the films, even the discourse of the director
and cinematographer, might suggest.

*The Long Goodbye*'s approach to the zoom is remarkable for the sheer frequency of zooms in the film—2.05 zooms per minute—an extreme outlier in
the context set but also well above Altman's median of 1.23. This marks the
approach to zooming in Altman's follow-up, *Thieves Like Us* (Figure 2.84), as
a departure. At 1.01 zooms per minute, *Thieves Like Us* uses the zoom less frequently than any of Altman's early 1970s films, undermining any notion of a
straightforward evolution in Altman's style. In some ways, *Thieves Like Us*, shot
by French cinematographer Jean Boffety, feels like a throwback film, with a far
staider zoom style than its predecessor or its successors—*California Split* and
*Nashville*. Altman made these films in rapid succession, and it seems significant that he chose to vary his approach rather than to follow a kind of stylistic
inertia. *Thieves Like Us* is, of course, a period film, set in the Depression-era
American South. So perhaps the reserved approach to the employment of
zoom technology here is part of a general attempt at "antiquing" the image,
though if so it is not one he employed on *McCabe & Mrs. Miller*.

It is also worth considering whether Altman may simply be alternating his
approach. *Images* mirrors *Thieves Like Us* in its average shot length (9.5 for
*Images*, 9.2 for *Thieves Like Us*). Both trail behind only *Nashville* (12.6) in this
metric. They also have fairly close zoom frequencies, with *Images* coming in
at 1.1 zooms per minute. Yet there are significant differences in key categories
of functionality. The restrained approach of *Thieves Like Us* is reflected in the
high percentage of reframing zooms (26.0%, the highest of the period) and in
its relative paucity of emphatic zooms (3.1% of zoom functions), one-third of

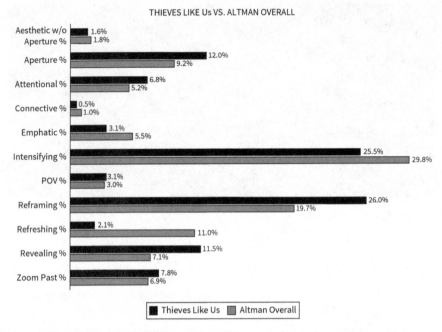

THIEVES LIKE Us VS. ALTMAN OVERALL

| Category | Thieves Like Us | Altman Overall |
|---|---|---|
| Aesthetic w/o Aperture % | 1.6% | 1.8% |
| Aperture % | 12.0% | 9.2% |
| Attentional % | 6.8% | 5.2% |
| Connective % | 0.5% | 1.0% |
| Emphatic % | 3.1% | 5.5% |
| Intensifying % | 25.5% | 29.8% |
| POV % | 3.1% | 3.0% |
| Reframing % | 26.0% | 19.7% |
| Refreshing % | 2.1% | 11.0% |
| Revealing % | 11.5% | 7.1% |
| Zoom Past % | 7.8% | 6.9% |

■ Thieves Like Us    ■ Altman Overall

**Figure 2.84** *Thieves Like Us* vs. Altman Overall

the proportion in *Images*. It is also distinct in its high percentages of revealing zooms (11.5%, second only to *M*A*S*H*'s 17.2%) and aperture zooms (12.0%, third highest and well above the overall of 9.2%). Thus, while there are, for Altman, comparably few zoom shots, they seem to be more aesthetically oriented. The high proportional incidence of revealing zooms suggests a strategy of slowly unfolding scenic space. This combination reinforces the general impression of a slower-paced, more restrained, and perhaps more refined zoom strategy. For instance, a forty-four-second long take that establishes the space for the gang's final bank robbery features a ten-second zoom out from an aperture framing of two of the thieves through the bank's front window (Figure 2.85). The zoom out reveals the interior of the bank in an overhead shot (Figure 2.86) that is likely an homage to Maurice Tourneur's *Alias Jimmy Valentine* (1915) (Figure 2.87). Instead of efficiency, a deliberate, slow-paced aestheticizing approach is employed.

Altman and his collaborators employ a similarly slow revelation of space in a subsequent scene ◉ (see the companion website for a video clip), beginning here with an aperture zoom back, framed through the mesh screen of a house vent, from a toy car pummeled by rain (Figures 2.88 and 2.89). A slight dolly back finishes the movement out, and a tilt up and pan left refocus attention on Mattie, whose bank-robber husband is in prison, leaving her to host his

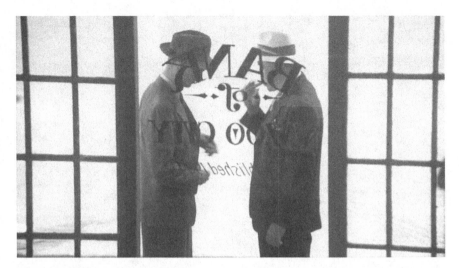

**Figure 2.85** *Thieves Like Us*

**Figure 2.86** *Thieves Like Us*

friends, as she cleans up after dinner (Figure 2.90). An episode of *The Shadow*, a radio program about a vigilante, plays on the soundtrack, and the next shot provides a revealing and connective zoom beginning on the home's radio then zooming out and tilting down to reveal Mattie's son, the owner of the toy car, playing on the floor (Figures 2.91 and 2.92). The boy's toys, including firecrackers and a toy pistol, are scattered around him, underlining his potentially criminal future as well as popular culture's role in shaping that future.

**Figure 2.87** *Alias Jimmy Valentine*

**Figure 2.88** *Thieves Like Us*

Figure 2.89   *Thieves Like Us*

Figure 2.90   *Thieves Like Us*

The juxtaposition also clearly ironizes the anticrime themes of the radio program. The beginnings of scenes in classical Hollywood cinema often provide an opportunity for overt narration, and here Altman uses his favored visual technique to playfully, but very deliberately, elaborate on his film's themes.

Altman's next film, *California Split* (Figure 2.93), shot by Paul Lohmann, makes more aggressive use of the zoom and represents a clear departure, rather than an evolution, from the zoom strategy on display in *Thieves Like Us*. Among Altman's films of the period, *California Split* has the highest

**Figure 2.91** *Thieves Like Us*

**Figure 2.92** *Thieves Like Us*

total number of zooms (278), the highest number of zoom functions served (346), and the highest number of zooms per minute (2.57). As with *The Long Goodbye*, for *California Split* Altman has provided a clear articulation of the film's zoom strategy:

> In *California Split* we had a rule—and there's always exceptions to these rules—that the zoom was always moved in. Because you get into a crap game in Las Vegas and you get to betting the money and watching the dice and suddenly they could take

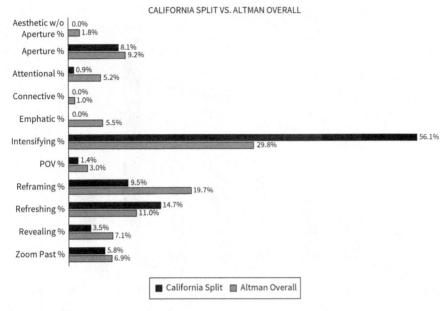

CALIFORNIA SPLIT VS. ALTMAN OVERALL

Aesthetic w/o Aperture %: 0.0% / 1.8%
Aperture %: 8.1% / 9.2%
Attentional %: 0.9% / 5.2%
Connective %: 0.0% / 1.0%
Emphatic %: 0.0% / 5.5%
Intensifying %: 56.1% / 29.8%
POV %: 1.4% / 3.0%
Reframing %: 9.5% / 19.7%
Refreshing %: 14.7% / 11.0%
Revealing %: 3.5% / 7.1%
Zoom Past %: 5.8% / 6.9%

■ California Split   ■ Altman Overall

**Figure 2.93** *California Split* vs. Altman Overall

Abraham Lincoln and George Washington and Winston Churchill and Adolf Hitler and put all these people around the table and you'd never notice them.[49]

Altman prefaces this by stating that, in general, the zoom is about "being able to focus attention." Altman's fuller statement, though, implies using the intensifying zoom to enhance audience engagement with the unfolding drama. This, rather than the definition of the attentional zoom based on picking out details, is what I take to be the stated aim of Altman's major zoom strategy in the film.

There is an obvious danger in taking the assertions of any filmmaker completely at face value. Intention (both stated and unstated) and practice, and practice and recollection, do not always tidily match up. We can, though, find evidence, contextualized by Altman's other films during the early 1970s, that supports and qualifies Altman's account (Figure 2.94). The ratio of zooms in to zooms out in *California Split* is a striking 5.2:1. The next highest ratio in Altman's early 1970s films is that of *The Long Goodbye*—approximately 2.2 zooms in for every zoom out. *California Split* is bracketed by films with ratios of 1.9:1 (*Thieves Like Us*) and 1.7:1 (*Nashville*). Altman states that there are always exceptions to rules filmmakers put into place, and in a film with 278 total zooms, even a ratio of 5.2:1 means that there are a significant number of zooms out in the film. In fact, *California Split*'s 45 zooms out exceeds *Images*'

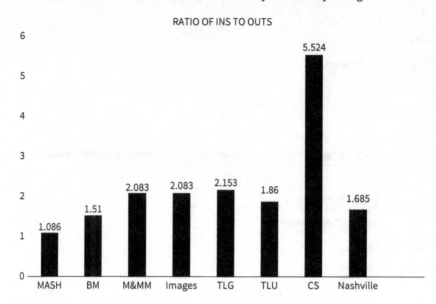

**Figure 2.94** Ratios of Ins to Outs

36 and almost matches *Thieves Like Us'* 43. The difference in strategy, then, is less about the absence of zooms out and more about the increased use of intensifying zooms in.

While Altman was overstating the extent to which he constrained his use of the zoom, the numbers bear out his claim of functional intent. *California Split* features far and away the highest proportion of intensifying zoom functions (56.1%), besting the next highest film, *The Long Goodbye*, by 20%. *California Split*'s status as a buddy film might explain its abundance of intensifying zooms in, providing two protagonist figures, rather than one, to zoom in on in most scenes. Yet *California Split* more than doubles the famously twenty-four-character *Nashville* (24.5%) in this category, so perhaps this does not entirely account for the film's distinctiveness. A more likely explanation is *California Split*'s reliance on the intensifying zoom to structure not just moments but entire scenes and sequences.

Altman and his collaborators accomplish this structuring using two strategies. First, more than in any of Altman's other films, a zoom in on a character will begin in one shot and, after a cutaway to a shot of something or someone else, will continue its intensifying trajectory in the shot that follows (Figure 2.95). Longer takes featuring a single intensifying zoom seem to have been broken down into multiple nonconsecutive shots. *California Split* features 87 such continuation zooms, more than double the number found in

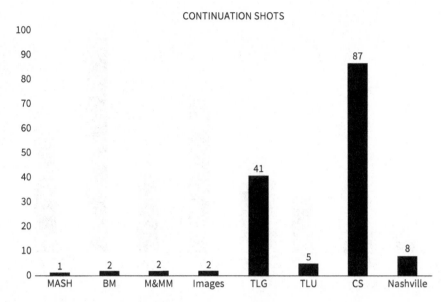

**Figure 2.95** Continuation Shots

*The Long Goodbye.* In fact, these two films represent blips in Altman's use of the technique in the early 1970s. None of the others exceeds single digits, and Altman's follow-up to *California Split, Nashville*—also shot by Lohmann—has just eight.

The second strategy is a well-established feature of Altman's zoom legend—the use of slow, "creeping" zooms (Figure 2.96). To avoid misleadingly reifying Altman's approach to the zoom across his films, this aspect of his profile requires qualification. In some sense, *California Split* represents the apogee of the creeping zoom in Altman's films of this period. It contains 217 zooms that could be described as slow, 78.1% of the total zooms in the film. Yet the incredibly extensive use of the creeping zoom should be seen less as a climax than as participating in an overall trend across Altman's films, possibly augmented by some of the factors—dual protagonists, continuation zooms—described previously. The next highest percentage of slow zooms is *The Long Goodbye*'s 57.9%, which, combined with the film's similarly high number of total zooms and high level of intensifying zooms, suggests some connection with *California Split*, although the two films have different cinematographers. *Nashville* has the next highest percentage of slow zooms (41.6%), and the rest of Altman's films run from 20% to 30%, with the exception of both *M\*A\*S\*H* and *Brewster McCloud* (approximately 4%). It is possible that Altman's use

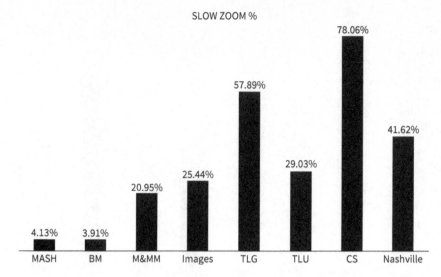

**Figure 2.96**  Slow Zoom %

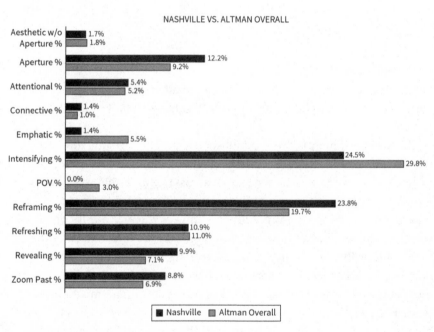

**Figure 2.97**  *Nashville* vs. Altman Overall

of the creeping zoom took off in earnest at this time, but its employment as a key descriptor of Altman's approach, particularly considering the prominent status of the comparatively noncreeping *McCabe & Mrs. Miller*, can be misleading.

*Nashville* (Figure 2.97), the final Altman film of the early 1970s and the film probably most cited as distinctively "Altmanesque," has perhaps also been subjected to the greatest amount of inaccurate zoom-oriented mythologizing. For instance, Byrne and Lopez describe its zoom strategy as, "comprised of extended panoramic zoom shots which sweep leisurely and relentlessly across wide, richly textured landscapes and eventually zoom slowly in on the main protagonists."[50] This statement likely seems fairly uncontroversial. Indeed, as discussed earlier, Altman is often described as the American leading the way in the "searching and revealing" movement, and *Nashville*, with its large cast and its focus on milieu rather than protagonist, is the ideal subject for this stylistic approach. Yet there are precisely zero shots in the film in which the camera pans across a landscape and then zooms in on a character—zero, in a film with almost two hundred zooms! The closest *Nashville* comes is in the previously discussed approach to shots of Tricycle Man's arrival at a location, though close examination reveals these differ significantly from Byrne and Lopez's account ◉ (see the companion website for a video clip). For example, almost a minute into the airport sequence Tricycle Man rides up to the arrivals area trailed by Hal Phillip Walker's campaign van. The camera, though, does not discover the character. Instead, along with some slight reframing zooms, the camera pans left with Tricycle Man (Figures 2.98 and 2.99), and as he gets off his motorcycle and walks rightward toward the airport entrance the camera begins to zoom in and pan to the right. When Tricycle Man passes by a minor character, a chauffeur named Norman who seems befuddled by Tricycle Man's appearance, the camera stops panning with Tricycle Man but continues zooming in on Norman's reaction (Figure 2.100). Because the zoom in, in combination with the halted pan, kind of "picks out" Norman, switching attention to him from Tricycle Man, the zoom serves an attentional function. But the attentional effect seems at least as dependent on the pan halting on Norman, and on Norman's reaction to Tricycle Man, as the use of the zoom. Here, attention shifts when character paths cross rather than as the result of an overt narrational decision expressed through a leisurely zoom. This approach to introducing a space does provide a bit of a panorama, but this hardly seems a novel use of the zoom, or of mobile framing in general.

A similar example of a pan followed by a slight zoom that is attached to a character's entrance accompanies faux-BBC journalist Opal's arrival at a Barbara Jean concert at the Grand Ole Opry theme park. Again, the camera pans right with a key character, Opal, then zooms in slightly as she sits down next to Private Kelly (Figures 2.101 and 2.102). The faces in the crowd are on display, providing some competition for attention, but no one is "picked out" from the kind of narratively neutral attentional starting point that the

**Figure 2.98** *Nashville*

**Figure 2.99** *Nashville*

**Figure 2.100** *Nashville*

**Figure 2.101** *Nashville*

**Figure 2.102** *Nashville*

standard account of Altman's "searching and revealing" approach implies. Instead, the narratively significant characters are identified through the coordination of mobile framing and blocking.

It is difficult to say why exactly this false perception of Altman's approach to the zoom in *Nashville* persists. It may be a result of the film's milieu-centric narrative. As was demonstrated in the chapter on Altman's narrative strategies, critics and scholars have tended to overestimate the narrative dispersion of the film, and in doing so they may have misremembered the film's visual style so as to make it consistent with their notion of its narrative approach. Another influence may be the ways in which critics, and sometimes Altman, have foregrounded the film's documentary-like qualities to mischaracterize the entire film. A good portion of the film is staged concert footage shot with multiple cameras, and the focus on milieu rather than a single protagonist is arguably documentarian, though only if one operates under a constrained notion of documentary form. As I will discuss in chapter 5, critics and scholars have generally misunderstood Altman's background in the nonfiction realm of industrial filmmaking, framing it as if he had been making proto-observational documentary.

Some, then, seem to have assumed that the *Nashville* camera operators largely stood back from the action and used that most observational of technologies, the zoom, to pick out details as they became salient, mimicking a vérité style. Altman has claimed that, "in *Nashville* more than any other film, what we did was sort of set up events and then just press the button and photograph them, pretty much like you would a documentary."[51] This seems very true of several of the musical sequences with big crowds, in which some of the zooms are a bit rough and halting, as if the camera operator was indecisive. But other events, like the freeway sequence, seem to have been more conventionally staged and shot. Indeed, that sequence, which features the majority of characters in the film, has only two zooms—one that captures the accident and then a reframing zoom of Tricycle Man as he rides away after the accident clears up. It is possible that zooms were used during the shoot but were then entirely cut out during the editing, but this seems unlikely.

Overall, the film's framings seem precise and consistent. Instead of reactive, improvisatory zooming, we get the kind of shortcuts one might expect in sequences requiring the coordination of shooting fictional music events with the management of large crowds. For instance, in the Grand Ole Opry sequence, set-ups and zooms are repeated as Tommy Brown and Haven Hamilton come onto the stage (Figures 2.103–2.106). Each instance utilizes a zoom out and pan left, following the performer from the backstage area to

**Figure 2.103** *Nashville*

**Figure 2.104** *Nashville*

**Figure 2.105** *Nashville*

**Figure 2.106** *Nashville*

a wide view of the stage and audience. In an AFI interview, Altman has said, "[on] *Nashville*, I didn't look through the camera very much. I wasn't very concerned about the shots being composed well, not that [the cinematographer] wouldn't compose them well, but that was not our intention. I was trying not to force anything. I was trying just to see things."[52] Yet *Nashville* contains a proportional use of aperture zooms (12.2%) exceeded only by *M\*A\*S\*H* and *Thieves Like Us*. The aperture framings at the end of the shots with Brown and Hamilton, for instance, heighten depth relations and create visual interest, though in a way that, while evidently planned, may have been fairly easy to implement. This may be one of the advantages of Altman's predilection for coupling aperture framing with his use of the zoom. The intensity of design can vary while the device itself remains a constant marker of craftsmanship, even if it is often overlooked in favor of the more functionally esoteric and, upon closer examination, ephemeral zooms conjured up by many scholars and critics.

This summary of the zoom in Altman's early 1970s oeuvre indicates a number of key revisions to his stylistic profile and in doing so illustrates the benefits of statistical analysis to historians of film form. While it seems likely, based on my sample, that during this period Altman's films did use massively more zooms than those of other Hollywood filmmakers, scholars have inaccurately described the typical purposes of these zooms. The "searching and revealing" description does not hold up to close scrutiny. It is possible that Altman's later films make more frequent use of the zoom for this function, but during this period the label is largely misleading. Since this misdescription seems to provide the basis for the majority of the claims about Altman's visual style as subversive or oppositional, such accounts should be reconsidered. Claims about Altman's use of the creeping zoom seem more accurate, but here, too, my analysis suggests a need to be more precise. The use of slow intensifying zooms varies dramatically over the half decade under examination. While a comparison of *Brewster McCloud* with *California Split* makes clear that in the early 1970s Altman and his collaborators eventually acquire the capacity to effectively coordinate slow intensifying zooms with the development of dramatic action, it is less clear that this solution resulted from the straightforward evolution of an underlying approach. The relative retreat from the technique in *Nashville* undercuts an unqualified evolutionary account.

As we have seen, each film represents a more or less distinctive approach to the zoom that is overlaid on some basic tendencies, including a predisposition to use the zoom where other filmmakers might rely on camera movement. While the evidence suggests that Altman is proportionally more likely to use the intensifying zoom than others in his cohort, it is in the use of zooms past and aperture zooms that his films seem most distinctive. This necessitates significant revision to Altman's image as an improvisatory filmmaker who cut his camera operators loose to shoot whatever caught their interest. Instead, the evidence indicates that these films regularly employed structured zoom shots with elaborative aestheticizing flourishes, most of which depended on heightening depth relations and providing a frame for the dramatic action.

Finally, critics and scholars need not look to the arcane or subliminal to explain Altman's zooms, or to admire them. Since critical esteem was necessary to ensure his continued ability to make films, Altman is arguably most deserving of admiration for having convinced journalists, reviewers, and scholars that such explanations were apt. What close analysis reveals is his use of the zoom as part of a larger project of multifunctional elaboration on and around classical Hollywood norms. Altman expands the functional aims of the zoom by compounding the narrative with the aesthetic and the intensificatory. These elaborations, though moderate compared to accounts of Altman as oppositional filmmaker, are significant departures from the zoom practices of his peers. The frequency, flexibility, and virtuosity with which Altman and his collaborators enact these zoom strategies need not and should not remain overshadowed by or shrouded in mystificatory metaphors.

# 3

# Elaborate Chaos

## Altman and Overlapping Dialogue

With the hugely successful release of *M\*A\*S\*H* in 1970, Altman finally broke out as a major feature filmmaker. Crucially, his new status was not just industrial—Altman as hitmaker. It was also critical—Altman as potential auteur. In addition to the innovative narrative approach discussed in chapter 1, *M\*A\*S\*H* is replete with novel stylistic strategies that provided critics on the lookout for significant new voices in American filmmaking with an array of features to latch onto. Alongside the zoom strategies discussed in chapter 2, foremost among *M\*A\*S\*H*'s innovations is a dense, layered soundtrack overflowing with overlapping dialogue. The *New York Times*'s Vincent Canby remarks that the film's "soundtrack is so busy it sometimes sounds like three radio stations in one."[1] Critics for *The Atlantic*, *Newsweek*, *Sight and Sound*, *The Nation*, *Commentary*, *Harper's*, and *The Village Voice* highlight the film's overlapping dialogue as worthy of praise.[2]

*M\*A\*S\*H*'s reception established key tropes that would prime future critical and scholarly responses to Altman's soundtracks. Significantly, few critics recognized the precisely designed nature of Altman's realistic artifice. *The New Yorker*'s Pauline Kael is exceptional, then, when she writes that the film has:

> some of the best overlapping comic dialogue ever recorded.... When the dialogue overlaps, you hear just what you should, but it doesn't seem all worked out and set; the sound seems to bounce off things so that the words just catch your ear. The throwaway stuff isn't really thrown away; it all helps to create the free, graceful atmosphere that sustains the movie and keeps it consistently funny.[3]

Compare that account to the one provided by *Newsweek*'s Joseph Morgenstern, who claims, "everyone jabbers at once."[4] Significantly, even this kind of (mis)characterization of *M\*A\*S\*H*'s overlapping dialogue as anarchic jabbering typically frames it as praiseworthy. In his largely negative review of the film, *Nation* critic Robert Hatch singles out the overlapping

*Robert Altman and the Elaboration of Hollywood Storytelling*. Mark Minett, Oxford University Press (2021). © Oxford University Press. DOI: 10.1093/oso/9780197523827.001.0001.

dialogue for plaudits, writing that, "whenever a conference is held or an order issued, all those present speak at once and then dash off in bursts of uninformed zeal."[5] Similarly, for Andrew Sarris it is the film's "anarchic overlapping of line readings," that allows $M*A*S*H$ to, "rise so prominently above its Sergeant Bilko sketches."[6] There is, if not a straight line, then a strong correlation between these initial descriptions of Altman's deployment of overlapping dialogue and the subsequent framing of Altman's work as a rejection of the classical Hollywood practice of manipulating sound to ensure narrative clarity and coherence. Even in relatively detailed overviews of Altman's sound aesthetics this discursive strain persists. Take, for instance, Jay Beck's characterization of Altman's sound practices in the 1970s as constituting "a radically new form of cinematic storytelling," which permits "a non-hierarchical structure of sound that liberates the multiple speaking voices in his films and gives them equal potential to be heard."[7]

There is, no doubt, pleasure in the thought of Altman as anarchic auteur thumbing his nose at Hollywood's cherished narrative clarity, but its drawbacks for understanding the dynamic history of sound design in moving image media are significant. Additionally, rejectionist accounts of Altman's approach to overlapping dialogue as radically oppositional provide little impetus for close attention to distinctions among the soundtracks of individual films in Altman's oeuvre. *Images*, for instance, one of Altman's "chamber dramas," contains very little overlapping dialogue. *The Long Goodbye* does make use of some overlapping (or underlapping, really) ambient conversational dialogue—most frequently, the chanting of Marlowe's New Age neighbors. But it also regularly foregoes opportunities for the more foregrounded and integrated use of overlapping dialogue found in some of Altman's other films. For instance, the sound of revelers during a party scene at the Wades' beach house is treated largely as undifferentiated and incomprehensible—a conventional technique known as "walla." When variation from film to film in Altman's oeuvre is acknowledged, technological-determinism tends to substitute for methodical examination. Hence, *California Split* and especially *Nashville*, with their use of Altman's proprietary Lions Gate 8-Track Sound System, are described as realizations or culminations of the dense approach initiated in $M*A*S*H$. In fact, within and between the films from $M*A*S*H$ to *Nashville* there is more diversity and less straightforward amping-up of overlapping anarchy than is often presumed.

As the revised account of Altman's use of the zoom indicates, individual films within Altman's early 1970s oeuvre make use of his signature techniques in ways that vary significantly in their characteristics and functions. This variation is often explicable through close consideration of the problems or goals set by the filmmaker. These problems are articulated largely in the context of the novel narrative material and production contexts (e.g., budget, personnel, and technologies) of a given film. The rather isolated characters in *Thieves Like Us*, for instance, are not as likely to be found in environments with dense mixes of diegetic sound and multiple zones of dialogue that might overlap. Altman, therefore, mainly layers that film's soundscape with period radio programming. The earlier *M\*A\*S\*H*, on the other hand, is replete with tents overflowing with characters and, therefore, with overlapping dialogue. Moreover, the employment of overlapping dialogue in *M\*A\*S\*H* is much more polished and proficient than it is two films later, in *McCabe & Mrs. Miller*, when Altman was given the freedom to exercise his practice-oriented preference and shoot on location rather than in the controlled environment of the studio lot.

That said, when overlapping dialogue is employed, there is a great deal of consistency in the ways in which Altman and his team handle this novel practice. As the preceding chapters have shown, Altman's means and goals are best viewed as augmenting the functional potential of Hollywood conventions. The layered soundwork in Altman's early 1970s filmmaking consistently displays a focus on directing audience attention and on making auditory space for narratively significant information. At the same time, the carefully manipulated use of overlapping dialogue displays an innovative and often virtuosic use of form. Altman and company open up multiple zones of interest in ways that replicate the complex soundscapes sometimes encountered in everyday life, allow for ironic commentary on the narrative situation, and encourage audiences to engage in effortful but rewarding acts of audition. In all of this, we once again find Altman elaborating on and around rather than rejecting Hollywood storytelling aims and practices.

Ironically, then, the problem set Altman actually seems to have consistently posed for his filmmaking teams is in some ways more robust than the standard critical account might suggest. He could not afford to simply ignore storytelling and narrative, to completely emancipate or confound his audience, even if he did want to (which is doubtful). Instead, Altman and his collaborators had to find ways to meld a concern with realism, an insistence on making films with a distinct, ironizing point of view, an intent to open up a film perceptually, and a practice-oriented preference for production sound with Hollywood's concern for storytelling and intelligibility. In doing so, Altman did not reject Hollywood storytelling; he enlivened it, innovating in a way that might make it more attractive to the younger, hipper, audiences that Hollywood targeted in the early 1970s.

Thus, while Altman's approach to sound may have been more challenging for the audience, it was certainly more challenging for Altman and the collaborators he pushed to innovate sound practices and technology. Rather than thinking of the sound design in Altman's films as actually chaotic, it is best to think of it as ambitiously structured, often in order to leave the impression of chaos while still imparting key narrative information. Rather than describing the sound design as dense, it is best to describe it as carefully and dynamically layered. Altman's teams often manipulate the levels of various sources in order to create what might be understood as the equivalent of the kind of deep focus found in the cinematography of Gregg Toland and praised by André Bazin. Altman's complex soundscapes can be usefully described as consisting of foregrounded, middlegrounded, and backgrounded sound elements, often placed in dynamic relationship with one another.

It seems likely that Altman read Bazin, since he was engaged in contemporary film culture and read film criticism throughout his early career. Regardless, this intertext illuminates his strategies and the critical response to them.[8] In his canonical essay, "The Evolution of the Language of Cinema," Bazin describes three ways in which deep focus "influences the interpretation" of a scene. First, it "brings the spectator into a relation with the image closer to that which he enjoys with reality." Second, it "implies, consequently, both a more active mental attitude on the part of the spectator and a more positive contribution on his part to the action in progress. . . . here he is called upon to exercise at least a minimum of personal choice." Then, Bazin, acknowledging that the third proposed influence, "may be described as metaphysical," goes on to argue that "depth of focus reintroduced ambiguity into the structure of the image if not of necessity . . . at least as a possibility. . . . The uncertainty in which we find ourselves as to the spiritual key or the interpretation we should put on the film is built into the very design of the image."[9] Substituting "sound" for "image" in Bazin's last proposition and removing Bazin's qualification of "at least as a possibility" we see here something like the essence of the rejectionist, oppositional account of Altman.[10]

It is crucial, though, to push back against the analogizing alignment of interpretation or felt experience and design features. Works of art are often celebrated when their form is perceived as reflecting or embodying their meaning or significance. Praiseworthy form, it is held, follows expressive function, either by offering itself up as another thematic element or by producing the interpretation or felt experience as a result of supposedly parallel features. One wonders, though, if this tenet actually functions to predetermine the description of style by extending interpretive heuristics more appropriate for use on subject and theme. When juxtaposed with standard accounts of

Altman's use of overlapping dialogue, the analyses offered in this chapter suggest that unstructured sound design is not required to provide the impression of liberation—that freedom is not necessary to feel free. A second lesson might be that neither the feeling of liberation from the shackles of narrative nor the availability of ambiguity are necessarily sufficient to account for the full range of a work's designed effects. They may just be the most vivid and memorable effects—perhaps because they are the most novel and/or the most desired—on an audience that has also been told a story. Moreover, reported impressions may not just be incomplete, they may be misleading—they may unintentionally exaggerate the size or scope of effects because they stand out for other reasons, such as novelty, or they may rule out or play down seemingly contradictory effects based on a flawed binary logic. This last possibility seems particularly important given my framing of Altman's purposes as additive and elaborative, and given the common critical positioning of Hollywood storytelling against the audience agency, ambiguity, and perceptual, psychological, and social realism associated with art cinema.

Indeed, Altman's deep focus sound, in tethering a targeted ambiguity to design features aimed at providing the auditor with substantive clarity and guidance—thereby moderating the risk to narrative comprehension—arguably tends more closely to the first two of Bazin's possible "influences" of deep focus. First, Altman gestures toward perceptual realism, simulating the reality of individuals' auditory encounters with everyday life, by creating a dynamic, multidimensional relationship between conventionally foregrounded sounds and elements that would normally be treated as background "walla." Second, Altman sometimes (although less often than is claimed) makes the verbal content of dialogue only "effortfully available" to auditors, which partly involves allowing them to choose among competing sounds. Again, though, he and his team accomplish this while largely maintaining key narrative aims of classical Hollywood storytelling. As a result, Altman's treatment of sound and dialogue is more usefully understood as part of the generally excessive approach to narration discussed in chapter 1.

Getting at the small-scale structuring and minute manipulation evident in the sound design of these films can be difficult. Individual scenes often have multiple dialogue arrangements, alternating between periods of overlap and no overlap, incorporating offscreen dialogue that is then moved onscreen, and mixing multiple dialogue sources in ways that make the "overlapping" label somewhat misleading. As a result, the approach used here emphasizes moment-to-moment analysis that tracks factors such as whether and how much dialogue is intelligible and/or audible and whether its source is identifiable. I also insist throughout on offering evidence in the form of dialogue transcriptions and, moreover, on providing dialogue transcriptions that attempt to reproduce not just verbal content but also the coordinated temporal development of multiple lines of dialogue. In doing so, I follow and build on Jeff Jaeckle's guidance, in his primer on analyzing film dialogue, to not only quote (rather than summarize) but to more robustly consider what accurately quoting film dialogue might entail.[11] Following Michel Chion's insistence that film is an "audiovisual combination," my analytic approach incorporates careful attention to the coordination of sound with the image track.[12] Finally, my analysis mobilizes its redescription of the overlapping dialogue in Altman's early 1970s films within a functionalist perspective influenced by the groundbreaking and influential work of Sarah Kozloff.[13] This methodology yields compelling evidence for the resituation of Altman and his collaborators' complex practices and aims as elaborative innovations rather than radical rejections. In doing so, it also indicates the need to move away from sound analysis based in the reductively impressionistic and abstracting metaphorization of sound practices.

## *M\*A\*S\*H*: Orders and Disorders

Self's canonical scholarly analysis of the sound design in Altman's films, which places particular emphasis on *M\*A\*S\*H*, emblematizes the rejectionist account of Altman. Self maintains that, in its first scene, *M\*A\*S\*H*'s sound disrupts "viewers' understanding of the initial situation of the story, which sets in motion the whole cause-effect chain of the narrative logic." Thus, "at the crucial stage of [the film's] beginning," causality is disrupted, seemingly catastrophically.[14] According to Self, this revolutionary departure from Hollywood norms occurs in the exchange between Colonel Blake and Radar that concludes the film's opening credits sequence ⊙ (see the companion website for a video clip). As a helicopter descends into the M\*A\*S\*H encampment with a fresh set of wounded soldiers, Blake and Radar exchange overlapping dialogue. Table 3.1 reproduces Self's transcription of this exchange.

Self characterizes this exchange as "incomprehensible," claiming that, "It is possible only after several listenings to decipher fully the content of their speech."[15] Self could also note, but does not, that the sound mix also includes the whirring of the helicopter's blades, although he does describe their visual presence in the shot in which the dialogue is presented. Attention to that sound effect, though, might have indicated that the filmmakers are, in fact, worried about intelligibility. While the helicopter begins as the foregrounded element in the mix, its volume is lowered significantly when the characters

**Table 3.1** Self's Account

| COLONEL BLAKE | RADAR |
|---|---|
| Radar, get a hold of Major Burns and tell him that we're going to have to hold a couple of surgeons over from the day shift to the night shift. Get General Hammond down there in Seoul; tell him we gotta have two new surgeons right away! | I guess I'd better call Major Burns and tell him to put another day shift in our night shift. I'll put in a call to General Hammond in Seoul. I hope he sends us those two new surgeons; we're sure going to need 'em! |

begin talking, thus making room for the dialogue and indicating a more complex strategy than Self acknowledges.

In requiring that dialogue immediately be "fully decipher[able]," Self sets a peculiarly high bar for comprehensibility and, unlike Altman, endorses a conventional Hollywood storytelling practice without fully considering whether that practice is necessary to meet Hollywood's storytelling aims. In everyday communication with others, total comprehension of every word in a conversation is not necessary to draw correct conclusions about meaning. Listeners, much like readers, make gap-filling inferences based on context cues provided by the situation and by the parts of the text or speech that are comprehensible. This is what matters for narrative comprehension as well.

To ask the more relevant question of whether the dialogue mix conveys narrative significance, we need a more accurate transcription than that offered by Self, which exaggerates simultaneity by compressing the temporal dimension. Drawing out the temporal axis, Table 3.2 better reveals the rhythm of the dialogue and the extent of the overlap.

This transcription reveals that pauses and tempo changes in dialogue delivery create space for individual phrases and words to stand alone and to echo one another. Even Self's hypothetical listeners, posited as stunned and perplexed by the overlapping dialogue, are given every opportunity to latch onto key verbal cues such as "Radar," "Yes sir," and "Major Burns." Kozloff identifies one of the key conventional functions of film dialogue as the "anchorage of the diegesis and characters."[16] "Narrative films," employ dialogue "to identify and create their time and space" and "also to name the most important elements of that diegesis—the characters."[17] Here, the dialogue's delivery is timed partly to ensure that it serves this important function. Radar is identified through the stand-alone portion of the exchange, and "Yes, sir" clarifies that he is subordinate to Blake. The dialogue names the quasi-antagonist of the film's first half,

Table 3.2  Revised Account

| COLONEL BLAKE | RADAR |
| --- | --- |
| Radar! | |
| | Yes sir! |
| Want you to get ahold of Major Burns. | I guess I'd better call |
| | Major Burns |
| And tell him that | and tell him to put another day shift in our |
| we're going to have to hold a couple of | night shift. |
| surgeons over from the day shift to the night shift. | |
| | |
| Get General Hammond | I'll put in a call to General Hammond in |
| down there in Seoul. | Seoul. |
| Tell him we gotta have two new surgeons | I hope he |
| right away! | sends us those two new |
| | surgeons. We're sure going to need 'em! |

Major Burns, as well as key figure General Hammond, and it also provides the orienting "Seoul" through the nearly simultaneous repetition of each. The exchange isolates and underscores elements that are key to the construction of the diegesis, a conventional function that contradicts Self's claim that it is essentially undermining and narratively subversive.

Self presumes that because the dialogue is overlapping the audience has necessarily missed what Kozloff describes as a "verbal event," where "speech acts are themselves pivotal links of the narrative chain."[18] But it is precisely this sort of "either/or" oppositional framework that Altman and his collaborators surpass. The end of the exchange isolates both "surgeons" and "We're sure going to need 'em!" The context of that exchange, with one military man speaking authoritatively to the other, and with the aforementioned isolation of "Yes sir," cues the audience that the narrative situation is one of providing orders. What might those orders be about? The final isolated bit of dialogue, especially, "two new surgeons," answers this question for the audience.

The bewildered Sgt. Major Vollmer, silently taking notes during the exchange, seems to be a sort of proxy for Self's ideal auditor when, after Radar's departure, he asks the Colonel, "What was that, sir?" Vollmer, though, is chronically perplexed in the film, and his unknowing, helpless, and eternally out-of-the-loop status is treated through a string of jokes of which this scene provides the first instance. Vollmer's befuddlement at the overlapping dialogue thus functions to ironize rather than endorse the notion that an auditor would be unable to keep up. Moreover, as any audience would undoubtedly be aware, $M*A*S*H$ is a comedy, and its overlapping dialogue is less likely to be viewed as narratively disruptive than as functioning in the service of humor. Indeed, a classic comic inversion—that the subordinate Radar understands the needs of the unit at least as well as his commanding officer, who seems unaware of his subordinate's superior competence, is dependent on the use of overlapping dialogue. The scene's punch line is Blake's response to Vollmer, "I gave everything to Radar." In fact, Radar already knew everything that was needed. To get this joke audiences need to get the gist of the overlapping dialogue—they must be made to understand that Radar's stated intentions are the same as Blake's orders.

Altman and his collaborators' use of sound is remarkable, then, not for its narrative disruption, but for the way in which the delivery of the dialogue has been skillfully tailored so as to reinforce genre aims, introduce characters, and propel the narrative. By making comprehension more difficult, the overlapping dialogue effectively serves as a wink to the audience and allows viewers to feel superior to characters in the film who require the imposition of order to feel secure or to operate effectively. The reward for the extra effort put into design and audition here is an ironizing humor that also reinforces the film's critique of US military adventurism. Thus, the use of sound in this scene could be said to serve as a model for one key aspect of Altman's approach to sound and overlapping dialogue. It overtly foregrounds Altman's ironizing authorial voice and at the same time contributes to the narrative.

There is an even more indicatively "Altmanian" use of sound in *M*A*S*H*'s initial mess hall scene, where Duke and Hawkeye, the unit's two new surgeons, arrive unannounced in a stolen jeep. This is the first prolonged instance in the film of the "realistic" sound design that critics typically underdescribe as "dense" and which is generally approvingly assumed to serve as a liberating distraction from the narrative. The term, though, can leave the misleading impression that Altman's scenes are enveloped in a kind of realistic sonic haze within which the audience can choose to pleasantly wander in whichever direction.[19] The key feature of Altman's soundtracks that initiates this discourse is a form of overlapping dialogue that relies on amplifying the use of the ambient conversational dialogue of noncentral characters. In the typical Hollywood film, this dialogue frequently remains inaudible or is handled as "walla," a sound effect best understood as a minimalist stab at realism that makes audible the conversations of a crowd while still, more often than not, rendering them as unintelligible.[20]

Distinguishing between *audibility* and *intelligibility* is crucial for grasping the covertly hierarchized sound strategies of Altman's films. A third factor is also essential—*sourceability*—that is, the extent to which cues are provided with which to infer the qualities or traits of the sound source. Whereas intelligibility is about understanding the verbal content of the dialogue, sourceability is about connecting dialogue to a speaker and, moreover, using the characteristics of the dialogue to infer the characteristics of the source. Walla, for instance, is often incomprehensible in terms of its verbal content, but it may be partly sourceable in that, for instance, the qualities of the voice might indicate whether the speaker is male or female, old or young. Along these lines, we might be able to infer from the tone of voice, even if the words are incomprehensible, whether the speaker is angry or calm, happy or sad. Thus, even unintelligible dialogue, all too easily overlooked as wallpaper, can communicate and contribute to narrative comprehension through its non-verbal qualities. The sound in *M\*A\*S\*H*'s initial mess hall scene is carefully designed with these factors in mind, manipulating dialogue that would typically be handled as walla so as to balance and intertwine Altman's narrative, expressive, and enhanced-mimetic concerns.

The scene opens with an interesting coordination of overtly expressive and covertly narrative sound design. The overlapping dialogue here frames interpretation of the narrative action and gives the impression of calamity but relies on sourceability to position the audience to anticipate the scene's narrative development. During Hawkeye and Duke's ride to the mess hall in a stolen jeep, the soundtrack is dominated by triumphant martial music—a deliberately clichéd bit of scoring that also plays over Hawkeye's earlier arrival at a military depot. The music's idiom is undercut at every point by the shenanigans on display, and its use here is indicative of Altman's broader strategy of employing juxtaposition to establish an overt if indirect ironizing narrational voice of the kind discussed in chapter 1. The music climaxes and concludes with the movement into the first interior shot of the sequence, a long shot of the row of tables and chairs inside the mess hall. The chow line is visible in the foreground right, with a Korean server on the very right of the frame. Colonel Blake and some other male officers are seated in the center left, with other groupings of officers positioned around them.

There are only a few scattered female officers visible in this initial framing, which is held for 2–3 seconds, but the only audible dialogue consists of a group of overlapping female voices engaged in a conversation. As the music is brought down in the mix, these identifiably female offscreen voices are brought up. So, while the initial framing emphasizes the male characters, the soundtrack emphasizes the conversation of an initially offscreen group of nurses. One could describe this as favoring realistic sonic chaos to the point of narrative decentering, since it is momentarily unclear which sounds or images will turn out to be important next.[21] Realism, though, does not require the audibility of the women's voices rather than the voices of the male officers. Moreover, the sound subtly calls attention to the nurses moments before they are displayed visually and narratively activated as the objects of

Hawkeye and Duke's desire. Importantly, this expansion is based not on comprehensibility but on sourceability. The onscreen sources can be ruled out because the dialogue is identifiably female, and the number of voices exceeds the number of women on display. Sound here anticipates narrative development, complementing an image track focused on the arrival of the protagonists.

By the end of this first shot, the image track catches up with the sound design, while also visually surveying the narrative landscape around which the scene's overlapping dialogue is designed. Since the olive drab flaps on the sides of the tent are pulled up, Hawkeye and Duke's arrival outside the tent is visible, tracked by a leftward pan and redundantly emphasized by a zoom in. This mobile framing does more than tend to the narrative event of arrival; it visually prepares the audience to comprehend the scene's soundscape, sweeping past male figures who will be introduced later in the scene and then past the group of nurses who are the source of the dialogue on the soundtrack. The final framing here places the nurse who will soon be labeled "Lieutenant Dish" in a close up in the right foreground of the frame, marking her as the most narratively significant of the group, while placing Hawkeye and Duke in the near background left and center-left of the frame. During this pan and zoom, the nurses' dialogue continues, as does the music, which concludes at roughly the moment the jeep and the pan and zoom come to a halt. The clattering of dishware and silverware is also audible, reinforcing a sense of messy realism.

As was established earlier, the audibility of the identifiably female voices is narratively motivated and actually a rejection of strict perceptual realism. The selective employment of intelligibility in the handling of the nurses' conversation is diversely functional. The women talk over one another, so that while multiple voices are audible and sourceable as female, it is difficult to comprehend what each voice is saying. The soundtrack blurs the distinction between dialogue and walla. As in the opening scene, the mix isolates and highlights some voices over others, punctuating the general din of conversation with intelligibility:

FEMALE VOICE 1: . . . total drag.
FEMALE VOICE 2: (loud) Where is she?! She's (incomprehensible)
FEMALE VOICE 1: (loud) Not another period! Another period!

At least one other voice can be heard alongside these two, and the image track reveals a group of four nurses sitting together talking. Whereas the selection of this conversation for audibility cannot be said to be motivated by realism, the treatment and content of the conversation arguably serve that function. That is, the decision to overlap the dialogue here replicates notions of how conversations are typically overheard. The intelligible aspects of the conversation, the verbal content plausibly available to the audience, fit the vulgar comic tenor of the film. The nurses seem to be gossiping about someone's menstrual cycle, and this is likely intended as outrageous humor, casually addressing a subject that is, at least on the public space of the cinema screen circa 1970, taboo. The casualness here also arguably amplifies the sense of the film's commitment to realism, since in "real life" some women do, in fact, discuss menstruation in casual conversation. The nominally excessive employment of seemingly digressive dialogue here also actually serves a key narrative function. In positioning the women as openly discussing what convention has deemed taboo it identifies them as potential allies to the rule-breaking men who serve as the film's protagonists. That these allies will lack the causal agency of the surgeons is unfortunately typical of Hollywood convention.

With a quick pan to the left moving Lieutenant Dish offscreen, the soundtrack similarly shifts from the nurses to the conversation between Duke and Hawkeye, multiply refocusing the scene on male-driven narrative development. The nurses remain audible, but are now largely unintelligible, their functional potential constrained, made subservient to the words and gazes of the men. The two men look offscreen right in the direction of the nurses through the majority of the shot, and an eyeline match cuts to a close up of Lieutenant Dish smiling and speaking, although the dialogue levels do not change with the cut; so even though Dish's lips move during the shot, her voice cannot be distinguished. Sound and image, aligned with the men, isolate her significance to that of a narrative object of male fascination, a status that could easily have been complicated by "democratizing" the soundtrack and elevating her voice in the mix. After a cut back to Duke and Hawkeye, the pair move into the tent with their lusty motivations made clear, and as they move left the camera pans left and zooms out to follow their movement.

With this movement, and with the end of Duke and Hawkeye's conversation, the mix becomes noisier. The ambient sounds of the M*A*S*H encampment, most prominently the roar of a truck shown driving by, are raised in volume. While the conversation of the nurses also seems to grow louder, this engine sound makes their speech almost entirely inaudible. When the truck drives off it leaves only a stark silence filled by Duke, who comments loudly on "that piece of scenery," namely, Lieutenant Dish. Another eyeline match and an emphatic zoom in on Dish show her turning her head, cueing the audience to understand that Duke's exclamation is audible and intelligible not just to Hawkeye and the audience, but also to its object—though the rest of the nurses do not seem to hear Duke's comment. After cutting back to Hawkeye and Duke entering the mess, the film again cuts to Dish. Her disdainful facial expression, with one end of her lips raised in a minor evocation of disgust, conveys the pertinent information about her subjective state.

The image track has isolated Dish from the nurses and presented her as annoyed object of the men's gaze. Meanwhile, the soundtrack has similarly isolated its contents to the expression of male desire around Dish but avoids the equivalent of direct redundancy with the image track—a slashing verbal response from Dish—in favor of overlapping dialogue that multiply rejects Duke's sexist overture. The conversation at the nurses' table returns to intelligibility here, a move that is purposeful and, perhaps, predictable in that it provides an opportunity for Dish to respond to Duke's harassment. Instead, not only does the initial intelligible line, "really a drag!" come from an off-screen character rather than Lieutenant Dish, but the speaker does not even seem to be aware of Duke and Hawkeye. This diegetically "coincidental" but clearly designed and narratively resonant juxtaposition of dialogue and situation indirectly characterizes Dish's feelings about Duke's comment—her lack of interest and her weariness with this form of sexual harassment. Using dialogue to provide information about a character's subjective state, what Kozloff labels "character revelation," is entirely conventional, whether the dialogue comes from the character herself or from a commenting character.[22] What is atypical here is that the diegetic dialogue from the offscreen nurse does not provide *her* comment on Dish's feelings or on the narrative situation— the nurse's comment is clearly directed elsewhere. Instead, with the selection of "really a drag!" for intelligibility, Altman and company seem to be indirectly commenting by employing the dialogue as a way to ironize Duke's overt sexism.

This dialogue provides a particularly interesting example of the persistently overt narrational voice found in Altman's early 1970s films. From the perspective of Kozloff's functional categories, this most resembles the use of dialogue to exercise "control of viewer evaluation and emotions."[23] The most typical form of this kind of dialogue, though, would be a sympathetic character directly characterizing a narrative situation and thereby providing an anchor for the audience's own evaluative or emotional reaction. Instead, the commentary here is subtly camouflaged within a stylistic technique, ambient dialogue, that conventionally functions to cue the "realism" response from audiences and critics. Critics who have recognized that Altman's use of sound is exceptionally dense and perhaps confusing because "in reality" soundscapes can be dense and are sometimes confusing have often left it at that. Yet as we have seen, the density and overlap here are hardly "natural"—the coincidence exists only at the level of the diegesis. Instead, Altman seems to be piggybacking an overt narrational voice onto his "exceptionally realistic" approach. Part of what is impressive about Altman's elaborative approach is the way in which it successfully integrates multiple and seemingly conflicting goals. Here, Altman and his team use "realistic" sound design to indirectly convey an ironizing expressivity.

The cut away from Lieutenant Dish and back to Duke, who moves further into the space of the mess hall, initiates another round of hierarchization of audio in coordination with the image track and narrative development. The shot is structured around a rightward pan that follows Duke's movement. The ambient sound of the nurses' dialogue continues, with Dish's first really audible and partly intelligible lines. The dialogue is at its most intelligible as the camera pans past Dish, and it becomes less intelligible as the pan continues, moving the nurses offscreen and coming to a halt on silverware bins. The clattering of the dishware here momentarily dominates the soundtrack, although a reproving "No, no!" pops into the mix above the generally unintelligible murmur of the nurses' conversation. Here, Altman's team is straightforwardly mixing the sound in coordination with the image track, although the overall track is probably more robust than convention demands. This is certainly not sonic haze or chaos.

As the camera tilts up from the dishware and Duke moves from the left of the frame to the right, Colonel Blake and two other officers are revealed in the background. Again, in a fairly conventional move this visual revelation is accompanied by audio access to Blake's conversation, with Blake inquiring as to the identities of Duke and Hawkeye, whom he mistakes for enlisted men. During the first part of this exchange the nurses' dialogue is only intermittently audible, but toward the end it is again raised in volume, anticipating the camera's return to the nurses with a pan left following Hawkeye's movement. With that movement, the sound mix fades down Blake's voice, again a choice that has nothing to do with realistic sound design and everything to do with focusing audience attention.

Though the volume of the dialogue is aligned with the scene's narrative center, the content and handling of the nurses' dialogue is still overlapping calamity. But the presentation of calamity here is afforded by and integral to conventional narrative purposes. Hawkeye takes a seat next to Dish, with Duke across the table, and the nurses carry on their overlapping conversations, with some intelligible lines about fainting in hallways. This conversation is interrupted slightly as Hawkeye slides in, with Dish instructing him to watch out for a nail on the bench (foregrounding their later romantic relationship), and then resumes, its topic shifting to Dish's recommendation that some unnamed woman ought to be using pHisoHex soap on her face. What soap has to do with fainting in hallways is entirely unclear, and the sonic milieu has the feel of uncoordinated improvisation. This seeming incoherence actually helps to perceptually align the narration with Duke and Hawkeye, who arrive mid-discussion and are wholly uninterested in the substance of the nurses' talk. In a way, the decision to include the nurses' voices as an incoherent element can be understood as analogous to the compositional, narrative disinterest in the coherence or intelligibility of their conversations. This alignment also offers an ideal opportunity to display a commitment to perceptual realism, since a late-arriving auditor would naturally be befuddled by the conversations' over-lapping content.

Moreover, this chaos, while possibly produced through on-set improvisation, was almost certainly made possible through postproduction manipulation of the soundtrack. Thus far, there have been several moments in this scene where functionally significant pieces of the nurses' seemingly improvised dialogue have been foregrounded by the sound design. Importantly, these have largely been delivered by offscreen speakers. This means that the dialogue did not necessarily have to pop-up in the natural flow of unruly improvised conversation and that their delivery did not have to be timed by the performers *in that space during that shot* to coincide with the on-screen narrative space with which they would be effectively juxtaposed. There are no moving lips for audience members to recognize as not in synch with the words on the soundtrack. In fact, throughout *M\*A\*S\*H*, Altman and his collaborators consistently find ways to remove lips from shots so that they can layer sounds in highly designed ways without having to worry about synch or about microphones that favor one speaker over another. Surgical masks, offscreen speakers, and distant framings are all employed in order to allow room to manipulate the deceptively "live" sound in postproduction.[24] This suggests that Altman and company are not particularly interested in production practices oriented toward critique of Hollywood storytelling as manipulative and antirealist. Instead, it indicates that their aim is to elaborate upon Hollywood practice, to engineer a storytelling solution allowing them to sidestep the conventional prohibition against partial coherence and troubled intelligibility that has been bound up with the general prohibition against overlapping dialogue.

The overlapping dialogue here also serves as a kind of bracket to the relative silence that punctuates a key narrative development. The nurses' conversation is brought to a full halt by Duke's repeated overtures to Lieutenant Dish and by Hawkeye pointing out that Dish is brandishing a wedding ring and is "definitely married." The stoppage isolates a moment of minor narrative conflict and the temporary resolution to Duke's courtship of Dish. It also provides the narrative and sonic space to quickly shift, with a cut, back to Blake, who declares that, "I'm the commanding officer, and I'm going to get to the bottom of this."

Blake's voice is temporarily the only really audible part of the soundtrack, but as he gets up and walks toward the men, overlap resumes. Unintelligible male conversational voices can be heard. When Blake finishes speaking, the officer Blake's dialogue previously labeled as Murrhardt expresses his disapproval by commenting to the other officer, whom Murrhardt's dialogue identifies as Bandini, that "they're eating here because they want to." With the camera panning left following Blake to Hawkeye, Duke, and the nurses, the sound of the nurses' conversation is again made audible, while Bandini and Murrhardt's conversation is removed as the pan moves them offscreen. Once more, sound design largely focuses on narrative development.

To be more precise, sound design largely, *but not exclusively*, focuses on narrative development, because once again Altman and his collaborators layer multiple functions through their manipulation of the multiple facets of film dialogue. As Murrhardt delivers his line, the p.a. system transmits an announcement that serves as a sort of bridge playing over the shift back to the nurses' end of the mess hall. Its function, though, is not merely neutral sonic gap-filling. Instead, it affords a return to the ironization of military order found in the scene with Radar, Blake, and Vollmer. Over Murrhardt's line, the p.a. announcer states: "Attention. Attention." And as he concludes his aforementioned critique of Blake with, "they want to," the p.a. overlaps his dialogue with, "Captain Murrhardt. Please report to the commander's [static]. To the office of the commanding officer." Of course, Blake, is, and (for the benefit of the audience) has just declared that he is, the commanding officer. Both men are in the mess, and Blake could obviously not have called for Murrhardt to meet with him, so the content of the message is absurd. It is as if the p.a. itself offers a rebuke to Murrhardt for criticizing Blake by calling him into Blake's office. The p.a. announcements (as opposed to the snippets of radio played over the p.a.) are delivered by Major Vollmer, who proves to be an ineffectual stickler for regulation. The surreal notion that Vollmer is watching over events and calling dissenters to account by summoning them into an empty office again ironizes military rules, regulation, and rank. The wordplay here, "the office of the commanding officer," reinforces the sense that the announcement should be regarded with comic skepticism. The p.a., then, becomes an avenue for indirect ironizing commentary on the film's central theme, but does so not through its content per se but through the juxtaposition of its content with the narrative situation.

Prior to the p.a. announcement, the overlapping dialogue in the scene has largely taken one of two forms. It has been placed within ambient or quasi-ambient speech—Altman's novelly middlegrounded walla such as the nurses' conversations—that audiences would normally not expect to be intelligible at all. Or, it has occurred between foregrounded speech, such as the conversation between Duke and Hawkeye, and ambient speech—again, the nurses' conversations. During the pan from one end of the table, where the nurses sit, to the other, where Blake sits, Altman has minimized overlap to some extent by handling the dialogue almost in the same way that a radio dial may be used to tune between two stations that are very close on the dial, with some interference in between them, but with one station brought into focus as the other goes out. This pattern alters with the introduction of the p.a. announcement, which is foregrounded and completely intelligible, as is Murrhardt's dialogue to Bandini, and as is Blake's dialogue to Hawkeye and Duke once he reaches the far end of the table.

The p.a. announcement, then, bridges the narrative space of Blake's transition, and it also serves as a kind of formal bridge into the final segment of the sequence, in which overlapping foregrounded dialogue, similar to Radar and Blake's previously discussed exchange, will dominate. This, as opposed to middle-grounded ambient dialogue like the nurses' conversations, is arguably the more conventional type of overlapping dialogue, and Kozloff suggests that:

> when a small group of characters engaged in one conversation all speak at the same time, the viewer may assume that no one is listening and that everybody is so emotionally involved in their own agendas that they are unwilling to cede the floor. . . . Generally, because the viewers' ability to hear distinctly is compromised, overlapping dialogue is used for realistic texture or comic confusion, not for an important narrative function.[25]

What Altman and his collaborators' elaborative approach rather sneakily provides, though, is a compounding of these conventional functions with thematic development. Moreover, through its virtuosic design, the overlapping dialogue here also presents a perverse elaboration of the kind of task that is at the heart of Hollywood's commitment to the principle of clarity—introducing a film's cast of characters. In M*A*S*H, this cast is relatively sprawling, and the task is handled incredibly efficiently through a technique praised by rejectionists for its inefficiency.

This scene's narrative function, then, is about introductions—diegetically between the characters but really to the audience. Its final segment effectively has two sets of these introductions ⊚ (see the companion website for a video clip). In the first, Blake discovers that Hawkeye and Duke are the surgeons he expected rather than rogue soldiers intruding on his mess hall, and Hawkeye inquires about the conditions at the base. During this conversation the nurses leave, making way for the second, larger, set of introductions. Their departure frees up space on the soundtrack and enables the establishment of a similarly open visual space, created by the framing and blocking of the shot, in which Duke, Hawkeye, and Blake occupy the left distant foreground of the frame. This leaves the right foreground empty, ready to be occupied by the other male officers on the base. Again, the image track and soundtrack are tightly coordinated. Overall narrative clarity, as well as other functional purposes, depend crucially on this moment-by-moment co-design, a fact occluded in many assessments of the storytelling in Altman's films of the period and by analytical methods assessing sound in relation to narrative situation rather than that situation's visual presentation.

The first set of overlapping introductions appears to fit modestly well with Kozloff's description of the conventional design and aims of overlapping dialogue—conveying the comic confusion of a group of individuals simultaneously pursuing their own agendas. Blake himself seems so preoccupied with going through the motions of his duty that he is oblivious to the absurd responses he receives to his inquiries. When he tells Hawkeye that he received a notification that he stole a jeep, he is quite satisfied with Hawkeye's reassurance that he couldn't have stolen the jeep because, "it's right outside." "So it is," says Blake, already turning to remind Duke that protocol dictates he should have immediately notified Blake of his arrival. Duke's response is that he and Hawkeye have been "boozing all day," and he continues speaking briefly although unintelligibly as Blake looks over Duke's orders and nods his head, saying "Good. Good. You've been working close to the front." The juxtaposition of the dialogue comically suggests that, given their proximity to the horrors of war, Blake approves of his new surgeons' boozing. But the image track and the overlap suggest that Blake is already oblivious to Duke's bad behavior and instead is positively assessing his resume.

But this bit of overlapping dialogue goes beyond mere comic confusion, since it also serves to reveal character, providing an exemplar of Blake's general tendency to overlook, ignore, or otherwise be oblivious to bad behavior and to be concerned instead with medical competency. Additionally, Blake—in spite of his puffed-up decision to confront Hawkeye and Duke about their presence in his mess—also proves to be fairly conflict averse, and his overlapping exchange with Hawkeye and Duke introduces this deflating character trait. The exchange is reproduced in Table 3.3.

Again, Blake seems to be primarily interested in his own agenda—attempting to complete what appears to be his standard statement on the challenges of being a military surgeon. Rather than enforcing military decorum, though, his yielding, laissez-faire management style seems to hinge on ignoring or managing the male officers' sexual pursuit of the nurses—an

**Table 3.3** Blake, Hawkeye, and Duke

| COLONEL BLAKE | HAWKEYE | DUKE |
|---|---|---|
| Now we have our slight periods here. But when the action starts you'll get more work in twelve hours than most civilian surgeons— | How many nurses do we have on the base sir? | |
| Seventeen. | | |
| Four . . . than a civilian surgeon . . . does in a month. Yes. I think it could be arranged. Yes. | How many nurses will there be in my— Can I select this young girl here [indicates where Dish sat]. [Unintelligible] think I could use her because, and the, um, girl over here. The blonde. | |
| Oh, Father Mulcahy! | | What the hell you mean ta . . . |

approach not ironized by the film's narration. Blake's sudden turn to Mulcahy, thereby beginning an extended round of introductions, can be understood not just as obliviousness to Hawkeye's ongoing requests but as a strategic attempt to shift topics to avoid confrontation about which surgeon gets which attractive nurse. It is also worth noting that Blake's shift comes just as Hawkeye requests the blonde nurse who will shortly be revealed to be Blake's mistress. Retrospectively, then, Blake's obliviousness may be understood as feigned, and his change of topic not just about avoiding conflict between Hawkeye and Duke but also between Hawkeye and Blake. The elaborative approach to the dialogue here not only functions narratively, thematically, and comically in the moment, but it also subtly provides an opportunity to appreciate clever design that is really only available on a second encounter, where an understanding of the narrative situation as comically chaotic likely persists but the functional range of the exchange expands beyond the thrills of realism to those of character insight and aesthetic appreciation.

Blake's call for Father Mulcahy shifts the action into the second half of the segment, which in some ways provides the quintessential instance of overlapping dialogue in the film. This set of introductions undoubtedly seems chaotic to the viewer, as multiple male officers talk over one another, make bad jokes, and glad-hand. The moment recalls screwball comedies, and *M*A*S*H* can be understood as an updating of the screwball form. According to Kozloff, overlapping dialogue in screwball comedies, "is used whenever several people are trying to straighten out some tangled mess . . . *to*

*show the characters' confusion, but never to confuse the viewer,* who has a superior understanding of all the concepts."[26] Close analysis of this second set
of introductions confirms that its design is largely geared toward signaling
rather than producing confusion. Many of this sequence's formal features
indicate Altman is concerned with fulfilling the narrative function of the
segment—the introduction of members of the film's large ensemble cast. The
findings of this analysis, though, depart from Kozloff's account in a minor
but significant way. At the beginning of this segment, audience knowledge is
largely, although not entirely, aligned with Duke and Hawkeye. The audience
is introduced to characters at the same time that they are—they share the
pair's inferior understanding. Altman's elaborative problem set, if Kozloff's
description of screwball comedy is accurate, would seem to surpass convention. The deployment of the overlapping dialogue must both signal chaos
and provide the audience with key exposition.

To accomplish this, Altman stages the shot in which the majority of the
introductions take place by opening up a large, central portion of the frame
in which to display the new characters (Figure 3.1). Hawkeye is framed in the
foreground left, and Duke is framed foreground right. The other officers are
arrayed in the middle of the frame, creating receding and converging lines
of figures that meet in the middle of the background. The new characters
will move into the foreground to be greeted, but, consistent with the comic
tone of the film, this movement is not uniform or regular. Instead, the new
characters lean in and push past one another. The framing and blocking,
though, have created a large enough space so that this disorder does not ob-
struct understanding.

Figure 3.1  *M\*A\*S\*H*

Crucially, the key feature of the film's sound mix during this segment is not the dialogue between Hawkeye and Duke and the new characters but instead the voice of Blake, who provides intelligible introductions while the other characters shake hands and exchange greetings. Blake is offscreen, and the quality of his voice sounds slightly different from the previous close-up shot of Blake as he called Mulcahy over, indicating that his dialogue may not be live production sound but instead may have been added in postproduction. The framing then, in addition to creating an adequate visual space in which the "chaos" can unfold with some clarity, also allows Altman the freedom to manipulate Blake's foregrounded dialogue, the loudest in the segment, in order to provide not just overlap but also a kind of safety net for the overlapping dialogue between the onscreen characters.

Blake, then, both initiates and helps to anchor the proceedings. His introductions initially alternate and then overlap with the greetings between the men. Table 3.4 attempts to capture most of the intelligible dialogue and to provide a sense of the rhythm of the exchange. "H" in the "MEN" column stands for Hawkeye, "D" for Duke, "M" for Mulcahy, "W" for Waldowski, and "B" for Black. Note the alternation, in which Blake's lines are generally given room in the mix or are not competing with voices of equal volume, and also note the redundancy of the dialogue. Waldowski repeats his nickname and his occupation, and Black's dialogue both makes a vulgar joke and, in doing so, restates his name and occupation.

With the introductions to nonestablished characters handled, there is an opportunity for the conversation to become more chaotically incoherent.

**Table 3.4** Introductions

| COLONEL BLAKE | MEN |
| --- | --- |
| Oh, Father Mulcahy!<br>I'd like you to meet Captain Pierce, our new surgeon. This is a Catholic chaplain.<br>And here's Captain Forrest. | H: [unintelligible] |
|  | M: [shaking hands with H] Dago Red!<br>H: [laughing] Dago Red?!<br>M&H: [lower and unintelligible] |
| Captain Waldowski, our dental officer! |  |
|  | W: Painless Pole! Better known as Painless. |
| This is Captain Black our anesthesiologist. | Pole! [simultaneous with M: Forrest? Hi.]<br>W: [to D] Painless Pole!<br>W: I'm a dentist here!<br>B: I'm John Black. I'll be passing<br>gas for you. [simultaneous with W: Duke?!<br>Welcome.] |

Even so, some fragments are intelligible, and most lines are effortfully accessible upon repeated screening, again creating room for a claimable "something more" beyond the immediate experiential "something more" of realistic calamity. With the characters that Blake has introduced now arrayed in an arc across the foreground, the previously named Bandini also moves to the foreground, filling what was an empty space in the middle of the frame. Bandini's reintroduction is treated with less clarity than the other officers' introductions—he introduces himself from offscreen after a cut to Blake. Even so, comprehension is hardly impeded by displacing the voice from the visual track, and other than Bandini's self-introduction, the cut back to Blake has no other truly foregrounded dialogue. The shot of Blake emphasizes his benign lack of true control over the behavior of the men, as he smiles and looks from side to side, intermittently obscured by the backlit silhouetted figures of his men in the foreground. Sonic chaos is again used as a background against which to highlight a key character trait.

Moreover, at a moment when genre convention and realism would aim only for chaos, Altman and his collaborators manage to establish key premises for a narrative chain that will have its blasphemous payoff in the film's "Last Supper" sequence. The film cuts back one final time to the shot of the men, with Murrhardt now seated in the lower right of the frame (Figure 3.2). Of the six men in the frame, all but Hawkeye deliver some dialogue during the shot, with at least three speaking at once. Superficially, this seems like the embodiment of comic chaos, but Altman again manages to have his chaos and defeat it too. Mulcahy is given the place and face of prominence as well as the voice of prominence in the shot. His dialogue is the loudest in the mix, while his brightly lit face is framed in the prime compositional location of the

Figure 3.2 *M\*A\*S\*H*

upper right intersection of the horizontal and vertical "rule of thirds" lines. Mulcahy, speaking to Duke and Hawkeye (who both ignore him), makes the following offer, "If ah, if you boys have any problems. Um, my um my tent is right—I was saying if you boys have any problems my tent is right there." This sets up the motivic comic treatment of Mulcahy as an inconsequential, if well-intentioned, presence (in contrast to the pompous religiosity of the as yet unseen Frank Burns). The sound design underscores this, placing Mulcahy's voice against the other men's talk. So, too, does the visual track, which cuts away to Blake, yelling loudly for Radar as Mulcahy tries to complete his offer. This dismissal is chaotic and comic but also establishes a key premise for the third act episode in which Waldowski will seek help with his erectile dysfunction from the bewildered Mulcahy, who will then turn to Hawkeye, who in turn convinces Waldowsky to commit "suicide" at a recreation of da Vinci's "Last Supper" after which he will be "resurrected" by the surprise sexual ministrations of Lieutenant Dish.

Blake's call for Radar initiates what is essentially a reprise of the comic bit that this analysis of *M*A*S*H*'s approach to overlapping dialogue and sound design began with. Once again, Radar anticipates Blake's instructions, with Radar here introducing himself and informing Hawkeye and Duke that they will be staying in Major Burns's tent and that he'll change the tags on the stolen jeep, all a half-second before Blake delivers his instructions. Radar's dialogue is narratively important because it provides the hook into the next scene—the trio's arrival at Burns's tent. Interestingly, there is less alternation than in the earlier scene, with Radar delivering his lines in a steadier, rapid-fire manner. But even with the added element of the off-screen officers' dialogue as a part of the mix, narrative clarity is maintained through raising the volume of Radar's dialogue and lowering the volume of Blake's. Although Blake is still intelligible and accessible, though only with effort, Radar's voice is clearly dominant and easy to follow. Indeed, Radar's dominant intelligibility underwrites the exclamation point put on the joke. Radar tells Duke and Hawkeye not to "worry about the jeep. I'll change the numbers," and then walks offscreen left. Blake, ever oblivious, calls after him, "Oh, and change the numbers on that jeep."

The sound design of this four-minute scene can fairly be characterized as dense, but it is far from the chaotic sonic haze or radically democratic forum assumed by most critics. Indeed, Altman and company manage to deliver the name of every male character in this scene at least twice without producing the feeling that the audience is being subjected to the kind of hackneyed exposition dump common to the set-up portions of Hollywood films. Altman, then, simultaneously fulfills and elaborates around the conventional aims of classical Hollywood. The careful design here serves the narrative and articulates a brand of sonic realism. It establishes and enhances the expected comedic elements of the film's genre while also permitting Altman to overlay a narrational voice that at times overtly ironizes his subjects. By carefully managing audibility, sourceability, and intelligibility through alternation and the manipulation of sound levels, and by coordinating the sound design with visual design, Altman and his collaborators innovate—expanding the resources and range and arguably augmenting the appeal of Hollywood storytelling.

## Interruptions, Innovations, and Intelligibility

It is reasonable to question whether the sound design of *M*A*S*H*, Altman's first major feature, and a film made on a 20th Century Fox studio lot, should be understood as setting a precedent for sound practices in the rest of Altman's early 1970s films, shot on location and largely outside direct studio control. Several of these films do not employ nearly the same degree of overlapping dialogue, instead substituting other sound elements in order to create a dense sonic mix. Moreover, *M*A*S*H* does not employ the much-discussed Lions Gate 8-Track Sound System. This system is often taken to be integral to Altman's sound signature, although it is used by only the final two of Altman's eight films during this period—*California Split* and *Nashville*. The coordinated trajectories of Altman's sound technologies and sound practices in relation to overlapping dialogue deserve attention. Rather than understanding technological advances as liberating Altman to finally liberate the soundtrack, we can see a relatively stable set of elaborative principles and practices guiding Altman and his team in the development and use of this technology.

The 8-Track advancement is often understood as working hand-in-hand with Altman's use of wireless radio microphones, specifically body mikes. However, the story of Altman's use of body mikes is muddled in the literature. It is sometimes assumed that Altman used them exclusively in all of his early 1970s films, but this is not the case. Self, for instance, follows sound scholar Rick Altman's observation that wireless microphones "pick up speech . . . *before* it is projected," and "can acquire spatial properties," to claim that Altman employed the technology on *M*A*S*H* in order to "distance the viewer from the three-dimensional wholeness of the narrative space and its personae."[27] The functional claim here will be addressed shortly, but more fundamentally, there is little evidence to suggest that *M*A*S*H* makes exclusive use of wireless body microphones as opposed to microphones (wired or wireless) concealed on the set and boom microphones. An examination of the features and production of the film that followed *M*A*S*H*, *Brewster McCloud*, suggests that Altman's use of the technique was less consistent and that his aims were more contingent. These aims were organized in part around practice-oriented preferences for production sound, and Altman's strategies were more considerate of convention than the standard account suggests.

Like M*A*S*H, Brewster McCloud's soundtrack features instances of complex layering, although it offers far fewer instances of overlapping diegetic dialogue. Where M*A*S*H seems to have generated its dialogue effects through a combination of on-set direction and postproduction manipulation, Brewster McCloud's equally interesting soundtrack relies far more on the latter—the juxtapositions and layering created by the ornithologist's voice-over serve as the prime example. Several factors might explain the difference in approach. Perhaps most fundamentally, the films' genres, narrative structures, and diegetic worlds differ. Chaos reigns in M*A*S*H, which takes place within an army encampment where surgeons and nurses work in close quarters. On the other hand, the parallel protagonist structure of Brewster McCloud has as one of its foci the film's titular loner—a decision that limits affordances for overlapping dialogue. The other protagonist, though, is out-of-town detective Frank Shaft, who must reluctantly coordinate an investigation with local authorities, and here Altman does seem ready to exploit the possibilities for overlapping dialogue. One of the parodic strategies employed in Shaft's narrative involves the interfering locals preventing him from being the sort of lone wolf police detective celebrated in the police dramas of the period. Altman thus surrounds Shaft with competing voices—the twin pairings of Captain Crandall and officer Hines, and Senator Weeks and his aide, Bernard, as well as the dim-witted officer Johnson who acts as Shaft's assistant. But even with the situational affordances provided by this strategy, the quality of the overlapping dialogue here seems different from M*A*S*H. More of the overlap is unintelligible, and the sense of general chaos is less extreme.

A second key factor to consider in explaining the differences between the two films has more to do with the pragmatics of filmmaking—a shift in the production context, in terms of both personnel and locale. Whereas M*A*S*H was filmed on a studio lot, Brewster McCloud was filmed on location in Houston. C. Kirk McClelland, a film student at the University of Southern California, was permitted to observe the film's production, and his book, On Making a Movie: Brewster McCloud, includes useful details about the sound recording on what seems to have been a fairly troubled shoot. According to McClelland, Doyle Hodges served as the sound mixer while Bob Kaplan "handle[d] the boom-mike," which McClelland notes was, "the primary mike in most every shot."[28] McClelland frequently describes the two men as having exceptional trouble with location sounds, as well as camera sounds. These problems culminated in at least one on-set confrontation between Altman and Kaplan. McClelland reports that, after a rehearsal for the scene in which Brewster does pull-ups while an admiring Hope masturbates to orgasm under a comforter:

> Altman is satisfied, commenting that the bit is "funnier than hell." Then Bob Kaplan says, "It's shitty for sound though." This seems to have been the wrong thing to say. Altman starts in on him saying, "God damn it, Kaplan—you're always saying that the shot is shitty for sound. You're a harbinger of bad news. Jesus, just do the best you can." Kaplan comes back with, "It's hard to do your best when you're not in the studio." Altman says, tensely, "Well, we're *not* in the studio. We never have been and you knew that we wouldn't be when we started. Just do the best you can."[29]

This exchange suggests both a trade-off of Altman's practice-oriented preference for location shooting—recording polished sound is difficult—as well as Altman's attitude toward what we might call the polished, studio film. That is, he is willing to accept imperfect audio or visual elements in exchange for the freedom of the location shoot and the additional creative opportunities enabled by his shooting method. We might make a useful distinction, then, between Altman as a producer of conventionally "polished" films, which he was not, and Altman as a polished or highly competent filmmaker, which he seems to have been. His priorities and habits, shaped largely during his time as an industrial filmmaker (see chapter 5), diverge from those of filmmakers accustomed to the Hollywood studio model of filmmaking.

McClelland's reporting also makes it clear that the filmmakers used a mixture of approaches to on-set recording, with the boom as the "primary mike in most every shot." Describing the recording of a scene in which Brewster pushes the wheelchair bound misanthrope Wright through one of his rest-homes, McClelland writes that Hodges, "used three mikes. Kaplan placed two mikes around the room and then held the boom-mike over Wright and Brewster as they travelled. [Kaplan] says that all of the microphones are unidirectional . . . and that he has a '4 pot' system under his Nagra IV recorder which he uses to control the levels of each mike."[30] In other situations, often crowd scenes with major characters placed in the middle, lavalier mikes were used, including a party scene in which Weeks and his assistant Bernard move through the party, mingling with guests.[31] Lavalier, or body, mikes were also used for a discarded scene in which Shaft arrives at a university laboratory but must first pass through a group of student protestors.[32]

Interestingly, though, the scenes with overlapping dialogue may not have been shot using lavalier mikes. For instance, in a portion of the manuscript not included in the published book, McClelland reports that Kaplan is often scapegoated for delays in shooting since he has to find exactly the right place for his boom. The example he offers is a scene that takes place in a Houston police lab where a bird shit sample is tested, and this scene is rife with overlapping dialogue. McClelland describes the scene as "typical of [Altman's] genius for incorporating about twelve different bits into one shot while still supplying information relevant to the film"—a nice summary of Altman's elaborative approach. McClelland offers the following account of the scene's shooting and recording:

> Since there are a lot of bodies in this shot and since there is a low ceiling, Mr. Kaplan is doing his usual bull in a china shop routine. His mike makes contact with virtually everything that is hanging down. He looks at me and says, "You have to be crazy to be a booman [sic]" . . . Personally, I think his trouble began about two and a half weeks ago when he started being extremely self-conscious about causing delays and holdups. Pearl [the script girl] calls him the scapegoat because everyone blames holdups on him. When Mr. Kaplan is in the process of finding the best way to record sound (and this is his trouble), the entire set is quiet. It is like walking on a tightrope with every eye in the place watching and waiting to see if you fall.[33]

Several inferences can be drawn from this account. The first is that Kaplan is not the best boom operator for location shooting—that his competencies do not match up with Altman's practical demands, and that this may have been a factor limiting the use of overlapping dialogue in the film. The second is that, in general, location recording of the kind of multiple competing sound sources that Altman employs in several of his films is difficult to accomplish with a boom. Altman's experience on *Brewster McCloud*, then, may have hastened his move away from the boom and toward greater use of lavalier microphones.

A third implication of McClelland's account is less about practice and more about the kinds of conclusions critics and scholars might fairly draw about the implications of lavalier recording for the film's audience. Claims for a distancing effect like Self's are based on assumptions not just about the kinds of technology used but about the different affordances of the particular technologies. It seems likely that Altman's films were recorded with a mixture of devices. Yet, there seems to be no review or public comment criticizing Altman's films for sound that oscillates distractingly from three-dimensional wholeness to distancing flatness. Surely sophisticated scholars and critics of the Hollywood Renaissance era would be predisposed to favor the identification of distancing effects and keen to note the intensified distancing effect likely to result from such swings? But no one appears to have noticed these shifts, or to care if they did, save perhaps for recording technicians and sound mixers. Instead, it seems likely that the antiperspectival effect of Altman's use of lavalier microphones is overstated. The entire question of precise sound perspective seems, in many cases, to be an interesting preoccupation of sound specialists that is then used as grounds for overreaching exegesis in search of the radical disruption of "illusionist" classical practices. But substituting a special class of auditors, focused on certain qualities of sound, for an average auditor watching a film is likely to yield flawed conclusions.[34]

Indeed, Tomlinson Holman, in his respected manual *Sound for Film and Television*, notes that "professionals and laymen differ on their level of perception and the annoyance experience from mismatches" between "the position of a sound source visually and aurally."[35] Holman's own writing on body mikes embodies the unresolved tension between specialist and nonspecialist auditors when he notes that even poorly placed booms "can still beat lavaliere [*sic*] microphones."[36] Why is this? Holman explains, "there is nothing natural whatsoever about the perspective reproduced by this arrangement. That is, if the performer turns away from the camera, his or her voice will not change quality in a way that we associate with people turning away from us and the sound will be very disembodied from the picture." Of course, Holman acknowledges, "many real-life television series depend on wireless microphones to limit the size of the crew to get usable sound from unscripted situations. It must be said here that the niceties of matching perspective between camera and sound to ensure verisimilitude give way to practical conditions of just getting any usable 'clear' sound."[37]

My guess is that the layperson's response to Holman's careful observations about differences in sound perspective is likely to be a resounding, "huh?" It may seem slightly strange to audiences that they can clearly hear a speaker turned away from the camera, but in the context of film, a representational medium where much of sound perspective does not exactly replicate the real world, and where the audience expects to hear comprehensible dialogue, a distanced response of "that's very disembodied" seems unlikely. The idea that this sort of response was a primary aim of Altman's, rather than a minor risk or "imperfection" he was willing to tolerate, seems even less plausible. It is much more likely that Altman, like the producers of unscripted television, was concerned with acquiring production dialogue that was usable for his elaborative purposes, that could be integrated into his films and manipulated for a variety of effects alongside and in coordination with a given film's narrative system. Altman wanted multiple voices, and he wanted them recorded on-set, but he also wanted discretion over what voices to include, highlight, and make intelligible.

The account provided to *American Cinematographer* by James E Webb Jr., who, beginning with *California Split*, mixed Altman's sound with the Lions Gate 8-Track Sound System, supports this understanding of Altman's sound strategies. According to Webb, "Multi-track recording for location film sound came about because of Robert Altman's desire to have more freedom in shooting style on the pictures that he makes." The immediate impetus for this technological innovation, according to Webb, was that Altman, "encountered certain frustrating restrictions in the area of sound during the filming of *McCabe & Mrs. Miller*." We will tend to *McCabe & Mrs. Miller* shortly, but it is worth noting that the immediate motivation cited by Webb is the liberation of the production team rather than the auditor.

In the same *American Cinematographer* article, Webb enumerates Altman's goals:

> Mr. Altman wanted to put together a sound system that would allow: (1) improvisation of dialogue during the scene, (2) the overlapping of dialogue as it naturally occurs in real conversation, (3) the ability to record all off-screen dialogue, and (4) the capability to record certain sound effects and "sub-conversations" in the scene that were normally lost in the effort to record the main dialogue.[38]

Combined, these goals paint a picture of a filmmaker inarguably concerned with certain kinds of naturalism—the replication of real conversational and perceptual practice and the notion of a potentially, though not necessarily, excessive soundtrack replete with intelligible conversations, both on- and off-screen, indicating a world extending beyond narratively central figures. Viewed in this light, we can understand Altman's demand for technological innovation as a recognition of Bazin's maxim that, "realism in art can only be achieved in one way—through artifice."[39] But as the earlier examination of Altman's use of overlapping dialogue in *M\*A\*S\*H* revealed, Altman's functional aims are multifaceted. Even if we were to take the naturalist potential of Altman's approach to overlapping dialogue as fundamentally liberating, which I would hesitate to do, its actual employment exceeds and complicates these mimetic affordances.

Additionally, underlying any goals, mimetic or otherwise, are key pragmatic principles. Perhaps the most important principle at play here is Altman's practice-oriented preference for the spontaneity of "on-set filmmaking," in terms of both directorial decisions and the actors' performances, over postproduction work. Certainly, part of Altman's success at maintaining a high degree of autonomy was based on his ability to keep his budgets down. But it is also true that Altman's sometime editor and friend Lou Lombardo has suggested that Altman just did not enjoy the experience of postproduction sound work. As was discussed earlier, it seems that much of what motivated Altman as a filmmaker was the creative work of production, the daily planning and problem-solving sessions, as well as the community experience of the evening dailies. As we will see in chapter 5, these aspects of his work have been important to him at least as far back as (and perhaps because of) his days working on location as an industrial filmmaker. The imperative to record live off-screen sound when it is easily recorded and added in post seems particularly indebted to Altman's belief in the creative potential of on-set filmmaking. So, in addition to functional motivations, Altman likely had distinguishable pragmatic and practice-oriented motivations for directing Webb to refine his sound recording capabilities. Indeed, Altman's use of overlapping dialogue in this period makes it clear that it is through this sort of complex matrix of differentiable types of goals that authorial decision-making and problem-solving is processed and that creative work is produced.

By Webb's account, *McCabe & Mrs. Miller* catalyzed innovation of the Lions Gate system, and the film did present some distinctive challenges. Working through these challenges likely motivated Altman and his team to develop more efficient solutions. *McCabe & Mrs. Miller*'s preview screening was marred by flawed sound reproduction, and the corrected version of the film still exhibits a lack of easy intelligibility in many of the backgrounded and middlegrounded tracks. This was likely an unintended result. According to Lombardo, the film's editor, Altman knew throughout production that the film's sound was not up to the standards set by *M\*A\*S\*H*. Lombardo, while visiting the set, was asked by Altman to provide his view on *McCabe*'s production. Lombardo gave him his unvarnished perspective:

> The sound was fucked, but he never changed it. I think he accomplished what he wanted to do with sound in *M\*A\*S\*H*—where it was audible but it was overlapped. He did it well. But on *McCabe*, it was recorded in there—a dirty track, a muddy track. It was like trying to get an out-of-focus picture in focus. I think [it was] because he was just tired and wet and cold, a lot of things, and Bob doesn't like to do looping and dubbing.[40]

Lombardo's account suggests that Altman's practice-oriented goals and preferences—his desire for location shooting, his aversion to looping—may have overridden the quality-oriented goals of providing a sound mix with polished clarity.

The lack of clarity in *McCabe & Mrs. Miller* seems attributable in part to problems with phasing, which occurs when multiple microphones are used to record a sequence. Holman describes the cause and effect of phasing as follows:

> if the source is not precisely centered between two microphones with overlapping pickup, then the sound will arrive at one microphone before the other. In this case, when the electrical output of the microphones is summed there will be constructive and destructive interference effects, leading alternately to peaks and dips in the frequency response of the sum. This may sound as though the source is being recorded through a barrel.[41]

Many of the sequences in *McCabe & Mrs. Miller* display this quality, which may have been what Lombardo meant by a "dirty" track. Jay Beck offers an alternative or complementary explanation for the murky sound: "Recording the dialogue with a large level of reverberation—something that was impossible to avoid because *McCabe*'s enclosed wooden sets lacked soundproofing—made it difficult to overlay the audio tracks in postproduction without the backgrounds adding up and partially obscuring the words."[42] Some critics viewed the muddy sound as a plus, and Altman was unrepentant. In an interview, he stated, "I could go back and show you some of Howard Hawks's early pictures and you'd find exactly the same effect. Somebody picked up on it in my films after *McCabe* because it irritated a lot of people; yet I've got a file of reviews and letters saying the sound track was the best thing in the picture."[43] The lack of polished clarity in the film's dialogue may have been less distracting and more seemingly coherent due to *McCabe & Mrs. Miller*'s complementary muddy setting and fuzzy visuals. Even so, stories abound about Warren Beatty's rudely expressed displeasure with the film's sound and the filmmakers' last-minute scramble to make corrections.[44]

Altman's experience with *McCabe* can be understood as an extreme, imperfect test of the theory of mind that likely shaped his approach to the problems of clarity and "bad" sound. Altman has said, "I think you have to train an audience that they don't have to hear everything. We go through life doing that. You look at somebody's face, you know what they're going to say. It's just a courtesy to let them finish."[45] This undermines claims that, for Altman, incomplete or effortful intelligibility are employed in service of narrative subversion. Indeed, Altman seems to feel that partial intelligibility can be managed without narrative loss. Additionally, Altman's idea of "training an audience" as expressed here does not seem to be about teaching the audience that they need to effortfully engage or even to be about teaching audiences how to listen to his films per se. Rather, it is concerned with training audience members to relax when they feel the anxiety of a perceived lack of clarity. They should relax, it seems, not necessarily because the narrative is unimportant but because they can comprehend the narrative as long as they make the natural inferences that they do in everyday conversational exchanges. In theory, minimizing the amount of dialogue necessary for narrative clarity would both sanction less-intelligible naturalistic dialogue and make room for dialogue aimed at other functions.

This seemingly more naturalistic, laid-back philosophy works in opposition to conventional Hollywood technique but not necessarily in opposition to Hollywood's primary storytelling aims, and it is far less radical than the rejectionist agenda often attributed to Altman.[46] It does, to some extent, make clarity less immediate, less easy, and possibly a little less passively immersive (though this effect of Hollywood cinema is often overstated). It would seem to depend, then, on a quick-thinking and open-minded audience. Indeed, Altman's rhetoric would appeal to the self-regard of the kind of hip, educated audience Hollywood temporarily targeted during the early 1970s. But Altman and his team clearly employ and develop strategies and technologies to ensure narrative comprehension. It also seems certain that the prescribed relaxed attitude does not necessarily extend to the entirety of Altman's production team. The file of approving letters and reviews for *McCabe* may have reassured Altman, but his experience making the film also gave him the impetus to collaborate to improve recording and mixing technology. While Altman's audience was encouraged to relax, and Altman's performers were perhaps given expanded, though still circumscribed, room for on-set improvisation (see chapter 4), Altman's team of mixers and recordists were pushed to innovate. The implementation of the resultant "technologies of artifice" required skilled craftsmanship and the development of new techniques to ensure narratively salient dialogue would still be highlighted amid the multifunctional elaborative space Altman's philosophy made theoretically possible. That this philosophy existed prior to the development of the Lions Gate 8-Track System is significant to assessing Altman's use of overlapping dialogue during the period. It helps refine our understanding of Altman's principles and explains the functional consistencies that underlay a period in which innovation removed technological constraints on the scope of these aims and the capacity for effectively achieving them.

Indeed, despite the existing technological challenges, *McCabe & Mrs. Miller* has a characteristically dense sound mix that remains consistent with Hollywood's storytelling imperatives. Take, for instance, the second sequence of the film, as McCabe first arrives at Sheehan's bar and moves through its interior and out the back door before returning to set up a poker table ⊚ (see the companion website for a video clip). The sound mix is filled with voices that are largely unintelligible, though they are, in hindsight, sourceable as various minor characters. Beck, following Kolker, has claimed that the off-screen status of many of the speakers results in "a liberating effect in the film," that "shift[s] the audience's attention away from the primary dialogue to the conversations among the secondary characters."[47] This shift in focus, though, is not the result of liberation but is directed through the coordination and manipulation of image and sound, with several key voices sequentially highlighted by the sound mix:

PATRON: [greeting McCabe] Evenin'.

SHEEHAN: [praying; after an eyeline match from McCabe] Holy mother of God keep me pure in thought word and deed.

PATRON 2: [offscreen] Laura what's for dinner?

MCCABE: [to drunk who offers his seat] (unintelligible) sit down.

PATRON 2: [offscreen] Laura!

MCCABE: Say, uh, that's the back door ain't it?

SMALLEY: Yeah.

SHEEHAN: [calling after McCabe] I . . . I was about to put up a bottle on the house.

PATRON 3: [offscreen] That'll be the day.

BARTENDER: Is he wearing a gun?

PATRON 4: [offscreen] sure didn't stay very long.

PATRON 5: [offscreen and as we see McCabe searching through his horse's pack] he ain't going nowhere. (unintelligible) out of his pack.

PATRON 6: [face offscreen] Hey, you know what kind of gun that was? That was a Swedish gun. Swedish.

SHEEHAN: Get a rag.

MAN AT BAR: So cheap he squeezes out the bar rag.

PATRON 7: [offscreen] . . . wearin' a gun . . .

PATRON 1: Wet enough for ya mister? Starts rainin' up here doesn't know when to stop.

MCCABE: Yeah . . . [as man helps put tablecloth on poker table] Hiya.

VARIOUS PATRONS: [as they gather around table] money . . . money . . . money . . .

This is actually a fairly focused, if linguistically fragmentary, soundscape. The one truly digressive offscreen line is a man's request to be informed about what will be served for dinner. Other than that, the intelligible dialogue establishes key premises that will be mobilized by the narrative. Four lines cumulatively characterize Sheehan as the cheap, dishonest, and hypocritical proprietor of the establishment. The others all revolve around the film's protagonist, who creates the disturbance in the status quo that kicks off the narrative line. Here, the intelligible dialogue focuses the audience on McCabe's traits and purpose by presenting greetings and speculation about McCabe's activity and his gun—a point of attention that will become particularly salient later in the film. Moreover, the majority of the sequence and its use of sound is organized around eyeline matches, beginning with McCabe looking offscreen at Sheehan and the patrons, continuing as McCabe moves through the bar and out the back door, and extending through Sheehan and his patrons' looks offscreen toward McCabe—the object of the majority of their comments. What is once again on display here is a distinct combination of realism and narrative work in which overlapping dialogue provides a naturalist complement to minimalized but effective set-up of character and situation. Beck acknowledges that "the background conversations present a strong sense of spatial verisimilitude and help establish the saloon and town," but this is only a partial description of what Altman and his collaborators accomplish.[48]

Many of the voices in this sequence do seem to have that "barrel" quality that Holman warns of, and perhaps different recording technology would have given Altman and his team the ability to capture more voices that met Hollywood's standards of technical clarity and quality. The Lions Gate 8-Track System developed for use on *California Split* helped solve this problem. The system augmented the ability of Altman and his team to maintain the separation of sounds such that they could manipulate levels and direct audience attention. In *California Split* it does seem as though the number of voices on the soundtrack has, in places, increased from earlier films, and that these voices are more intelligible. It is still apt to describe them as effortfully available, but they demand less effort and are more available. In chapter 1, I discussed how Altman relies on what Buckland terms multizone staging to generate digressive moments. He sets up and cuts between distinct subspaces within a larger scenic space in which separate groups of characters interact, often in ways that do not obviously develop the narrative chain of cause and effect. Often, but not always, key to this technique is Altman's use of what might be called multizone sound, in which separate sets of characters audibly interact, often simultaneously. Here, we might recall Webb's stated third and fourth Altmanian goals: "(3) the ability to record all off-screen dialogue, and (4) the capability to record certain sound effects and 'sub-conversations' in the scene that were normally lost in the effort to record the main dialogue." We have already seen an example of multizone staging in the sequence from *M\*A\*S\*H* analyzed earlier. While there were multiple zones of sound in that sequence—Hawkeye and Duke outside the tent, the nurses, and Colonel Blake—the filmmakers typically manipulated the levels in coordination with mobile framing to make the sound of the onscreen characters audible and intelligible and to make the voices of the offscreen characters largely inaudible or unintelligible, with limited but significant exceptions.

The second sequence in *California Split*, in which Bill and Charlie coincidentally meet in a bar, offers another key example of this kind of sound, but it presents an important variation ⊛ (see the companion website for a video clip). Multiple zones overlap, remaining simultaneously audible *and* largely, if effortfully, intelligible. The opening of this sequence is particularly revealing. It consists of one forty-three-second long-take. The shot begins with a pan left, following the movement of a bartender. The bartender moves behind the bar, passing behind two men sitting with their backs to the camera, although one has his head turned in profile. The bartender then asks Bill, whom the pan reveals, if he would like another beer. Once Bill is framed screen left the pan stops (Figure 3.3), and the camera zooms out, eventually displaying two women talking in the left foreground, one of whom is a nude dancer sitting, bottomless, on top of a piano. When the two women, gradually revealed to be mother and daughter, are framed in medium shot the camera pans left again, shifting the man in profile at the bar partly offscreen right. The zoom out continues until the bottom of the bottomless woman's buttocks is level with the lower frame line. The final framing has Bill in long shot centered in the background, looking at the two women speaking in the foreground left (Figure 3.4).

Absent sound, we might think that there are two key zones in the shot, the first with one of our protagonists at the bar, and the second occupied by the two foregrounded women. But through the soundtrack Altman's team has layered in a third significant zone—that of the two men at the bar. In spite of these multiple sound zones, though, the sequence does not become incoherent, and it certainly does not have the feeling of calamity common to overlapping dialogue in classical Hollywood cinema. Table 3.5 helps to reveal why this is the case, breaking down the opening of this sequence in a way that represents the temporal aspect of the dialogue delivery. As we saw with the treatment of the overlap between Radar and Colonel Blake at the beginning of *M\*A\*S\*H*, there is significant temporal design to the treatment of the multiple voices. Whereas Radar and Blake's voices were carefully alternated to ensure enough cues were given to maintain clarity, here the design is focused on introducing the multiple voices in a phased manner. First, we hear the offscreen voice of the mother. Then, we hear the bartender asking Bill about a beer, after which we get the final significant component—the conversation between the two men at the bar. This phasing in of multiply-zoned sound

**Figure 3.3** *California Split*

**Figure 3.4** *California Split*

design allows key lines in the dialogue to be understood and makes it easier to distinguish between zones.

Additionally, there is some manipulation in the relative volumes of the conversations, although it is less significant than that observed in the parallel scene in *M\*A\*S\*H*. Intelligibility is largely maintained, but there is some movement between foreground and middleground sound, coordinated with prominence in the frame. As a result, the conversation between the men becomes less intelligible as the zoom out reveals more of the mother and daughter. With the final pan left the men are marginalized, and their conversation becomes only intermittently intelligible, to the point that the substance of the conversation is lost. The fact that Bill's conversation with the bartender is so limited also helps moderate the complexity here.

Altman provides just enough sound to mark out the zones for audience attention, but not so much as to make it a truly competitive sonic space. The

**Table 3.5** Overlapping Dialogue in the Bar

| Image Track [and Other Voices] | Mother and Daughter | Men | Bill and Bartender |
|---|---|---|---|
| Pan left | Mother: Didn't have enough money behind me. Goddamn it I would have beat their ass! | | |
| [Woman: Well, I don't.] | | | |
| | | | Bartender: Sir, would you like another beer? |
| | | Man 1: See, I . . . I bet it on Notre Dame because I kind of felt | |
| Pan stops. Zoom out. | Mother: There's no question I can beat that [unintelligible] game. | Notre Dame was gonna pull it off, because they beat UCLA before when they had so many games going straight. | Bill: No. Bill: Yeah. |
| | Mother: You know I'm opposite [unintelligible] player. Baby, this particular game is duck soup. | And uh, you know it's similar to, to the Miami Dolphins. I mean the fact that they won seventeen games straight last year . . . | |
| | Oh come on I need that goddamn miserable game. Don't make me beg | And, uh, this year they still have a [unintelligible] | |
| Mother's face visible. [Daughter: Mother keep your voice down please.] | for a stinking thirty dollars! Daughter: Momma please. | [unintelligible] [unintelligible] . . . coupla people . . . [unintelligible] Man 2: You can't [unintelligible] You just told me that | Bartender: take it outta, six. |
| Pan left | Mother: You know, your attitude just pisses me off sometimes button nose. | [unintelligible] | |

audience is left with the impression of three conversations but really has just two conversations to choose from. Even then, the image track and some manipulation in the levels of each conversation work to guide audience attention. The fact that the protagonist stares at the women in the foreground, that their dialogue is foregrounded, and that one of the women is bottomless all work to encourage the audience to tend to the mother/daughter duo. Again, we have some dialogue (between the men at the bar) that is effortfully available, if only partially.

Overall, the dialogue does not radically disrupt the audience's narrative expectations, but it does give the flavor of such a digression. It offers a gesture toward intensified mimesis by mobilizing ambient dialogue but does so in a way that advances central themes and underwrites character. Bill is a mopey gambler, depressed and uncertain, and in the bar he is listening to two gambling addicts' rationalizing accounts of failure. The foregrounded dialogue between the mother and daughter provides a vignette that is not causally related to Bill and Charlie's narrative action, but it does inform the audience's perspective.[49] The first of the situation's ironic reversals, with a mother asking her child for money, reinforces the second irony, one that works both with and against arguably misogynist stereotyping, that a gambling addict can be more pathetic than a stripper. This, in turn, provides a context from which to evaluate Bill and Charlie's gambling. The use of sound here recalls and participates in the sort of overt interpretive priming discussed in chapter 1 with regard to Altman's authorially expressive narrational strategies.

One can certainly say that the Lions Gate 8-Track System makes more dialogue intelligible with difficulty, an effect we might call effortful availability, rather than the more unintelligible mix of overlapping dialogue that crops up in several scenes in *McCabe & Mrs. Miller*. But if we ask what that effort yields, the function of the dialogue is neither entirely unconventional nor wholly digressive. What does tend to be somewhat exceptional, though, is the process of listening, the effort Altman requires for those elaborative rewards, even if the level of difficulty is often overstated. On the whole, Altman continues his larger strategy of using complex sound design to integrate his elaborative aims with conventional storytelling demands, rather than employing strictly conventional storytelling devices. On *California Split*, the Lions Gate 8-Track System works to makes the rewards both more fulsome and more available, providing extra incentive to auditors and critics to give in to Altman's unconventional storytelling practice.

## *Nashville*: Oppositional Analysis and the Parthenon Paradox

*Nashville*, Altman's follow-up to *California Split*, with its advertised cast of twenty-four major characters and its elaborate use of the Lions Gate 8-Track System, has been crucial to accounts of how the filmmaker's approach to sound was pushed further and further away from the aims and techniques associated with classical Hollywood practice. Rick Altman has produced the canonical scholarly article on the film's sound, in which he argues that Robert Altman actually "model[ed]" his twenty-four-character narrative:

> on the 24-track recording technology commonly used within the music industry.... Altman's metaphor for cinema creation is thus based neither in film direction nor in cinematography, but on the process of mixing sound. Created as an ode to country music for the American bicentennial, Nashville is also a tribute to the twenty-four track sound technology that dominates the music industry.[50]

Rick Altman offers no concrete evidence for this hunch, nor does there seem to be any. Jan Stuart's *The Nashville Chronicles*, which provides a narrative of the script's development and the ballooning of characters from screenwriter Joan Tewkesbury's original eighteen to the eventual twenty-four, does not mention 24-track recording technology as an inspiration. And, in fact, Altman's team did not record any of the sequences in the film on 24-tracks. Even the musical numbers in the film were not recorded with 24-track technology. Instead, according to editor Sid Levin, the team used a 16-track recorder.[51] For the dramatic sequences, Altman's team used a Stevens portable 8-track recorder, with "one channel being reserved for a sync pulse."[52] According to Stuart's account, "If there were more than seven actors speaking in a scene, some crafty sharing was the order of the day. 'In the big scenes I had to talk into Keith's shoulder,' recalls Allan Nicholls." Furthermore, according to Stuart, "Not all of the sound [was] processed by body mikes. In the airport scene, for example, an old-fashioned overhead boom captured the Franklin High School Band and ambient noise while television reporter Bill Jenkins announced Barbara Jean's arrival into a live hand mike."[53]

The discrepancy and confusion between practice and interpretation in some ways emblematizes misunderstanding of Nashville's sound strategies. Critics have claimed big things for and found deep meanings in the sound design, but these often require overgeneralizing description of the film's employment of overlapping dialogue and interpretive heuristics that squeeze reflexive and symbolic significance out of multifunctional moment-by-moment design decisions. While I have described the sound practice in Robert Altman's early 1970s films as an elaboration rather than rejection of classical Hollywood practice, Rick Altman sets Nashville in diametric opposition to classical practice, which he characterizes as the "intermittent approach" to sound design. According to Rick Altman, this approach is "based on [a] narrative-oriented hierarchy," where "the highest rank among diegetic sounds is accorded to sounds that contribute to the elaboration of the narrative." It is intermittent because, "each of the separate sound components looks like a line drawing of Monument Valley," in which music and sound effects drop out to make room for narratively significant sound elements and where "Dialogue occurs irregularly, typically usurping all available volume when it does. Within any given dialogue passage, the same alternating strategy obtains, with each speaker studiedly keeping silent while another is speaking."[54]

I do not wish to dispute this account of the prototypical Hollywood soundscape. Where the account goes wrong, though, is in its characterization of Robert Altman's approach as standing, "in direct opposition" to Hollywood norms. As the article puts it:

> Altman's radio-miked inputs are often mixed in a non-hierarchical fashion, producing sound tracks that are complex, thick, multi-layered. . . . Altman refuses to accommodate one sound source to another. Far from reducing ambient sound to assure comprehension of dialogue, Altman often begins a second dialogue while the first continues, with both mixed at the same volume. . . . Instead of forcing all auditors into the same experience of the film, Altman's layering of multiple sound sources opens up the sound track to a variety of divergent hearings. Multiple screenings of a film like *Nashville* are unlikely to be repeatedly perceived in the same way. . . . Altman's sound mix thus replaces Hollywood's familiar intermittent sound editing patterns by alternation of attention on the part of the auditor.[55]

The agency, in Rick Altman's account, is placed in the hands of the listener, rather than the filmmaker who, he claims, "studiedly avoids hierarchy, charging individual auditors rather than the sound mix with choosing the sound actually heard."[56]

Rick Altman is not entirely wrong. Altman's soundtracks are accurately characterized as frequently thick and multilayered and, as such, extend choices to audience members—embedding diverse functions that are likely only available with effortful attention and/or repeated screenings. But the sound design of *Nashville* hardly lacks hierarchy, and the essay offers a sweeping overgeneralization of the film's sound design, claiming that its nonhierarchical design stretches "from beginning to end," while providing no close description or analysis to support such a claim. Nonetheless, Rick Altman places at the crux of his analysis of *Nashville*'s sound design the claim that the film's culminating scene at Nashville's Parthenon disappointingly betrays the liberated auditor, giving in to the oppressive demands of narratively determined hierarchization, resulting in what he terms "the Parthenon paradox."[57] The sense of paradox, I maintain, is generated less by the film than by the critical hyperextension of the politicized form-equals-function interpretive heuristic discussed earlier.

Accounts by those who worked on the film frequently emphasize the work done to hierarchize, to manipulate audience attention, often by coordinating sound and image. For instance, Stuart describes how *California Split* served as a "laboratory" to develop workable approaches to the new mixing system:

> Among the techniques that Webb would discover . . . was the "sound zoom," in which the sound volume adjusts to reflect the movement of the camera. "There were three desks in a room, and George Segal and Elliott Gould have to sell their insurance to raise quick cash. Segal is sitting at the last desk, [there's] a conversation going on at the second desk, and something going on in Spanish at the first desk. Three distinct things, so I miked each desk. Later on watching the dailies, I notice the camera starts at the first desk—that's the first track—the camera zooms to the second desk—the second track—and onto to [*sic*] George's conversation at the third. So I went back and literally did a 'sound zoom' at the same time and speed as the camera."[58]

The scene that Webb discusses here does not seem to have made it into the final cut of the film. However, this account of the "sound zoom," which manipulates the levels of the sound in coordination with the image, nicely tracks the shifts in levels and intelligibility described during the zoom out accompanying the long take at the bar in *California Split*, and it also conforms to the structured approach this chapter has described. In qualifiedly preserving options for the motivated auditor, the sound zoom is more open than the strictly intermittent approach Rick Altman ascribes to Hollywood. To that extent, it is best seen not as a replication of Hollywood sound design, but as a revision that accomplishes the goal of directing attention while allowing for the kinds of elaboration that have been discussed previously. In *Nashville*, part of that elaboration involves the multiplication of conversations—a carefully manipulated simulation of the "cocktail party effect" where auditors can choose, or at least feel they are choosing, between multiple available conversations.

According to Stuart's interview with Webb, the sound zoom approach and "related techniques" would also be used on *Nashville*, where:

> Altman would be able to shift the sound emphasis from one area of a room in which a number of conversations are occurring to another area. "We found out at the Picking Parlor in *Nashville*, where you have Henry Gibson talking at a table and then it goes over to Bob Doqui yelling across the room at Timothy Brown, that while you

can't isolate what everybody is saying (because there's always a leakage between mikes) what you can do is tip the balance of the scene one way or another."[59]

In fact, the Picking Parlor scene, which features a theoretically ideal situation for Altman's democratic auditory excess—seven key characters, multiple zones of character interaction, a musical performance, and a calamity—is actually subject to a great deal of careful sonic manipulation prior to the sound zoom that Wells describes. It begins with an exterior shot of the parlor, during which the sound of a bluegrass band, the Misty Mountain Boys, can be heard foregrounded in the mix. With the cut to the interior of the club, the music continues at an identical volume. The first interior shot pans right and zooms out to reveal the band, with Lady Pearl in the lower right of the frame standing next to the stage. The second shot pans right past a few patrons and zooms back to reveal Doqui's character, Wade. As the band's vocalist sings that he has "a cute little gal," Wade's voice can be heard saying, "Oh yeah, he has." Interestingly, Wade's voice is heard while Wade's face is largely in shadow—it is difficult to make out whether the line is live sound or was added in post. Additionally, once the pan is completed and Wade is more clearly visible it becomes evident that his lips are moving as he chats up the two women next to him while his dialogue is now largely inaudible. Altman's team seem to have momentarily highlighted a key character's voice by manipulating levels, and perhaps even by adding dialogue in postproduction. Rather than reflecting an interest in non-narrative conversation, the decision to highlight Wade's interjection primes the audience for more of the same—he will eventually cause a disturbance that empties out the club.

Two more sonic spaces are established visually with cuts to Haven Hamilton and the black country star Tommy Brown seated at one table and then to Bill and Mary seated at another table. Again, narratively significant dialogue is emphasized. As Bill and Mary argue with one another, their dialogue is foregrounded, and the level of the band is brought down slightly in the mix. As the last of the scene's major characters, Kenny, arrives, the film cuts to him by the entrance, where Lady Pearl instructs him to sit down. Her dialogue is middlegrounded now, lower than the music, but still easily accessible. This is partly because as the visual track shifts its focus to Pearl and Kenny the musical number moves into a breakdown segment, eliminating the song lyrics as a possible competitor for the audience's auditory attention. As Kenny is seated next to Bill and Mary he apologizes to the pair, and the exchange is slightly lower in volume than was previously the case. Mary turns to whisper to Bill that Kenny looks like Howdy Doody, and the dialogue plays out at the same level as Kenny's remarks to the table. Kenny, though, does not seem to hear it—clearly, strict realism is not a major goal of the sound design. Instead, in the first segment of this sequence we have highly conventional sound design, with the volume of the diegetic music lowered to make space for the conversation of major characters. What is unconventional here is not the use of sound per se, but the multiply focused narrative situation that Altman has tasked himself and his collaborators with portraying in a way that ensures narrative clarity while conveying a sense of naturalism.

When the band finishes its performance and Lady Pearl introduces Tommy Brown to the crowd, Wade, apparently motivated by Brown's assimilationist persona, loudly interjects. Lady Pearl attempts to intervene while Hamilton tends to Brown's departure, and Webb's sound zoom transitions between the pairs along with the image track, crafting a qualified clarity within situational chaos and the general din of unintelligible crowd noises. Importantly, this is not a sonic stab at observational realism, and the audience is not tasked with mixing nonhierarchized sounds, even if they are free to effortfully "remix" the soundscape by tending to available but de-emphasized sounds. Instead, we have a highly constructed soundtrack, partly produced in postproduction, with a sound zoom providing clarifying guidance even at the most calamitous moment in the scene. This is not to say that the audience is left with the remembered experience of clarity. Indeed, leaving an impression of nonhierarchized calamity like the one reflected in Rick Altman's claim can be taken as a marker of success for Altman and his collaborators' large and small-scale strategies. *Nashville* consistently displays an elaborative approach that allows for narrative digression and some potential for digressive auditor agency while still carefully managing the telling of a story.

The film's denouement, then, can hardly be seen as a regression, even if Rick Altman's description of it were accurate, which it is not. Altman's article complains that, as political operative John Triplette arrives at the Parthenon and is confronted by an unhappy Barnett (who has spotted a political banner Triplette earlier agreed would not be present), "the image clearly reveals that multiple conversations are underway, yet we hear only the dialogue between [the featured characters]."[60] But as Triplette arrives, accompanied by his "man in Nashville" Del Reese, the low unintelligible conversations of the other people on the stage *can* be heard. And Barnett's arrival is signaled by his intelligible remarks, "settin' up, huh?" and "Whoo! It's gonna be a scorcher," both of which overlap with Reese's also intelligible recounting of the Parthenon's history in Nashville. This creates three layers of sound. The only intelligible layers are those provided by the main characters, but as we have seen, this is entirely in line with earlier practice in the film. The unintelligible background voices do slow to a trickle, but not because of overt manipulation of the mix.

Instead, their silence is narratively motivated. Barnett, shouting and pointing at the offending banner, creates a scene, which (quite naturally) causes everyone else on the stage to stop, stare, and even take pictures.

After cutting away to Mrs. Green's funeral, the film returns to the Parthenon for the concert, already in progress. Here, too, Rick Altman finds fault in Altman for, "eschewing his common strategy of broadening space by consistent use of off-screen sound," and "treating his characters as separate vignettes rather than as simultaneously present tracks of a complex sound mix." According to the article, the image track "cut[s] one-by-one to the principal characters arriving," and the soundtrack generally refuses to include any of their dialogue, in spite of the fact that the image track shows their lips moving in conversation or song. This leaves the audience "hear[ing] nothing but the featured song and a low rumble of crowd noise."[61] In fact, what we get at the beginning of Barbara Jean's number are the offscreen voices of Barbara Jean and Haven over a shot of the American flag, followed by a revealing zoom out and tilt down to a wide shot that establishes the presence of ten of the film's featured characters on the stage. And what of the disconnect between characters talking and/or singing along and the absence of sound? All of the individual characters featured approaching the stage are not speaking, with the exception of Mr. Green and Kenny. It is true that on the stage Triplette can be seen speaking to Reese and that this dialogue is inaudible, but this is hardly a marker of extreme departure from previous practice.

If we moderate Rick Altman's general point—that sound is handled here in a more direct and less layered manner than previous scenes because it is the film's climax—then it may be largely true, but what we see and hear is hardly worthy of the "paradox" label. Possibly because of the unwieldy large concert format, background dialogue is not recorded, but Altman still incorporates footage from multiple cameras zooming in and out on multiple subjects. Rick Altman downplays this point, claiming that during Barbara Jean's final number characters other than Barbara Jean and her assassin, Kenny, have no "place in the image."[62] In fact, there are two slowly panning shots across the right and left wings of the stage that show the characters in various states of attentiveness. This is not to deny that there is also a steadily intensifying alternation between Barbara Jean and Kenny, but the focus is not as incredibly narrow as the article suggests. Additionally, at the end of the song Haven is featured strutting out to deliver a bouquet of flowers to Barbara Jean before she is shot, providing a moment of pause between the climax of the song and the climactic shooting. While many of the details of Rick Altman's account are wrong, the general thrust, if moderated, is, as I have stated, moderately valid. The filmmakers employ various strategies to increase narrative intensity during the climactic moment of the film. But then again, Altman and his team are constantly modulating narrative intensity throughout the film.

Any real difference, or lack thereof, between sound practices here and in prior sequences might become more evident if the Parthenon number is compared to another large-scale musical number, rather than a club scene. Barbara Jean's aborted appearance at the Opry Belle is the most proximate of these. The sequence picks up a dangling cause presented in an earlier scene, in which Haven Hamilton has indirectly instructed Triplette that to secure his appearance at the Parthenon he must first secure a commitment from Barbara Jean to appear. The lead-up to Barbara Jean's appearance on stage presents Triplette and Reese pursuing Barnett backstage. Contra Rick Altman, the sound design here is largely hierarchized, with inaudible or unintelligible dialogue from non-feature-characters to an extent even greater than that found in the Parthenon sequence. As Barnett departs for the stage along with Barbara Jean, Reese assures Triplette that he is going to "stay after him like a rodent, man," and the film cuts to Barbara Jean walking on stage, with the music and the audience's applause the only elements in the mix.

Here we get to the meat of the comparison. Will the numbers be layered with multiple digressive, "simultaneously present" tracks? During Barbara Jean's first number, an exuberant song extolling "the loving of a hard-driving cowboy man," the self-proclaimed BBC reporter Opal is shown arriving, and she takes a seat next to Private Kelly, who has been watching over Barbara Jean throughout the film. As in the Parthenon sequence, her arrival is dialogue-free. As Barbara Jean finishes her first number, there has been no addition to or layering of the sound mix. Here, too, she is greeted with applause.

The second number is "Dues," a romantic ballad much softer and slower than the first song, and it creates some space on the soundtrack for intelligible intrusions ⊛ (see the companion website for a video clip). The future assassin, Kenny, now arrives at the performance, and, in a departure from the handling of Opal's arrival, his footsteps are marked out on the soundtrack. Why? One motivation might be to gently indicate that the film is opening up another sound zone, perhaps pre-consciously preparing the audience for the addition of another layer to the mix. It also emphasizes Kenny's arrival, indicating his narrative significance. This indication is followed up on three shots later as the film presents a rather poetic intensifying zoom in on Kenny that begins as a three-shot of Kenny, Private Kelly, and Opal. Initially, as Barbara Jean sings, "I'd give a lot to love you the way I used to do," the men's faces express adoration. Kelly's face maintains this appearance, but as the zoom in singles out Kenny, and as Barbara Jeans sings, "you've got your own private world," Kenny's expression becomes quite anxious and sad. The juxtaposition of the lyrics with the visual track and performance here provides a powerful example of Robert Altman's indirect approach. He intensifies the narrative moment in a way that nicely foreshadows the handling of the Parthenon sequence, creating a suggestive and retrospectively ironic juxtaposition.

When the zone around Kenny is opened up as a sonic space, it is Private Kelly and Opal who interact, and whose conversation the sound design caters to. Barbara Jean's number is middlegrounded in the mix, and Opal's questioning of the private is foregrounded. "Have you been in Vietnam?" she asks, and Kelly looks confused and then turns his attention back to the stage, nodding arrhythmically, either in response to Opal or along with the music. Opal makes the implausible claim that she can tell by his face that he has, and then we return to Barbara Jean and to the foregrounding of the music. There is no real competition here between layers of sound. It is clear where auditor attention should be directed. As we return for another exchange between Opal and Private Kelly, the change in the mix is repeated. Interestingly, both moves to this side conversation are coordinated with a movement from lyrics to humming. In the first instance, this is followed by another verse during the exchange, but in the second instance, Barbara Jean's singing is entirely nonverbal. If providing an audience-liberating competition between nonhierarchized layers of sound is one of Altman's goals, this is a strange choice.

Opal and Private Kelly's final intelligible interaction during the number, foregrounded in the mix and competing only with the nonverbal vocalizations of Barbara Jean for attention, is also less than narratively digressive. Opal asks Kelly if Vietnam was awful, and he replies, shaking his head, that it was "kinda hot and wet." This is immediately followed by a shot of Kenny, whose facial expression changes slightly and who then turns to look up at the soldier. Once again, we get a subtle foreshadowing of what is to come. A soldier has been asked about his experience of war and violence, and this seems to hold special interest for Kenny, who turns back to look at Barbara Jean before the film cuts away. That cut is to a dialogue-free shot of Barnett, Triplette, and Reese standing in the wings of the Opry Belle, with Barnett raising his hand to emphasize for Triplette and Reese the high note that Barbara Jean is capable of reaching. This moment of salesmanship is clearly linked to Triplette's narrative line. The shot plays out with the men entirely inaudible, although Altman and his team easily could have provided lines to the men, especially if Altman was incredibly concerned with delivering self-mixing opportunities to the auditor or with digressing for the sake of digression.

Instead, placing the sonic emphasis on Barbara Jean's poignant song of betrayal, loss, and longing for love provides an effectively multivalent juxtaposition with the looks of profound if ambiguous fascination, the infantilizing solicitousness, and the economic and political exploitation aimed at her. Kelly's distracted weather report response to Opal's questions about Vietnam could be read as a critique of music's ability to distract from serious subjects, but the film has constantly undermined taking Opal seriously, and the time and place of her questioning suggests her reportorial mindset is even more banal than Kelly's response. The potential power of Barbara Jean's music to serve as an effective emotional and thematic agent would likely have been undermined by too much sonic interference. The musical numbers here, then, are treated as emotionally and thematically engaging and narratively situated performances, with brief though thematically resonant digressions that are connected to larger narrative strands that will be resolved at the Parthenon. In retrospect, one wonders if the song's tale of disillusionment might echo the feelings of Kenny, so transfixed by Barbara Jean's performance, upon seeing her abilities put to work in service of empty political pomp at the Parthenon.

Barbara Jean's nervous breakdown and monologue immediately follow— an event made even more traumatic because of the preceding musical poignancy. The sequence arguably presents a parallel to the trauma of Barbara Jean's assassination, and it provides Altman with a similar opportunity for sonic calamity. But Barbara Jean's rambling is initially accompanied only by stunned silence. The second time she stops the song, the film emphasizes the silent discomfort of the onlookers by bringing in low sound effects, including footsteps, an ambient engine noise, and sounds from the theme park. Barnett intervenes after she stops the music a third time to tell a story from her childhood, and it is only as Barbara Jean is helped off the stage that the audience erupts in a chorus of displeasure. The handling here is entirely conventional, with only a few of the angry voices intelligible, and none competing with Barnett's voice as he speaks through Barbara Jean's microphone, telling the crowd that they will be able to see Barbara Jean for free at the Parthenon. This gives the sequence a clear narrative climax, which continues as Barnett walks up to Triplette and they quickly negotiate terms, again entirely intelligibly and again foregrounded in the mix. This sequence is, then, every bit as narratively oriented as the Parthenon sequence, and the handling of the sound is also almost completely in-line with that of the later sequence. Altman's "oppositional approach" seems to have been a sonic mirage.[63]

In his essay, Rick Altman concludes that "as long as Altman and his sound crew are dealing with preliminaries, everything is possible. . . . Once narrative necessity takes hold, however, innovative sound techniques go out the door," and *Nashville* "subordinat[es]" innovation to "narrative imperative."[64] His disappointment is that of the betrayed supporter of the radical opposition party when his favored candidate, lacking courage or conviction, sells-out and joins the assimilationist party. Or, as Barbara Jean would put it, "I'd give a lot to love you the way I used to do." But that radically oppositional Robert Altman never existed. The oppositional camp misdescribes, misunderstands, and underestimates what Altman and his team are up to.

What Robert Altman and his team do provide in *Nashville* is another example of innovative elaboration, another instance in which careful sound design enables something extra to be added to the storytelling. In Altman's final film of the early 1970s what is added is often musical performance and its sometimes ironic, sometimes subtly foreshadowing, emotionally and thematically charged juxtapositional effects. At other moments in the film, and in Altman's early-1970s oeuvre, the storytelling is amplified by a narrationally excessive sense of a realistic narrative space, and by an overt, ironic narrational voice. Indeed, while *Nashville*'s broad canvas might be seen as an evolutionary endpoint in which technology and narrative concept allow Altman to finally depart from the classical norms of sound design, Altman's sound goals and techniques during this period actually seem to be relatively stable, if also relatively expansive. Technological developments allowed him not to wholly reject traditional storytelling but to better fulfill his established, multifaceted aims. The statements of his collaborators and close analysis of Altman's use of sound during this early period in his career reveal an agenda of problem-setting and problem-solving that is far less oppositional and far more classical than has previously been acknowledged. His team's repertoire of strategies facilitated an approach that could appeal to a younger, educated audience who likely appreciated the challenges embodied in effortful availability and desired something more than the same old stories. As with his approach to narrative and visual design, Altman's sound strategies were designed to give his audience something more *and* to tell a story. This is not rejection but elaborate and elaborative addition and expansion.

# 4

# Improvisation, Transposition, and Elaboration

## Altman Unscripted?

Since the birth of Hollywood cinema, filmmaking has depended on the sacred authority of the script. As Janet Staiger writes in *The Classical Hollywood Cinema*, "the detailed continuity script was normal practice by 1914." Intended to serve as "the blueprint from which all other work was organized," the script, in its multiple incarnations, was integral to the production management practices adopted by Hollywood, with "trade papers and 'how-to' handbooks help[ing to] standardize its format." As the studio system became larger and more complex, scripts became even more crucial to Hollywood's drive toward efficiency and control.[1]

In contrast, since his emergence as a major film director during the Hollywood Renaissance, accounts of Robert Altman's filmmaking process have been tied to allegations, confessions, and exaltations of his disregard for the script. In a 1971 interview with *The Times* of London that describes Altman's production methods as "freewheeling," the filmmaker proudly declares, "If there's one group that are not fans of mine . . . it's writers."[2] David Denby's review of *M\*A\*S\*H* for *The Atlantic*, titled "Breakthrough," celebrates Altman's sacrilegious attitude. Denby claims that "Many elements in this production," especially the "acting style . . . are innovative in ways that could be important for the big studios." Here, Denby refers specifically to the freedom Altman gave his performers on-set to improvise departures from the script. Denby offers two justifications for Altman's approach. First, he emphasizes that Altman took a script that "other directors had turned . . . down," suggesting that the film's difficulty in finding a director may have been because of weaknesses in the script that therefore made it unworthy of reverence. Denby also provides the kind of form-equals-expressive-function justification discussed in previous chapters by declaring, "In a movie devoted to the destruction of pretense, overelaborate or florid readings [of the script] . . .

*Robert Altman and the Elaboration of Hollywood Storytelling.* Mark Minett, Oxford University Press (2021). © Oxford University Press. DOI: 10.1093/oso/9780197523827.001.0001.

would be all wrong." Naturally, Altman "had to throw a lot away" in order to get the "craziness and pacing that more anxious preparation kills."[3] The critical impulse here to interpret this aspect of Altman's production practices as determined by a specific film's subject matter would, of course, undergo modification as Altman moved on from the military screwball comedy of *M\*A\*S\*H* while retaining his disregard for his source material as well as his concomitant liberation of actors. These practices would provide critics with grounds for an interpretive framework through which to understand and praise Altman's expressive project—his commitment to an expansive realism freed from the pretense demanded by Hollywood norms.

Altman's reputation for an improvisational, highly collaborative production practice dependent on scriptual infidelity contributed to the distorted accounts of each of the practices reassessed in the previous chapters. What were his films' auditors liberated from, if not listening to conventional scripted dialogue? What were his alleged roving zooms wandering away from, if not the scripted action? A 1970 *Time* profile of Altman clarifies the connection between Altman's relationship with the script and claims of plotlessness, stating that prior to the success of *M\*A\*S\*H*:

> What used to trouble Hollywood about Altman was that he turned the totalitarian trade of film directing into democracy, if not anarchy. Far from strutting around on the set with a riding crop, Altman is likely to operate the clapstick himself and encourage suggestions from second assistants and electricians. An Altman film is more like an improvisational encounter group than a showcase for stars and plot.[4]

Altman's films may not be a "showcase" for plot, but, as chapter 1 makes plain, the standard account claiming his early 1970s films lack coherent narratives is largely incorrect. In fact, the majority of his films from this period exhibit classical narrative structures organized in conventional ways around goal-oriented protagonists. Even the more episodic or sprawling films like *M\*A\*S\*H* and *Nashville* hybridize their innovations with substantial narrative structures and significant, if perversely employed, classical features. Of course, it is hypothetically possible that these conventional narrative structures could have resulted from improvisation or drastic, repudiating revisions of the films' scripts. The analyses in chapter 1 are based on examinations of the finished films and are therefore silent on this question.

What still remains to be addressed, then, is the established account of Altman's production practices promulgated by *The Times* of London, *The*

*Atlantic, Time,* and the majority of writing on the director, and which has served as a key component of the filmmaker's identity as an oppositional Hollywood Renaissance auteur. As the standard story goes, Altman so detested Hollywood filmmaking that he denied himself its most important managerial and storytelling tool. In critics' focus on Altman's use of improvisation, they implicitly and explicitly aligned him with the practices of European filmmakers and with independent American filmmakers.[5] In doing so, they framed Altman's films as intensely improvisational rejections of Hollywood norms. Altman himself encouraged this rhetoric, perhaps cashing in on what J. J. Murphy describes as a postwar "emphasis on spontaneity and improvisation" that "formed a subversive discourse against the prevailing corporate liberalism of the postwar period."[6]

Instead, we might take seriously Denby's assertion that Altman was an innovator whose use of improvisation offered an example of how to open up Hollywood cinema to new possibilities that might appeal to a more cine-literate and socially engaged audience. Steven Maras, drawing on Staiger's work, writes about Hollywood's employment of the screenplay as, "organized around the separation of the work of conception and execution." According to Maras, this led to a persistent state of affairs in which "the script is commonly seen as a kind of blueprint, with production being modelled closely on the building of a house," and in which, "the script is supposedly written and then shot as planned."[7] Altman's approach presented a significant revision to this model, relocating, allegedly indiscriminately, creative acts conventionally understood as conceptional to the domain of execution.

However, closer examination of Altman's relationship to the script in his early 1970s filmmaking proves to be revelatory, once again demonstrating that his practices are best understood not in terms of radical opposition to Hollywood but as additive and elaborative. It is clear that Altman's films do not wholly conform to their scripted "blueprints," and that his filmmaking aims were difficult to fully assimilate under the conventional values and mode of production of Hollywood filmmaking. At the same time, though, Altman and his collaborators did largely rely on the conceptional work provided in their scripts, and they did so to an extent obscured by his biographical legend. Altman used the preproduction script as the substantial basis of a production process of ongoing conceptualization that expanded the content, techniques, and ambitions of classical Hollywood filmmaking. In doing so, he departed from the fusty allegiance to fully replicating the script standardized by past practice. Ian W. Macdonald, in his work on the poetics of screenwriting, argues against continuing to view the script as the only appropriate vehicle for the conception of a film, claiming that the notion persists, "for no reason other than convenience within the film industry, and against considerable evidence [to the contrary]."[8] This is a critique Altman seems to share, but the transpositional innovations he undertook were elaborative and desanctifying rather than repudiative.

## Altman's Elaborative Transpositional Method

The production process, with its on-set problem-setting and problem-solving constituting the "transpositional" movement—the replications, revisions, and rejections of premises and structure—from script to finished film, has always been difficult for film historians to reconstruct. The distance of years, failures of recollection, and scarcity of documents all pose substantial obstacles for researchers. Obviously, the scope of transpositions to be accounted for is broadened when significant changes to the premises and structure of a preproduction script are evident in the final film. In these cases, rather than delineating only the manner in which scripted elements were executed through cinematic technique per se, the reconstruction must also account for transpositional practices that are both exotic, or exoticisable given the historically central role of the script in production, and self-evidently obscure. As Virginia Wright Wexman points out, while "many films make use of improvisation, it is usually difficult, if not impossible, to obtain accurate documentation about precisely when and how the improvisation occurs."[9]

While the process of transposition obviously extends beyond on-set activities such as performance and into postproduction, this chapter will seek to interrogate an oppositional account of Altman that largely rests on a (mis-) characterization of his on-set transpositional practices. Recovery of Altman's transpositional practices, at least in part, is made possible here through the close comparison of the preproduction scripts of Altman's early 1970s films, held by the Wisconsin Center for Film and Theater Research (WCFTR) as well as the Altman Archive at the University of Michigan, with the release versions of the films. This helps to clarify what features of the final film are retained from the preproduction script, establishing what might be termed an "improvisatory ceiling" for each project. This comparative analysis is supplemented by further archival material, interviews, and the statements of Altman and other production personnel.

Unless clear evidence suggests otherwise, transpositions are attributed to Altman, or to Altman and his collaborators, though such attribution should generally be understood to indicate authorization rather than origination. This seems appropriate given that Altman exerted a great deal of control over his productions during this period, often receiving writing and producing credits, taking advantage of the freedom to emulate the European model of auteurism that Hollywood's stab at reaching a cine-literate youth audience afforded. Indeed, Altman even complicated a keystone of his own emerging biographical legend by admitting that his approach was "regal" rather than fully democratic, although he did reassure the interviewer that he was "a good monarch."[10] Furthermore, certain transpositional strategies are repeated across Altman's early 1970s films, and while this period of his career is characterized by a fairly stable set of collaborators behind-the-camera, this fact would seem to support the default attribution of at least some portion of credit for the conception, if not necessarily a particular execution, of these strategies to Altman.

This chapter traces out these consistencies in Altman's transpositional practices, beginning with the somewhat speculative case offered by the materials available for *McCabe & Mrs. Miller*. It then moves on to confirm and extend those tentative conclusions by examining *The Long Goodbye*'s more proximate preproduction script. The chapter then traces these transpositional practices back through Altman's approach to *Brewster McCloud* and Ring Lardner's Academy Award–winning script for *M\*A\*S\*H*. The chapter concludes by jumping forward to Altman's transpositional strategies after *The Long Goodbye* on *Thieves Like Us*, *California Split*, and *Nashville*. These analyses clarify the continuities in Altman's approach, while also—in the latter two films—revealing innovations in screenplay form meant to anticipate and accommodate Altman's practice-oriented preferences.

While retaining almost all of the large-scale narrative structure as well as most of the scenic structure of his films' preproduction scripts, Altman also finds ways to embellish, amplify or mute, and redirect the conventional aspects of their dramatic and thematic content. He and his collaborators make targeted use of actorly improvisation and selectively improvised revisions to character traits, behavior, and dialogue in response to his films' casting. Altman's transpositional strategies rely on and create affordances for the elaborative practices laid out in the previous chapters. Revisions to production scripts often provide the grounds for experimentation with the excessive description of milieu, ironizing expressivity, depth composition, and overlapping dialogue. We find in Altman a consummate problem-solving filmmaker, devising ways to integrate his own novel aims and preferences and to synthesize them with Hollywood storytelling traditions.

## Transposition, *McCabe & Mrs. Miller*, and the Elaboration of a Biographical Legend

Chapter 1 has already pointed to the formative influence on Altman's reputation of Aljean Harmetz's 1971 *New York Times Magazine* profile framed around a visit to the set of *McCabe & Mrs. Miller*. Harmetz's account primed future discussion of Altman's relationship to narrative, quoting Altman as saying that a good film requires, "taking the narrative out, taking the story out of it." It also built on Altman's quickly forming reputation with regard to the related topics of improvisation and the place of the script in his filmmaking practice. After all, what would the story be taken out of, if not the script? Altman, his intentions framed by a desire for greater realism, is described as wanting to, "catch the accidents of life and fling them on the screen"—a description that easily lends itself to accounts of Altman's sets as rife with actorly improvisation that camera operators and sound recordists attempted to catch on-the-fly.

Beyond claiming a general disregard for story, Altman's statements in the piece frame him as blithely indifferent to scripts and the labors of screenwriters. According to Altman, "It's not words we're dealing with in the films I make, not clever dialogue." Harmetz's article elaborates on this point

> Most of the writers on Altman's films have ended up as his more-or-less bitter enemies. By the time one of his films is finished there's nothing left of the original script except a couple of soup bones of plot and a few expletives. "Bob," says [*McCabe & Mrs. Miller* screenwriter] Brian McKay, "considers a script simply as an instrument, as the tool you sell the studio."

It is worth considering whether McKay's characterization of Altman's attitude toward the script actually matches Harmetz's rather hyperbolic description of Altman's practice, but Harmetz supports this characterization by recounting Altman's run-ins with the writers of *M\*A\*S\*H* and *Brewster McCloud*. Bill Cannon, who wrote the original screenplay for *Brewster McCloud*, states, "[Altman] claimed I should take my name off the screen since he, himself, had written most of the film." Ring Lardner, writer of *M\*A\*S\*H*'s screenplay, for which he won the Academy Award (and failed to thank Altman in his acceptance speech) complains that "Mr. Altman does not treat a script very carefully," and Harmetz lets the reader know that, "his private opinions are considerably more vitriolic." In the article, Altman's response to this accusation of negligence is to declare that he is "interested in the behavior patterns of the characters, not in what they say. In my films, the actors can be creative.

I don't think one person can write dialogue for 15 people." Apparently un-interested in amicably resolving this dispute, Altman summarizes his own contributions to *M\*A\*S\*H* as, "the basic concept, the philosophy, the style, the casting, and then making all those things work. Plus all the jokes, of course."[11]

Before testing these transpositional claims about *M\*A\*S\*H*, it is worth first spending some time investigating the transition of *McCabe & Mrs. Miller* from script to screen, testing Harmetz's claims, including that only, "a couple of soup bones of plot and a few expletives," remain from its screenplay (eventually credited to Brian McKay *and* Altman). According to Harmetz and others, the script was radically revised, or perhaps immediately discarded, with the great bulk of the film resulting from collaboration and improvisation. Of all the films covered in this chapter, *McCabe & Mrs. Miller* has the least proximate preproduction draft available. The WCFTR holds what is marked as a "First Draft" script dated December 7, 1969. The Altman Archive at the University of Michigan also holds a script, though dated January 19, 1971, and marked "REV. FINAL." Because the film was well into production at this time, with Harmetz's set visit taking place in December of 1970, and the film actually beginning production in mid-October and concluding in January,[12] it is likely that the Michigan script is what Steven Price, following James F. Boyle, calls the "set" script. The set script can be either "a retrospective record of any changes made during improvised scenes," or of "all of those revisions made *during* production but before the shooting of the scene."[13] Given the date, the script is most likely the former. Even though the "First Draft" script was produced ten months before the start of production, and it therefore seems likely that production began with a revised version of the script, a comparison between this script and the revised final version of the script, and with the film itself, is revealing. While there are major differences between the versions, it is highly inaccurate to claim that this first draft was merely discarded, or that only fragments of plot and scripted expletives remain.

Harmetz writes that there was an "organic relationship between Altman and his script, his actors, his sets and the final film." She quotes the film's set designer, Leon Erickson, who oversaw the construction of Presbyterian Church during production, as stating, "The town grew as the script grew. . . . Lots of things in the town changed because of the script; lots of things in the script changed because of the way the town was built. Everything happened organically."[14] Furthermore, "throughout the picture, it was rare for Altman to know on one morning exactly what he was going to be filming the next morning. Often the next morning's scene had not yet been written." As an example, Harmetz offers an anecdote about the preparations for a funeral scene, when "an offhand suggestion by [Altman's] secretary of 'Asleep in Jesus' as the epitaph for [Bart Coyle's] gravestone led to a frantic search through old hymnbooks and, in Friday morning's cold mist, to a painfully affecting scene." Harmetz concludes the anecdote by declaring, "none of it had existed—even in Altman's head—24 hours earlier."[15]

Harmetz's account of the organicity of the set/script/actor relationship (several actors reportedly lived in the constructed town during shooting) seems intended to be understood as emblematic of Altman's intuitive and spontaneous filmmaking philosophy. According to Altman biographer Patrick McGilligan's characterization, though, other factors played a role in decisions to revise or reject elements of the script. For instance, interpersonal issues with Altman meant that Brian McKay "was a pariah on the set. So, the filming of *McCabe* saw the director presiding over collectivist revisions," including contributions by Warren Beatty and "Hollywood script doctor" Robert Towne (by telephone). According to script supervisor Joan Tewkesbury, Altman "simply turned [Mrs. Miller's] stuff over" to actress Julie Christie, so that she could "take these scenes and redo them as a woman would do them in this position." Tewkesbury describes the typical on-set practice as follows:

Then what Bob would do is rehearse [the script revisions] and see what would come out of the rehearsal. Then I would write all the stuff down and they would all be asked to repeat their own lines. On occasion, on Saturdays, he would dictate to me a couple of the scenes he wanted done, specific ways, and this stuff would be embellished by the actors. What I began to realize is, all Bob really needed to work was a strong spine for the story. If you could create scenes that had strong purposes—a way to get in and a way to get out, and it moved the story along—what happened in the middle would depend on the environment.[16]

McGilligan's description (via Tewkesbury) of Altman's production practices is certainly a more moderate rendition than Harmetz's. According to Tewkesbury, it was in the middle of the scenes and in the dialogue where the flexibility for improvisation was located. Moreover, the contingencies of that particular production helped determine the nature and extent of the collaboration that took place. We can contrast this form of "organicity"—a responsiveness to contingency and a qualified openness to collaboration grounded in a core narrative structure—with Harmetz's suggestion that after the script had been used to sell the production to the studio, it would then necessarily be abandoned within a couple of weeks in favor of "whatever accidents of weather or actors' improvisations fate has chosen to bring him."[17]

While there are obvious and major changes between the first draft of the *McCabe & Mrs. Miller* script and the revised final version, which recorded the revisions made over the course of production, the Harmetz account proves to be misleading. The film did not essentially begin anew at the start of production, although it does appear as though the tone was shifted significantly. Instead, Altman and company seem to have worked closely from the large scale and scene-by-scene structure of the first draft. While the two versions of the script do not completely line up scene-by-scene, there is a high degree of resemblance between the two. In fact, a segmentation of each, placed side-by-side for comparison (Table 4.1) reveals extensive correlations.

It is difficult to argue, based on this evidence, that Altman simply gave in to fate and improvisation when so much remains from a first draft finished over a year before production began. For instance, even after a fairly major change in the plot—the transformation of McCabe's flat refusal of any offer by the mining company in the first draft into an ill-fated and overconfident attempt at negotiation in the revised final draft—much of the remainder of each script is very similar. Indeed, the final act confrontation between McCabe and the hired killers plays out almost identically in each script.

There is also no evidence here to support Harmetz's assertion that over the course of the film's production Altman "clipped several great chunks of plot out of the film," thereby leaving "a number of puzzling but undefined characters to wander—mostly in long shot—in and out of the background."[18] Chapter 1 addresses the question of narrative structure in *McCabe & Mrs. Miller* in particular. To summarize, *McCabe & Mrs. Miller* actually displays a fairly classical narrative structure that is elaborated on according to Altman and his collaborators' other concerns and practices, such as providing an ironizing narrational voice and digressive interludes. These, in tandem with aspects of Altman's biographical legend, can work to give the impression of a film that is somehow narratively lacking. Hypothetically, *McCabe & Mrs. Miller*'s narrative structure could have been constructed in an improvised manner during the film's production. The side-by-side analysis, though, clearly indicates that it was not. It also does not indicate that Altman reduced the narrative content of his preproduction script in any particularly notable way. There are no significant "chunks of plot" missing between the first draft and the revised final version of the script.

So, if we accept that Altman did not engage in a thoroughgoing process of narrative reduction, how are we to describe the differences between the first draft of the script and the revised final, and the range of improvisations and transpositions that may have taken place during production? First, we can say that the production process seems to have been elaborative and additive rather than subtractive. The revised final version of the draft actually has more named characters than the first draft. For instance, the first draft includes

**Table 4.1** *McCabe & Mrs. Miller* Script Comparison

| *McCabe & Mrs. Miller First Draft* | *McCabe & Mrs. Miller Revised Final* |
|---|---|
| Framing device with a modern setting established and a bulldozer moving dirt overtop of a crumbling church. Then move back in time to 1800s. | |
| McCabe arrives at Presbyterian Church. | McCabe arrives at Presbyterian Church. |
| McCabe sets up a card game at Sheehan's; plans to sell opium to Chinese residents and open saloon and whorehouse. | McCabe sets up a card game at Sheehan's; plans to buy land. |
| McCabe goes to Bearpaw, sets terms for opium supply and negotiates for three prostitutes; glimpse of Mrs. Miller. | McCabe goes to Bear Paw, sets terms for opium supply and negotiates for three prostitutes; glimpse of Mrs. Miller. |
| | McCabe returns to Presbyterian Church with prostitutes. Brief skirmish between miners and prostitutes. McCabe appears flummoxed by his new prostitutes. |
| The town's development is established as men line up for prostitutes operating out of a tent. Preacher passes by. | The town's development is established as men line up for prostitutes operating out of tents. Preacher passes by. |
| Sheehan asks McCabe to conspire with him to keep competitors out. Interrupted by brawl in a prostitute tent, which a confident McCabe breaks up. | Sheehan asks McCabe to conspire with him to keep new competitors out. Interrupted by a prostitute stabbing a man, which a bewildered McCabe stops. |
| Wagon brings foreman Bob Webster and his wife, Ida, to town, along with Mrs. Miller. | Steam tractor brings Ida, laborer Bart Coyle's cousin/bride to town, along with Mrs. Miller. |
| Mrs. Miller proposes a partnership with McCabe in McCabe's saloon. | Mrs. Miller speaks with McCabe in his saloon, asks where she can get some food. |
| | McCabe has difficulties managing a prostitute who is stealing. |
| | New boarders arrive at Sheehan's. |
| | McCabe and Mrs. Miller begin a conversation at Sheehan's. |
| | Bart asks for help for Ida, who is bleeding. |
| | Mrs. Miller proposes a partnership with McCabe. |
| | McCabe gets drunk in his room. |
| Men build bathhouse and anticipate new prostitutes, including "Chinese princess." | Men build bathhouse and anticipate new prostitutes, including "Chinese princess." McCabe, going to visit Mrs. Miller, stops to talk to them. |
| McCabe scratches on Mrs. Miller's tent flap. Mrs. Miller tells him to go away. | McCabe knocks on Mrs. Miller's door. Mrs. Miller tells him to go away. |

*Continued*

**Table 4.1** *Continued*

| McCabe & Mrs. Miller First Draft | McCabe & Mrs. Miller Revised Final |
| --- | --- |
| The new prostitutes arrive. | The new prostitutes arrive, along with Sumner Washington, the new barber, and his wife. The prostitutes take a bath. |
| The men take baths before moving over to the new prostitutes, who still operate out of a tent while the whorehouse is under construction. McCabe enters to wish them well, and Mrs. Miller asks if he has taken a bath, thinking he is there as a customer. McCabe asks if Mrs. Miller is available and then leaves, dejected, hearing the men enthusiastically ask for Mrs. Miller. | The whorehouse is operational. McCabe enters, looking for his foreman, and Mrs. Miller asks if he has taken a bath, thinking he is there as a customer. The men ask what Mrs. Miller's price is and agree to it. McCabe leaves, dejected. |
| McCabe in empty saloon having problems with his ledger. Mrs. Miller arrives and after McCabe complains about costs shows him the first day's take. She reprimands him on his bookkeeping and offers to help him with his ledger. | McCabe in empty saloon having problems with his ledger. Mrs. Miller arrives and after McCabe complains about costs shows him the first day's take. She reprimands him on his bookkeeping and offers to help him with his ledger. |
| The prostitutes enter the finally completed whorehouse while three boys look on and comment. | Bart Coyle gets injured in a fight with another miner his wife is mistaken for a prostitute. |
| The town's transformation is highlighted, with McCabe getting a shave from Sumner Washington and a wrestling match taking place. | Mrs. Miller prepares for a birthday party for one of her prostitutes. |
| Sheehan hosts Sears in his bar and expresses his resentment of McCabe. | Bart refuses help for his injury, and Sheehan points out McCabe to Sears. |
| Sears introduces himself to a drunk McCabe. They move into his saloon, where Sears offers to buy him out. McCabe refuses. | Continuing from previous, Sears and his partner, Hollander, introduce themselves to McCabe. They move into his saloon, where they offer to buy him out. McCabe refuses their offer and tries to bargain them up. |
| There is a party at the whorehouse and McCabe is conspicuously absent. Mrs. Miller is disappointed by his absence. | The birthday party at the whorehouse begins, with disappointment expressed at McCabe's absence. |
| McCabe sobers up in the bathhouse. | McCabe sobers up in the bathhouse. |

**Table 4.1** *Continued*

| *McCabe & Mrs. Miller First Draft* | *McCabe & Mrs. Miller Revised Final* |
|---|---|
| Mrs. Miller is about to smoke opium, when McCabe knocks at her door. She hides the opium and lets him in, expressing skepticism that he has had a bath. They kiss. | Mrs. Miller is about to smoke opium, when McCabe knocks at her door. She hides the opium and lets him in, expressing skepticism that he has had a bath. McCabe tells her about the offer from the mining company. She is upset that he refused and warns him that they will kill him. Sears and Hollander come to whorehouse to make counteroffer, which McCabe refuses, offering to meet them the next morning to discuss further. McCabe returns to Mrs. Miller, who has been smoking opium. |
| The next morning, McCabe asks Mrs. Miller to be his woman. He tells her about the offer from the mining company. She is upset that he refused and warns him that they will kill him. She kicks him out and is insulted when he needles her by offering to pay her fee. | |
| | Sears and Hollander in Sheehan's. They decide to leave without negotiating further. |
| | Mrs. Miller, much sweeter than before, is pleased that McCabe now seems to have them negotiating. McCabe puts her fee in her music box before getting in bed. |
| McCabe packs his bag and holsters his gun in preparation for his trip to Bearpaw. He looks longingly toward Mrs. Miller's window. On his way out of town he tells the preacher that God is dead. | At McCabe's saloon, men discuss Bart's waning health. McCabe learns that the mining company men have left town. |
| Ida discovers her husband's mangled body at the sawmill, while Mrs. Miller smokes opium. | |
| McCabe meets with a lawyer at Bear Paw, who encourages McCabe to stick it out so he can become a symbol. | McCabe goes to Bear Paw to intercept Sears and Hollander, but fails. He meets with a lawyer, who encourages McCabe to stick it out so that he can become a symbol. |
| McCabe is scared off his horse when a shot rings out on his way out of Bear Paw. It is a false alarm. | McCabe tells Mrs. Miller about his plan to stick it out. She is upset with him. |
| Only a few mill hands attend Bob's funeral. Ida asks the preacher what she will do now, and he turns away. Ida's question provides a dialogue hook into the next scene at Mrs. Miller's. | The town attends Bart's funeral, where Mrs. Miller exchanges meaningful glances with the widowed Ida. McCabe leaves early when he hears a rider is approaching. He confronts the cowboy and is relieved to learn he is in town only to use the whorehouse. It is a false alarm. |

*Continued*

**Table 4.1** *Continued*

| *McCabe & Mrs. Miller First Draft* | *McCabe & Mrs. Miller Revised Final* |
|---|---|
| Mrs. Miller sees McCabe return from Bear Paw. | |
| McCabe and Mrs. Miller are in bed together after having made love. They are initially happy but begin to argue. McCabe tells Mrs. Miller about his plan to stick it out. She is upset with him. | |
| At McCabe's saloon, Sheehan gloats over McCabe's impending demise. | |
| McCabe's visit to the assay office reveals that the mining company is short rating the zinc from Presbyterian Church in order to make the miners unhappy with McCabe. When he leaves the office, he is again paranoid and runs to his room to get his gun. It is another false alarm. | |
| In McCabe's saloon, men tell him the killer is coming to town on the Bearpaw trail. McCabe tracks him far out of town and watches him ride. | |
| In the whorehouse, prostitutes disgruntled with the downturn in business angrily discuss Ida joining their ranks and the mining company's impending takeover of the town. | In the whorehouse, Cowboy enjoys his time. McCabe wants to deliver a package to Mrs. Miller but is told she is with someone and leaves dejectedly. Mrs. Miller prepares Ida for her life as a prostitute. |
| Mrs. Miller visits McCabe to do his books and they discuss the danger he is in. | |
| McCabe again watches the rider, who has set up camp. | |
| McCabe in Mrs. Miller's bedroom, telling her about the camp. She encourages him to ride to Bearpaw and tell them he reconsidered. He tells her that he doesn't expect her to understand. | |
| McCabe scopes out the town for the best positions in case of a gunfight. | |
| McCabe watches the rider approach. | |
| McCabe rides into town and prepares for the rider's arrival. When he does arrive, he confronts the cowboy and is relieved to learn he is in town only to use the whorehouse. It is a false alarm. | |
| McCabe and Mrs. Miller discuss the impending arrival of the real killer and argue about McCabe's refusal to leave town. | |

**Table 4.1** *Continued*

| McCabe & Mrs. Miller First Draft | McCabe & Mrs. Miller Revised Final |
| --- | --- |
| McCabe wakes up in a panic and sees that the killers have arrived at Sheehan's. He gets his gun and sets up in the saloon. | The killers arrive at Sheehan's, disrupting the town drunk's dance on the ice. McCabe watches the three killers (Butler, Breed, and Kid) as they scope out the town. Butler tells Breed to stay away from McCabe. |
| McCabe discusses the killers with his bartender. Shortly after, the three killers (Butler, Breed, and Kid) come to the saloon with Sheehan. They ask McCabe if he shot Bill Roundtree and engage in a tense conversation before leaving. | Mrs. Miller visits McCabe in his saloon and tries to convince him to leave town. McCabe learns that the killers have refused his invitation to come to his saloon and negotiate. |
| The killers take shots at townspeople to intimidate them and put pressure on McCabe, who makes plans. | McCabe goes to Sheehan's to attempt to negotiate, but Butler tells him he doesn't negotiate. He then asks McCabe if he shot Bill Roundtree, and they engage in a tense conversation before McCabe leaves. Sheehan seems to enjoy seeing McCabe humiliated, and one of McCabe's prostitutes is in attendance. |
| McCabe sees two of his prostitutes defect to Sheehan's. | |
| The killers engage in impressive target practice and continue their intimidation while McCabe listens, becoming more and more anxious, and continues his preparations. | The prostitutes, including Ida, say goodbye to Cowboy as he leaves the whorehouse. At Sheehan's Kid engages in target practice. Kid tricks Cowboy into showing him his gun and shoots him down. |
| Kid tricks Cowboy into showing him his gun and shoots him down. | |
| McCabe goes to Sheehan's to confront killers. He makes a wager with them and Sheehan that he will survive. | McCabe prepares himself for confrontation with the killers, while speaking aloud as if to Mrs. Miller, who is not present. He mutters that he has "poetry in his soul." |
| McCabe visits Mrs. Miller for one last night together. He tells her how he feels and apologizes. He declares that he has poetry in him. They make love. | McCabe visits Mrs. Miller for one last night together. He tells her how he feels and apologizes. She holds him. |
| McCabe leaves the next morning while Mrs. Miller is still asleep. | Mrs. Miller leaves the next morning while McCabe is still asleep. |

*Continued*

**Table 4.1** *Continued*

| *McCabe & Mrs. Miller First Draft* | *McCabe & Mrs. Miller Revised Final* |
|---|---|
| McCabe engages in a game of cat and mouse with the killers. He goes up to the church steeple to survey the scene, returns to find the preacher holding his shotgun on him, and is forced to leave without it. | McCabe engages in a game of cat and mouse with the killers. He goes up to the church steeple to survey the scene, returns to find the preacher holding his shotgun on him, and is forced to leave without it. |
| McCabe shoots Kid in the back and is shot in the leg. | Butler shoots the preacher and the church is set on fire. |
| Butler shoots the preacher and the church is set on fire. | McCabe shoots Kid in the back and is shot in the leg. |
| McCabe shoots Breed through a window. McCabe is shot by Butler, feigns death, and then shoots Butler in the forehead. | The townspeople, including the prostitutes and led by Sheehan, rally to put out the fire at the church. |
| Sheehan finds McCabe on the ground and shoots and kills him. | McCabe shoots Breed through a window. |
| | McCabe is shot by Butler, feigns death, and then shoots Butler in the forehead. |
| | While the townspeople celebrate their achievement, McCabe bleeds to death in the snow. |
| The prostitutes try to tell Mrs. Miller that McCabe is dead and learn she is in an opium den. | |
| In the opium den, an oblivious and uncomprehending Mrs. Miller is informed by a Chinese resident of McCabe's death. | While Chinese residents shout about McCabe's death outside, in an opium den an apparently oblivious Mrs. Miller stares at a snuff bottle. It produces a prism of color in which one can see what looks like the face of McCabe. |
| In the barbershop, Sumner prepares to shave McCabe and is told they want the body at Sheehan's for pictures. | |
| At Sheehan's, photos are taken of McCabe while Sheehan declares that the town will no longer be a one-man town but a Company town with Sheehan as their point man. | |
| Reprise of the bulldozer framing device from beginning. | |

Bob Webster—McCabe's foreman, whose death leaves his mail-order bride, Ida, a widow, thereby leading her to join Mrs. Miller's stable of prostitutes. In the revised final version of the script, this character is split into two separate characters—Jeremy and Bart Coyle, and both characterizations have been elaborated beyond the traits found in the initial script. For instance, Jeremy's "full of shit"-ness and his propensity to use workers' diarrhea as an excuse for delays in construction are absent from the Bob Webster character. Likewise, Bart Coyle's physical disability, probably originating in Altman's casting of

Bert Remsen, whose back was broken in an on-set accident in the early 1960s, is added to the Webster character, as is his defensive and ill-tempered nature. In the first draft of the script, Bob Webster dies in an accident at the sawmill. In the revised final version, Coyle is killed after he is injured during a fight he starts over a misunderstanding about his wife.

Plot-cutting aside, Harmetz's linked assertion that "a number of puzzling but undefined characters ... wander—mostly in long shot—in and out of the background," might at first glance seem plausible, but it requires a good deal of revision. First, many of these "background" characters are in fact given "highlighting" moments, such as Owl and Smally's conversations about facial hair at Sheehan's bar. Indeed, what might make these characters "puzzling" or, more probably, objects of gentle curiosity and amusement for the audience, is the fact that many are given foregrounded moments that are sometimes, but not always, narratively digressive. Thus, these characters do not "wander" into frame so much as they are "middlegrounded"—spotlighted by Altman and his collaborators. Furthermore, these characters have not been left narratively stranded, either by cuts to the script during the production process or as discarded footage left on the editing room floor. Instead, they provide additional points of emotional interest (the pathos generated by the town drunk, for instance) and sources of humor, and they deepen and elaborate on the general milieu. What they do not do, and never did, is impinge in a significant way on the film's plot—on its large-scale or scene-to-scene narrative structure.

Although Altman and his collaborators retain the essential narrative structure of the script, they are also apt to improvise and revise around the film's major characters. For instance, McCabe's *refusal* to negotiate with the mining company in the first draft of the script becomes McCabe's *failed attempt* to negotiate with the mining company in the revised final version. The effectual yield in both versions, though, is more or less the same. While this revision's impact on the causal chain is nil, it is still indicative of a fairly extensive and significant set of changes to McCabe's character. In the first draft, McCabe is a fairly macho type, and he is written as more direct and competent than his revised incarnation. He makes love to Mrs. Miller more frequently, sometimes even without paying. He is just as bad at bookkeeping and figures, but he more easily fits within the western type of the heroic gunslinger, even if he is perhaps less eager to employ violence, or the threat of violence, than is typical.

For instance, the first draft of the script interrupts Sheehan's entreaty to McCabe to collude against competition with a brawl among the miners in the prostitutes' tent, rather than with the film's stabbing of a miner by a prostitute.

Instead of a bewildered McCabe struggling to hold back a rail-thin prostitute, the first draft of the script gives us the following:

> [McCabe] is fully dressed, his Navy Colt strapped to his side at the ready. He walks slowly and deliberately to the area near the tent and stands quietly. At first, his presence is only felt by a few of those nearest him, but soon the fighting begins to slacken off until it stops totally. When it is quiet and all eyes are on him, McCabe singles out Tiny [who is actually gigantic] and directs his words to him, hand poised over the butt of his gun.
>
> McCABE
>
> Tiny—you want to fight somebody, you can fight me.
>
> All eyes are on the two. Tiny hovers over McCabe, but McCabe wears the difference.
>
> TINY
>
> Except I ain't got a gun.
>
> McCABE
>
> Go get one.
>
> Tiny is cornered and has to back off.
>
> TINY
>
> Listen, Mr. McCabe—I don't want to mess around with you. Hell, I didn't mean no harm—Honest—I don't want to get no gun.

The script tops off this moment by indicating the offscreen sound of a church bell—prompting a self-satisfied McCabe to triumphantly declare, "I don't never want to kill nobody on Sunday."[19]

At the time that the first draft was finished, the project was titled not *McCabe & Mrs. Miller*, nor even *McCabe*—the title of the Edmund Naughton novel from which the film and its first draft were adapted—but *The Presbyterian Church Wager*, commemorating a climactic scene in which McCabe enters Sheehan's saloon and bets the mining company's hired killers that he will survive their attempt to kill him. This moment of bravado is absent from the revised final version of the script, which condenses the premise of McCabe going into Sheehan's to talk to the killers with another moment from the first draft, in which McCabe (in his own bar) holds his own against the killers with a shotgun. This revision again rejects elements indicating McCabe is in control, as well as those projecting his macho competence and confidence. For instance, the first draft of the script has McCabe respond to the head-killer, Butler's, assertion that he knew and liked Bill Roundtree (a man McCabe admits to having shot) by declaring, "Bullshit.—Roundtree was . . . never nothin' but a pennyante card cheat."[20] In the revised final version of the script, when McCabe is asked whether he killed Butler's "best friend's best friend"

Bill Roundtree, he claims, "I was in the poker game when he got shot but I did not do it." The Kid challenges McCabe on this point, asking him if he is calling Butler's friend a liar, and McCabe immediately retreats, saying, "I ain't calling nobody a liar." The revised and condensed version of these scenes concludes with Butler, watching McCabe retreat across the bridge, confidently asserting, "that man never killed anybody."[21]

Of all of the scripts surveyed for this chapter, *McCabe & Mrs. Miller's* changes to its central figure seem to have been the most extensive and essential. This may be because the only available preproduction script of the film is the first draft, and that later drafts incorporated more significant changes, but aspects of the historical record argue against this and suggest that the revisions to the character were made on set. For instance, Patrick McGilligan, who conducted extensive interviews with key personnel on the film, writes that Altman, "encourag[ed] Beatty (who had helped transform the brutal bank robber Clyde Barrow into a sexually confused outcast in *Bonnie and Clyde*) to turn the character of McCabe inside out."[22] It seems likely that these revisions were at least partly contingent on Beatty's antimacho star persona. Beatty himself claims that he "watched the rushes" on the film "to see what the hell we should do next. . . . We kind of discarded the original script and I found myself writing most of the scenes. I wrote all my dialogue."[23]

Other evidence suggests that changes to Sheehan, the major antagonist in the first draft of the script, were made after production was underway. In the revised final version of the script, as in the first draft, he comes to terms with the mining company, but in the first draft he is a much more vicious and venal character. Sheehan mocks McCabe after he has been marked for death by the company and, in the script's climax, shoots and kills the wounded McCabe. He then orchestrates a triumphant photo session with McCabe's corpse, at the end of which he takes charge of the town on behalf of the mining company, instructing the photographer to place the body on ice so they can, "run him down to Bearpaw and make some money," presumably by making it a paid attraction.[24] René Auberjonois, who played Sheehan, has said that his experience on the film taught him:

a big lesson . . . about Bob and why you should never read a script of a film that Bob is about to direct. It's a waste of time and it's counterproductive to you as an actor. In the script, my character . . . was supposed to come upon . . . .McCabe and find him wounded and finish him off. I remember Bob taking me aside and saying, "We're not going to do that." That was deep into the film. I was deeply disappointed because I thought that completed the arc of the character.[25]

Auberjonois's description of the revision to Sheehan's character indicates that at least some of the first draft's character premises had been retained at the start of production. That these changes were made "deep into the film," after the actor had formulated his view of the character, makes their improvisatory status even more likely and in some ways more remarkable.

We should not, though, overstate the narrative significance of these changes, since they do not change the outcome for the film's protagonist. McCabe still dies. Moreover, Sheehan still becomes the leader of the town. The precise way in which this transfer of leadership is handled, though, points to another significant aspect of Altman and his collaborators' approach to the preproduction script. In *McCabe & Mrs. Miller*, Sheehan is a key node in the film's thematic structure. The ostensible change in Sheehan's character arc that so troubled Auberjonois is, then, a decision to shift the handling of the film's thematic materials from a direct approach embodied in narrative conflict to a more indirect approach. This indirect approach relies on an overtly ironizing narrational voice that mobilizes thematic elements through crosscutting between Sheehan, who emerges as a town leader by orchestrating the town's fight against a church fire, and McCabe, dying alone in a snow drift. The first draft of the film's script handles the thematic material more directly, not just in the narrative action—having Sheehan shoot McCabe—but also in the dialogue. Immediately before Sheehan instructs the photographer to put McCabe on ice, Sheehan tells the townspeople, "Nobody's gotta worry no more. This ain't gonna be no one-man town like it was. Company'll be coming and there's gonna be the good life like it was before <u>he</u> came. (beat) I'll be acting for the Company and you know you can always get a square shake from Patrick Sheehan."[26]

The script's placement of this dialogue in its final scene and on its final page indicates its intended thematic significance. As Kozloff points out in her discussion of the thematic function of film dialogue, "as a general rule, dialogue in a film's last scene carries particular thematic burdens, either reinforcing the film's ostensible moral or resisting closure."[27] Sheehan's scripted dialogue is clearly designed to reinforce the film's anticorporate moral message, and in doing so it works against the closure without comprehension strategy that, as discussed in chapter 1, Altman generally favored in the early 1970s. It is possible that Altman decided on his revised indirect approach in postproduction. The revised final version of the script does not specifically indicate the crosscutting on display in the final film. It does, though, elaborate on the firefighting in a way the first draft does not, and it also does more to emphasize the simultaneity of McCabe's situation and the townspeople's activities. Perhaps most importantly, it omits the dialogue from Sheehan transcribed previously.

As we shall see, this move toward an indirect approach to theme, and to character drama, is a consistent aspect of Altman and his collaborators' overall approach to the transposition of the preproduction script. And as the Sheehan example illustrates, this shift is often (but not always) carried out through changes, be they revisions or wholesale rejections, to scripted dialogue.

This close comparative analysis can help us better understand what Altman might be articulating in his declaration to Harmetz that, "It's not words we're dealing with in the films I make, not clever dialogue," and that he is, "interested in the behavior patterns of the characters, not in what they say. In my films, the actors can be creative. I don't think one person can write dialogue for 15 people." Rather than concluding that Altman is discarding the entirety of the script in favor of a process in which the actors fully improvise their parts and their words, we can understand him as inclined to permit limited improvisation by actors and to enact his own improvised, but strategic, rejection of scripted elements (since it seems to have been Altman who chose to eliminate the first draft's final scene with Sheehan) in service of a general preference for a more indirect approach to presenting narrative action, characters, and thematic material. In spite of changes like these, and rather than reducing or eliminating narrative structure and narrative elements, as some accounts have suggested, Altman and his collaborators seem to have elaborated on the script's narrative elements during production—adding minor characters, premises, and vignettes, and thereby thickening the storyworld or milieu. Interestingly, the move away from a conventional approach based in conveying theme directly through conventionalized storyworld proxies such as character dialogue requires an overt narrational voice and/or an audience seeking art cinema expressivity. In this way, Altman relocates credit and control of the film's thematics from the script to the production process and from the screenwriter to the gatekeeping "auteur" presiding over said process. By emphasizing his scriptual infidelity, implying wholesale rejection of the script and a fresh, organic, start Altman's biographical legend runs on a modified version of auteurist notions of origination, thereby obscuring a more complicated transpositional strategy of qualified rejection and intense elaboration.

## Transpositional Elaboration or *The Long Goodbye* to the Preproduction Script?

The available preproduction script for *The Long Goodbye* offers a chance to test some of the above hypotheses about Altman and his collaborators' transpositions and improvisations. The WCFTR copy of *The Long Goodbye* script—credited to Leigh Brackett—contains handwritten notes, including the words "Altman" and "keep close" on its cover. Significantly, written beneath the typed date "May 22, 1972," is the handwritten date "June 21, 1972"—six days *after* the official start of production. This version of the script, then, seems an ideal document with which to measure the extent and nature of Altman and his collaborators' overall revisions, rejections, or simple enactments of scripted elements. What is revealed confirms but also thickens the account of Altman's strategies indicated by the review of the *McCabe & Mrs. Miller* documents.

As with *McCabe & Mrs. Miller*, the large scale and scene-to-scene narrative structure of *The Long Goodbye*'s script is kept largely intact. In both script and finished film, a visibly injured Terry Lennox asks Marlowe, whose cat runs out on him, for a ride to the Mexican border. After dropping Lennox off, Marlowe is rousted by the police and thrown in jail, where he learns that Lennox is believed to have killed his wife. Upon his release, a newspaper reporter tells Marlowe that Lennox has confessed to the crime and committed suicide in Mexico. Marlowe is then hired by Eileen Wade to find her missing alcoholic husband Roger, whom Marlowe quickly discovers at Dr. Verringer's clinic. After he returns Roger Wade to his home, Marlowe is accosted by Marty Augustine and his gang. Augustine is looking for money Lennox has stolen from him and threatens Marlowe, displaying the lengths to which he'll go to get his money by smashing his girlfriend across the face with a Coke bottle. Marlowe follows Augustine to the Wades' beach house, where he learns that there is a connection between Lennox and the Wades. Upon visiting the Wades the next day, Marlowe has a conversation over drinks with Roger during which he asks him about Augustine and Lennox. At a party at the Wades' beach house, Dr. Verringer returns to request payment for his services, humiliating Wade in front of his guests. During the fallout, Marlowe questions Eileen Wade about connections between Lennox, his wife, and Roger Wade, and the evening climaxes with Roger Wade committing suicide. Afterward, Eileen tells Marlowe that she believes Roger killed Sylvia Lennox. Marlowe is rebuffed when he reports this to the police, and he is told that Roger Wade's alibi—that he was at Dr. Verringer's clinic—holds up. Once again, Marlowe is confronted by Augustine, who finds a $5,000 bill on Marlowe that he received in the mail from Terry Lennox. Marlowe is rescued at the last minute when Eileen Wade returns the stolen money, and as Marlowe tries to chase her down to talk to her he is hit by a car and hospitalized. Upon leaving the hospital, he returns to the Wades' Malibu home to find that it has been put up for sale and that Eileen has left town. Marlowe then travels to Otatoclan, where Lennox died, to re-interview the coroner and police chief, or "Jefe" (in the script the first interview takes place after Marlowe talks to the reporter, while in the film this is relocated to after Marlowe's "drinking party" with Roger Wade). The Otatoclan authorities accept the bribe Marlowe offers and reveal that Terry Lennox is, in fact, still alive. Both script and film conclude with Marlowe confronting and shooting Lennox after he calls him a loser, and with Marlowe then wordlessly walking past Eileen Wade as she returns to Terry.

Altman described *The Long Goodbye*'s narrative as, "merely a clothesline on which to hang a bunch of thumbnail essays, little commentaries."[28] And, as was suggested in chapter 1, this clothesline metaphor—to the extent that it might suggest a sparse or underdeveloped narrative—does not do justice to the classical narrative structure on display in the film. That the core causal chain is essentially replicated wholesale in the move from script to screen reinforces the conclusion that while Altman's rhetoric assigned narrative a secondary status, this does not seem to have meant that he viewed it (at least during the early 1970s) as disposable. Instead of being cynically, or cannily, used to sell a project to financiers and then rejected in favor of a surprise oppositional project and process, the scripted narrative clothesline provided the necessary support around which Altman's elaborative ambitions could be fulfilled. Granting that the script's narrative spine has not been tossed aside but remains more or less intact in the final film does not mean setting aside an understanding of Altman as improviser, collaborator, or innovator. Instead, it provides a warrant for closer examination in order to generate a more plausible account of Altman's transpositional rejections, revisions, and elaborations.

Many of these changes signal a drive toward efficiency through the cutting of narratively inessential or redundant actions. These transpositions are best viewed not as principled opposition to dominant norms but as the sometimes perversely economic means with which to simultaneously achieve Altman's conflicting or complementary practice-oriented, realist, and expressive aims. As one example of this transpositional imposition of efficiency, we can point to the film's treatment of the aftermath of Roger Wade's suicide. Interestingly, while the fact of Wade's suicide is retained in the film, the means have been revised in the transpositional process. Where the script indicates that Wade shoots himself in the head offscreen, Altman and company stage Wade's suicide on the beach of the Wades' Malibu Colony home, as Roger Wade wades out into the sea, recalling both "Cuchulain's Fight with the Sea" by the Irish poet W. B. Yeats,[29] and more proximately—in a reflexive thematic improvisation that will be discussed shortly—Norman Maine's suicide attempt in Cukor's *A Star Is Born* (1954).

More relevant to our purposes here, though, is that the structure and features of the script's handling of the suicide's aftermath underwent consolidation in the transpositional process. In the script, Marlowe's discovery of the body is immediately followed by a scene in the Wades' living room in which a police detective reads Eileen's statement aloud and then asks Marlowe and Eileen about their relationship. The scene ends with Marlowe leaving to accompany the detective to police headquarters, where he is to give his official statement, but before he departs he promises Eileen that he will come back later that night. A second scene has Marlowe returning to the living room to interrogate Eileen, which ultimately yields her admission that she believes Roger killed Sylvia Lennox, with whom he was having an affair. A third scene features Marlowe in Lieutenant Farmer's office at police headquarters, where he demands that, based on this new evidence, the police reopen the Lennox case. Farmer, though, informs Marlowe that the police already knew about Roger and Sylvia's affair and had eliminated Wade as a suspect because he was under sedation at Verringer's clinic at the time of Sylvia's death. Marlowe, unsatisfied, declares that Wade paid Verringer for his alibi and then storms out of the office.[30]

While the script takes three scenes and eight pages to move through this narrative material, Altman and company virtuosically condense it into just one scene and four-and-a-quarter minutes ⊚ (see the companion website for a video clip). Following the film's revision and restaging of Wade's suicide, all of the aforementioned narrative action has also been moved to the beach, which—in the aftermath of Wade's suicide—is now replete with uniformed policemen and onlookers. The dialogue in the scene begins with the police officer restating Eileen Wade's statement, using some of the dialogue from the script. Marlowe, though—holding an unscripted bottle of booze and a coffee cup—now interjects, haranguing the police and the onlookers, and at one point proclaiming that "everybody's drunk!" Rather than leaving with the officers, Marlowe shoos them away, encouraging one officer to, "get a couple of sand crabs and stick them up your nose and just disappear and go take a leak or something." When the police do leave, Marlowe's interrogation of Eileen begins. After Eileen essentially tells him that Roger killed Sylvia, Marlowe marches up the beach to where Lieutenant Farmer is overseeing the investigation. They argue, as in the script, and Farmer dismisses Marlowe's new information, citing the Verringer alibi. Instead of delivering the scripted, "I'll see you later," Gould's Marlowe storms off, shrouded in a blanket and with the bottle of booze in his hand, declaring, "you don't deserve to be alive, you fucking pig!"

Here, we get a qualified version of the sort of organic revision Harmetz proposed. Altman and company take advantage of the beachside setting of the Wades' home to revise the means and location of Roger Wade's suicide. They then take advantage of the new location's expansive physical space to create a single, but multiply zoned, dramatic space that efficiently encompasses the essential narrative action that, in the script's conception, required three separate spaces. By adding alcohol to the mix and overlaying a tone of drunken impulsiveness and hysteria on Marlowe's part, the film's version makes the increased pace—the stacking up of narrative events without ellipsis—seem appropriately and expressively frantic rather than like hackneyed expositional efficiency.

Altman's efficiency seems motivated by nonstandard—if not nonclassical—elaborative aims. The condensation here, perhaps counterintuitively, creates opportunities for addition, both in terms of a setting that can be crowded with characters and in terms of adding practice-oriented value for Altman, who can now exercise his preferences for improvisation and collaboration. Indeed, while retaining the core narrative action of the script, the film's postsuicide scene seems to be intensely improvised, with Gould and Steve Colt—the actor portraying Farmer—sometimes barely able to conceal their grins at Gould's articulation of the drunken Marlowe's high dudgeon. That very little of the scripted dialogue is replicated in the film raises the question of the extent to which the actors on Altman's films had free-reign to wander off-script, to fully improvise and revise their characters and their dialogue. According to Altman, "A lot of [Marlowe's stream-of-consciousness wise-cracking] was improvised, and [Gould] came up with that phrase, 'It's OK with me.' And we sort of used that as the key thing with all of these things that were happening."[31] Gould seems to have been a particularly welcome and enthusiastic partner in improvisation. He would later refer to himself as "the first American jazz actor."[32]

Historically, though, the problem with accounts of Altman, actors, and improvisation has been both overclaiming about the quantity and imprecision about the nature of the improvisation. For instance, stories about improvised monologues like Barbara Baxley's homily to the "Kennedy boys" in *Nashville* are sometimes viewed as the tip of an improvisatory iceberg constituted by Altman's entire oeuvre, rather than something more akin to the shark fin strapped to the young prankster's back in *Jaws*.[33] But as the examination of *Nashville*'s preproduction script later in this chapter reveals, it seems like this kind of actor-generated dialogue and character enhancement are best understood as a qualified form of improvisatory elaboration on top of a narrative structure largely retained from the script. Attempting to set the record straight, *Nashville* screenwriter and frequent early 1970s Altman collaborator Joan Tewkesbury has asserted that, "contrary to popular belief the whole movie was *not* improvised." Henry Gibson has similarly stated, "There's a tremendous misconception. . . . 'Oh, but it was all improvised, wasn't it?' Bullshit."[34]

Altman has also retreated from describing his approach in the expansive terms on display in the Harmetz article, telling one interviewer that:

> Now I get accused a lot of using improvisation, but that's a misunderstanding. For me improvisation is a rehearsal tool. Once we go to shoot the film, everyone pretty much knows what's going to happen, unless it's some scene with three hundred people, and we say, "OK, fire! Everybody run!" Then, that's usually improvised. Most of all, I just encourage actors to feel comfortable.[35]

Altman's comments here, and those specifically about Gould in *The Long Goodbye* earlier, suggest a more qualified version of improvisatory practice, one in which actorly improvisation is not only targeted and contingent but is encouraged and considered during rehearsals rather than captured "live" during shooting.

To some extent, then, even Gould's fairly limited—in terms of narrative impact—but plausibly "live" improvisations of dialogue for the postsuicide sequence in *The Long Goodbye* might be understood as an extreme case, the exception rather than the norm. In general, there is a lack of evidence that any changes resulting from rehearsed or live improvisations in Altman's films from this period were allowed to undermine causally essential features of the films' narrative designs. Indeed, a thorough comparison between the dialogue in the script and the dialogue in the film reveals that, even with Elliot Gould doing his best to present a manic Marlowe, causally salient portions have been retained. For instance, part one of the scene—while reducing the dialogue from the corresponding section of the script from four pages to around half a minute of screen time, and while adding the aforementioned drunken interjections by Marlowe—replicates the following lines of scripted dialogue:

Detective

[reading Eileen Wade's statement to her]

. . . suicide on a number of occasions. I think he had been under some kind of psychiatric care. Question, Don't you know? Answer, He kept . . .

Detective

[a second detective in the film]

Is this list of witnesses to your husband's behavior at the party substantially correct?

Eileen
Yes.


Detective
Your husband was upset about Verringer's visit, he threw everybody out of the house, passed out, and then he left you alone with Marlowe . . . [in the script, "passed out, and then he left," is "came back and found . . . "][36]


Detective
And there was no more definite motive you can think of, Mrs. Wade, that he might have had for killing himself? Marital problems, perhaps?

It is around this dialogue that Marlowe interjects and that Gould's performance elaborates. In the scene's second segment, almost all of the scripted dialogue is rephrased or replaced—except for Eileen's narratively crucial admission to Marlowe about Roger and Sylvia's affair, which implicates Roger in Sylvia Lennox's death. Likewise, the third part of the revised scene most closely tacks to the script when Farmer rebuts Marlowe's charges with the Verringer alibi. It seems clear, then, that Altman made improvisatory freedom conditional on retention of the narratively essential, on the maintenance of a coherent clothesline.

We also find in this revised sequence another of Altman's transpositional strategies—the multiplication and addition of narratively inessential characters. Whereas the script has a single detective interrogate Marlowe and Eileen Wade, the film provides two police officers who take turns asking questions. More incidentally, the beach is littered with onlookers talking over one another. This additive approach is on display throughout *The Long Goodbye*, as two new age female neighbors in the script become five in the film, although only two seem to actually have lines. Likewise, the number of hoods in Marty Augustine's gang is increased first by one, when they roust Marlowe at his apartment, and then again, with the addition of Arnold Schwarzenegger, in the film's final act. These excessive additions add nothing to the narrative function of the police department, Marlowe's neighbors, or Augustine's gang, but they do allow Altman to improvise riffs, or "essays," on new age living and multiculturalism, as each of Augustine's hoods represents a different race, religion or ethnicity. In each case they provide a surfeit of available and, at times, emphasized detail elaborated around the script's narrative spine.

These on-set elaborations are fairly minor excessive touches compared with the more thoroughgoing revisions that take place around the film's two male leads—Elliott Gould and Sterling Hayden. As with Beatty's star image reshaping McCabe, the casting contingencies associated with both actors likely played as significant a role as Altman's predisposition for scriptual in-fidelity. Extensive on-set revisions to Roger Wade's traits and narratively in-essential actions were most likely the result of the late casting of Hayden after the death of *Bonanza* star and Altman friend Dan Blocker, originally set to play the part. According to Brackett, the role had been written specifically for Blocker before Altman was attached to the film, and "when Hayden was cast the whole plot was thrown off base.... I had written Blocker in as a large cow-ardly type who would strike his wife. A big man with nothing inside. When Bob came to do the scenes between Marlowe and Wade, he had Gould and Hayden ad-lib most of the dialogue."[37]

It is not entirely clear why, as Brackett implies, Hayden could not play a big man with nothing inside, or how his casting threw the whole plot off base. In the script, Wade beats his wife offscreen, which he does not do in the film. It is hard, though, to believe that Hayden could not have performed this act, and the shift might actually have more to do with the revisions to Marlowe, who in the script bravely and successfully intervenes to stop Wade. What is clear is that the change in casting gave Altman, and therefore Hayden, reason and license to depart from the script. This may have been due to the late date at which Hayden replaced Blocker, who died May 13, 1972—just nine days before the typewritten date on the script and just a month before shooting began. Altman may have been busy enough and may have trusted Hayden enough to let him improvise key aspects of his part without calling for an of-ficial revision to the script. Much of the surrounding structure of Marlowe's visit to the Wade home—his talk with Roger, and Roger's interactions with Eileen—is substantially revised in the film. In general, Hayden's Wade is a somewhat gentler, somewhat more sympathetic loser figure than the script's bullying bastard.

Marlowe is similarly softened in the transposition from script to screen. For instance, the script describes Marlowe's sexual interest in Eileen Wade, while in the film it is almost inconceivable that Marlowe would sexually pursue any woman. In both script and film, Marlowe returns to Mrs. Wade after his initial encounter with Dr. Verringer. He is described as taking "what he hopes is an opening" and asking Eileen for a drink. She refuses him, with her demeanor described as "iceberg."[38] In the film, though, any notion of sexual tension is defused when Marlowe reveals to Eileen that he can't eat the dried apricots she offers because they give him diarrhea. According to Brackett, the "Gould-Altman character" is "pure Altman . . . Bob built up his character from the bar and cat scenes. Gould isn't tough at all. He looks vulnerable. You have to work with what you have. Marlowe isn't what he was in *The Big Sleep*, but

Elliott Gould isn't Humphrey Bogart."[39] Like Blocker, Gould was cast before Altman came on the picture, at the request of initial director Brian Hutton, but apparently he was also cast after Brackett had completed a draft of the script. Brackett recalls that, "Bob and I spent a lot of time talking over the plot. . . . I wrote one script, and then had to change the construction later. Bob wanted Marlowe to be a loser."[40] In spite of Brackett's revisions, the distance between the pre- and post-Gould Marlowes remains evident when comparing script to film. The script's Marlowe truly seems as though he had walked out of the 1940s or 1950s. At least in the preproduction stage, it does not look like much revision was done to "work with what [they] had," which meant that it was up to Gould and Altman to improvise, or "ad-lib" the character while maintaining the script's narrative spine.

One related on-set transposition revealed by this comparative analysis is surprising given that it involved Altman's excision of scripted material that developed what he has publicly proclaimed to be *The Long Goodbye*'s key thematic framework. As Altman put it, "I said, 'Let's take this guy out of the forties because there's no such thing as these private eyes. They don't exist as such.' And we put him in 1973. We called him Rip Van Marlowe. He was still in the forties, but suddenly he was in this period. And we made that the main kind of texture we were trying to deal with."[41] Yet this "texture" is hardly as uncomplicated as the statement makes it seem. As opposed to a classical-era Hollywood star like Robert Mitchum, who portrayed Marlowe in the 1978 adaptation of *The Big Sleep*, Gould seemed to epitomize the early 1970s. This posed a problem of thematic incongruity since the script that Altman took into production is replete with scenes and lines of dialogue that emphasize the distance between Marlowe and his times.

Based on the handwritten notes on the WCFTR's copy of the script it seems clear that this issue was not resolved even as production was underway. For instance, the second page of the script features a handwritten change in the dialogue that actually adds extra emphasis to the notion of Marlowe as a man out of time. The exchange between Terry Lennox and Marlowe, in which they discuss Marlowe's female neighbors was originally written as follows:

Terry
You must have some new neighbors since I was here.

Marlowe
A couple of real swingers. They keep the place lively.

The written notes suggest this dialogue be changed to the following:

Terry
We could have had some fun in the old days.


Marlowe
I don't know, there's something about unhooking a brassiere that I'd miss.

Here, the late revision actually makes this section of the script more thematically consistent, since reminiscences about the good old days and moments
when Marlowe is placed in stark contrast to the world around him are
scattered throughout the screenplay. In the very next scene, Marlowe and
Lennox's arrival at the Tijuana border is described as follows—"The border
Cops are really shaking down the cars with the long hairs in them. When they
see Marlowe and Terry Lennox, with suits and haircuts, they wave them on
through."[42]

Altman's transpositional solution to these incongruities was to adopt
a strategy similar to that employed on *McCabe & Mrs. Miller*. He and his
collaborators replaced most of the script's very direct approach to thematiza-
tion with an indirect approach. The dialogue (including the original versions)
and the details of the Tijuana border discussed earlier are both eliminated from
the final film, as are several other scenes whose focus seems to be on the Rip
Van Marlowe contrast. In the script, after Marlowe gets his assignment from
Eileen Wade he visits a corporatized private investigatory firm, The Carne
Organization, Inc., which has a placard on the front of its building declaring
its business to be "Confidential Enquiries"—in response to which Marlowe
declares, "Kee-rist." The interior of the building is described as "reeking of
chrome-steel efficiency," and the employees "are proper gentlemen, neatly
dressed, emphasizing Marlowe's shabbiness." The script specifies that, "from
O.S. we HEAR the SUBDUED CLATTER of business machines."[43] Marlowe
is visiting the Carne Organization in order to make use of what he describes
to their uncomprehending secretary as their "barred-window file," which he
goes on to explain is "the list of doctors who specialize in treating rich alco-
holics and borderline psychos." After the woman retrieves the information he
is looking for, he thanks her and in doing so invokes the classic image of the
private investigator—"Just like that. Think of the time and shoe leather if I'd
had to track them down myself." Her response is a humorless, "We consider
ourselves efficient Mr. Marlowe."[44] The entire scene is completely direct in its
thematic intent. It is also inessential to the plot, and so it seems that Altman,
generally favoring the indirect approach, felt safe in removing it, along with
several similar incidents in the script.

What remains of this thematic strand is more indirect and is largely incorporated into the mise-en-scène: Gould's rumpled suit and his refusal to take his tie off; his 1948 Lincoln Continental, which apparently actually belonged to Gould;[45] and his tendency to chain-smoke. Perhaps less concretely but most importantly, Altman also retained the character's core values, particularly his naïve trust in his best (nonfeline) friend. In some ways, this paradoxically makes the "man out of time" thematic less direct and substantial while also providing it greater focus. It is not the times per se but an aspect of Marlowe's most important relationship that marks him as out of touch. "It's OK with me," the line repeated by Marlowe throughout the film, reinforces this sense of his apartness from the attitudes and behaviors of his contemporaries, and as was established above, it was added by an ad libbing Elliott Gould during production.[46]

But Altman did not just reduce and revise the script's existing overt thematic elements over the course of production. He also elaborated, adding multiple motivic elements and several thematic threads. Importantly, their development is not entirely coherent—significance remains vague. Instead of conveying a thematic point, they seem to be part of an excessive narrational design intended to add layers of resonance to the film, provoking interpretation in a way that might be said to manifest the ambiguity and authorial expressivity of the art cinema. The film displays several of these improvised motivic structures, including incompletely "domesticated" animals, reflexive references to Hollywood, and contemporary left politics.

Brackett makes it clear that the idea for the film's opening sequence with Marlowe's cat originated with Altman, and the opening pages of the script, which alternate between Lennox driving from the Malibu Colony to Marlowe's apartment and Marlowe trying to please his hungry cat, are marked "A"–"D" rather than numbered as the rest of the script pages are, suggesting they were added later. As at the end of the finished film, the cat motif returns at the end of the script, which describes Marlowe's confrontation with Lennox, with Marlowe self-identifying to Lennox as a "loser. I even lost my cat," before shooting him. These final three script pages also have unusual markings, with "6.1/72" toward the top of each page, perhaps indicating the date of revision. The final page of the script, where we find the cat line, is actually numbered "90–91," suggesting that it condenses two pages from a previous draft. These special notations would seem to indicate that some of Altman's on-set transpositions were actually continuations of a process begun in preproduction and carried over into production because of time constraints.

In any event, Marlowe's cat should be understood as just the most prominent element in the film's larger unscripted animal-related motivic structure, which also, of course, prominently features dogs. While the inclusion of the film's dogs may also have originated with Altman, the canine elements, unlike the cat premise, seem to have been inserted into the film only after the beginning of production. In every instance, the dogs in the final film are absent from the script. Eileen Wade's constantly barking Doberman, who harasses Marlowe and Roger Wade throughout, is not mentioned in the script. Likewise, a stray dog that Marlowe refers to as Asta—a reflexive reference to the dog in *The Thin Man* detective films—as well as the dogs who are wandering in front of traffic as Marlowe first arrives at the Malibu Colony, are missing from the script. The previously mentioned revision of Roger Wade's suicide provides an opportunity for concluding the Doberman's arc—he is last seen roaming the beach, carrying the drowned man's cane in his mouth like a trophy. Finally, stray dogs roam the streets of Otatoclan—most prominently the two dogs whose presence was, according to filmmakers, coincidental and who engage in a supposedly spontaneous (again, according to the filmmakers) sex act. Interestingly, the shot that captures this coupling is preceded by a clearly staged shot of Marlowe getting off a bus and being followed by a dog as he walks through the village (Figure 4.1). It is a cut to a closer framing of Marlowe that captures the climactic canine reproductive act with a zoom in (Figure 4.2). The fornication may have been improvised, but the shot in which it takes place was at the very least staged and framed so that a group of dogs would be featured in the background. It seems likely that at most only the sex, rather than the presence of the dogs, was improvised by Altman's canine collaborators while the camera was rolling, and we might remain skeptical about even this.

What does this improvised motivic structure add up to, though? Given the status of dogs as "man's best friend" and the faith in friendship that deludes

Figure 4.1 *The Long Goodbye*

**Figure 4.2** *The Long Goodbye*

Marlowe into believing Lennox, it is possible that this domesticated animal backdrop offers resonance with the major moral themes of the film. The fact that, immediately before his best friend exploits him, Marlowe is deserted by his own pet over something as petty as a cat food brand, and that Marlowe references that loss right before killing his friend seems significant. Perhaps the wild dogs of Otatoclan can be understood as metaphors for Lennox's nondomesticated behavior, since he has killed his wife and violated the ethical code of friendship. Coincidental or not, the image of one dog mounting another until the bottom dog, having had enough, finally snarls and throws him off summarizes the Lennox/Marlowe relationship nicely. But the symbolic and thematic significance here is fairly indirect compared to the more thematically loaded scripted scenes and dialogue discussed earlier. Even the delivery of the final installment of the cat motif at the film's climax feels more absurd than thematically weighty.

Likewise, the reflexive references to Hollywood are more provocative than coherent, and they, too, are completely absent from the script. As with Marlowe's lost cat, the most direct aspect of the motivic structure—the "Hooray for Hollywood" song—brackets the film, appearing over the United Artists logo at its beginning and then returning for Marlowe's long walk away from Lennox's corpse and past Eileen Wade. But its function is fairly obscure, as are: the references to Al Jolson in blackface, the ineffective Malibu Colony guard's preoccupation with impressions of classic Hollywood stars, the borrowing of the suicide attempt and use of reflection shots from *A Star Is Born*, a hoodlum's reluctance to take off his clothes because George Raft never had to, the "invisible man" whose face is wrapped in bandages and shares Marlowe's hospital room, and the restaging (and reversal) of the ending of *The Third*

*Man* as Eileen Wade drives past Marlowe in a jeep while he ignores her. Again, none of these are in the script. According to Elliot Gould, Altman allowed him to improvise the entirety of his exchange with his hospital mate, but the fact that his "I've seen all your pictures" line is just one part of this larger motivic set suggests that Gould was improvising within a broader concept established by Altman. As was discussed in chapter 1, some critics have seen a critique of Hollywood in these reflexive motifs, but Altman has protested that he wished only to call attention to the film as "just a movie." What is perhaps more interesting here than any interpretive yield generated by careful scrutiny of this motivic patterning is the fact that it was done "on the run," as it were. This may explain any particular set of elements' difficulty in cohering, although clearly Altman was making use of some classical principles of construction with the opening and closing cat and "Hooray for Hollywood" framing. It also reinforces and makes more precise Altman's insistence that his work came on top of character and story, which these motivic and thematic additions may inflect but do not substantially impact. Moreover, this approach lines up with Altman's practice-oriented appreciation for day-to-day problem-setting and -solving. Improvising ways to extend a motif originated on-set would seem to be a particularly appealing challenge for someone with that preference.

As with the layers of reflexive, canine, and feline patterning, the less ostensibly indirect, politically relevant material in the film seems to have been added after the film's production was underway. This includes the grocery store clerk's reappearance at the police station, where Marlowe asks him about his girlfriend and he declares that his girlfriend "got busted at a protest rally," leading him to "bust the pig that busted her." The interrogation scene that immediately follows this exchange also adds political thematics not previously present in the script, as Altman once again multiplies the number of characters indicated in the script, adding a black police officer and a second, overtly homophobic, white detective. In the script, the white Lieutenant Farmer handles the entirety of the interrogation, while in the film Farmer waits in an observation room with the black officer while the white detective asks Marlowe a series of questions about his name and background, providing Elliott Gould a chance to improvise an Al Jolson impression and responses to accusations of homosexuality. Meanwhile, Farmer and the black officer have an exchange in which Farmer reprimands the black officer for calling Marlowe a "cutie pie" rather than what is, to his thinking, the more correct "smart ass." When Farmer finally enters the interrogation room and the other white detective declares Marlowe to be "a real cutie pie," Farmer says nothing. The black officer, still watching through the one-way mirror, responds to this double standard by commenting to himself that, "He's the cutie pie, Lieutenant. You're the smart ass you little honky bastard."

The handling of the interrogation scene is entirely in line with the previous improvisatory practice at the beach discussed earlier. Altman adds characters, and then allows for improvisational elaboration around the narrative core of the scene—the interrogation of Marlowe by Farmer. In terms of its fidelity to the script, the scene is remarkably bifurcated. Before Farmer enters the interrogation room, the film departs entirely from the preproduction script, with the added detective and Marlowe apparently ad libbing their lines inside the interrogation room while Farmer and the black officer add commentary and contribute to the film's political thematics as they look on through a two-way mirror. After Farmer enters the interrogation room, with the exception of the cutaway to the black officer's line the scene plays out with remarkable fidelity to the script, conveying all the important premises about Marlowe and Lennox's relationship and the death of Sylvia Lennox. As an additional bonus, this elaboration around the scripted elements also allows Altman to shoot a large portion of the scene through the scratched and ink-stained two-way mirror of the observation room—an instance of the aperture framing, filtered look, and depth effect chapter 2 established as integral to his visual approach.

Perhaps unsurprisingly, Marlowe's time in jail provides a key focal point for the film's political content. After the interrogation, Marlowe is shown being released from his jail cell. In the script, Marlowe is "alone in the cell,"[47] while in the film Altman and company have once again added another character, Socrates, played by David Carradine in an uncredited role. Socrates's recounting of his harassment by the police is interrupted by the arrival of the warder, and he then changes the subject of his monologue to how prisons are full of people who smoke marijuana rather than rapists and murderers, complaining, "Possession. Possession is what you get here now. Possession of noses. Possession of gonads. Possession of life. It's a weird world. Listen, someday—someday all the pigs are going to be in here, and all the people are going to be out there." Marlowe agrees and, in a break with the "man out of time" framing of his character, leaves his cellmate with a new age gem— "Remember, you're not in here. It's just your body. See you when you get out." A fairly digressive interlude, this scene resides alongside the narrative action rather than having been integrated with it. On its own, then, this exchange seems the opposite of indirect, both in terms of its overt insertion into the narrative and its straightforward commentary on the contemporary political situation. But from the perspective of its contribution to large-scale motivic patterning and an overarching thematic statement, the role of this exchange is less straightforward, more one-off.

More conventionally indirect is Altman's handling of Marlowe's first view of the interior of the posh Malibu Colony where the Wades reside ⓓ (see the companion website for a video clip). While the script has nothing to say about the milieu of the Malibu Colony, the film prefaces Marlowe's interview with Eileen Wade with a sequence in which he surveys the private neighborhood on his drive from the gated entrance to the Wades' home. In a series of three quasi-eyeline matches, Marlowe observes an Asian maid walking dejectedly in a stereotypical uniform (Figure 4.3) and then sees a black man in white jacket and tie sweeping the walk in front of a home (Figure 4.4). This is followed by a shot of the "guests" entrance to the Wades' home (Figure 4.5). As he pulls into a parking space, four white women—dressed smartly in their tennis whites— pass by (Figure 4.6). Marlowe looks them over suspiciously and then makes a point of turning and locking his car door (Figure 4.7). This brief bit of word- less social commentary is a subtle contribution to Altman's improvised por- trayal of social and racial tensions in contemporary Los Angeles, providing

**Figure 4.3** *The Long Goodbye*

**Figure 4.4** *The Long Goodbye*

**Figure 4.5** *The Long Goodbye*

**Figure 4.6** *The Long Goodbye*

**Figure 4.7** *The Long Goodbye*

one of the set of "thumbnail essays" hung on the script's narrative clothesline over the course of its transposition.

Altman makes the final socially "relevant" alteration to the film's script during Marlowe's return to Otatoclan, where he offers a bribe to the Mexican officials. This is in some ways a troubling plot point, since it plays into othering stereotypes of corrupt Mexican officials. The script addresses this straightfor-wardly, as the "Jefe" protests Marlowe's bribe of $5,000, asking, "Mr. Marlowe, why do you persist in this attitude that all Mexicans are corrupt? Why do you come here with your insults . . . ?" Marlowe responds, "I don't think that Mexicans are one bit more corrupt than white Anglo-Saxon protestants . . . WASPS to you . . . and all I want to know is what really happened to Terry Lennox." But when Marlowe offers him another $500, "Jefe" relents, telling him, "I pride myself that I am absolutely incorruptible, I never sell out a man for less than he paid me. You have topped Lennox by $500."

We can compare this attempt to have it both ways with the revised solu-tion in the film. Instead of taking place in an office, this conversation occurs in a rather sad looking police car. The scene begins with the Mexican officials insisting that they want to show Marlowe their town. The move to the police car adds a level of visual interest and movement to the sequence, a strategy we can see on display as far back as Altman's first industrial film, *Honeymoon for Harriet*, discussed in chapter 5. The revision also provides an opportunity for some qualifiedly digressive description of milieu, as the car tours the poverty-stricken town. This is only "qualifiedly digressive" because Altman has lever-aged the elaboration of milieu into a compositionally motivated plot point (or vice versa) and a motivic element, as the officials intend the tour to illustrate the need for improvements in the community. Marlowe takes the hint and offers his bribe as a "donation to the people of this town" rather than a payout to a selfish official. This could still be viewed rather cynically, providing a cover for what is understood by Marlowe to be a more straightforward kind of bribe, but the overall tone the film takes in regard to the Mexican officials is much lighter and gentler than the tone found in the script, in which the officials are full of false bravado. The spotlighting of the poverty of America's neighbor to the south and the movement away from the stereotype of the greedy and corrupt Mexican official serves to reinforce the liberal political and racial thematics that Altman has elaborated around the film's narrative line.

Whereas a comparison of *McCabe & Mrs. Miller* to a version of its prepro-duction script simply suggested many of Altman's improvisatory strategies and practices, a comparison of *The Long Goodbye* with a much more proximate version of its preproduction script offers more concrete confirmation of their use. Moreover, this examination displays Altman and company employing these transpositional strategies with a high degree of sophistication and skill. Altman and his collaborators have maintained not just the essence but the bulk of the narrative structure found in the script. This narrative structure serves as a strong support on which Altman and his partners can elaborate and improvise in several characteristic ways. Cuts and revisions made to the narrative action of the film during production, such as the changes made to Roger Wade's suicide, often serve to enhance Altman's unconventional or deconventionalized approach to the subject matter and genre and also provide more improvisatory opportunities. Key actors are permitted, because of trusted relationships and/or because of the contingencies of production, to revise aspects of their characters (probably under the direct guidance of Altman) and to improvise behavior and dialogue.

While this improvisation may take place, Altman and his collaborators also ensure that key links in the causal chain are maintained, often through retaining the narratively central dialogue from the script in order to deliver kernels of plot. The overall strategy of elaboration around the narratively essential includes multiplying and then foregrounding lower-tier or conventionally backgrounded figures such as Marlowe's neighbors, police officers, cell mates, etc., and then sometimes, but not always, allowing them to make their own apparently improvised contributions. These changes to character and characters, and the improvisations that they depend on and also extend are often put in the service of one or several improvised motivic and thematic structures. The seemingly offhand structures are themselves elaborated around and on the retained narrative structure, although they tend to be relatively indirect and are unlikely to cohere in a way that conforms to classical norms. Kristin Thompson discusses the use of motifs in Hollywood storytelling as a means of attaining "overall unity and clarity." Such motifs are repeated systematically, often to "add emotional resonance," to provide a "means of exposition," and, with visual motifs, to "help add redundancy without the need for heavy-handed dialogue."[48] Altman's less structured motifs are sometimes substituted for the more classical motivic and thematic material present in the script, as with the elimination of the bulk of the direct "Rip Van Marlowe" material in favor of a more politically engaged and socially conscious set of materials. What we find overall, though, is largely a supplementing of story and script rather than their abandonment. Altman's departures from standard practices are substantial, but they are also targeted and bounded rather than wholly subject to a pragmatic principle that requires complete organicity.

## Before and After: Consistent Inconsistencies and the Anticipation of Elaboration

*The Long Goodbye* provides a clear example of the kinds of transpositional practices suggested by the comparative analysis of *McCabe & Mrs. Miller*, but it also displays a degree of sophistication in the employment of these practices that implies a long history of experimentation and refinement. Examining the feature film immediately preceding *McCabe & Mrs. Miller—Brewster McCloud—*and then tracing Altman and his collaborators' work back through *M\*A\*S\*H*, makes it clear that Altman's strategies are fairly consistent, with the details of their employment varying with the narrative and production contingencies of each film.

The Altman Archive's copy of *Brewster McCloud*'s script, dated May 11, 1970, just eleven days prior to the start of production,[49] is largely consistent with the finished film. Probably the most significant thematic elaboration beyond the film's script is around the ornithologist's lecture, discussed in previous chapters. In the script, the ornithologist does not transform into a bird-man and is instead present strictly as a voice on the radio. Furthermore, while the lecturer's presence is extended throughout the finished film, in the script it is limited to the opening montage sequence with Brewster and Wright. In accounts of the film's production, the lecturer has been described as a last-minute addition improvised by actor René Auberjonois and Altman. According to Auberjonois, "In one day, we shot like thirty-six different scenes of me turning into a bird. I did my own makeup, my own costume—feathers in my hair—and we put birdseed in the chalk tray in front of the blackboard. At the end of that day Bob said to me, 'I don't know. I'm shooting this to be safe, and I don't know if any of this will be in the film.'"[50]

These late additions significantly changed the subject and tone of the lecture. In the script, as in the film, the lecturer does begin by discussing the motivation for man's long-standing fascination with flight, with "tales of flying spirits scientifically explained today as artistic and religious sublimation's [sic] of man's frustrated dream of flight."[51] But he then goes on to recount a fairly straightforward, if colorful, history of the pursuit of flight. We can contrast this with the wide-ranging, multifunctional lecture delivered in the film, which, as discussed in chapter 1: primes the audience for interpretation, indirectly clarifies narrative premises, encourages narrative-oriented hypothesizing, and offers ironic commentary. Much of this functionality arises from the juxtaposition of the lecturer's description of the behaviors of specific kinds of birds with characters in the film, and in his account of the film's production McClelland describes being asked to look over several books on birds: "[Altman] asks, 'You know the relations of the characters to the movie pretty well, don't you?' I nod. 'Well, I need someone to go through these bird books that I've got here and find birds to match the characters. René Auberjonois begins his lecture Monday and I haven't even started writing it.'"[52]

Altman and his collaborators also add a series of political references to *Brewster McCloud* along the lines of those found in *The Long Goodbye* comparison. The script does not indicate the race of the band members whom Heap lords over in her Astrodome rehearsal of the national anthem, and it also has Brewster annoyedly turn off a monitor displaying the rehearsals. The film, on the other hand, depicts Heap shouting down a black marching band, and has Brewster play the "Black National Anthem" over the Astrodome p.a. system. Later, when Heap is feeding her white doves and Brewster's raven flies into the scene, the script indicates only that, "She becomes very upset and hits at the bird."[53] In the film, though, she shouts a racial epithet at the raven. The cumulative import of these additions serves to suggest that Heap's subsequent strangulation is motivated by antiracism.

A complementary Spiro Agnew motif was also elaborated during the film's production. The film shows Brewster's raven shitting on a newspaper with the headline, "Agnew: Society Should Discard Some U.S. People," at the end of the opening sequence with Heap, but in the script the raven simply, "squawks as CAMERA GOES to it on its perch."[54] Likewise, Altman and company improvised a thematic use for the scatologist investigating the excrement found on the murder victims. In the script, a police scientist recommends that Shaft visit an unnamed scatologist at a university.[55] In the film, though, the scientist offers Shaft a name, or an attempt at a name, "—uh, Agnew, Agnok," thus connecting the vice president to an "expert on excrement." Through these revisions to the script, then, Altman indirectly incorporates the political— none of the characters discuss contemporary politics directly.

As with Altman's subsequent films, *Brewster McCloud* retains the essential narrative spine of the script and most of its scenes. There has been some rearranging to create interesting juxtaposition and, presumably, to improve pacing. But much more is added than is cut, and no essential element of the film's narrative structure is removed. Instead, Altman and his team once again elaborate around the scripted elements. For instance, officer Hines' courtship of the widow of the abusive and corrupt Detective Breen was added during production, as was the play with Captain Crandall's constant misidentification of Hines as "Hanes." In the script, the character, played by Corey Fischer, is called Grimes, a name that does not lend itself to the (homophonic) ketchup/ underwear brand confusion that Crandall seems to be suffering from. That

Altman would allow Fischer to improvise such an extensive elaboration during production is a testament to Altman's belief in the actor. In fact, during the production of *M*A*S*H* an exasperated Altman, pointing toward Fischer, asked Elliott Gould, "Why can't you be more like him?"[56]

Fischer's account of the production of *M*A*S*H* is helpful for clarifying the principles underlying Altman's approach, both to improvisation and to the elaboration of the narrative structure of the script:

> People talk about improvisation in Bob's movies, but it's often a misnomer. It wasn't as if people were improvising on camera. What Bob loved to do was to create a scene that had a lot of density, a lot of levels going on, all these simultaneous conversations and overlaps. He liked having more than one center to a scene or a shot.... [By] the time he actually got to [shooting a scene], it would have been set. He would have made suggestions, tinkered with it, and signed off on it. With Bob I have this image of a Renaissance painter, where Michelangelo would be working on the main figures and his helpers would be working on the figures at the edges. I think that's what Bob wanted and needed, this entourage of actors who were not playing primary characters who would enliven those edges.[57]

This enlivening of the edges, the conditional and situational entrusting of his collaborators to improvise, along with the approval process that these improvisations had to go through, paints a very different picture from that of the entirely organic, laissez-faire image of Altman that is often articulated as a significant part of his biographical legend.

As Fischer's statement indicates, even under the presumably more constrained production circumstances of *M*A*S*H* there is still evidence that Altman's improvisatory and transpositional practices are consistent with his approach in later features during the early 1970s. Aside from the qualified improvisational process that Fischer and others were permitted to engage in during production, the very presence of several of the secondary characters in the film was prompted by Altman. According to Altman, "Originally, it had only eight characters who had speaking lines, and I just filled it with people ... from an improvisational theater group in San Francisco, and I had to write a line in for each one in order to get them hired."[58] We should be circumspect of Altman's claim that the screenplay initially had only eight characters with speaking lines. However, in a letter from Ring Lardner to Ingo Preminger on his final script revisions, Lardner writes, "I realize I inserted the added characters Bob wanted without really integrating them, and I think what he's done with Murrhardt, Bandini and Leslie is all to the good."[59] Lardner's letter indicates that there was a collaborative back and forth between writer and director during the preproduction of the film, with each suggesting and making changes and augmentations. This would seem to differ from Altman's later account, which essentially claims total authorship and acknowledges collaboration solely with the actors.

Altman's basic strategy of additive elaboration is indicated by a comparison between the film and its "Final Screenplay," part of the WCFTR's Robert Altman Papers, dated February 26, 1969, but including Lardner's revisions as an addendum. Many of the changes made during production, or postproduction, are common parts of the film's legend, such as the addition of the punctuative public address announcements that function much like the lecturer in *Brewster McCloud*, or the extension of Hot Lips's presence beyond the infamous shower/hair color incident because Altman was so impressed with Sally Kellerman's performance. McGilligan's biography of Altman does an effective job of categorizing many of these changes in the process of partially discrediting Altman's aforementioned totalizing authorship claim.[60] McGilligan's conclusion, though, that "Altman started out pretty much where he ended up," understates the extent of the revisions, perhaps because his gauge was the thoroughgoing improvisation and departure promised by Altman's biographical legend. It is true that much of the narrative content of the script is retained, but Altman's approach recognized that narrative structure could provide the backbone, or "clothesline," for thoroughgoing and impactful elaboration.

Altman's tendency to redirect the thematics of the scripts is certainly on display as early as *M\*A\*S\*H*. Whereas the script condenses most of the gory surgery which was so important to Altman into a montage sequence immediately after Hawkeye and Trapper return from Japan, the film interweaves these elements throughout, creating a consistent backdrop that qualifies and contextualizes its hijinks rather than serving as a more concentrated focal point directing the audience to contemplate the consequences of war. Furthermore, Altman eliminates a thematically weighty character goal and subplot from the script, in which Hawkeye is focused on getting Ho-Jon, the camp's "native" houseboy, into Androscoggin College. In a section of the script seemingly excised during production, Ho-Jon is weighed down with explicit thematic import, as he questions Duke and Hawkeye's suggestion that he round up "a few of the boys" to serve as "native bearers" for Trapper, who has been promoted to chief of surgery. Ho-Jon's response, "And if I go to New York, the natives there will carry me? I don't think so," leads the men to rethink their request and apologize.[61] Whereas the film says goodbye to Ho-Jon when he fails to fail his army induction physical, in the script Ho-Jon returns to the M\*A\*S\*H unit after he is injured in combat. Indeed, the winnings of the inter-Army football game are meant to go toward putting Ho-Jon through college, until he unexpectedly dies from a medical complication. It is not clear how much of this material was shot, if any, but this goal and these premises did not make it into the final cut of the film, perhaps because of Altman's general tendency to avoid direct and foregrounded thematic "significance" and perhaps because he was wary of the postcolonial critique Hawkeye's goal could engender—although given the film's questionable sexual politics this would have been a rather arbitrary acquiescence to political responsibility.

M\*A\*S\*H provides strong evidence that from early on Altman's transpositional strategy of de- or rethematization of the script was complemented by a dedramatization of the script. Certainly, some have suggested, probably accurately, that the elaborative "layering" that Fischer and others have talked about decenters the dramatic action of the script, limiting audience engagement and sympathy. While I discuss in chapter 1 how some of these claims need to be qualified, the comparative analyses conducted for this chapter do reveal consistent movement toward limiting intense or, less generously, clichéd and histrionic dramatization that might be present in the scripts. For instance, the dialogue from McCabe's famous, "I got poetry in me," monologue, delivered as a soliloquy in the film, is largely present in the script, but there it is delivered to Mrs. Miller, as McCabe fully and expansively opens up to her for five pages during their last night together. The original scene ends with Mrs. Miller declaring, "Love me, John. Love me."[62] Likewise, the preproduction script for The Long Goodbye features Marlowe heroically rescuing Eileen Wade from one of Roger's beatings.[63] In his transposition of M\*A\*S\*H, Altman makes similar revisions. For instance, he removes a scripted scene in which Lieutenant Dish is so distraught after an abdominal surgery that she has to leave the operating room. Hawkeye goes out to comfort her and succeeds—"Smiling, tears gone, ready to go to work," she thanks him, saying, "You helped me pull together when I needed it."[64] It is this interaction that sparks their relationship in the script, whereas in the film Dish and Hawkeye flirt during a leg amputation. The excision of Ho-Jon's collegiate subplot serves similar purposes. For instance, while the film retains the visual content of a scripted post–football scene, where Hawkeye, sitting at a poker game, turns to watch Ho-Jon's body taken away, with the film's removal of the Ho-Jon subplot the covered body becomes anonymous. A specific and conventional pathos has been replaced with a more generalized melancholy.

The above examination of M\*A\*S\*H and Brewster McCloud clearly demonstrates a consistent set of elaborative transpositional practices prior to Altman's much publicized (if also misrepresented) work on McCabe & Mrs. Miller. Similarly, moving past The Long Goodbye and comparing the preproduction scripts of *Thieves Like Us, California Split*, and *Nashville* to the finished films reveals that these transpositional approaches seem to have largely endured throughout the early 1970s period. As with the other examples in this chapter, Altman retains the core narrative structure and causal chain, excises exposition, and engages in the dedramatization and dethematization of each film. Doing so clears the way for the elaborative layering of contingent improvisational opportunities for performers, middlegrounding of typically backgrounded characters, and improvised thematics discussed earlier. However, with *California Split* and *Nashville* the construction of the scripts themselves also integrates strategies responsive to Altman's practice-oriented preferences. These innovations in script format, novel even in the context of Altman's early 1970s practice, can be understood as participating in what Steven Price has described as a general loosening of the rules governing screenplay construction in post–studio system Hollywood. This was a period in which writers and writer-director auteurs "were able to write their scripts in more idiosyncratic ways than would have been possible under the old order," not just in terms of "thematic or generic concerns," but also in terms of "the formal properties of [the] screenplays" themselves.[65] Altman's innovative collaborations with his screenwriters on these films take advantage of this shift in Hollywood's industrial and craft practices.

Unfortunately, the Altman Archive's copy of Joan Tewkesbury and Altman's script for *Thieves Like Us*—dated February 1, 1973, but with interior pages dated March 10, 1973, and with handwritten notes on the pages and on small scraps of paper that are appended—is incomplete, missing pages 36–68. Even so, comparative analysis of the extant script with the final film indicates general consistency with the transpositional practices described previously. Interestingly, *Thieves Like Us* displays less improvisational departure from the scripted dialogue and fewer significant revisions to the main character's traits than in the previous films. Still, many of Altman's regular strategies have been applied to the film's revisions, and this is particularly evident in the excision of roughly twenty pages (112–131) of the script's final act.

The removal of these pages, though, does not significantly alter the film's narrative structure. The excised pages cover the visits of the film's male and female leads, Bowie and Keechie, with a sympathetic and corrupt Mississippi judge in an attempt to acquire his assistance in getting Bowie's partner in crime and Keechie's cousin, Chicamaw, out of prison. They also include the couple's trip to a movie theater and beauty parlor. The scenes with the judge are mostly talk and serve only a very limited role in advancing the narrative's causal chain, providing mainly a kind of false start since Bowie decides to abandon his attempt to get the judge to secure legal representation for Chicamaw in favor of breaking him out. That said, as part of his shift in strategies, the scripted Bowie does write the judge a letter requesting a forged bench warrant and a sheriff's badge. The excision of this causal link from the finished film leaves Bowie's possession of these items unexplained. Likewise, the excised scenes outside of the movie theater and beauty parlor make only minor contributions to the film's romantic plotline, with the pair discussing marriage but deciding against it and reiterating their established plan to escape to Mexico.

Whether or not these scenes were abandoned entirely during production or whether they were shot and then left on the cutting room floor is an open question. In the film, Keechie's hair does mysteriously transform from straight to curly from one scene to the next (from the pair's arrival at the Grapes motor hotel to Bowie monologuing to the sleeping, sickly Keechie in their cabin). The excised portion of the script describes Keechie as coming out of a beauty parlor with a Ruby Keeler style haircut. Moreover, the dialogue in the film explaining why Keechie is sleeping is delivered as Bowie and Keechie move to their lodgings with their backs to the camera, freeing the filmmakers to insert the dialogue in postproduction.[66] At the very least, the discontinuity in Keechie's hairstyle suggests the filmmakers may have planned to shoot the excised portion of the script. In any event, the excisions arguably demonstrate Altman's previously discussed drive toward efficiency. Here, scripted action whose narrative purpose is inessential or simply expositional is treated as expendable.

Importantly, though, the removal of these scripted scenes also reflects Altman's strategies of dedramatization and dethematization. While Bowie is waiting outside of the beauty parlor, he engages in a confrontation with a drunk that seems intended to demonstrate Bowie's increasing callousness. The confrontation reaches its dramatic climax with Bowie knocking the drunk down with his car door, getting out of the car, ripping his shirt, kicking him, and threatening to stomp his head in.[67] Such a starkly valenced incident, with the protagonist bullying a helpless drunk in order to illustrate a character arc, seems to have run against Altman's preference for a less direct approach to characterization.

The dethematization of the *Thieves Like Us* script comes partly in the film's excision of an overt discussion between the judge and Bowie about social injustice—including one potent anecdote about a rich man killing a poor man's dog—and the glamorization of criminality found in the mass media.[68] It comes, as well, in the removal of the fairly direct critique of the fantasy sold to depression-era audiences by Hollywood that is relayed in the scenes outside the movie theater and beauty parlor. Altman's removal of these sequences undermines accounts of his expressive project as focused on the reflexive critique of Hollywood and also attenuates the sexist implications of depicting Keechie as unreflexively enamored of the aforementioned Ruby Keeler, lost in female fantasy while the man bears the burdens of real-world responsibility.

Rather than eliminating the social justice thematic, the film displaces it to a revised version of the scripted sequence in which Bowie, impersonating a sheriff, arrives at the prison and meets with the prison head, Captain Stammers ® (see the companion website for a video clip). The script describes a prison office whose exterior "is a squat, brick building . . . a barrack-looking building with stone foundations and whitewashed," and whose interior smells of disinfectant. Bowie's meeting with Stammers is unremarkable, except for the fact that Stammers is suffering from neuritis, giving him an aura of pathos.[69] The film, though, discards almost everything about the encounter except Bowie successfully clearing the narratively significant hurdle of getting Stammers to buy into his ruse. Stammers is shown as keeping a home on the prison grounds, and Bowie meets with him on his screened-in porch, which serves as a dining area. Stammers is about to eat his lunch—served by a black prisoner—as Bowie arrives, and the small table on the porch is overloaded with meats and sides. The direct discussion of social injustice found in the excised scene with the judge is replaced in the film by the implications of this meal and by the unpolished, seemingly improvised, discussion of gravy, mashed potatoes, and weight gain by Stammers and his wife. Bowie waits in his car while Stammers finishes his meal, where he promptly and somewhat implausibly falls asleep. He is awakened by the baying of the dogs kenneled next to the house as Stammers' wife feeds them the meal's substantial leftovers. This revision nicely conveys the injustice of the social system, with the dogs, whose purpose it is to hunt down escaped men, ironically eating better than the men themselves. At the same time, the presence of the unscripted dogs fits nicely with Altman's established preference for elaboratively adding animals during the production of his films. Here, he does so even as he removes the script's overt allegorical comparison of dogs to women and the poor.[70]

Altman's robust set of transpositional strategies, including the dedramatization and rethematization evident in the transposition of *Thieves Like Us*, is also present in *California Split*. However, Joseph Walsh's script is remarkable in its attempt to anticipate—and arguably preclude—a key aspect of Altman's on-set transpositional method. Specifically, Walsh claims he was asked to write dialogue for background conversations about a month before the start of production. The request, and Walsh's fulfillment of it, would seem to mark a step backward from Altman's challenge to the standard Hollywood logic, articulated earlier by Maras, that demanded the separation of conception and execution. The University of Michigan's Altman

Archive holds a copy of the script dated December 18, 1973 (though some pages are dated as late as February 4, 1974), that reflects this strategy.[71] For instance, page 11A of the script, marked at its top with "January 8, 1974," notes, "THE ACTION DESCRIBED IN SCENES 4, 5, AND 5A IS HAPPENING SIMULTANEOUSLY." Scenes 4 and 5 encompass Bill and Charlie's first meeting at the bar, and scene 5A covers the discussion between the stripper and her gambler mother.[72]

The film's version of the scene is described in chapter 3, and there are several points of interest raised by a comparison of the script to the finished film which suggest Walsh's unconventional work was more of a compromise than a retreat from Altman's innovative on-set practices. First, while the script's approach to the scenes does indicate an attempt to plan for or build-in Altman's preference for the middlegrounding of typically backgrounded characters, there is actually a third, unscripted, additional zone of dialogue in the filmed scene—constituted by a pair of men who discuss betting on basketball. This expansion could be explained in part by Altman's interest not just in the presence of middlegrounded characters for the purposes of a realistic robustness of milieu but in the transpositional practice of improvising a layer of action during production. In this sense, Altman's practice-oriented preference for on-set improvisation may have meant that pre-scripted realism was inadequate to satisfy him as a filmmaker. His stated principle that a single writer could not adequately capture the voices of all of a film's characters may have also played a role here. A second, related, point of interest is that the script provides no guidance or suggestion on how the simultaneity of the dialogue was to be executed, leaving it up to Altman and his collaborators' on-set transpositional approach. Finally, much of the scripted dialogue has not been transposed to the final film without significant alteration. Some of it may have been shot but then removed during postproduction.

Altman, then, did not abandon his past practice even with Walsh's novel contributions. Though it seems to cut against a key aspect of Altman's approach to transposition, which emphasizes the elaborative layering of middlegrounded dialogue during production, it could also be argued that Walsh's additional work on California Split's script—in its consecutive delineation of simultaneous events and scripting of dialogue that would normally be treated as walla—is, in and of itself, an interesting departure from standard Hollywood practice. This departure was likely prompted by Altman's elaborative notion of what constituted realistic film dialogue, and also, perhaps, in order to provide a more substantial preplanned framework for the early deployment of the technologically innovative Lions Gate 8-Track System.

Beyond modifications even to Walsh's prescripted elaborative layers of middlegrounded dialogue, it seems clear that Altman once again permitted his lead actors a great deal of freedom for elaborative improvisation around core narrative material. This should come as no surprise since Charlie is played by Elliot Gould. However, George Segal, playing Bill, was also told by Altman to "make it up," and to "say something, whatever you'd say." This provided the impetus for Segal to conceive of Bill's drunken stabs at recalling the names of Disney's seven dwarves and the pair's intense if incoherent discussion of the taboo status of the black crows in *Dumbo*.[73]

The addition of this material in the improvised dialogue seems to have also opened up the possibility for Altman and his collaborators to improvise unscripted motivic patterns in the film of the sort found in Altman's earlier work. Both the seven dwarves and *Dumbo* specifically recur in the film, but there is also a more elaborate motivic extension of elements related to minstrelsy and the stereotypical depictions of African Americans. The two men's drunken discussion of the negative reactions among black Americans against the anthropomorphic animal minstrelsy in the Disney film presumably leads to their unscripted performance of "Rufus Rastus Johnson Brown" as they dance toward Bill's car in the bar's parking lot. The next day, at the racetrack, Charlie compliments Bill on his skillful escape from work by saying he gave his employer, "a little razzle dazzle. The minstrel man strikes again!" A subsequent scene at a boxing match is scripted for "two Mexican fighters,"[74] but was cast with one black and one Latinx fighter. It is unclear whether the racial aspect of the shift was intentional or not, but it leads to an unscripted bit where Charlie and Bill decide to bet on "the black guy" but cannot figure out what his name is. Charlie suggests it is "Mose," apparently a reference to the Uncle Mose stereotype, and then giggles at his remark.

As in *Thieves Like Us*, the Altman team also revises the setting and set design for a key scene to advance a thematic motif through unconventionally indirect means. In a scripted scene, Bill goes to a backroom poker game in a desperate attempt to win money to pay his bookie. The script describes the setting simply as a furnished room without personality. The host's family "are watching TV," and when Bill arrives he "passes the 'TV people' and begins to nod 'hello,' when he realizes they couldn't care less."[75] The film relocates the scene to the backroom of a massage parlor, where Bill is guided by a black prostitute who suggests he consider spending some of his winnings on her. On his way, he moves through a space with the host's white children in bunk beds watching television. The program they're watching, undesignated by the script, is counterculture animator Paul Gruwell's short promotional film for Cheech and Chong's song, "Basketball Jones." The video features a variety of over-the-top, racially stereotyped caricatures of blacks. For instance, the singing cheerleaders featured in the portion of the video on display in *California Split* have tiny eyes, huge lips, and giant afros. Their cheerleader skirts are incredibly short, exposing their panties, and the film provides a shot of them waving their rear-ends back and forth in time to the music.

Perhaps because of its unconventional deployment, it is difficult to discern what the overall thematic significance of this particular motivic pattern might be. Is the film participating in a hip white cultural appropriation of and delight in minstrelsy, or is it critiquing it? The pathos of Bill's walk to the poker game and the inappropriateness of the animated film (and the overall living quarters) for the children in the scene suggests critique, but Charlie's string of remarks is certainly not framed as an indictment of casual or historical racism. The implementation of this improvised thematic strain is consistent with Altman's past transpositional practice, but it also indicates a risk to the approach.

The transpositional intensification of the depressing aspects of Bill's walk to the poker game also provides another example of Altman and his collaborators working to dramatize the plight of characters in a way that is less direct, and less conventional, than the approaches on display in the preproduction scripts. A similar instance is provided in the film's elimination of a scripted scene in which Bill breaks into his former home to steal his alimony check back from his ex-wife. While there, he shares a heavily sentimental moment with his dog, who flops at his feet and emits a "soft cry."[76] The scene is omitted from the final film, and it is likely that the overt sentimentality of the moment was too much for Altman, who seems to have preferred a more spontaneous and unconventional approach to the incorporation of animals. Altman also removes an extended sequence that takes place after a retained, though significantly revised, scene in which Bill and the young prostitute Susan almost have sex. In the script, a drunken Bill, "eyes vacantly staring ahead," gambles with his life by intentionally driving through multiple red lights, comes to a stop in front of a sign marked "WRONG WAY—DO NOT ENTER," and then goes through a "Jekyll and Hyde" type transformation, and violently assaults his car's interior and exterior.[77]

While Walsh sought to anticipate and accommodate Altman's transpositional practices by scripting background conversations on *California Split*, Joan Tewkesbury takes a different approach in her script for *Nashville*. The Altman Archive's copy of the 160-minute film's script runs just ninety pages, including the title pages and two pages that inventory the overall cast and the "HIGHWAY LINEUP" of characters who would appear during that famous sequence. It seems that Tewkesbury's script was designed to realize, in the document itself, Altman's proclaimed perception of his films' scripts as rough blueprints, deliberately incomplete conceptions that, nonetheless, delineate his films' essential narrative spines. Indeed, Tewkesbury's ninety-page script incorporates almost all of the narrative events included in the final film, though the details of most have undergone at least some elaborative revision during the transpositional process.

Tewkesbury's script innovates, then, in that it seems to build in elaborative and improvisatory opportunities throughout, sometimes designating narrative situations without specifying all or most of their details. The film's six-minute highway sequence is given just three pages in the script, with most of that space occupied by one or two-line descriptions of each character's interactions (for instance, "SUELEEN talks about her audition") rather than scripted dialogue.[78] Another example is provided by the film's scene encompassing: Opal witnessing the unscripted monologue by Barbara Baxley—as Lady Pearl—about "the Kennedy boys," a performance by Connie White, an uncomfortable exchange between Connie and Barbara Jean's husbands/managers, Norman and Bill discussing Mary's possible infidelity, and Haven Hamilton's indirect specification to Triplette of the conditions under which he might perform at Hal Philip Walker's fundraiser. Through strategies discussed in the previous chapters, the film efficiently handles all of this in under eight minutes, but the script treats this material in a single page, one-third of which is used to provide a rough description of the outlines of Opal's conversation with a phone operator and the group's departure from the lounge—events excised from the final film. Three lines of dialogue are specified for Norman and Bill's exchange, but the remainder of the scene is described as follows:

NEW ANGLE
The elevator door opens and CONNIE WHITE and her group step into the lobby. The M.C. in the lounge spots her and coaxes her into taking the stage and singing one of her hits. When she finishes, BARNETT walks up and thanks her. Meanwhile, HAVEN, who is there with BUD and PEARL, tells TRIPLETTE that CONNIE and BARBARA JEAN will replace each other, but never appear on the same bill. After BARNETT exits, CONNIE leaves with HAVEN, BUD, PEARL and TRIPLETTE. OPAL is still on the phone, now speaking in ITALIAN.[79]

This approach to the handling of a scene is obviously unconventional. It indicates the narrative gist of character exchanges while refusing to specify their verbal content. In doing so, it treats scripted dialogue not as the substance of a script but as a recommendation for execution that may or may not be included as needed.

It is interesting to consider how these innovations in script format coincide with the innovative approach to multitrack recording initiated by *California Split* and extended here. It may have been the greater confidence and expertise that Altman and his collaborators now had in the Lions Gate 8-Track System, along with their success in incorporating improvisation on top of Walsh's scripted "extra" dialogue for *California Split*, that encouraged them to move forward with a script that demanded elaboration rather than merely afforded it—or that simulated it in the manner of Walsh's additions.

To be clear, *Nashville*'s script does not treat every scene in the same spare manner. Indeed, there is still a good deal of dialogue present in the script. But, perhaps surprisingly, this does not mean that Altman and his collaborators regarded the scripted dialogue as essential. Indeed, even with the script's generous accommodation of Altman's transpositional predispositions, a comparison of the script with the final film suggests a deliberate excision of dialogue that served exposition and conventional drama. A good deal of the dialogue that lays out character backstory is removed, including, as one example, Wade's discussion of his past with an uninterested Linnea during the Exit Inn scene where Tom performs. Perhaps the clearest instance of this general strategy, though, is provided by the transposition of the climactic Parthenon sequence. In the script, after Kenny assassinates Barbara Jean, he shouts:

> I could have got that Walker bastard before. I've been closer, closer than this, but my Nash broke down and somebody kept stealing my things. I wanted to get him the day before, then Mrs. Brown's wife died, so this was the right time. I love the President of the United States. I love him.[80]

Even this fairly threadbare explanation of Kenny's motivation is removed from the film, in which he is tackled while still firing his gun. The last line of dialogue in the script is given to presidential candidate Hal Philip Walker who, as in the finished film, has been waiting, unseen, in his limo. Whereas in the film Walker drives off, still unseen, in the script he exits the limo and walks up to an ambulance taking Barbara Jean away, saying to Triplette, "What'd she do, faint again? I'm getting tired of waiting in the car." Triplette "belts him" in response.[81] This pointed rejection of American popular politics through the action of what has until then been its narrative avatar, Triplette, is replaced in the film by Triplette taking a moment to collect himself and then simply walking alone off the Parthenon stage.

The continuities in practice made evident by this series of contextualized comparative analyses between scripts and final films strongly supports a more qualified understanding of Altman's use of on-set improvisation and of his alleged misuse or disuse of the preproduction script than is commonly articulated. Indeed, these practices were far more restrained than is suggested by the "improvisational encounter group" comparisons first made during the early 1970s. Altman retained the vast majority of scripted narrative material, and—as Joan Tewkesbury and others have pointed out—he largely made and/ or vetted revisions himself rather than leaving these decisions solely or primarily to his actors. It seems that Altman's confession that his productions were more "benign monarchies" than democracies is fairly true. We might also add that, as monarch, Altman did indeed promulgate laws and principles to which his subjects were bound. Rather than allowing freewheeling departure from Hollywood storytelling and wholly rejecting the institutionalized primacy of the script, he largely required adherence to his scripts' large scale and scene-to-scene structures and ensured the replication of their key narrative premises as the stable core of his elaborative approach.

Even so, Altman, as monarch, clearly viewed the script as a tool rather than the kind of sacred scripture that some accounts of Hollywood norms might suggest. This meant that he was open to on-set improvisation, but on a contingent basis. Scripted dialogue, whose precise phrasing always seemed to be desanctified on the sets of Altman's productions, might be altogether excised if deemed too direct or purely expositional. Likewise, narrative situations that illustrated character dilemmas or related thematic premises too overtly or too conventionally were at risk for removal—probably to create space for the elaborative improvisation of more indirect illustrations of theme and character and for the filling out of the narrative milieu by middlegrounding usually backgrounded characters. The movement in the scripts for *California Split* and *Nashville* away from traditional scripting practices and toward accommodating Altman's on-set preferences is particularly interesting. Their coordination with the innovation of recording and on-set mixing technologies suggests they resulted from a willingness to experiment with scriptedness or nonscriptedness in anticipation of what seems to have been an intensification of key elaborative strategies. They also reflect an industrial context that permitted and may even have encouraged experimentation in approaches to the form, constraints, and uses of the screenplay.

The revisions to the standard account of Altman's early 1970s transpositional practices offered here provide evidence that Altman's approach to the script and improvisation was one of robust but strategic innovation within, though sometimes against, the broader and broadening norms of Hollywood

practice. Altman, then, provides one model for how filmmakers might challenge key aspects of Hollywood's historically circumscribed approach to the
screenplay in pursuit of their own ends. Macdonald has cited J. J. Murphy's
observation—in relation to the American avant-garde and independent
filmmakers whose work frames Altman's early 1970s oeuvre—that, "the
written screenplay can be an obstacle to the cinematic idea" and to what a
filmmaker might consider to be the "fun stuff" of filmmaking.[82] This chapter
demonstrates that Altman did not need to wholly eliminate the screenplay
from his screen practice in order to have his fun. Instead, he had his fun
*with* the screenplay, using it (or, from the perspective of some of his films'
screenwriters, abusing it) as a springboard for the extension of collaborative
conceptional authorship throughout the production process.

# 5

# Institutional Elaboration

## Altman's Training Grounds

The surprise success of 1970's *M\*A\*S\*H* is often taken as a starting point for serious critical consideration of the maverick director's career. Indeed, it is where I begin this book's repositioning of "Early Altman." There is, though, an "Earlier Altman" who had been involved in filmmaking since he was cast as an extra in the 1947 Danny Kaye movie *The Secret Life of Walter Mitty*. Over the next twenty-five years, Altman went from easily overlooked Hollywood extra to celebrated Hollywood Renaissance auteur. During this time, he directed approximately sixty industrial films for the Kansas City–based Calvin Company. He also wrote, produced, or directed more than 110 episodes of television, including episodes of *Alfred Hitchcock Presents*, *Bonanza*, and *Combat!*. Additionally, he directed or codirected five films: *The Delinquents* (1957), the documentary *The James Dean Story* (1957), *Once Upon a Savage Night* (1964), *Countdown* (1967), and *That Cold Day in the Park* (1969).

This earlier period in Altman's career receives its most substantial coverage in two richly detailed popular biographies of the filmmaker. Patrick McGilligan's *Robert Altman: Jumping off the Cliff* and Mitchell Zuckoff's *Robert Altman: The Oral Biography*. These books provide a good deal of information that is useful both for reconstructing the institutional contexts in which Altman worked and for assessing the principles, practices, and purposes behind the formal features of the works themselves. This chapter builds on and expands their work not only through its close analysis of specific works but also through its mobilization of extensive archival research into the contexts and production histories of Altman's filmmaking in these industries. It also uses as its foundation the significantly revised account of "Early Altman" offered in the previous chapters. Placing Altman's work in relation to this revised account allows us to see more clearly the complexity of the relationships between Altman's early 1970s practices and his earlier work.

Until recently, the scholarly and critical literature on Altman has provided comparatively little consideration of, and frankly misleading conclusions

*Robert Altman and the Elaboration of Hollywood Storytelling.* Mark Minett, Oxford University Press (2021). © Oxford University Press. DOI: 10.1093/oso/9780197523827.001.0001.

about, Altman's career during this period.[1] Commonly, Altman's career before *That Cold Day in the Park* and the emergence of the disruptive auteur "Altman" via *M\*A\*S\*H* is treated as the first term in a binary, oppositional, pair. Take, for instance, Robert T. Self's compounded reductionism in describing the key transformation in Altman's filmmaking as the "aesthetic difference" between, on the one hand, Altman's entire body of work up to and including the 1968 low budget WB film *Countdown*, and, on the other hand, 1970's *M\*A\*S\*H*. Self articulates this difference as an opposition between two modes of film practice—the classical Hollywood cinema and the art cinema.[2] The notion that industrial film or filmed television might be anything other than a shadow of generic Hollywood feature filmmaking appears to be unthinkable.

There are importantly paradoxical features of accounts of Altman in relation to each of these training grounds. On the one hand, filmed television is described as bland and conformist, exhibiting "zero-degree style" or an "attenuated continuity" approach that mechanically follows baseline classical Hollywood norms.[3] This position is hard to reconcile with assertions about the distinct influence of a background in television leading to aesthetic grandstanding by Altman and several of his New Hollywood peers (though as chapter 2 makes clear, there is actually scant evidence to support a consistent relationship between a training ground and its graduates' approaches to the zoom). To summarize the underlying paradox, Altman's feature work is presented as displaying a novelty impossible in the character-less form of television, which trained Altman in the base-level norms that he departs from in his feature work in ways partly explicable by the characteristic nature of television directing. Critical and scholarly accounts of Altman's time in industrial filmmaking are equally conflicted. Altman's work for the Calvin Company in the early 1950s, producing twenty-minute "sponsored" films that largely served promotional purposes, is seen as the source of Altman's allegedly "documentary" approach. At the same time, the Calvin Company is described as the ideal training ground for future Hollywood filmmakers.

These conflicts are not irresolvable, although the proffered solutions tend to be based on inaccurate premises. Take, for instance, the suspect causal chain in which television's limited opportunities for directorial authorship and its rigid adherence to formula lead to reflexive subversive embellishment, which, upon Altman's departure from television, leads to the all-out rejection of formal norms. As the previous chapters established, Altman's work in the early 1970s is not a radical rejection of Hollywood norms. Moreover, as I will demonstrate in this chapter, the institutions under discussion here are not as narrow, as possibility-constraining, or as dissimilar as they are often made out to be.

By reconstructing, through the use of trade publications and archival documents, the institutional contexts of these training grounds, and by closely analyzing available examples of Altman's work at the Calvin Company and his work on the filmed television series *Troubleshooters* and *Combat!*, this chapter provides a more substantial foundation for understanding this period in Altman's career. Altman's filmmaking during these years exceeds the implications of the "training ground" framework so often employed to explain it. It displays more than a developing mastery of the core competencies of Hollywood storytelling, and it does not conform to assumptions about what standard work in either field should resemble. Once again, we find Altman working with underestimated institutional norms while also elaborating around them according to his own aims and preoccupations. Altman developed solutions to the problems he found interesting with the institutional resources and authority he could acquire. While this account does not offer a straightforward story of a filmmaker's evolution, the findings here do provide a larger continuity with the revised account of Altman offered by the book thus far. We find in his work during this earlier period the origins and implementation of his elaborative transpositional approach, of the negotiation of unconventional sound and image strategies—including the kind of intensification of depth and movement that marked Altman's work with the zoom—and of his experimentation with an overt and ironizing narrational voice.

## Industrial Filmmaking as Training Ground

Before making his successful move in 1956 to filmed television in Hollywood, Altman spent approximately six years writing and directing industrial (or sponsored) films for the Calvin Company in his hometown of Kansas City. Altman has said that Calvin served as a "great training period"[4] and that "everything he ever learned, he learned at Calvin."[5] Thus, an approach to Calvin as training ground has found its way into the literature on Altman. This "training ground" label has largely served as a placeholder for close critical attention. Altman's biographical legend also frequently mobilizes his time at Calvin as evidence of his experience and interest in "realist" filmmaking. In a 1971 interview, Altman describes Calvin as a "documentary outfit."[6]

This credential has likely served as a critical rationale for the description of Altman's work as documentary-like. Richard Corliss, writing about *M*A*S*H*, claims that Altman, "mixes comedy situations with a documentary rigor almost worthy of Wiseman."[7] Jan Dawson's *Sight and Sound* article on the making of *Images* asserts, implausibly, that, "In view of [Altman's] reputation for realistic detail and his origins in industrial documentaries, he's very anxious to prevent his audience viewing *Images* as a clinical documentary about insanity."[8] Pauline Kael describes *Nashville* as, "a documentary essay on Nashville and American life."[9] This critical trope demonstrates a desire to mark Altman as separate from Hollywood so as to legitimize him as an object of attention. With the rise of observational documentary in the 1960s as a consecrated mode of filmic expression, associating a director with documentary filmmaking lent him credibility with cine-literate audiences.

The precise context of background norms and practices with which Altman interacted at the Calvin Company has yet to be established. Likewise, there has been almost no close analysis conducted to identify the formal features of Altman's films at Calvin. Most of Altman's Calvin output from the period and most of the Calvin Company's films have yet to be recovered. Calvin ceased operations in the early 1980s, and its papers seem to be lost.

This chapter offers a reconstruction of the immediate institutional context in which Altman worked by drawing on new archival research, industry publications, and close analysis of available examples of Altman's work at Calvin. It uses McGilligan and Zuckoff's work but goes beyond it in several ways. First, it supplements the information in McGilligan's published book with his original, unedited, interviews, accessed at the Wisconsin Center for Film and Theater Research. Second, pertinent documents have recently been made available as part of the Robert Altman Archive at the University of Michigan, including a binder detailing the 1955 Calvin Workshop—a training seminar for industrial filmmakers across the country. This chapter also makes use of a decade's worth (1948–1958) of Calvin's monthly newsletter, *The Aperture*. Three of Altman's Calvin films are analyzed in depth. *Honeymoon for Harriet* (1950) is Altman's first directorial effort, made for International Harvester—a manufacturer of tractors, trucks, farm equipment, and home appliances. *The Perfect Crime* (1955) was made for Caterpillar in cooperation with the National Safety Council. Finally, *The Magic Bond* (1956) was produced for the Veterans of Foreign Wars, or VFW. In order to develop a sense of the context of industrial filmmaking during the 1950s, when Altman was working for Calvin, more than a dozen films by a variety of producers that are part of the Wisconsin Historical Society's International Harvester collection have also been surveyed. By using these resources, this chapter provides a substantial understanding of the development of a celebrated Hollywood Renaissance filmmaker and the industrial organization and formal norms of a generally denigrated tradition of filmmaking. It provides an overview of Calvin as an institution, interrogates whether Calvin trained Altman in Hollywood competencies, considers how Bob Altman, the novice filmmaker, used Calvin to become Robert Altman by pursuing his own experimental agenda, and asks which novel features of his later filmmaking practice may have been derived in part from the unique opportunities provided by the Calvin Company.

Accounts of the Calvin Company tend to describe it as a production company. For instance, Rick Prelinger's excellent *Field Guide to Sponsored Films* describes Calvin as "Kansas City's high-rise motion picture factory."[10] In fact, Calvin is more accurately described as a hybrid service/production company, and it likely generated more than half of its revenue through its service division. Calvin did make industrial films—probably around thirty pictures a year—but its focus seems to largely have been on services like processing, editing, recording, and equipment.[11] Their productions provided a revenue stream, but they also provided the service department with a sales hook. One article in *The Aperture* argues that the fact that the Calvin Company was a leading producer of 16mm films meant that they provided a "hidden" secondary service to producer-clients and guaranteed that, "the man who sits in with him for a reading of his script against the edited workprint is a man who has himself written, directed, edited, and produced films." According to Calvin, "this is the factor . . . that makes this producing company a strong 'partner' for other producers. No one can understand a producer's problems as well as another producer.[12] The free annual production workshops that Calvin offered shared the company's production techniques with other 16mm producers, and the hundreds of attendees included some of the biggest producers of industrial films—competitors and also potential service accounts.

Contra Calvin's sales pitch, Altman actually began in their service department before moving to production. He likely edited films sent to Calvin and proofread and revised the scripts for the films' voiceover narration.[13] He came to Calvin with no experience in film production, even though he spent time in Hollywood after the war, where he sold a treatment that became the Lawrence Tierney film noir *Bodyguard* (1948) but was never given access to the film's set.[14] In spite of this inexperience, and probably because of his abilities as a writer, Altman was soon given a job as one of Calvin's writer-director-editors.

Calvin's organization of production during this period most resembles the director/producer or the director-unit systems that Janet Staiger describes as dominant in American filmmaking from 1907 to 1914. Director/producers, according to Staiger:

> made most of the major and minor decisions involved in the filming of the product . . . either furnish[ing] the idea for the film or rewr[iting] one the firm had available. He selected his stage settings and gave directions to the carpenters,

painters, and property men. If any research was needed, he would do it. He selected the people from the stock company; he found locations.... Once the cameraman or laboratory staff developed the film, the director edited it.[15]

Exhibitors' demand for "twenty or thirty new films per week" led production companies to augment the director/producer system by hiring multiple directors who were put in charge of their own units.[16]

In a parallel manner, Calvin employed four or five separate producer-writer-director-editors, with Barhydt serving as the overall head of production. Barhydt claims Calvin:

operated on the idea that the guy who directs the show ought to be the guy who writes it. They did this for economic reasons in part, but also because if you're going to have to produce it yourself you're not going to write stuff that isn't producible. You're going to be thinking of difficulties and the expense of producing the picture.... If a guy's assigned a picture he's assigned to write it, direct it, cut it and everything.[17]

Calvin's was a mode of production that followed an integrated model of authorship organized around a central creative figure who oversaw the conception, budgeting, and every stage of production for each project.

A Calvin director averaged less than a film a month and made a broad range of types of films, none of which resembled observational documentaries. For pricing purposes, Calvin recognized three categories: the all-voiceover film—voiceover narration over actuality footage; the all-dialogue film—"dramatic" sequences in the style of Hollywood; and the hybrid part-voiceover, part dialogue film.[18] Calvin also categorized films by their uses, including: direct sales films, sales promotion films, human relations films, indoctrinations, industrial or personnel relations, sales or job training, high-speed and other studies, safety films, and public relations films.[19]

The emphasis on categorization by function here underlines Calvin's insistence that industrial films should be thought of as, "a tool, chosen for a purpose," and designed with a specific audience in mind. Their position was supported by later studies, such as an Association of National Advertisers report, that showed no correlation between the entertainment-value generated by an industrial film and its rhetorical effectiveness.[20] Many clients could be fuzzy on who their target audience was, but Calvin insisted that pinning it down was the only way to make effective films, which helps to explain the astonishment expressed by Barhydt when Altman later told Barhydt's son, a writer on Altman's late 1970s films, that he should forget his audience and make films for himself.[21]

This sketch, brief as it is, of Calvin's organization and institutional prerogatives is useful in addressing the "training ground" perspective on Altman's development, the core assumption of which seems to be that the formative role played by a culturally inferior motion picture industry was limited to the provision of hands-on work that allowed them to become competent in Hollywood standards. There are good reasons to handle this claim with caution. A survey of the International Harvester films held by the Wisconsin Historical Society suggests that Calvin films, though certainly not the least technically proficient in the industry, often failed to meet certain technical standards valued by Hollywood, particularly the maintenance of an immediately clear and comprehensible spatial continuity.

Kristin Thompson has described the importance of the principle of consistent screen direction to the classical continuity system employed by Hollywood filmmakers, particularly for dialogue scenes.[22] Scenes were shot and edited so as to maintain consistent relative figure position between characters, so that Character A, when looking at or moving toward Character B, always moves right and Character B always looks or moves left toward Character A. The range of set-ups employed during a scene was generally constrained to one side of an axis of action—an imaginary line through the key figures that bisected the 360-degrees of scenic space. The so-called "180-degree rule" served as a kind of sacred minimum Hollywood standard, allowing filmmakers to ensure that audience members would never be distracted from the story by spatial confusion.

Altman's films at Calvin, though, only irregularly adhere to the standards of continuity editing. Altman's first-ever directorial effort, *Honeymoon for Harriet*—meant to promote International Harvester's farming equipment and, through a final twist, their household appliances—takes an "all-dialogue" approach to salesmanship, narrativizing its pitch. The film's story features an elderly country mailman training his replacement. Along their route, the senior mailman tells an elaborate story, presented in flashback, about the travails of local couple Joe and Harriet Miller. With approximately half of the film constituted by dialogue scenes between the two mailmen, *Honeymoon for Harriet* provides evidence that, if Calvin did serve as a training ground for Hollywood filmmaking, it was one that neglected to ensure Altman met Hollywood's key minimum standard.

Sequences that depict the two mailmen in conversation include frequent jumps of the axis of action, creating inconsistencies in relative figure position. For instance, as the mailmen arrive at the Millers' whale-shaped mailbox,

Altman provides a slightly high-angle establishing shot looking down on the two mailmen in medium to medium long shot (Figure 5.1). The camera looks past the mailbox which, positioned in the lower right foreground, provides a nice sense of depth to the shot and displays the kind of ornamental use of depth composition that, as we have seen in chapter 2, would characterize his use of the zoom. The young mailman, who occupies the passenger's seat, is positioned on the left in the middleground, while the elderly mailman, who looks left to speak to his apprentice, is positioned slightly behind him and to his right in the center of the frame. From this, Altman cuts to a closer framing of the elderly mailman, taken roughly from the rear passenger side of the car (Figure 5.2). In this new set-up, though, the older mailman is now on the left side of the frame and looks right, rather than left, as he talks to the younger man, who is now situated in the bottom right corner of the frame. The sequence's third shot, which again focuses on the older man, jumps the axis of action once more (Figure 5.3), as do its fourth and fifth shots (Figures 5.4 and 5.5). Somehow, Altman has managed the remarkable achievement of breaking down this scenic space without once respecting the axis of action and the standards of continuity editing.

**Figure 5.1** *Honeymoon for Harriet*

**Figure 5.2** *Honeymoon for Harriet*

**Figure 5.3** *Honeymoon for Harriet*

**Figure 5.4** *Honeymoon for Harriet*

**Figure 5.5** *Honeymoon for Harriet*

Furthermore, while Hollywood practice tends to repeat the employment of the same set-ups as part of the shot/reverse shot approach to scene dissection, Altman never repeats a set-up in this sequence. Instead he provides practically every possible permutation of vantage point, shooting from each car door. It seems that Altman was far more interested in providing visual variety than with ensuring continuity. Altman's camera frequently jumps into the back seat rather than simply alternating between framings taken from the front passenger and driver's side doors (Figures 5.6 and 5.7) in a manner that would respect continuity standards. He provides, for instance, high angle framings looking down at the elderly mailman, whose black cap bulges into the top left foreground (Figure 5.8). Another backseat shot is strikingly symmetrical, with the carmaker's logo, "Plymouth," compositionally dead-center (Figure 5.9). While the standards of continuity editing were not upheld in *Honeymoon for Harriet*, this should not necessarily be taken as evidence that the film's spatial relationships were wholly confusing. Instead, the product feels effective but also unrefined.

According to Thompson, the stability of the rules and devices of continuity editing was ensured by the relatively slow process of developing studio directors by socializing young filmmakers with more experienced filmmakers

**Figure 5.6** *Honeymoon for Harriet*

**Figure 5.7** *Honeymoon for Harriet*

**Figure 5.8** *Honeymoon for Harriet*

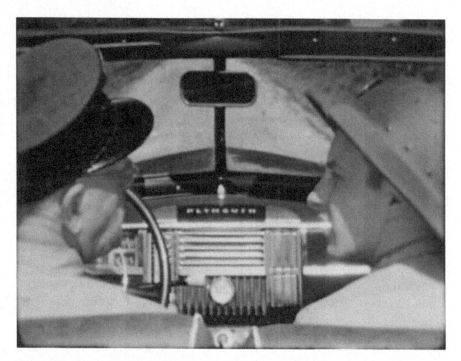

**Figure 5.9** *Honeymoon for Harriet*

and through professional organizations that "encouraged filmmakers to gather and see each other's work."[23] The need for these mechanisms suggests that certain conventions were not necessarily obvious. One factor, then, beyond Altman's own preoccupation with visual variety, that likely contributed to the discontinuity found in some scenes in *Honeymoon for Harriet* was Altman's accelerated advancement and Calvin's hands-off managerial structure. Calvin's writer-director-editors were given freedom and opportunity, but this on-the-job and on-their-own training likely meant a long learning process and, by Hollywood standards, unpolished products.

In Hollywood, the director-unit system dominated from 1909 to 1914, prior to the establishment of a standard classical Hollywood style. The central producer system that followed the director-unit system "centralized the control of production under management of a producer," who, unlike Barhydt, "used a very detailed shooting script, the continuity script, to plan and budget the entire film, shot-by-shot before any major set construction, crew selection, or shooting started." Importantly, Staiger proposes that this system was partly the result of the fact that "the techniques for achieving continuity . . . coalesced," requiring more extensive production planning and quality control. This coalescence seems not to have taken place at Calvin. Interestingly, Staiger claims that the move to the central producer system was also partly due to the lengthening of film duration from "an average of eighteen minutes," in-line with a Calvin film, "to seventy-five minutes or more."[24] It becomes then, a bit of a chicken-and-egg question. With little central control and only limited apprenticeships Calvin's means for maintaining or even teaching the conti-nuity system were likely insufficient. And with no expectations of Hollywood-style continuity, there was no need for a central producer to ensure standards or the training to meet those standards. There are also obvious implications here for Altman's subsequent attitude to the sanctity of the script.

Because of how difficult it is to see Altman's full body of work at Calvin, it is hard to say how, when, or if his ability to construct a sequence with con-sistent screen direction improved. A subsequent Altman industrial film, *A Perfect Crime*, also displays problems with continuity. This "hybrid" indus-trial film begins with a sequence depicting the robbery of what is literally a Mom and Pop corner store by a deranged gunman who knocks Pop uncon-scious and then guns down both Mom and the little girl unfortunate enough to be in the store buying candy. This multiple murder, as will be discussed later, is not the titular crime, but it does provide Altman with one of the few opportunities—in a film whose runtime is dominated by footage of roadways, construction, and car crashes—to test his ability to capture dramatic action. Altman manages to adhere to continuity standards through most of the se-quence, but he punctuates the violence with jarringly short shot durations that risk audience comprehension. More problematically, when the gunman fires at his last victim—the standing, shrieking girl—mismatched eyelines make it appear that he is pointing the gun at her kneecaps (Figures 5.10 and 5.11). In some ways, the film's editing is more disjunctive than *Honeymoon for Harriet*'s, but here it seems expressively appropriate and less like the inci-dental result of compositional experimentation. Even so, a similar effect could likely have been attained in a more polished manner, one at less risk of sig-naling incompetence rather than intent. As a display of filmmaking bravado, and of a willingness to experiment with convention in service of ambitious aims, Altman's award-winning work on *The Perfect Crime* is successful. On the other hand, as a calling card meant to display adequate training in the minimum standards of continuity editing, the opening scene would not pass muster. Either way, Altman's relative "failure" here raises questions about the adequacy of characterizations of Calvin as a training ground.

If we turn briefly from moment-by-moment style to large-scale structure, *The Perfect Crime* offers an opportunity to consider Altman's work in relation to the industrial film industry's own standards. A 1956 article in *The Aperture* cautions against even attempting the kind of ostentatiously dramatic scene,

**Figure 5.10** *The Perfect Crime*

**Figure 5.11** *The Perfect Crime*

referred to as a "Big Opening," that Altman builds into the opening of *The Perfect Crime*:

> The BIG OPENING is another trap into which the producer sometimes strays. It takes two forms. One is the opening sequence which may be very well done, very effective in itself—except that it has no connection whatsoever with the main subject matter of the film. The opening is purely a come-on and we can almost hear the narrator say, "Well! Now that that's out of the way, we can get down to business!" ... The other Big Opening fault may utilize subject matter directly connected with the film's main subject, but lacks a smooth transition from the opening to the following body of the film. Here again, the Big Opening betrays sufficient lack of planning during the scripting stages, or lack of good judgment on the part of the producer or sponsor.[25]

Altman does take some steps, discussed later, that may have headed off criticism of his film based on these concerns, but the sensationalistic opening murder in *A Perfect Crime* seems undeniably to constitute a Big Opening. As such, it is a marker of Altman's ambition and his willingness to violate Calvin's articulated standards, to reach beyond Calvin's training.

Altman's ability to undertake this is multiply suggestive. Perhaps Calvin's distinctive structuring of authorship afforded him the opportunity to disrupt or innovate on the company's stated standards. Perhaps the advice against Big Openings in *The Aperture* was one that the Calvin itself adhered to only contingently. Either option implies that as an institution industrial filmmaking was less constrained and more open to innovation than one might expect. Here, Altman expands on the routine purposes of the Calvin Company in order to present a dramatic flourish displaying his (not yet entirely competent) craftsmanship and his attempt at expressive style. Calvin, then, provided Altman a forum for the development of the elaborative approach outlined in previous chapters.

The skepticism outlined earlier about Calvin's ability to train its filmmakers in Hollywood's formal standards is not intended as a criticism of Calvin or its brand of filmmaking. Many producers of industrial films underused continuity conventions. For instance, Great Lakes Productions' *Double Ringer* (1950), which compares the satisfactions offered by International Harvester's milking system to the special feeling of achieving a "double ringer" toss in a game of horseshoes, is replete with continuity errors. On the other hand, the Wilding Productions' farm safety–oriented re-imagining of *It's a Wonderful Life* (1946), *Miracle of Paradise Valley*, consistently displays a polished look. The film is also remarkable in that it is one of the few International Harvester films that, like *Honeymoon for Harriet*, is thoroughly dramatic, with no doc-umentary footage per se in the film. The scarcity of dramatic sponsored films suggests another reason why Calvin may not have trained Altman in Hollywood standards. Whereas Hollywood style was oriented around character-driven storytelling and the presentation of psychologically moti-vated chains of cause and effect,[26] sponsored film style was developed around serving whichever of the variety of rhetorical purposes the sponsor demanded. Most of these demands did not require scenes depicting conversations be-tween characters, limiting the utility of mobilizing resources to ensure its filmmakers mastered Hollywood's formal standards. Given Calvin's high rep-utation within the field, their looser approach met their institutional needs.

If the core competencies of continuity editing were not taught by Calvin, what was? An examination of the 1955 Calvin Workshop binder provides an extensive list of rules and suggestions to attendees, although conventions like the axis of action are never explicitly mentioned. An outline of the lecture on "Editing Technique" includes sections on "Field Areas," the Calvin term for shot scale or framing distance, and "Camera Angles."[27] Rules included guidelines for breaking down a sequence by employing a long shot, medium shot, close-up pattern that "corresponds to the three stages through which the human eye unconsciously views action or subject matter."[28] A caveat emphasizes that this pattern, "may be changed to add interest," and a quo-tation that precedes the lecture's outline states, "The classic formula of LS-MS-CU is merely the ABC of the beginner's guide. Much of the best 'editing' achieves results by departing from the formula." Penciled-in above and to the right of this quotation is the name of the session's lecturer, "Bob Altman" (ironically, one of the first tips is to avoid cutting "too short—remember, you know the story better than the audience").[29] The closest the outline comes to delineating rules of continuity is a statement that "Camera angles may be planned to . . . maintain orientation (the 'natural' angle)."[30] Just what exactly a "natural" angle might consist of is left unexplained by the outline. The fact that Altman was responsible for the session on editing suggests that by 1955 he had reached a high level of what we might call "Calvin competency." These competencies were not as formalized as Hollywood's standards, but there does appear to be some overlap (the lecture, for instance, recommends the use of re-establishing shots).

Calvin, then, did serve as a place in which Altman could train in certain core competencies of filmmaking—standards expressed in *The Aperture* and in the Calvin workshops, even if Calvin competencies did not perfectly overlay Hollywood standards. But this does not mean that Altman was simply training in a system. Instead, the relative freedom provided by Calvin—where

Altman taught others that the best filmmaking comes from "departing from the formula"—provided a forum for Altman's pursuit of his own initiatives and interests. Perhaps Altman insisted on elaborative autonomy in his later work because he became accustomed to this freedom at Calvin. There, Altman explored techniques that would later come to distinguish his storytelling. He pushed against common Calvin practice and helped to push Calvin's practices in new directions. Two particular techniques are worth focusing on here: multiple camera shooting and camera movement.

Altman and Calvin cameraman Charley Paddock shot several films using multiple cameras, and Altman encouraged Paddock to develop lighting that could be used with this approach. McGilligan reports that the Altman-directed *The Dirty Look* was the first Calvin film that featured the technique, and he suggests that the idea may have come from the film's star, William Frawley.[31] Frawley played Fred on *I Love Lucy*, which made use of multiple camera shooting. While a print of *The Dirty Look* has yet to be uncovered, Altman's early use of this technique is on display in the opening sequence from the VFW-sponsored *The Magic Bond*, featuring a group of World War II G.I.s who take shelter in a bombed-out home. Shot on a sound stage and employing what largely sounds like live dialogue, the film feels like a live television drama.

In his career as a feature filmmaker, Altman often shot scenes using several cameras, with one covering the action from a distance and another reportedly serving as a sort of roving eye, seeking out interesting details and performances. There are good reasons to be skeptical that this secondary eye was truly a rover. More likely, the second camera strategically, if also somewhat flexibly, picked up rehearsed "improvisation" by middlegrounded characters secondary to the core narrative action, indulging Altman's interest in fleshing out the dimensionality of his narrative milieu and providing him with secondary footage from the same take. Such a practice fit the need for efficiency likely instilled in Altman by the exigencies of industrial filmmaking and that was later a basis of his freedom to innovate in feature filmmaking. In any event, *The Magic Bond* seems to provide a clear early instance of Altman engaging in what would later become a regular feature of his elaborative approach.

Altman's preference for the more flexible lighting system required for multiple camera shooting also persisted in his feature film work, though in discussion of his distaste for what he described as "Rembrandt" lighting, Altman emphasized the affordances greater flexibility leant to camera movement.[32] A willingness to renegotiate standard practice to accommodate mobile framing strategies was a part of Altman's approach at the Calvin Company, where he consistently worked with cameramen to incorporate more camera movement. Altman made a point of teaming up with Paddock, who shared Altman's interest. According to Paddock, the two believed that movement brought a film to life by giving it a three-dimensional effect.[33] Unfortunately, Calvin's approach to production was utilitarian—they would spend only as much as the project demanded. Incorporating camera movement would expand the resources spent on productions while resulting in little that the client would recognize as valuable.

Altman overcame this institutional obstacle in two ways. First, he built movement into a film's concept. Because of Calvin's organization of production, his role as writer-director-editor meant that he could try to execute the idea so long as he accepted the consequences of failure. Altman has said that he received his first assignment, *Honeymoon for Harriet*, because he wrote an appealing script that no one else could figure out how to execute. According to Altman, "They couldn't figure out how to shoot dialogue in a car, as this was before tape was used—the sound went directly on to the film. So I 'invented' looping, which of course they had done in Hollywood, but I suspected that and just kind of made it up."[34]

Looping was required because of the premise's integration of movement, and Altman not only successfully developed a parallel system for looping dialogue (particularly interesting, given his reputed distaste for looping in his feature filmmaking), he also, according to Barhydt, developed a rig that could be attached to the exterior of the car that would allow him to film the mailmen's conversation in motion, and to thereby achieve his aim of a constantly mobile camera.[35]

Altman also overcame institutional indifference to camera movement by inspiring his crew to expand their work hours to help him pursue his experiments. Barhydt remembers Altman working into early morning with his cast and crew, none of whom were being paid overtime, in order to successfully execute an ambitiously arcing camera movement for an otherwise pedestrian project (the client, says Barhydt, never noticed).[36] This was made possible by Altman's leadership abilities but also by the fact that that Calvin's workforce was non-union and workers were paid a regular salary. The "family atmosphere" that management strived to create meant that everyone kept irregular hours.[37] After his move to Hollywood, Altman voiced a great deal of frustration with union crews, and his disposition toward what he viewed as their inflexible attitude was likely rooted in his time at Calvin.

Calvin, then, provided Altman with a forum for elaborating on the institutional norms of the company by pursuing his own filmmaking interests, even though they sometimes required modifying Calvin's existing practices.

Again, this can be seen as prologue to Altman's approach in the early 1970s. At the same time, though, Calvin's institutional prerogatives arguably shaped Altman's feature filmmaking practices. In particular, the qualified documentary aspect of industrial filmmaking—going into the field and shooting on location—likely contributed to Altman's future practices in several important ways.

First, the exigencies of location shooting meant that a different attitude had to be taken to scripting industrial films, and Calvin promoted an approach in which the shooting script should not be regarded as scripture. This, according to Calvin, was a common mistake of inexperienced producers. While the shooting script should be as complete as possible, it should also be revised according to the realities discovered on location. We can see in this advice the seeds of the transpositional flexibility discussed in chapter 4. Altman, infamous among his screenwriters for his disregard for the sanctity of his scripts, has stated, "I try to make the film knowing that I have the script as a platform, something to fall back on. It's like an architect's rendering on a blueprint."[38] Calvin, in their 1955 workshop binder, uses similar language, describing the script as "a blueprint"[39] that must be adapted to "actual shooting conditions and new information."[40] While the description of the film script as a "blueprint" was fairly common in Hollywood, Calvin's insistence on this specific understanding of the script is significant. The workshop binder also emphasizes that the script is primarily "a business and production tool."[41] This echoes McCabe & Mrs. Miller screenwriter Brian McKay's account of Altman's view of the script, "simply as an instrument, as the tool you sell the studio."[42] Framing the script in this way liberated Altman to pursue his elaborative interests at Calvin and in his feature career.

Beyond its modifications to the role of the script, the fact of location production also meant, under Calvin's organizational structure, that Altman was forced to learn how to effectively and efficiently manage a shoot on his own. A preference for and skill at directing location shoots would become one of Altman's hallmarks. Not only did it eventually help him land work in television—Altman was employed as a location producer on the Hitchcock television series Suspicion because of this expertise—but it also gave him a taste for the creative autonomy provided by distance from one's supervisors.[43] Later on, Altman would be severely disappointed when he learned that M*A*S*H would not be shot in Korea but at the Fox studio.[44] After that film's success, Altman ensured that his subsequent films would be shot on location. The critical tendency is to view a preference for location shooting as motivated by an interest in realism, but we should recognize the other advantages location shooting held for someone with Altman's practice-oriented preferences.

Perhaps the most intriguing contribution Calvin plausibly made to Altman's filmmaking practice is connected to the central role that the narrator plays in industrial films. *The Aperture* spends a great deal of time discussing how to write and record effective narration and very little time on how to shoot or write "dialogue" sequences. In the language of *The Aperture*, the narrative script is the script read by the narrator, not the script used to guide dramatic shooting. Voiceover narration was a condition imposed by the distinct rhetorical uses for which industrial films were most often made. It is this rhetorical dimension of Calvin's industrial filmmaking, rather than some critically surmised fly-on-the-wall observational documentary approach, that influenced Altman's later practice. While none of his feature films make use of voiceover narration per se, many contain consistently overt narration— strong signs of a controlling authorial voice working to integrate the material, guide interpretation, and set a mood. The integration of the ornithologist's lecture in *Brewster McCloud* provides the most obvious manifestation of this tendency, and the one that most closely resembles voiceover narration. But we might also think of: the use of the public address announcements and radio broadcasts in *M\*A\*S\*H*, the Leonard Cohen songs in *McCabe & Mrs. Miller*, the multiple variations on the theme song for *The Long Goodbye*, the old-time radio in *Thieves Like Us*, the Phyllis Shotwell songs in *California Split*, and the Hal Phillip Walker speeches blaring from campaign vans in *Nashville*. In interviews, Altman has described his use of these techniques as "punctuation," comparing them to "commas, pauses, and dashes that also comment on what you're seeing at the time."[45] Altman also frequently used crosscutting to create ironizing juxtapositions, and in his films' opening sequences he regularly primed his audiences to interpret rather than to merely comprehend or emotionally engage with narrative. Rather than attributing these strategies to the influence of European art filmmaking, we might consider the influence of Altman's time at the rhetorically oriented Calvin, where an overt narrating voice was required to "provide a mood," "guide attention," and "aid in the transition from idea to idea."[46]

At Calvin, Altman was consistently generating elaborative approaches to the standard problem of the narrator. In *Honeymoon for Harriet*, a comedic framing story is used to present the sales pitch. The elderly mailman narrates the core story about Joe, a man who spends his honeymoon money first on a whale-shaped mailbox, and then—because an International Harvester dealership is on the way to the travel agency—on more and more farming equipment. Harriet, his beleaguered wife, accidentally wins an all-expenses-paid honeymoon by coincidentally crying out her preferred destination, "Niagara Falls," at the same time that a radio quiz show has called and asked her to identify a "mystery sound" that turns out to be the sound of the famous waterfall. This concludes the elderly mailman's story, but when he and his replacement learn that Joe and Harriet have not left for their honeymoon as expected, the shocked postal workers race to their home. Here, the framing story and its narrator meet the sales story and its subjects. The mailmen learn that it is Harriet who has passed up the chance to go on her honeymoon this time. Frustrating Joe, she has decided to accept the radio show's offer of a variety of International Harvester home appliances and houseware in lieu of the vacation.

In *A Perfect Crime*, the conjoining of narrator and narrative subject also serves as a vehicle for surprise, though with a very different affective overtone. The opening violence is resolved with the capture of the murderer and the brandishing of a newspaper with a banner headline screaming, "BANDIT SLAYS 2; GETS $14." The narrating voice tells the audience that "public indignation" meant the killer would be caught, preventing his crime from achieving the titular perfection. It then asks the audience to consider another crime, "this time, a perfect crime," and the next sequence shows an automobile accident in which a woman and child are killed, leaving the male driver badly injured but still alive. This hard pivot, an apparent attempt to motivate the film's elaborative Big Opening, seems ham-fisted, but it does provide evidence of Altman's concern with integrating the murder with the more institutionally normative "safety film" business of the car crash. As the ambulance drives away, an insert shot returns to the aforementioned newspaper, this time zooming in to a much smaller headline, "Highway Crash Fatal to Two," just above the fold. The crash, the on-screen narrator explains, is the result of "bad roads," and the body of the film combines rather mundane safety tips with a sales pitch arguing that better roads are needed to save lives. The audience members are culpable in traffic deaths, the narrator contends, because they fail to demand these better roads. At the film's climax, the narrator reveals that he has the credibility to deliver this rather scathing judgment because he is the lone survivor of the film's initial car crash. Altman again presents the earlier images of dead, bloodied bodies with white sheets covering them, but now with the addition of a shot of the narrator on a stretcher. "Yeah, that's me," the voiceover narration declares. "That's why I can talk. My wife and daughter died on a bad road. I killed them. You helped. But what good's a confession now? It was a perfect crime." It is hard to imagine Altman designing this revelation with a straight face, although it is not difficult to imagine him anticipating its effectiveness. It is the opportunity to play with the conventions of rhetorical framing that most likely interested him, and that interest would be sustained through his early 1970s feature work.

Finally, Altman's *The Magic Bond* features a man pounding away at a typewriter in the bottom right foreground of the first shot of that film's Big Opening (Figure 5.12). The typewriter's clacking can be heard even after the camera tracks past it and into the dramatic action. At the conclusion of the five-minute long dramatic sequence, the filmmakers return to a framing in which the typewriter can be seen in the lower right (Figure 5.13). An insert shot shows a dateline being typed out, followed by the name of the war correspondent Bob Considine (Figure 5.14). This is followed by a graphic match to another page on another typewriter, this one typing out, "On the Line," the title of Considine's International News Service column (Figure 5.15). The graphic match has transported the viewer to the present day, and from this temporal position Considine provides the narration for the film's celebration of the VFW and the bond between servicemen. This is probably the least interesting of the three examples and a far cry from the p.a. announcements of *M\*A\*S\*H*. That said, this framing of *The Magic Bond*'s endorsement of the VFW goes beyond the standard approach in its visual integration of narrator and dramatic action, expressively suggesting a permeable boundary between past and present that underwrites the logic of the sponsor.

**Figure 5.12** *The Magic Bond*

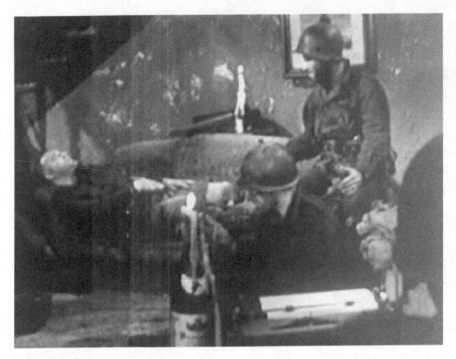

**Figure 5.13** *The Magic Bond*

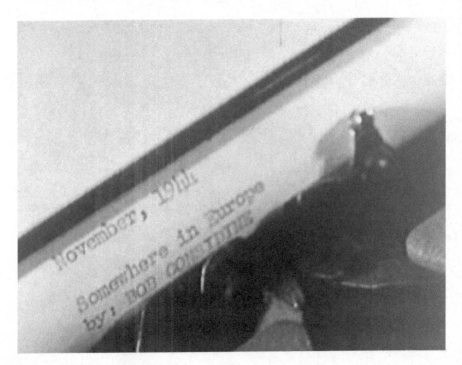

**Figure 5.14** *The Magic Bond*

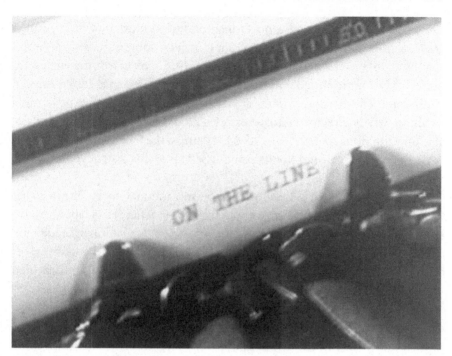

**Figure 5.15** *The Magic Bond*

It would be irresponsible to claim that the narrator requirement of industrial filmmaking necessarily led to the novel narrational devices that held together and set the mood for Altman's later films. Even so, a causal relationship is plausible, especially if we understand industrial filmmaking as involving more than just applying a set of minimum standards to shifting subject matter and instead consider it a dynamic and creative process of problem-setting and -solving. Altman was trained to make films in a context that more often than not required a narrational voice, but the method for incorporating that voice was not set in stone—the functional affordances one could build into and around that device were not strictly delimited. Altman could and did elaborate. Moreover, the centrality of the narrator problem in industrial filmmaking likely primed Altman to think about the possibilities of narrational voice in relation to narrative filmmaking. At Calvin, Altman realized such a voice could actually be a useful tool for adding unexpected interest to subject matter, both for the audience and for a filmmaker whose practice-oriented preferences favored the adventure of playful problem-solving.

Even after eliminating the misleading though legitimating conflation of industrial filmmaking with observational documentary, we can see that there is much of interest remaining in Altman's time at the Calvin Company. The

Calvin Company provided a novel institutional context in which Altman could, as part of his regular duties, train in at least some of what Hollywood supposed to be the basics of filmmaking. But Calvin competencies required only contingent adherence rather than rote allegiance to the rules of Hollywood. The division of labor at Calvin consolidated creative power in a producer-writer-director-editor, creating a kind of industrial auteur answerable only to a film's sponsor. This afforded Altman the freedom not only to experiment with Hollywood standards but also to push his craft beyond Calvin's conventional practices.

At Calvin, Altman could elaborate upon institutional norms in ways that bear broad and specific resemblance to his later practice. His elaborative insistence on mobile framing, for instance, anticipates his later heightened use of the zoom. Beyond Calvin's division of labor, the specific demands of industrial filmmaking shaped Altman in lasting ways that the training provided in another institutional context probably would not. Calvin set him loose on locations, likely stoking his later preference for on-location shooting. It also encouraged its filmmakers to be open to reconceiving their films in response to what they found on those locations, positioning the script as flexible blueprint rather than sacred regulatory control—a perspective Altman extended into his feature work. The form's commercial and rhetorical requirements both burdened and invigorated Altman with material and practices that, at least for a filmmaker of his ambitions, required innovation to enliven. Thus, we see in Altman's work at Calvin plausible precedents for Altman's later creative solutions to the presentation of an overt narrational voice. The specificity and multidimensionality of Altman's time at Calvin undermines the one-dimensionality of its standard framing as training ground. Although sponsored filmmaking may be a culturally denigrated form, its interest to historians of American media, and its significance to Hollywood feature filmmaking practice, cannot be reduced to the provision of a vague terrain on which "Earlier Altman" drilled.

## Expanding Television Aesthetics and Authorship: *Troubleshooters* and *Combat!*

Outside of McGilligan's thoroughly researched popular biography and Zuckoff's oral biography, Altman's time in his filmed television "training ground" has historically received little sustained attention. However, recent work on the subject by Anthony Williams and Nick Hall, though displaying some of the traditional misconceptions of "Altman," complements this chapter's project.[47] Hall, for instance, rightfully observes that the common use of the term "bland" in describing Altman's television 1950s–1960s work "suggests that television can be dismissed as commerce irrelevant to Altman's later art" and "discourages scholars and enthusiasts from investigating the potentially revealing details and textures of Altman's work." Moreover, Hall cannily points out, "it ignores the fact" that Altman's feature work "would be interfered with by studios, prefaced by commercial messages and attended by an audience as variously rapt or distracted as they might be at home."[48] In other words, critics have too often presumed differences in institutional contexts, flattening out the dynamism within and obscuring similarities between key aspects of feature film and filmed television.

One example of the pervasiveness of this "blandness assumption," is provided by Kolker's account of Altman's earlier years, which gives only passing mention to Altman's television work, claiming that until *That Cold Day in the Park*, Altman worked solely in, "what could be called the Hollywood anonymous" mode, in which, "there is no space for the inflection of style."[49] This recalls David Thompson's complementary account of Altman's transition from television to film, cited in chapter 2, in which Altman's "surviv[al]" of "the constraints of little time and money in delivering hours and hours of generic television series clearly showed him exactly what needed to be done, just so that he could later undo it. Once liberated from the standard demands of master shot and close-ups to be handed over to an unseen editor, Altman began to allow himself to roam free."[50]

Beyond, or perhaps alongside, these hierarchizing assumptions about media forms three key premises are at work in standard accounts: that Altman had no authorial control during this earlier period because television directors were uniformly constrained; that all filmed television style was capable only of providing training in something like Caldwell's "zero degree style" or Butler's notion of "attenuated continuity"; and finally, that Altman's feature filmmaking strategies (post-*Countdown*) mark a clean break from his work in television. These assumptions are, to some extent, understandable. Christopher Anderson has discussed the factory-like conditions that characterized Warner Bros. Television production of the period, quoting WB producer Jules Schermer's claim that, "Most directors don't even take the trouble to understand the script or to understand what they are doing. . . . They're more concerned with meeting a schedule than getting values out of a script."[51] According to Anderson, directors were "hired on short-term contracts . . . assigned to individual episodes, and . . . responsible primarily for shooting the script in the prescribed amount of time."[52] But Anderson also claims that WB's approach failed because it stifled creativity—its shows were deemed *too formulaic compared to those of its competitors*. This implies that WB's creative constraints should not stand in for a more robust account of industry norms.

Newcomb and Alley have argued that it is television producers who have tended to wield the kind of creative power that is conventionally regarded as authorial.[53] Moreover, even when Newcomb and Alley acknowledge that "good, important, even great television is not always the result of the creative producer's controlling hand, eye, and ear," directors are left off their list of possible creative agents.[54] In his *Television: The Director's Viewpoint*, Ravage offers a description of the director's role that is based on its presumed creative limitations: "Since the creative control of content is the prerogative of others, the director searches for fulfillment where he [*sic*] can find it. He often makes a game of his job, delighting in the mastery of technical skills and creative short cuts that will not consume too much time."[55] Whether or not a particular production was as factory-like as at WB, the odds were that the director was left "attempt[ing] to create interest and vitality by an artful edit or a sly expression, tucked away where the producer's inquiring eye might miss it."[56]

Ravage's perspective on possible creative interventions is a useful starting point for analysts wishing to locate directorial contributions. Perhaps they should search for moments of aesthetic or expressive experimentation rather than the kind of thoroughgoing and expressive stylistic regularities that critics trained in auteurist analysis are primed to expect. Given the evident creative constraints, a directorial aesthetic of largely disconnected stylistic flourishes actually makes a great deal of sense. Even in the absence of the desire for creative expression, there is also a pragmatic need for the television director to create work that signals to prospective employers not only competency but distinction. The ability to effectively execute the scripted material while also producing added value in the form of visual interest and aesthetic quality would likely be attractive. As we shall see, looking for this kind of small-scale elaboration in Altman's early television work proves fruitful.

This perspective, though, rests in part on an overly general notion of the division of labor and television authorship. The scholarship discussed earlier provides useful premises for assessing authorship within television production, but it is also somewhat limiting. Most problematically, reliance on institutional norms occludes the importance of establishing specific production contexts, with particular, sometimes peculiar, authorship formations. Institutional norms are not necessarily hard and fast rules but can instead encompass a dynamic range of more or less likely options. It is crucial to ask whether common practices were followed on a given project.

Altman's work on the obscure engineering adventure series *Troubleshooters* (1959–1960) illustrates the problems with accepting standard accounts of filmed television authorship. Altman directed fourteen of the show's twenty-six episodes, sixteen-millimeter prints of which are available at the Wisconsin Center for Film and Theater Research. *Troubleshooters* follows the crew of the Stenrud Construction Company as they travel around the world, completing major projects and overcoming action-packed and frequently outlandish obstacles. Filmed entirely in Southern California, the show starred feature film character actor Keenan Wynn as the crew's "top push," Kodiak, and gold medal winning Olympic decathlete Bob Mathias as his engineer and righthand man, Frank Dugan. In addition to Kodiak and Dugan, four crewmembers were regularly featured in episodes, although their prominence waxed and waned in ways that hold significance for consideration of Altman's authorship. The series was produced by Meridian Pictures for United Artists Television, purchased by Marlboro cigarettes, and "slotted on NBC Friday nights."[57] It debuted in a particularly difficult timeslot, facing off against the popular Western series *Rawhide* on CBS and *Walt Disney Presents* on ABC, helping to explain why the series ran just twenty-six episodes.[58]

According to the *Los Angeles Times*, the concept originated with Wynn, who felt television might be the proper venue for his heretofore undervalued talents.[59] McGilligan writes that Altman and producer-screenwriter Allen Rivkin were brought on board at Wynn's request. They developed and cast the show, providing Altman an unusual amount of authorial responsibility for a director. According to McGilligan, Rivkin described the experience as:

> one of the worst of his life. . . . Altman changed dialogue and scenes and was filming straightaway without the producer's approval. The pace was so relentless—two episodes a week—and the budget so minimal that after a time Rivkin threw up his hands. No matter what he did, Altman would be out in the hills somewhere, simulating some exotic locale, and doing exactly what he liked.[60]

Altman claims that during his early television days he worked so fast that his crew would often finish early and rather than starting on the next episode, "the trick was to stay out almost all day, so we started doing reflection shots and all kinds of complicated stuff just to fill the day out."[61] Put another way, by completing core storytelling work efficiently, Altman created the opportunity for creative elaboration. This clearly foreshadows Altman's subsequent approach to storytelling efficiency and economy, as described in previous chapters.

Clearly, attempting to account for authorship across *Troubleshooter*'s sole season by focusing on a creative producer is misguided. Compounding the issue of Altman's evident, if partially usurped, authority is that while Rivkin produced thirteen of Altman's fourteen episodes (one episode, strangely, does not have a credited producer), Frank P. Rosenberg is credited with producing the remaining twelve episodes of the series. Additionally, the show's credits list two executive producers, John Gibbs and Richard Steenberg, and declares the show both a Meridian Pictures Production and a United Artists Television Production. Which of these is the "creative producer?" It seems likely that Gibbs and Steenberg were the studio producers appointed to the job by United Artists. Day-to-day running of the show, by Rivkin's account, seemed to be in the producer's hands, but only to the extent that he could handle Altman. Credit for the show's "creative vision," though, has been claimed by Wynn and also asserted for Rivkin and Altman by McGilligan. Furthermore, McGilligan claims that it was Altman's connections with Calvin Industries that set the show up with its extensively featured Caterpillar construction equipment. Obviously, then, a production can be much more wild-and-wooly than an organizational structure suggests. In this case, it seems as though the overall concept and style of the show can be attributed to Wynn, Rivkin, and Altman, while Altman and Rivkin contested its management.

Applying Butler's concept of "attenuated continuity" to describe *Troubleshooters* would not be entirely inappropriate. The series consistently makes straightforward use of continuity editing conventions, and the scoring by Raoul Kraushaar, who worked at Republic composing for B films in the late thirties, conforms to the norms of classical Hollywood practice while adding the typical cues to bracket the show's commercial breaks. A voiceover provided by Wynn at the beginning of each episode delivers concentrated exposition about each location and job, as well as a hint of the problem that the team will encounter. Most of the framings are straight-on and average height. Camera movement is fairly limited, consisting mainly of simple pans left and right that either reframe important figures or follow figures and vehicles as they move past the camera. The relative lack of sophistication or expressivity in camera movement can likely be attributed to the show's small budget. This factor, as well as the heavy reliance on exterior shooting necessitated by the show's premise likely played a role in the show's lighting—almost always flat and high key.

However, "attenuated continuity" fails to capture *Troubleshooters'* consistently heightened use of deep focus, depth staging, and distant framing. To some extent, the scale of the show's featured construction projects and equipment might be understood to motivate the distant framings. Depth staging and deep focus also allow for the display of these objects behind the dramatic action for reasons of verisimilitude and, perhaps, product placement. All three of these choices, then, might be understood as primarily motivated by the show's premise, but the consistent employment of depth staging and deep focus also suggests that the show's design may have been reaching for the kind of "quality" Hollywood look associated with these features. In either case, these features are best understood as multiply motivated and multifunctional *choices* rather than industrially predetermined outcomes. For instance, the show's provision of constant, legible reminders of location and busy backgrounds also enables what McGilligan describes as the series' "Hawksian" milieu, emphasizing "the camaraderie, the action, and risk-taking of a cadre of professionals."[62] In other words, *Troubleshooters'* stylistic strategies are tailored not just to the subject but so as to afford a particular perspective on the subject.

The notion of a Hawksian milieu brings us to perhaps the most obvious aspect of Altman's creative contribution to the show—the greater prominence of the four supporting construction workers in his episodes. Each has a distinct, though not necessarily interesting, characteristic: Jim is the strongman, Scottie is the rough ladies' man, Slats is a beanpole, and Skinner is the elder crewmember. The crew gets its largest number of lines at the climax of the Altman-directed "Gino" when the men's table talk at a poker game ratchets up the pressure on a coworker who has stolen the payroll and believes he has escaped suspicion. In the climax to the Altman-helmed "Harry Maru," the men are foregrounded again, as they conduct an operation to rescue Kodiak from a Japanese military officer who refuses to acknowledge the end of World War II. The crew members brave enemy fire as they drive their Caterpillar bulldozers through the outpost's front gates, while Olympic decathlete Mathias, as Dugan, pole vaults over the rear fence so as to sneak up on Kodiak's distracted captors. Altman's foregrounding of the men culminates with the series' final episode, in which the crew puts on a circus that allows each member to display a talent.

McGilligan describes Altman's use of the cast as a "multiplayer ensemble—the first of its type on the director's list of credits," but this is an overstatement.[63] *Troubleshooters* is far from *Nashville*, and in practice the men's presence serves more to suggest a Hawksian atmosphere than to fully articulate one. Rather than a first instance of ensemble narrative structure in Altman's oeuvre, we can see here instead an early instance of Altman's elaborative transpositional approach of multiplying and middlegrounding background characters. In interviews, Altman has identified this as a conscious strategy employed during his time in television and carried over into his work in the early 1970s. For instance, while describing his addition of characters to *M\*A\*S\*H*, Altman tells Fuller:

> I had started doing that same kind of thing in television. I had a bunch of guys I called "panics," who were utility actors, and I would write one line into the script for them, and hire them as a reporter or whatever, to give some sense of reality to it. By that time I was seeing Italian films, and I was striving toward that kind of neorealism. It seemed to me these things should be done that way.[64]

The extra emphasis the director was able to place on the four supporting players seems to confirm Altman's unconventionally extensive agency on the series. Indeed, one of the men, Slats, was played by Chet Allen—a former set designer at Calvin.

This elaborative narrative approach accompanies a more subtle locus of Altman's authoring contributions—the heightening of aspects of the series' three main visual hallmarks, which were also likely originated by Altman. Altman's more extensive and, for *Troubleshooters*, virtuosic use of deep focus, depth staging, and distant framing is identifiable in his handling of conversations. Typically, one character stands in the foreground plane in a medium shot or medium close-up while a second stands in a background plane on the opposite side of the screen in longshot or medium longshot. Such staging is perhaps not uncommon in Hollywood cinema, and Altman is likely working well within the norms of filmed television. However, his episodes display this spread much more consistently than those of other directors on *Troubleshooters*, which suggests a particular interest in depth composition consistent with his early 1970s predilection for accompanying zooms with aperture framing.

Altman is also more likely to use fairly complicated blocking in combination with this depth staging. For instance, in one such shot in "The Cat-Skinner" Kodiak sits at a picnic table under an umbrella in longshot in the distant foreground screen right while Dugan's jeep can be seen driving forward from the distant background. A Caterpillar bulldozer drives across the screen in the distant background (Figure 5.16), and Dugan's jeep emerges from its dust trail (Figure 5.17). The camera first pans left to follow the jeep as it arrives in the foreground and then pans rightward as Dugan exits the jeep and takes a stance in a medium shot in the near foreground (Figure 5.18). Kodiak then walks from his seat at the table to stand next to Dugan (Figure 5.19). In the broader context of Hollywood style, such a shot might not stand out as particularly exceptional, let alone particularly expressive, but it does

**Figure 5.16** *Troubleshooters* "The Cat-Skinner"

**Figure 5.17** *Troubleshooters* "The Cat-Skinner"

**Figure 5.18** *Troubleshooters* "The Cat-Skinner"

**Figure 5.19** *Troubleshooters* "The Cat-Skinner"

stand out as a significant aesthetic elaboration within the terms set by the series as a whole. It may be attenuated, but it is also distinctive.

Indeed, other directors working on the series employ this kind of relatively complex depth staging with greater irregularity. The closest approximation comes from John Brahm, an Old Hollywood feature director who directed two episodes of *Troubleshooters*. Aspects of these episodes suggest that Brahm's directorial style may also be distinctive. Like Altman, he stages scenes in exceptional depth, but Brahm's staging involves less complex blocking and usually occurs in interiors. It also frequently serves expressive rather than simply decorative purposes. For instance, in "Pipeline" Brahm shoots a scene set in a Persian prince's office by placing a medium shot of the prince at his desk in the foreground with his back to the camera while Kodiak and Dugan, framed over his shoulder, emerge from a doorway in the background in extreme long shot. Their relative size and the long walk up to the prince's desk emphasize both the grandeur of the palace and the intimidating status of the prince. In "Tunnel to Yesterday," the crew discovers a hidden Nazi bunker. Brahm frequently positions his camera at one end of a corridor while placing the actors at the far end in extreme long shot, thereby emphasizing the size of the bunker and the vulnerability of the crew, who encounter a group of bearded Germans who refuse to believe the war is over.

Brahm's work with depth brings to mind Ravage's suggestion that a television director might focus on the incorporation of flourishes, and analysis of the entire season of *Troubleshooters* suggests that the work of a given director might be characterized not so much by a specific type of flourish but by the frequency with which flourishes appear in their episodes. As can be expected from Altman's account of his typical shooting days, where he "finished" early and spent the rest of the day experimenting, Altman's episodes display more frequent, and more experimental, flourishes. For instance, Harry Maru surrenders only after he is sent into shock by the resemblance of a Caterpillar bulldozer to the tanks he encountered in the war, conveyed by Altman through a match cut of the bulldozer with newsreel footage of a tank. A montage of combat footage is then superimposed over the traumatized Maru, who shrieks and begins to tear apart his wicker chair. His screeching combines with the sounds of combat to create the most psychologically jarring moment in the series, and Altman's use of sound montage is as distinct as his use of visual montage.

This account of *Troubleshooters* relies on a somewhat cursory summary of the series' formal design and production context, but its specification of concrete consistencies with Altman's later work, its identification of a distinct series style, and its establishment of a contested context of authorship clearly challenge the basic assumptions underwriting the standard account of Altman's television work. In particular, the unchecked application of the "creative producer" model of authorship proposed by Newcomb and Alley to questions of television authorship seems unwise. These conclusions are supported and expanded on by the more developed account of the ABC series *Combat!* provided by greater access to the show's production documents, mobilized in tandem with a dynamic framework of authorship based on distinctions found in the world of both business and, appropriately enough, the military. This framework is particularly useful in examining "iterative cultural production"—a broad range of practices including genre cycling, adaptation, and the franchising of intellectual property as well as, and more relevant for this chapter's key questions, those processes of repetition and revision that occur in series-based media-making such as television.

This framework distinguishes between five overlapping realms of authorship—*sanctioning, missioning, strategy, tactics,* and *implementation*. Sanctioning consists of enabling and circumscribing the general conditions, especially financial and content-related conditions, of the endeavor. Missioning involves deciding on aims and establishing narrower parameters within the broader sanctioned conditions. Strategic authorship concerns authoring the method and plan for achieving those aims—conceiving of and developing key narrative, stylistic, and thematic premises, and determining a basic structure for managing the project. Strategy and missioning constitute the conceptual core or hub of the iterative project, which for television would be the series. The tactical level involves similar conceptive and managerial activities but deals with the shorter-term demands of a specific *iteration*—for television, the episode. Authorship at the tactical level often means developing a specific plan that will then be implemented at the "ground level" by the kind of cultural labor that tends to be elided in discussions of creativity and authorship. Distinctions between these realms can, in practice, become hazy. Authoring agents can often have responsibilities that are distributed across these areas. However, using these distinctions as a point of reference provides a level of abstraction and a degree of flexibility that is useful for contrasting and comparing different modes of iterative production and for understanding the authorship dynamics of television.[65] When applied to the first season of *Combat!*, on which Altman served, intermittently, as director, writer, and producer, and on which a good deal of heretofore unexamined archival resources will be brought to bear, the framework allows us to more robustly account for the methods and modes of Altman's elaborative television authorship.

The missioning-level conceptive authorship of *Combat!* likely began with Selig J. Seligman, the head of Selmur Productions. Seligman authored a document titled "Military Show," presumably distributed to ABC, of which Selmur was a subsidiary, that seems to have served as a rough proposal for the as yet untitled series.[66] In the proposal, he argues for a "dogfaces" approach that focuses on the infantry and "gives us more flexibility in cast, in types, in action, in mood, in identification, in contact, girls, etc." Seligman's sole authorship, though, is complicated by the next line of the proposal, "Pirosh gets top credit, his and mine personal experience." Robert Pirosh was a writer/director/producer who had won an academy award for his screenplay for the 1949 WWII film *Battleground* and written the screenplay for the 1962 war film, *Hell Is for Heroes*. The second page of the proposal briefly describes six main characters for the proposed series. It seems likely that these were formulated through collaboration with Pirosh, who would be hired to write and produce the pilot. This document, then, proposes a mission (a military television series), conceives of key aspects of the strategy for fulfilling that mission (a cast of recurring characters), and suggests the management team of Seligman and Pirosh.

Here we have Seligman and Pirosh collaboratively engaging in the conceptive authorship of "originating" and developing ideas for the series. However, a closer examination of the archival record complicates the meaning of "origination" in relation to the authorship of highly iterative cultural productions. In his proposal, Seligman is not originating the concept of the series in the romantic sense of the term but proposing ABC participate in a cycle of intense generic production. He cites the "Upsurge in motion pictures of great stature on war recently, includes D. Day Story, the Longest Day by Zanuck, Hell is for Heroes, Guns of Navarone, etc. (see attached list)." In an interview, Seligman gets more specific, claiming that *Combat!* was a response to the success of the 1955 war feature *To Hell and Back*. "The box office picture," he explains, "was so out of kilter [with the film's modest budget] that we were forced to make note of it." Furthermore, Seligman claims, "it's my job as president of a wholly-owned subsidiary of ABC-Paramount to experiment. Studios such as Four-Star, Screen Gems, Desilu, etc., are placed in the position of compromise. Their business is programming, per se, where we on the other hand, as a TV arm of a network and a movie company have the umbrella of corporate relationships as protection."[67] Seligman's assertion that studio ownership allowed him the freedom to try out the untested television format of the war series is an interesting wrinkle on how scholars usually think of the constraining power of corporate ownership. In any event, *To Hell and Back*'s shared constraint with television production—its modest budget—suggested that a war series might also be profitable. In this way, the film served as a discursive node across which to transmit the war genre to television, a pillar for an argument for ABC to exercise its sanctioning authorship and to allow Selmur to experiment with a "new-to-television" genre.

ABC seems to have been persuaded, and its proposed agreement with Selmur reveals the simultaneously enabling and constraining functions the network served in sanctioning *Combat!*'s mission and strategy.[68] The most obvious form this two-sided circumscription takes is in setting the budget—here a respectable $125,000 per episode. The agreement also circumscribes the series' narrative approach as episodic rather than serial, requiring that, "each program shall be a separate and complete story of first class entertainment value based on and up to the quality of the elements of the program." Other circumscriptions were vague but still significant, such as article fourteen's requirement that, "The programs shall comply with governmental requirements, ABC's network policies, and the business policies of our customers." More specific were requirements that Rick Jason and Vic Morrow serve as the "stars," that four other named actors would serve as "principal performers," and the designation of Pirosh as the script supervisor for the pilot and "as the script writer for at least three (3) out of every thirteen (13) of the programs."

Pirosh, though, would not go on to write any produced scripts for the first season of *Combat!*, perhaps because ABC's audience testing resulted in below average scores. This suggests a further authoring contribution by ABC to the series' mission and strategy. One significant aim of any television series is assembling an audience that could be sold to advertisers. ABC's scheduling of *Combat!* from 7:30 to 8:30 implies that the series mission would be to appeal to both youth and older audiences. Indeed, while the network's summary of the testing acknowledges its below average reception but then goes on to state, "the major asset of the program is that it appears to have appeal for both adults and children." Adults appreciated the combination of appeals, including "humor, realism, action," and "the touching human responses." After restating the importance of "humor" in adult reactions, the summary states that, "as might be expected, the youngsters found the action and broad comedy parts the main attraction."[69] In highlighting these appeals the network can be understood as providing strategic direction.

After expressing his own dissatisfaction with the pilot, Seligman hired as series producer screenwriter Robert Blees, who had produced 20th Century Fox's unsuccessful television adaptation of the film *Bus Stop*. Blees's first act was to innovate a key aspect of the series strategy, and perhaps of television's standard mode of production, by hiring Altman, with whom he had worked on *Bus Stop* during the previous television season, as the "series director"—a role that Blees has described as a television first.[70] In a DVD commentary,

Altman offers a number of reasons for taking the job, which he chose over another combat series, "The Gallant Men," whose pilot he had directed. One reason was financially pragmatic. *Combat!*, according to Altman, paid a salary, while "The Gallant Men," because it was at WB, "paid scale minimum." The second reason was that, based on his familiarity with Blees, Altman estimated that *Combat!* presented a better opportunity for exercising authorial control beyond the kind of limited tactical or implementive tasks typically assigned to television directors.[71] Indeed, Altman, while on the series, would direct every other episode, and he would also be given time between episodes to plan the approach to his next episode. This innovation to the organization of television production allowed Altman to implement his desired strategy of handling each episode as a mini, or "imitation," movie.[72] Altman expected not just to implement the shooting of an episode in a pro forma manner but also to take up each episode as an opportunity for tactical planning, conceiving storytelling strategies, and, apparently, revising aspects of the scripts. The series' script status reports describe Altman as "polishing" several scripts before they went into production, including scripts that he did not go on to direct.[73] Additionally, he wrote one episode, "Cat and Mouse," himself. Altman also received a producer credit for five of the episodes he directed—a formal signal of the expanded range of authoring roles Altman took up over the course of *Combat!*'s first season.

Altman's authorship also extended to collaborating on the initial, post-Pirosh, revisions to the core strategy of the series. Altman, along with director of photography Robert B. Hauser and star Vic Morrow, worked with Blees to develop and initiate what they described as a tone of greater realism. In spite of the fact that Seligman enthusiastically pitched Pirosh's participation to the network as a guarantor of realism, this quartet dismissed Pirosh's pilot as "the Rover Boys in Normandy" (the Rover Boys being a popular children's book series about the hijinks of a trio, and then a quartet, of teenagers in military school).[74] This conception of the shift, though, which would seem to indicate a contradiction of, or at least a complication to, the strategic emphasis on humor proposed by ABC, implies a contestation of the series strategy whose implications would be felt during the first season's production.

This creative revisioning by a quartet scattered across production domains also complicates the creative producer account's emphasis on a singularity of vision. Even so, with the series core revised, Blees remained in charge of managing the execution of that vision, and so might be understood to have been the dominant author. Two factors, though, problematize this account. First, at least two participants in the first series, star Rick Jason and writer Gene Levitt, have described Altman as the dominant creative personality. According to Jason, Altman "Sherman tanked" Blees.[75]

The second complication, which we can link to Blees's departure from the series halfway through the first season, has more to do with management structure than personality. Two of Newcomb and Alley's possible producer roles seem particularly pertinent to an account of *Combat!*'s authorship. The first is the "independent producer," or "a person committed to a single product or series." The second is the "production company," formed by a producer who wishes to produce a number of shows and "in which the chief executive happens to function primarily as a business executive."[76] Seligman, as head of Selmur and the chief executive heading his own production company who functioned primarily as a business executive, would seem to fit within the latter model, while Blees plays the role of creative producer of one of the production company's series. The problem here is that *Combat!* was, in fact, the only Selmur series during its first season, and that Seligman, with only one series to oversee, may have seen himself as more akin to an independent producer, thereby impinging on Blees's turf while also not fulfilling all of the creative producer's day-to-day responsibilities. In correspondence between Blees and ABC explaining his dissatisfaction with Seligman, Blees complains:

> No one at the moment is running the operation. [Seligman] is making many decisions . . . but he is not accepting all of the responsibilities which the day-to-day producer must accept. . . . At the same time, I am not being allowed to function in the manner which I believe the network has a right to expect from me as Producer. . . . I am also being placed in the position of having to accept responsibility for what I think are mistakes, without having the authority to correct them.[77]

In interviews, Blees has offered a less pragmatic but more artistically respectable explanation for his departure, claiming that he was removed because Seligman found his approach to the show too bleak, putting the series' mission at risk by moving the strategy away from humor and by contradicting another aspect of Seligman's authorship—his framing of the series, in interviews with the press and in correspondence with ABC, not just as realistic but as patriotic and uplifting. Seligman summarizes and reiterates this frame in a letter to the network, to which he attaches a *Variety* interview where he employs the rhetorical strategy. In the letter, Seligman states, "if the column were . . . disseminated widely . . . it could . . . help to forestall the promulgation of uninformed criticism of the war series. . . . The recalling of the exploits of free men in a hot war for the preservation of democracy if handled correctly can be a true service to our country."[78]

The "criticism" that Seligman's effusive description of *Combat!*'s social contributions sought to head off focused on claims that the military genre was a backdoor for TV violence. ABC had just gone through the spectacle of Senate subcommittee hearings attacking ABC vice-president Oliver Treyz for ABC's action-adventure-heavy programming strategy and its presumed threat to young audiences. This seems to have raised concern in Seligman that ABC might withdraw its sanction of *Combat!* in order to protect itself from the possible sanctioning power of the US government. Framing *Combat!* as a patriotic service, then, can be understood as a ploy to forestall criticism of a genre which, as the first line of Seligman's military series proposal put it, had as its primary (or at least first-stated) benefit, "Action adventure in new TV form. No restriction on violence. Clearcut enemy . . . Patriotic basis."

Whether sincere or cynical, this frame, which Seligman likely assumed had been integrated into the mission and strategy of the series, holds implications for pervasive claims summarizing Altman's time in television as subversive. Altman's own statements frequently place subversion at the center of what he learned from his televisual training ground. At an AFI seminar in 1975, Altman stated that his time in television was:

> very, very positive. I mean, you never stop learning but . . . you're not allowed to do exactly what you want to do. You've got to work underground, so you learn to do things. The whole business . . . of what this art is is just solving problems . . . until the last day you're solving a bunch of problems. You set up a goal and then you start cutting your way through the underbrush to get to it. And you really learn how to fight dirty in television.[79]

In other interviews, Altman has claimed that he wanted to make *Combat!* as realistic an account of war as possible, but "because the star of *Combat* [*sic*], Vic Morrow, couldn't be killed off, I'd take an actor, establish him as an important character in one segment, use him three or four times more, and then kill him early in the next script, offscreen, in a way that had nothing to do with the plot. That was unorthodox. It made them nervous. I used to get fired for it."[80]

After Blees was dismissed from the show, Altman was briefly made the series producer (an incredibly misguided move if bleakness of tone was Seligman's problem with Blees), and then he was indeed fired—but not necessarily, the evidence suggests, for killing off characters. In one account of his removal, Altman reports that he was fired for putting into production, without telling Seligman, an episode, "Survival," that had been deemed too brutally downbeat to be produced.[81] Half of the episode's runtime consists of Morrow's Sergeant Saunders staggering alone through the French countryside, delirious from third-degree burns inflicted when allied artillery set fire to a French farmhouse where he was being held by the Germans. Other accounts suggest that Altman lost his job after insulting Seligman at a party.[82]

However, financial rather than strictly creative or personal motivations may have been the dominant factor in Altman's departure. Creative work is not just visionary expression but also a pragmatic and strategic investment of labor, and it is worth noting that Blees has said that Altman was secretly negotiating a contract with MCA Universal to become a producer-director for their *Kraft Suspense Theater* at the time he was fired. Blees and Altman were dissatisfied with Seligman not only for creative reasons but also because he was not receptive to the spin-off proposals the pair were developing and in which they would have a financial stake. In an interview with McGilligan, Blees relates that he and Altman had plans to become the equivalent of Aaron Spelling, the head of a production company that oversaw a veritable empire of television series. Seligman, though, was off tending to a pilot starring William Shatner as Alexander the Great.[83]

There are other reasons we should be wary of wholeheartedly embracing Altman's self-description as subversive, even if we grant the possibility that on some series, and even in some circumstances on *Combat!*, he was "sneaking" things into his episodes. While Altman's time on other series may have conformed to Ravage's constrained account of television directors' authorship as tucking embellishments away where producers won't notice, Altman's authorship of *Combat!* was not limited to a narrow form of implementation, or even just to implementation. Instead, Altman had a voice in reformulating not just episodes but the core strategy of the series, particularly its tone and look.

Moreover, the central illustration of Altman's claimed subversive realism—the killing off of cast members—is dubious. For one thing, this "subversive" idea may have originated with the show's executive producer, albeit in a more pragmatic formulation. As part of Seligman's enumeration of the benefits of a military show in his proposal, he includes, "Flexible and colorful casts; kill off guys who don't play." More important, though, is the simple fact that in practice this strategy was never actually employed. Only two previously foregrounded soldiers die in Altman's episodes on the show, neither in circumstances that can be described as "casual." Temple, played by John Considine, initially appears as an ill-prepared ballet dancing squad replacement who proves himself in "Rear Echelon Commandoes" and then does not appear again until he dies a long and featured (rather than offscreen) death in "I Swear by Apollo." In his biography of Altman, McGilligan provides Considine's account of the turn of events that led to the resurrection and death of Considine's character. Considine and Altman ran into one another in the

MGM commissary just before the actor was to begin shooting his part in *The Greatest Story Ever Told*. When Altman found out Considine would be occupied, he expressed disappointment, stating that he had been thinking about using him again. Considine, though, told the director that he had six days before he began shooting, to which Altman responded, "Well. Maybe I'll just kill you off."[84] Though Altman's decision to bring back and then kill Temple seems to have been fairly casual, the handling of the death itself was actually heavily dramatized, contra Altman's claim of significant subversive fatalities. The same can be said for the death of the other recognizable recurring character, who dies in *Survival*—shot while ill-advisedly putting his stolen pair of boots on before escaping the Nazi camp that the squad had stealthily infiltrated.

There is concrete evidence that Altman "misbehaved" at least once during the shooting of *Combat!*. An attempt was made to constrain Altman's authorial discretion as a result of an implementive elaboration during his second assignment, "The Forgotten Front." Interestingly, the authority he ran afoul of seems to have been the Department of Defense—a key sanctioning author of *Combat!* that also held influence at the other four levels of authorship. Seligman's proposal for the series includes a hand-written note, "stock footage—cooperation of service already set—stories galore." Access to this stock footage would save the production a great deal of money (essentially enabling it to be made) and, or so Seligman believed, would also provide a patina of realism to the show. These affordances came at a price, not just in dollars per foot of combat film but in the yielding of key areas of authorial control to the military. Seligman's papers contain a copy of a Department of Defense directive for cooperating with media producers, and the directive lists several stipulations that speak to the conception of *Combat!*'s mission and strategy, including that the series must benefit the department while also being accurate and authentic (as defined, of course, by the Department of Defense).[85] To ensure these stipulations were met, the Department of Defense required submission of scripts and a print of each episode.

Its stipulations, then, required a particular management scheme (the logistics of which are negotiated at length in the archival documents) and placed constraints on the kinds of stories the series could tell. Indeed, at least one script, "Conscientious Objector," seems to have been blocked from enactment by the Department of Defense for obvious reasons. The revisions required by the Department of Defense, though, seem to have largely been about realism in the sense of accuracy. For instance, suggested revisions for "No Time for Pity" include corrections to the description of squad formations, army terminology, and technology.

A more meaningful change was required when General Dodge, Chief of Information of the US Army, visited the set and screened what was to be the series' premiere episode, "The Forgotten Front." In the episode, a squad member accidentally reveals intelligence to a German prisoner claiming to be a deserter, and when the arrival of a German tank eliminates the squad's ability to escape with the German prisoner they must decide whether to kill him or leave him alive. Caje, the squad member who must make the decision, seems to execute the German offscreen, but he later confesses to Morrow's character, Sergeant Saunders, that he could not do it since he did not feel right about "playing God." In the version of the episode that aired, Saunders expresses his sympathy, and according to Blees this was also the case in the final draft of the script. In an interview with McGilligan, Blees states that when Altman, the episode's director, shot "Forgotten Front" he had Morrow tell Caje that he should have shot the German anyways.[86] Apparently, this version of the episode is what was screened for Dodge.

In a letter to Seligman, Dodge notes that the episodes looked, "fine except for the scenes about the 'shooting' of the German prisoner which I feel strongly must be revised. . . . It seems to me that . . . an elimination of the part of the last scene that very definitely fixes on Sergeant Saunders the desire and intent that the prisoner be shot would make it acceptable."[87] While it is not evident from the correspondence included in Blees and Seligman's archival papers, Blees states that the Army threatened to remove cooperation over the episode's ending, effectively eliminating a key enablement to the series, and so the episode was altered.

Blees claims that Altman was chastened by this incident and never went off script in a similar manner again.[88] We should be skeptical about this, but the archival record indicates at least one concrete change to the series' core managerial strategy. Final drafts of scripts for episodes that went into production after Dodge's visit have an added feature—a caution at the bottom of the title page reading, "The changes which have been made in this script, from previous drafts, include changes requested by Continuity Acceptance and by the Department of Army, and MUST BE COMPLIED WITH."[89]

Another interesting feature of the "Forgotten Front" incident can be found in the way in which storytelling style is implicated in Altman's subversive strategy. Although the original cut of the episode is unavailable, it is worth noting that the key exchange between Saunders and Caje takes place with Saunders speaking while turned away from the camera, his lips largely unseen. There is no compelling dramatic reason to have shot this moment this way, although one could argue that it signals Saunders' thoughtfulness. We might posit that this framing provided Altman, aware of the risk he was taking, with a strategic safety net that would ensure "correction" of his subversion required only the recording of new dialogue rather than reshooting.

This archivally supported account of the first season of *Combat!*'s dynamic context of distributed authorship indicates that Altman was qualifiedly constrained in a way that bears only intermittent resemblance to what standard accounts of television norms might suggest, and that he was not particularly subversive, at least in the ways suggested by Altman's biographical legend. How, then, are we to summarize his work on *Combat!*? A third option posed by some, including Davidsmeyer, McGilligan, and television scholar Tise Vahimagi, was that Altman was an innovator. This seems like a more apt characterization, but it raises the question of what the innovations actually consisted of—a particularly pertinent question given the previous chapters' demonstration of the need to rein in claims about the oppositional nature and revolutionary extent of Altman's innovations. Four major innovative stylistic features have been claimed for *Combat!* during its first season, and each has been partly credited to Altman. Vahimagi's entry on Altman in Newcomb's *Encyclopedia of Television* identifies handheld camerawork, low-key lighting, and overlapping dialogue, all of which are also purported to have been introduced to television by Altman—a claim that, particularly in the area of low-key lighting, we should be dubious of but that, absent further evidence, we shall set aside.[90] Davidsmeyer and McGilligan seem to concur on these first three features and claim a fourth—clutter, in terms of both cluttered foregrounds and cluttered framings more generally. Close analysis of *Combat!*'s first season, though, reveals that claims for each of these aspects require qualification or revision.

First, overlapping dialogue is present in just one scene in all of Altman's ten episodes. In the opening act of "The Volunteer," the titular French child appears at the squad's temporary headquarters with a rifle slung over his shoulder and pauses in the doorway. The presence of multiple overlapping conversations among the squad functions fairly conventionally, conveying the kind of chaos or calamity conventional to overlapping dialogue scenes discussed in chapter 3 and reinforcing the confused perspective of the child. None of the dialogue is narratively significant.

Instead of sustained innovation in overlapping dialogue, Altman's episodes of *Combat!* display a consistent attention to experimentation with sound design that is not evident in other episodes.[91] In particular, Altman-helmed episodes tend to reduce the prominence of the score to make room for the expressive use of environmental sound. So, for instance, the tension in "Cat and Mouse" as G.I.s hide from German soldiers in an abandoned windmill is reinforced not by background music but by the middlegrounded squeaking of the windmill. In a DVD commentary recorded forty years after production, Altman articulates a further storytelling motivation, recollecting that the noise of the windmill was "put up quite high so it would plausibly disguise" the voices of the soldiers from the Germans.[92] Similarly, when the badly depleted squad attempts to rob a German camp in "Survival," the soundtrack deploys an unusually loud wind whipping through trees to cover the sounds of movement while also creating tension. These kinds of departures from standard practice in the service of enhancing narrative and expressive aims would come to characterize Altman's feature work in the early 1970s.

Sometimes, Altman's episodes temporarily set aside not just the conventional interpretation of action by music but the rule that the mix must ensure maximal clarity of the dialogue track. The most striking example occurs in a scene set in a rainy cemetery in "Escape to Nowhere," in which a captured Hanley is used as part of an escape attempt by a German officer who had participated in a failed plot to assassinate Hitler. The two, clothed in German uniforms, are discovered in a cemetery by a group of child resistance soldiers and a priest. Whereas standard practice would require placing the sound of rain beneath the characters' voices in the soundtrack's hierarchy, here the rain is elevated to a status equal to or even slightly louder than the dialogue track, muffling everyone's voices. The combination of the image of pouring rain and the unconventional sound mix expressively conveys an environment that is violently out of control, literally hampering communication. It is precisely this problem with communication that keeps the French youths from understanding the men's explanation and culminates in the shooting of the priest.

As one of Altman's early 1970s sound recordists would put it, he "demands a track which will 'color, highlight, and augment his story.'"[93] *Combat!* reflects those demands, and in doing so provides evidence that filmed television, given the right conditions, could serve as more than a simple training ground in which a director's role was constrained to the execution of the basics of Hollywood style. Conventionally, the television director did have little control over the sound of his episodes. In one interview, Altman recounts the shock he felt when he bumped into an actor coming out of a looping session on the Universal lot that he knew nothing about.[94] However, it seems likely that on *Combat!*, a series which Altman chose in part to strategically expand the domain of his opportunities for authorship, he made a point of asserting greater control over sound style.

Robert Reed Altman recounts an anecdote his father told about *Combat!* that further supports this assertion while specifying yet another novel on-set strategy consistent with Altman's later "middlegrounding" transpositional practices:

Vic Morrow would walk down a crowded street with a hundred and fifty extras and no one could talk except that one actor and the guy that was with him, because they were being paid to do that. And my dad would go to the extras every morning and say, "Who wants a line today?" And the assistant directors were like, "No, no, you can't do that!" My dad would pick five people to shout things out as Vic walked down the street.[95]

*Combat!*, then, seems to have provided the director with a dynamic forum in which he had enough control over tactical and implementive decision-making that he could pursue what would become some of his favored long-term formal experiments.

The second of Altman's claimed innovations on *Combat!*—the show's purportedly low key lighting style—is more apt but also misleadingly imprecise in its application, as it is often used poetically to frame *Combat!* as a figuratively *and* literally dark exploration of war. The series does use some low-key lighting, but the lighting is also frequently high-key. The variable that seems to determine the lighting scheme is the tone and subject matter of the specific scene and episode, a relationship that is actually fairly consistent with classical Hollywood lighting practice. *Combat!*'s production budget, while not extravagant, allowed it to display a higher quality look, with the attention to detail in lighting and situationally determined variation in lighting schemes within and across individual episodes that goes along with it. It does, perhaps, make greater use of effects lighting or night scenes than other series, but the show is not regularly lit to resemble a film noir—the impression left by the claim.

Much has also been made of the supposedly "verité" camerawork on Altman-helmed episodes, including a claim by McGilligan that, "as often as not, the camera was handheld."[96] These kinds of claims are broadly inaccurate. While some episodes do display handheld work, it is usually limited to a few brief shots during combat sequences or in moments intended to emphasize chaos, including a few scenes in which the squad is greeted by the euphoric liberated French. One or two episodes, such as "One More for the Road," do make more frequent use of handheld camerawork, but even in those cases the handheld shots constitute a tiny percentage of the episodes' total footage. That said, there is arguably an arc of development to *Combat!*'s use of the handheld camera—an intensification in the handling of characters' sunlit woodland wanderings in "The Volunteer" and a culmination in Morrow's delirious shambling across the countryside as the suffering Saunders in "Survival."

The intermittent growth of the use of the technique across Altman-directed episodes suggests that he may have been innovating, but focusing on handheld shots when describing the camerawork on Altman's episodes is misleading.

The occasional use of handheld certainly does not seem to have provided the template for camera movement at the level of series style, which is instead notable for its fairly extensive use of cranes and dollies. The camera regularly moves within shots to connect spaces and soldiers and to follow the narrative action, and we are more likely to find examples of the kind of fluid and structured camera movement on display in the opening shot of "No Time for Pity," directed by Bernard McEveety. Here, the camera cranes from an extreme long shot looking through an open city gate revealing a bombed out French village (Figure 5.20) into a medium shot of Hanley and Saunders discussing their plans (Figure 5.21) and then tracks back with a pan right to reveal the rest of the squad (Figure 5.22). These relatively intricate camera movements are also often used for expressive effect, as in the previously discussed scene from Altman's "Escape to Nowhere." After one of the child soldiers shoots the priest, Hanley and the German get back into the German's luxury sedan and drive off, and the camera pans left and cranes up from a long shot of the car (Figure 5.23) past and over the cemetery's fence (Figure 5.24) to an extreme long shot, framed through the "V" of a dead tree, of a child kneeling over the dead priest (Figure 5.25).

**Figure 5.20** *Combat!* "No Time for Pity"

**Figure 5.21** *Combat!* "No Time for Pity"

**Figure 5.22** *Combat!* "No Time for Pity"

**Figure 5.23** *Combat!* "Escape to Nowhere"

**Figure 5.24** *Combat!* "Escape to Nowhere"

**Figure 5.25** *Combat!* "Escape to Nowhere"

It is a bit puzzling why so much confusion should exist on the point of *Combat!*'s camerawork. It is tempting to attribute this inaccuracy to attempts to unify Altman's oeuvre, to connect *Combat!* to Altman's biographical legend—particularly his reputation as a former documentarian and the reading of his later films as documentary-like and dominated by an anti-Hollywood realist aesthetic. It is also plausible that because Altman's episodes of *Combat!* featured more use of handheld camerawork than other filmed television series they have been misremembered as not just displaying difference but as primarily constituted by this difference.

As the previous description of the shot through the trees from "Escape to Nowhere" implies, Davidsmeyer and McGilligan are correct when they assert that the foregrounds in Altman-helmed episodes of *Combat!* are often occupied by an assortment of objects. They describe this as producing a "cluttered" look. This "cluttering" is often attributed to Altman's interest in realism (in that it reflects the messiness of everyday life), or, for Williams, to the creation of a claustrophobic atmosphere that expresses the anxiety of the characters.[97] However, Altman's use of "foreground clutter" on *Combat!* is less about messy realism or anxiety than it is about elaborating aesthetically interesting, suspenseful, and sometimes poetic frames around the narrative action.

Take, for instance, a scene in Altman's "Survival" in which two members of the squad creep up on a German sentry. Altman initially frames the men in medium shot in the middleground through the gnarled branches of a foreground tree, with the German soldier's legs momentarily visible as he walks away (Figure 5.26). Then, as one of the men gets up to stand behind the tree, the camera rises up, with the foreground tree moving to the bottom and left edges of the frame (Figure 5.27). The German is momentarily nowhere to be seen, but he then emerges from behind the tree in the background as the American soldier prepares his garrote. As the German approaches, the American leaps out to strangle him, and the camera reframes to the left, creating an aperture framing with the foregrounded tree on the bottom and left of the frame and the middleground tree on the right of the frame (Figure 5.28). The two men then fall to the ground offscreen. Here, the aperture framing affords opportunities for suspenseful concealment and revelation, while also providing an aesthetically appealing composition.

**Figure 5.26** *Combat!* "Survival"

**Figure 5.27** *Combat!* "Survival"

**Figure 5.28** *Combat!* "Survival"

We can identify a continuity here with a key aspect of Altman's visual style in his early 1970s filmmaking. Chapter 2 established that Altman's films consistently displayed the employment of aperture framings in his zoom shots, highlighting depth relations and providing the zooms with structured and frequently decorative touches. This interest in heightened depth seems to have been part of Altman's self-determined problem-set at least as far back as his television work. Altman has said that he and Hauser, "worked a lot on creating depth in the image."[98] This extra effort suggests that, as in his time in industrial filmmaking, Altman was pushing the norms of institutional style—possibly with an eye toward elaborating the kind of quality look that might provide an appealing calling card for a move into features.

As with *Troubleshooters*, Altman's directorial style on *Combat!* is marked by a generally heightened, virtuosic approach to the show's broader norms. Altman consistently uses more distant framing and more complex depth staging than other directors of *Combat!*'s first season, all of whom also worked with Hauser. It is informative to compare, for instance, McEveety's aforementioned initial presentation of *Combat!*'s squad through camera movement and medium shots with the depth-staging approach that Altman takes in "Any Second Now." Altman begins his episode with an extreme long shot of the squad in a churchyard (Figure 5.29). Saunders drives up in the distant middleground in a jeep (Figure 5.30), and we cut to a close-up of Saunders in the jeep, drifting off to sleep, followed by a shot with the squad in the background in extreme long shot and Saunders in the foreground right dozing (Figure 5.31). Rather than McEveety's revelation of the squad through camera movement, we get a presentation that focuses on depth staging and forces us to look past the foregrounded Saunders.

As in *Troubleshooters*, Altman's handling of conversations and two shots consistently focuses on emphasizing depth. Take, for instance, another scene in "Any Second Now," as Hanley, trapped beneath a collapsed beam in a church, talks with a British bomb specialist who has lost his confidence but must defuse a German time bomb. Altman frames the scene with the specialist in the foreground left in a medium shot and Hanley in the lower right background, his head visible in long shot. The bomb on the right side of the screen creates an aperture framing of Hanley (Figure 5.32). Altman breaks this space up with cuts to a close-up of Hanley and a medium shot of the specialist, but even in the specialist's close-ups Altman inserts objects in the background like a candelabra to further emphasize depth (Figure 5.33). Altman combines this depth with camera mobility by concluding the scene with an unexpected flourish—a crane up and left from the initial framing to an overhead view as sirens begin to wail (Figure 5.34). Williams is right in characterizing the

**Figure 5.29** *Combat!* "Any Second Now"

**Figure 5.30** *Combat!* "Any Second Now"

**Figure 5.31** *Combat!* "Any Second Now"

**Figure 5.32** *Combat!* "Any Second Now"

**Figure 5.33** *Combat!* "Any Second Now"

**Figure 5.34** *Combat!* "Any Second Now"

visual approach in this sequence as "claustrophobic," but it also participates in a broader, functionally dynamic, visual strategy of depth compositions and aperture framings.[99]

This elaborative strategy even provides a central structuring device for the Altman-scripted "Cat and Mouse." Saunders and another G.I. are trapped in a windmill when Germans, unaware of the Americans' presence, decide to use it as a forward operating base. Saunders must hide in the workings of the windmill to avoid capture, and a hole in the wall offers a framed floor-level view of the German command center, around which Altman designs a series of shots. The first two depict Saunders and then Saunders and the other G.I. in close up on either side of the hole, which a cat sits next to (Figure 5.35). The camera then tracks forward past the men to shoot directly through the hole, with cobwebs framing the action (Figure 5.36). This set-up returns later—as a POV shot of a German officer holding his newly adopted pet (Figure 5.37). When the G.I. drops his walky-talky through a hole above the command center, another POV shot from this set-up shows it hit the floor and catch the cat's attention (Figure 5.38). As the G.I. surrenders, Saunders watches through the original hole, and we get the same POV set-up as before, followed by an axial cut looking over Saunders's shoulder (Figures 5.39 and 5.40). As the American is interrogated, he drops his pen, which rolls toward the hole, and when he is ordered to pick it up this framing allows the viewer to see both Saunders's nervousness and the G.I. giving him the thumbs-up signal (Figure 5.41). After the G.I. sacrifices himself to create a diversion so that Saunders can escape, Altman returns to the hole one final time for a four-planed shot of: the dead G.I.'s hand holding a gun in the foreground, his bloody head in the middleground, the cat looking through the hole at Saunders in the distant middleground, and a silhouetted German in the background (Figure 5.42).

This kind of systematic and virtuosic depth staging is largely absent from non-Altman-directed episodes. Moreover, this attention to stylistic display is evident in almost every Altman episode, though not necessarily in the same form. For instance, Altman's extensive use of the POV shot in "Cat and Mouse" is not repeated in his work on the series. It seems as though Altman selected and developed (or, in the case of "Cat and Mouse," wrote) individual scripts that would give him the opportunity to experiment, and this experimentation is as much a marker of his authorship as heightened attention to depth.

*Combat!* also displays continuities in what chapter 4 termed Altman's "transpositional" or "implementive" strategies—his approach to moving from final draft of a script to filmed work. Chapter 4 argued that the extent of Altman's on-set improvisations in his early 1970s films has been overstated by the filmmaker and critics. So, it is unsurprising that the claim which Altman makes

**Figure 5.35** *Combat!* "Cat and Mouse"

**Figure 5.36** *Combat!* "Cat and Mouse"

**Figure 5.37** *Combat!* "Cat and Mouse"

**Figure 5.38** *Combat!* "Cat and Mouse"

**Figure 5.39** *Combat!* "Cat and Mouse"

**Figure 5.40** *Combat!* "Cat and Mouse"

**Figure 5.41** *Combat!* "Cat and Mouse"

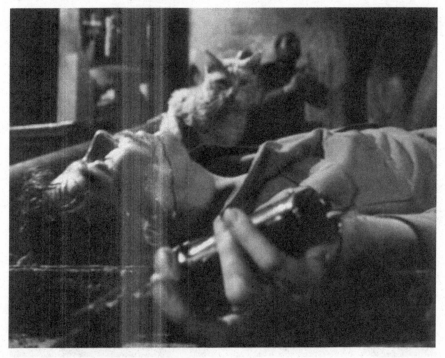

**Figure 5.42** *Combat!* "Cat and Mouse"

on *Combat!*'s DVD commentary that, "we pretty much improvised those things," is contradicted by an examination of several final script drafts, dated for the beginning of production. We can, though, find evidence for a qualified improvisatory practice that elaborates around the core narrative structure of episode scripts in order to serve a range of elaborative interests. For instance, in "Any Second Now" Altman elaborates on the milieu by giving extra lines to an American soldier and his French lover as they huddle together in an improvised bomb shelter. This middlegrounding of typically backgrounded characters—an extension of the anecdote provided above regarding giving lines to extras who were told to yell at Vic Morrow on the street—is in line with Altman's future transpositional practice.

Anyone who recalls the cat-centric opening sequence of *The Long Goodbye*, which Altman added to Leigh Brackett's original script, or that film's fornicating dogs, is familiar with another of Altman's transpositional practices also on display in his episodes of *Combat!*—his late-stage integration of animals. Unscripted animals appear throughout "Any Second Now," with shots of dogs in the street replacing a dialogue sequence, and with the addition of a cat to the milieu of the café and its basement bomb shelter. In "Rear Echelon Commandos," Altman foregrounds ducks, and the German soldiers later intent on mowing down our heroes are first shown carefully tending to unscripted kittens, complicating the naively patriotic good/bad storytelling that Seligman seemed to envisage for the series. Altman scripted "Cat and Mouse" himself, but even in this case, the final draft of the script makes no mention of the cat who looks through the hole in the wall at Saunders and who is cared for by that episode's Germans. A few added pages of revisions dated during the episode's shooting indicate only a portion of the cat's role, suggesting it was a late elaboration.

"I Swear by Apollo" provides examples of the kind of overtly ironizing transpositional elaboration that would characterize Altman's later work, and it confirms that Altman's television work could be expressive in a way that shares narrative characteristics with his feature work. In the episode, the squad is forced to bring their wounded to a convent. Altman uses the setting to lace the backgrounds of his shots with nuns and crucifixes, creating darkly ironic juxtapositions within shots (Figures 5.43 and 5.44). At one moment, a graphic match is employed as an ironic transition (Figures 5.45 and 5.46) from the sacred—a dying soldier reclines horizontally in the foreground, with nuns praying at an altar in the background, to the vulgar—the foot of an Army doctor preparing to treat his own blister. While the scene with the doctor is present in the script, his blister is not indicated, strongly suggesting that this narrational provocation was added during production.

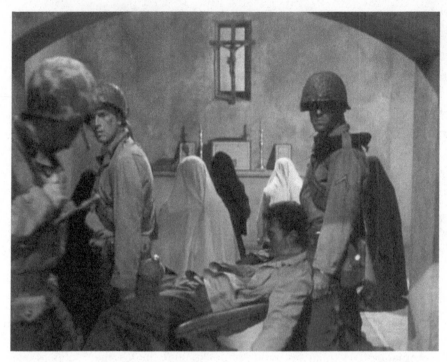

**Figure 5.43** *Combat!* "I Swear by Apollo"

**Figure 5.44** *Combat!* "I Swear by Apollo"

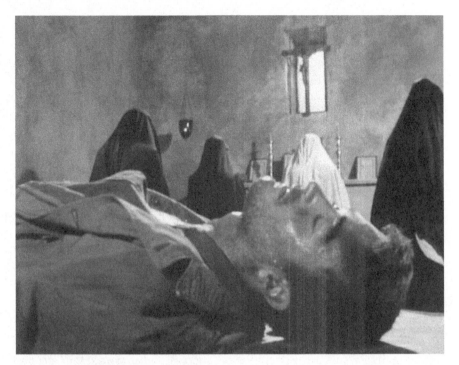

Figure 5.45 *Combat!* "I Swear by Apollo"

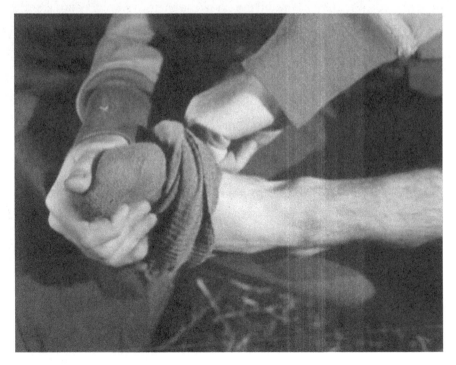

Figure 5.46 *Combat!* "I Swear by Apollo"

Davidsmeyer quotes Altman as saying that he took the *Combat!* assignment because he saw the show as "a think piece," an assertion that does more for his auteur reputation than the previously discussed financial and careerist explanations Altman provides on the series' DVD commentary.[100] Even so, many, though not all, of the episodes that Altman chose to work on display a distinctly "thoughtful" perspective. In doing so, they tend to leave the audience with a central irony or ambiguity that resembles what chapter 1 termed the "closure without comprehension" strategy on display in Altman's early 1970s features. Causal chains are perversely resolved—providing closure to the story, but in ways that trouble the kind of straightforward emotional comprehension that the Hollywood happy ending provides.[101] For instance, in "I Swear by Apollo," the American surgeon with the blister dies of a heart attack en route to the convent. Thus, Saunders has to capture a German surgeon and force him to try to save the life of a dying French resistance member who has knowledge of secret German plans. The German intuits the situation, realizes that saving the man will cost German lives, and with ambiguous motivation— perhaps to save his countrymen, but perhaps because of legitimate medical concerns—insists he cannot operate. Saunders, in a low voice, threatens to shoot him if he refuses. The operation is a success, and afterward the German, in one of Altman's deep two-shots, asks Saunders if he would have worked so hard to save the man's life if he did not know the enemy's secrets. Saunders tells the German that there is "a war going on," which means that he doesn't necessarily "like it. But I do what I have to do. Like you." Then, Saunders turns the question back on the German, "if I hadn't put a gun up to your head, would you have operated? *Doctor*?" This jettisoning of moral certainty and responsibility culminates in an evocative close-up of Saunders with a crucifix, altar, and skull looming in the background (Figure 5.47).

Saunders is placed at the center of another ambiguity-foregrounding wrap-up in the Altman-written "Cat and Mouse" when the intelligence-gathering mission that the G.I. heroically sacrifices his life for turns out to have been redundant. Saunders returns with the vital intelligence only to discover that the same information was already revealed when the Americans broke a German code the same day. Likewise, in "The Volunteer," a young French boy with a rifle wants to join the squad. They refuse, but in the end need the boy's help. He saves the life of an American by shooting a German, and he initially celebrates—until he recognizes the German as the same one who, earlier in the day, offered him chocolate and showed him a picture of his son. The boy, disillusioned with war, puts away his gun while the squad marches to the next battle. The episode's humanization of the German soldier complicates moral certitude once again.

**Figure 5.47** *Combat!* "I Swear by Apollo"

The notion that an episode of *Combat!* would leave its viewers unsettled, and that this vision of realism—in place of one focused on convincing footage of artillery and tanks and the accurate depiction of military procedure— would dominate the series was likely disturbing to Seligman. It placed his framing of *Combat!*, grounded in an uncomplicated patriotism, at risk. "The Volunteer," in which an impressionable youth rejects naïve militarism and the excitements of war, practically embodies the threat Altman and his collaborators' vision of realism posed to the mission and strategy authored by Seligman and ABC's report on audience testing. To the extent that Altman— guaranteed a significant portion of strategic, tactical, and implementive authorship over half of the first season's output—posed a challenge to the authorial aims of Seligman and put the continuing support of the Department of Defense and ABC at risk, it is easy to understand how, despite the complex of contingencies and contestations described earlier, the ultimate resolution of the struggle for *Combat!*'s ongoing authorship was never in doubt. Altman was removable. He could contribute to the conception and enactment of the mission, but he did not control the sanctioning institutions that enabled and constrained it. Perhaps, then—at least in terms of this aspect of Altman's contributions to *Combat!*—he truly was engaged in a project of institutional subversion, though one that took place more or less in the open, and in which filmed television served as a strange battlefield rather than a bland "training ground."

As we have seen, though, Altman's creative contributions to *Combat!* and *Troubleshooters* goes well beyond subversion. Much like his early 1970s feature filmmaking, his television work innovates on and elaborates around institutional storytelling norms, and as with his feature work it does so in part because the institutional context was dynamic enough to accommodate these elaborations. Combining this account of Altman's early television work with the account of industrial filmmaking offered in the first half of the chapter, we can see where the standard narratives of Altman's pre-1970s work have gone wrong. Industrial film has been mistaken as a realist-driven documentary medium, and as one where Altman's training was focused only on core competencies. Filmed television of the 1950s and 1960s has been described as a restrictive mode of filmmaking that produced only aesthetically bland work and in which a constrained Altman was forced to elaborate only through subversive touches until he could be liberated by a career in feature filmmaking. This chapter's reconstruction of specific institutional and production contexts, as well as its close analysis of even a limited set of Altman's work in these fields, suggests that what we might call "Earlier Altman" is more complicated than previously acknowledged. Not only have the institutions been mischaracterized, but Altman's work within them exhibits a range of continuities with his later elaborative filmmaking tendencies and concerns. Altman's time in industrial film and filmed television constituted not just a learning period but a period of experimentation in problem-setting and problem-solving that is not as dissimilar from his feature film career as has previously been acknowledged. Crucially, the "significant" yield of this experimentation is arguably not just Altman's subsequent early 1970s oeuvre but also his denigrated industrial films and episodes of filmed television.

# Conclusion

Grounded in an evidence-based approach that requires historical contextualization, close description, and functionally robust analysis, the account presented here calls into question the faux-comprehensive and narrowly interpretive tendencies of authorship criticism that have all too frequently treated undersupported assumptions about formal design as the starting point for assertions about personal vision and political import. In spite of the experiential exhilaration that Altman's early 1970s oeuvre offered audiences, critics, and scholars, we should hesitate to account for these films' innovations by ascribing revolutionary intent or impact, whether political or formal, to their design. It may have once been a thrilling notion that radical power resides in overlapping dialogue or open narrative structures. Such claims now seem reductive and misguided. A better understanding of the multidimensional operations of media industries, works, and audiences is necessary for any project of political or artistic engagement.

A historically targeted rethinking of Altman broadens the field of questions we might ask about the possibilities of Hollywood authorship. In its argument for elaborative authorship as a position within Hollywood filmmaking practice, the account presented here requires rethinking the nature of Hollywood norms. Given the deceptively clear "difference" of Altman's approach to filmmaking, it is tempting to view his work during the Hollywood Renaissance as a kind of test case for the limits of Hollywood's capacity to house certain forms of deviation. Rather than reading Altman as a liberated anti-Hollywood art cinema auteur in order to justify critical attention, or claiming his work's novelties are fully assimilable to the standard Hollywood aims, I would argue that we should understand Altman's novelty in the context of a Hollywood cinema whose norms have always been a work in progress on multiple levels. It is not only Hollywood's formulas—its conventions and techniques—that are constantly in play, contingently open to a range of modifications and renegotiations, but also the formulation of its underlying principles and aims.

This book has argued that Robert Altman's negotiation of Hollywood storytelling during the early 1970s has largely been misdescribed and misunderstood. Critics and scholars from the rejectionist camp have exaggerated the extent to which Altman's work in this period departed from classical Hollywood norms and resembled modernist art cinema. This book has

*Robert Altman and the Elaboration of Hollywood Storytelling.* Mark Minett, Oxford University Press (2021). © Oxford University Press. DOI: 10.1093/oso/9780197523827.001.0001.

established that it is more accurate to describe Altman as participating in an elaborative relationship with institutional norms in which Altman more often than not worked around and on standard Hollywood storytelling practice. In doing so, he expanded the range of popular cinematic storytelling in a way that incorporated aesthetic, realist, and expressive aims likely to appeal to the hip, cine-literate audience sought after by Hollywood during the early 1970s. While Altman's post-*M*A*S*H* films from this period frequently met with only limited, if any, financial success, it seems clear that Altman sought to take advantage of the window of opportunity afforded by the shift in the industry's prospective consumers. He made films that might appeal to audiences and critics looking for, as the advertising for *Brewster McCloud* put it, "Something else from the director of *M*A*S*H*."[1] But of what did this "something else" consist? Was it something completely different, something less, or something more than the standard story told the standard way? This book makes a strong argument for the "something more" position.

During the early 1970s, Altman's elaborative narrative strategy was based on the utilization of classical storytelling techniques, both at the level of large-scale structure and in his films' moment-by-moment narration. However, this Hollywood classicism, and particularly its methods for achieving expositional efficiency, served both classical aims and a perverse economy that allowed for the elaboration of multidimensional and frequently sprawling milieus around a clothesline of classical narrative structure. He embellished and punctuated his narratives with an overt, reflexive, and frequently ironizing narrational voice that provided his audiences with interpretive frameworks through which to understand the films' subjects. Likewise, although he followed the classical standard of providing his films' narrative lines with closure, he paired that closure with art cinema ambiguities that troubled and complicated emotional and intellectual comprehension. The result is not the dissolution of classical narrative but its vitalization. Altman may have publicly proclaimed a desire to "take the story out" of his movies, but his elaborative filmmaking practice in the early 1970s found another way to "[make] a good movie," one that relied on a foundation of classical narrative rather than discarded it.

Some have located Altman's "something else" in his novel employment of specific stylistic techniques, particularly his intensified use of the zoom and his innovations in overlapping dialogue. But whether that something else refers to the describable features and patterns of these devices' deployment in the films or whether it refers to the functions that they served, the record has been tainted by the circular logic of political modernism's interpretive mechanisms. Misdescriptive claims about form have followed from reductive heuristics about function, generating an account of Altman's stylistic tendencies that frames his innovations as oppositions to classical Hollywood's conservative ideologies of spatial coherence and auditory autocracy. Rather than striking a blow at the foundations of the regime, Altman's use of the zoom and overlapping dialogue represents a nonconformist rejection of its old-fashioned standards, an effort at revitalization perhaps motivated by the recognition of his inescapable position as a subject within Hollywood, but also one based on a belief in the flexibility and capacity of technologies and audiences.

Altman's preference for the zoom certainly exceeded that of his cohort during the early 1970s, but his application of this technology has been misdescribed and mischaracterized. Rather than overt or improvisatory attentional interventions that somehow both probe and dissolve diegetic though narratively neutral spaces, Altman's zooms frequently serve as pragmatic substitutes for the less exotic functions and technologies of the mobile camera, while also creating affordances for aestheticizing and dramatically intensificatory elaborations. Furthermore, the close, quantitative analysis conducted in chapter 2 reveals a contingent approach rather than one driven by dogma, varying its emphasis based on subject matter and the parameters and problems that Altman and his collaborators might devise for any given project. Thus, while supposed signatures like the "creeping zoom" might dominate some of Altman's work during the period, Altman's zoom style fluctuated from film to film in a manner that was neither entirely evolutionary nor entirely predictable. This provides an alternative to the common model of understanding a filmmaker that depends on reification or reduction and oversimplifies the more complex and contingent trajectories of problem-setting and problem-solving that make up a filmmaker's career.

This heretofore underexamined complexity is also made evident by the book's redescription of Altman's employment of overlapping dialogue. The densely layered sound designs of Altman's early 1970s films prove, on close inspection, not to display the film-by-film, track-by-track progression toward sonic discord and antinarrative anarchy that some accounts suggest. Instead, we see a fitful movement toward a greater technological capacity to achieve Altman's fairly consistent goal of augmenting narratively functional dialogue with ambient and sometimes overlapping dialogue in service of a number of elaborative aims—most commonly expressive and realist. This augmentation may add some degree of effort to auditor comprehension, but the analysis conducted in chapter 3 shows how Altman and his collaborators aimed to maintain narrative clarity by manipulating the different layers of sound. They employed techniques like the "sound zoom" and the carefully timed alternation of "overlapping" dialogue to direct auditor attention and promote the uptake of key narrative premises. Again, the approach was flexible and pragmatic, offering audiences a more robust set of experiential options than the standard soundtrack while securing them to the film's narrative "clothes-line" through subtle though evident strategies that coordinated composition, performance, and sound design.

The celebrated contemporary American filmmaker Paul Thomas Anderson has said that Altman's influence on his own work, "isn't something within his films. It's not overlapping dialogue; it's not zooms. . . . the biggest thing is just the attitude [of the undertaking]."[2] While chapters 2 and 3 focused on these more concrete aspects of Altman's filmmaking in the early 1970s, they also suggested that practice-oriented preferences helped to shape their execution, though sometimes in ways that seem to vary from long-standing accounts of Altman's productions as realms of wholesale improvisation. Chapter 4's archivally supported redescription of Altman's transpositional practices and his films' "improvisatory ceilings" provides a more plausible, though still nec-essarily incomplete, understanding of Altman's on-set improvisations, which seem to have been more limited and controlled than some "free-wheeling" ac-counts have suggested. Altman's desanctification of the script may have been viewed as defilement by some of his early collaborators and as a dethroning of classical Hollywood storytelling by some film scholars, but it is a move best understood as repurposing the script as a tool for elaboration. Altman and company provided actors with the opportunity to depart from the precise language of scripted dialogue, enabled select performers to add elaborative improvisations around the narrative core of certain scenes, and consistently added background characters that could then intermittently be foregrounded. Furthermore, Altman and his collaborators frequently improvised thematic revisions and additions—substituting, revising, or augmenting direct and structured thematic content with several looser thematic chains responsive to the contingencies of the production and the immediate social context.

The rejectionist account of Altman positions his early 1970s work on the far side of a stark shift from a filmmaker held prisoner by Hollywood con-vention to a liberated art cinema auteur. However, chapter 5's re-examination of Altman's time in the twin training grounds of industrial film and filmed television undermines this standard framing of the filmmaking practices of "Earlier Altman." Removing the twin blinders of the standard account of "Early Altman" and the standard approaches to the developmental history of an "auteur" filmmaker, we once again find Altman working not just within institutional norms, but also on and around them to pursue his own interests, setting and solving novel goals that expand the techniques and aims of the in-stitutional contexts. In reconstructing these production contexts, we find that even these culturally denigrated industries display a robust set of affordances for creative authorship and resist reductive generalizations.

The Calvin Company served not as a realm within which to experiment in observational documentary technique that presaged Altman's use of the zoom and his preference for realism. Nor did it function as a blank training ground in which Altman simply learned the core competencies of narrative filmmaking. Instead, Calvin served as a field in which Altman could work relatively independently, frequently on-location, to pursue the directed aims set by a given client and to elaboratively experiment with visual and sound techniques and overt narrational approaches. In a similar manner, assumptions about filmed television of the late 1950s and early 1960s as an aesthetically bland, wholly constraining institution led to a misapprehension of the possibilities for Altman's exercise of creative authorship. If not always thorough-going patterns, directors of filmed television could create brief flourishes of formal experimentation and expressivity. Moreover, as the chapter's examination of *Troubleshooters* and the first season of *Combat!* confirms, Altman pursued and found authoring opportunities that went beyond not only the rote implementation of scripted elements assumed of television directors but also the typical duties of many feature film directors. Additionally, Altman-helmed television episodes display both broad and specific continuities with this book's redescription of his early 1970s oeuvre. Altman amplified the role of the supporting cast on *Troubleshooters*, adding and then middlegrounding characters who might otherwise be treated as background. His consistent experimentation with aesthetically and sometimes expressively oriented depth composition recalls a key aspect of his later zoom practice, and his work on *Combat!* regularly displays the ironizing narrational voice, closure without comprehension strategy, and transpositional elaboration that would become key features of his filmmaking in the early 1970s.

Even in his filmmaking prior to the 1970s, then, Altman was providing commercial clients, television producers, and audiences with "something else," often whether they wanted it or not. This suggests both Altman's persistence and the underestimation of the dynamics within and resemblances between the filmmaking institutions in which he labored. As creative as Altman was, both as visionary storyteller and as pragmatic climber, he could not create the institutional contexts in which he worked. Instead, he was tasked with navigating norms whose constraining powers were more regularly assumed or defended than challenged, and institutions whose capacity for enabling meaningful innovation has been disavowed or delimited in ways that this accounting of Altman's work would seem to refute. The assertion by Bordwell, Staiger, and Thompson of a classical core to Hollywood filmmaking has sometimes been mistaken for a totalizing account of its storytelling, both by those who would frame Hollywood as other than classical and by those who would frame Hollywood as only classical. Instead, we might see the classical core as Robert Altman appears to have—as a configuration that could be flexibly employed within the dynamic system of a given film and, more broadly, within a given institutional system that is itself constantly subject to (and may from time-to-time invite) processes of reformulation and revision.

In the context of Hollywood's reorientation in the late 1960s and early 1970s, Altman was able to make room to pursue a novel set of elaborative formal strategies and to set aside select standards of filmmaking practice. In doing so, he took advantage of affordances for innovation whose precise instantiations were contingent and constrained but whose general availability would seem to be a feature rather than a bug of the Hollywood system. Although my findings led me to label Altman as an innovator and to designate his innovations as both elaborative and novel, I do not intend to suggest either that Altman's elaborative innovation of classical Hollywood filmmaking practices is necessarily novel or that elaborative innovation was alien to Hollywood prior to Altman. Altman's augmentation and reformulation of classical Hollywood's hierarchized aims—risking clarity for realism and ironizing expressivity, and doing so partly in service to his practice-oriented preferences—may be distinct, but it is not likely to be solitary or unparalleled given the fluctuating socioeconomic context in which the institution operates.

This account of an elaborative Altman, as an alternative to the rejectionist/assimilationist binary, might, therefore, usefully be applied to other Hollywood filmmakers, as well as to those operating in other institutions and modes of filmmaking practice such as art cinema. By arguing for an understanding of Altman as a filmmaker whose distinctiveness expands the possibilities of a filmmaking institution, I make explicit a third way of describing Hollywood filmmakers that has been implicit in a good deal of work on the industry's most prominent directors. Many of these filmmakers elaborated their own concerns and priorities on top of the Hollywood formula by deprioritizing or discarding constraints and standards they deemed outdated or unjustified, and they did so in the forms and to the extent that the contingencies of their filmmaking contexts allowed or possibly even encouraged.[3]

The research and findings presented here constitute just a first step in the reconsideration of Altman's incredibly full career. Much of the excitement and interest I found in this project was generated by the extent to which close examination of Altman's work required the overturning of reified accounts of "Altman." As chapter 5 suggests, the method and implications of this book's redescription of the canonically "Altmanesque" work of the early 1970s might fruitfully be extended both backward to the still largely unexamined body of work that predates *M\*A\*S\*H* and forward to the filmmaker's death in 2006. The variations of technique and practice on display within even the six-year window of filmmaking examined in the book's first four chapters suggests that further research might reveal multiple avenues of experimentation and development, and it might also expose aspects of Altman's problem-setting and problem-solving practices that have yet to be fully recognized or understood. The small-scale dynamism evident in the film-by-film progression of Altman's filmmaking strategies in the early 1970s, his constant innovation—responsive to contingency and subject—likely contributed to his longevity as a filmmaker. Moreover, it suggests a model for how transformative innovation might be integrated into dominant filmmaking paradigms—not through grand gestures of dogmatic contrarianism but rather through dogged and pragmatic elaboration.

# Zoom Context Films
## (Organized Chronologically by Director)

*The Landlord* (Hal Ashby, 1970)
*Harold and Maude* (Hal Ashby, 1971)
*The Last Detail* (Hal Ashby, 1973)
*Shampoo* (Hal Ashby, 1975)
*Leo the Last* (John Boorman, 1970)
*Deliverance* (John Boorman, 1972)
*Zardoz* (John Boorman, 1974)
*The Godfather* (Francis Ford Coppola, 1972)
*The Conversation* (Francis Ford Coppola, 1974)
*The Godfather: Part II* (Francis Ford Coppola, 1974)
*10 Rillington Place* (Richard Fleischer, 1971)
*The Last Run* (Richard Fleischer, 1971)
*See No Evil* (Richard Fleischer, 1971)
*The New Centurions* (Richard Fleischer, 1972)
*Soylent Green* (Richard Fleischer, 1973)
*The Don Is Dead* (Richard Fleischer, 1973)
*The Spikes Gang* (Richard Fleischer, 1974)
*Mr. Majestyk* (Richard Fleischer, 1974)
*Mandingo* (Richard Fleischer, 1975)
*Taking Off* (Milos Forman, 1971)
*One Flew over the Cuckoo's Nest* (Milos Forman, 1975)
*I Walk the Line* (John Frankenheimer, 1970)
*The Horsemen* (John Frankenheimer, 1971)
*The Iceman Cometh* (John Frankenheimer, 1973)
*99 and 44/100 Dead* (John Frankenheimer, 1974)
*The French Connection 2* (John Frankenheimer, 1975)
*The Out-of-Towners* (Arthur Hiller, 1970)
*Love Story* (Arthur Hiller, 1970)
*Plaza Suite* (Arthur Hiller, 1971)
*The Hospital* (Arthur Hiller, 1971)
*Man of La Mancha* (Arthur Hiller, 1972)
*The Crazy World of Julius Vrooder* (Arthur Hiller, 1974)
*The Man in the Glass Booth* (Arthur Hiller, 1975)
*Dirty Dingus Magee* (Burt Kennedy, 1970)
*Support Your Local Gunfighter* (Burt Kennedy, 1971)
*The Deserter* (Burt Kennedy, 1971)
*Hannie Caulder* (Burt Kennedy, 1971)
*The Train Robbers* (Burt Kennedy, 1973)
*THX 1138* (George Lucas, 1971)
*American Graffiti* (George Lucas, 1973)

*The Last of the Mobile Hot Shots* (Sidney Lumet, 1970)
*The Anderson Tapes* (Sidney Lumet, 1971)
*Child's Play* (Sidney Lumet, 1972)
*The Offence* (Sidney Lumet, 1973)
*Serpico* (Sidney Lumet, 1973)
*Lovin' Molly* (Sidney Lumet, 1974)
*Murder on the Orient Express* (Sidney Lumet, 1974)
*Dog Day Afternoon* (Sidney Lumet, 1975)
*The Ballad of Cable Hogue* (Sam Peckinpah, 1970)
*Straw Dogs* (Sam Peckinpah, 1971)
*Junior Bonner* (Sam Peckinpah, 1972)
*The Getaway* (Sam Peckinpah, 1972)
*Pat Garrett & Billy the Kid* (Sam Peckinpah, 1973)
*Bring Me the Head of Alfredo Garcia* (Sam Peckinpah, 1974)
*The Killer Elite* (Sam Peckinpah, 1975)
*Macbeth* (Roman Polanski, 1971)
*What?* (Roman Polanski, 1972)
*Chinatown* (Roman Polanski, 1974)
*Prime Cut* (Michael Ritchie, 1972)
*The Candidate* (Michael Ritchie, 1972)
*Smile* (Michael Ritchie, 1975)
*Colossus: The Forbin Project* (Joseph Sargent, 1970)
*The Man* (Joseph Sargent, 1972)
*White Lightning* (Joseph Sargent, 1973)
*The Taking of Pelham One Two Three* (Joseph Sargent, 1974)
*Boxcar Bertha* (Martin Scorsese, 1972)
*Mean Streets* (Martin Scorsese, 1973)
*Alice Doesn't Live Here Anymore* (Martin Scorsese, 1974)
*Two Mules for Sister Sara* (Don Siegel, 1970)
*The Beguiled* (Don Siegel, 1971)
*Dirty Harry* (Don Siegel, 1971)
*Charley Varrick* (Don Siegel, 1973)
*The Black Windmill* (Don Siegel, 1974)
*The Sugarland Express* (Steven Spielberg, 1974)
*Jaws* (Steven Spielberg, 1975)
*Bedknobs and Broomsticks* (Robert Stevenson, 1971)
*Herbie Rides Again* (Robert Stevenson, 1974)
*The Island at the Top of the World* (Robert Stevenson, 1974)
*One of Our Dinosaurs Is Missing* (Robert Stevenson, 1975)

# Notes

## Introduction

1. Academy of Motion Picture Arts and Sciences, "Academy Awards Database—AMPAS," http://awardsdatabase.oscars.org/ampas_awards/DisplayMain.jsp?curTime= 1262832683008 (accessed January 7, 2009).

2. See, for instance, Robert T. Self, *Robert Altman's Subliminal Reality* (Minneapolis: University of Minnesota Press, 2002) and Robert Kolker, *A Cinema of Loneliness*, 3rd ed. (Oxford: Oxford University Press, 2000).

3. David Bordwell, Janet Staiger, and Kristin Thompson, *The Classical Hollywood Cinema: Film Style and Mode of Production to 1960* (New York: Columbia University Press, 1985), 372–375.

4. In this respect, this book's closest peer is Gayle Sherwood Magee's *Robert Altman's Soundtracks: Film, Music, and Sound from M\*A\*S\*H to A Prairie Home Companion* (Oxford: Oxford University Press, 2014). That book is similarly grounded in archival research and close analysis. While its historical scope does encompass Altman's entire career, its analytic scope is narrowly focused on his use of music.

5. See also Warren Buckland's *Directed by Steven Spielberg: Poetics of the Contemporary Hollywood Blockbuster* (New York: Continuum, 2006).

6. Stephen Crofts, "Authorship and Hollywood," in *The Oxford Guide to Film Studies*, ed. John Hill and Pamela Church Gibson (New York: Oxford University Press, 1998), 320.

7. As scholars such as Berys Gaut have pointed out, attributing authorship of a film's features to a single individual risks misstating the collaborative nature of filmmaking. For a filmmaker such as Altman this would seem to be especially problematic. In place of the "ideology of single authorship" Gaut proposes a "multiple authorship" default position that allows for a variety of collaborative structures, including "the dominant collaborator film . . . when one individual has dominant creative control over a film." This, perhaps surprisingly, seems to apply to Altman. Even as he played up the collaborative, improvisatory nature of his productions, he also insisted that his approach was "regal" rather than democratic, though he reassured one interviewer that he was "a good monarch." That said, we should take Gaut's caution to heart as much as possible. I would like to leave open, to a reasonable extent, the possibility that the origination of specific applications of narrative or stylistic techniques may not reside with Altman, even while it is important to acknowledge that primary accounts of Altman's productions demonstrate that he served as a gatekeeper and censor as well as an enabler and instigator of collaborative opportunities. Consistencies in the use of specific strategies and solutions across his body of work also suggest they are likely attributable to Altman. Therefore, I will still credit these features to Altman, or to Altman and his collaborators, except where specific evidence suggests a technique's origins lie with a specific collaborator. I am utterly open to the possibility that other scholars may present evidence that challenges attribution of authorship to Altman, but in the absence of such evidence, it seems reasonable to presume Altman's authorship as a default. On collaborative authorship,

see Berys Gaut, *A Philosophy of Cinematic Art* (Cambridge: Cambridge University Press, 2010), 128–129. And for the "good monarch" framing of Altman, see Michael Billington, "The Monarch after M.A.S.H.," *The Times* (of London), February 4, 1971.

8. See, for instance, Justin Wyatt, "Economic Constraints/Economic Opportunities: Robert Altman as Auteur," *The Velvet Light Trap* 38 (1996), 51–68.

9. David Bordwell, "Poetics of Cinema," in *Poetics of Cinema* (New York: Routledge, 2008), 12–13.

10. Bordwell, "Poetics of Cinema," 23.

11. Bordwell, "Poetics of Cinema," 25.

12. David Bordwell, *Figures Traced in Light: On Cinematic Staging* (Berkeley: University of California Press, 2005), 41.

13. Bordwell, "Poetics of Cinema," 28.

14. Self, *Robert Altman's Subliminal Reality*, vii.

15. American Film Institute, "Robert Altman Seminar," *Dialogue on Film* 4, no. 5 (February 1975), 12.

16. Stephen Altman, interview by author, August 1, 2012.

17. Bordwell, "Poetics of Cinema," 14–15.

18. Bordwell, "Poetics of Cinema," 20–21.

19. Meir Sternberg, "Reconceptualizing Narratology: Arguments for a Functionalist and Constructivist Approach to Narrative," *Enthymema* 4 (2011), 40.

20. David Bordwell, "Neo-Structuralist Narratology and the Functions of Filmic Storytelling," in *Narrative across Media: The Languages of Storytelling*, ed. Marie-Laure Ryan (Lincoln: University of Nebraska Press, 2004), 204.

21. See James J. Gibson, *The Ecological Approach to Visual Perception* (Boston, MA: Houghton Mifflin, 1979). For one example of media studies' appropriation of Gibson's concept, see Marie-Laure Ryan's introduction to *Narrative across Media: The Languages of Storytelling* (Lincoln: University of Nebraska Press, 2004), 1–2.

22. Self, *Robert Altman's Subliminal Reality*, 26–28.

23. Self, *Robert Altman's Subliminal Reality*, 28.

24. Self, *Robert Altman's Subliminal Reality*, 46.

25. Self, *Robert Altman's Subliminal Reality*, 29.

26. Self, *Robert Altman's Subliminal Reality*, 44.

27. Kolker, *A Cinema of Loneliness*, 338.

28. Nick Hall, *The Zoom: Drama at the Touch of a Lever* (New Brunswick, NJ: Rutgers University Press, 2018), 150.

29. Hall, *The Zoom*, 36–37.

30. Jon Lewis, *Whom God Wishes to Destroy . . .* (Durham, NC: Duke University Press, 1995), 165n.

31. Murray Smith, "Theses on the Philosophy of Hollywood History," in *Contemporary Hollywood Cinema*, ed. Steve Neale and Murray Smith (New York: Routledge, 1998), 3.

32. Diane Jacobs, *Hollywood Renaissance* (New York: Delta Books, 1977).

33. Jacobs, *Hollywood Renaissance*, 4.

34. Steve Neale, "'The Last Good Time We Ever Had?': Revising the Hollywood Renaissance," in *Contemporary American Cinema*, ed. Linda Ruth Williams and Michael Hammond (London: McGraw Hill, 2006), 91.

35. David A. Cook, *Lost Illusions: American Cinema in the Shadow of Watergate and Vietnam: 1970–1979*, History of the American Cinema (Berkeley: University of California Press, 2000), 67–69.

36. Paul Ramaeker, "A New Kind of Movie, Style and Form in Hollywood Cinema 1965–1988" (PhD diss., University of Wisconsin–Madison, 2002).

37. Mark Shiel, "American Cinema, 1965–1970," in *Contemporary American Cinema*, ed. Linda Ruth Williams and Michael Hammond (London: McGraw Hill, 2006), 34.

38. Neale, " 'Last Good Time,' " 92.

39. Thomas Schatz, *Old Hollywood/New Hollywood: Ritual, Art, and Industry* (Ann Arbor: University of Michigan Research Press, 1983), 204.

40. James Bernardoni, *The New Hollywood* (Jefferson, NC: McFarland & Company, 1991), 117.

41. Elsaesser has insightfully framed this period as essentially one of "crossover" between "Old" and "New" Hollywood, European art cinema, the avantgarde, genres, and political ideologies. See Thomas Elsaesser, "American Auteur Cinema: The Last—or First—Picture Show?," in *The Last Great American Picture Show*, ed. Thomas Elsaesser, Alexander Horwath, and Noel King (Amsterdam: Amsterdam University Press, 2004), 37–69.

42. Self, *Robert Altman's Subliminal Reality*, xvi–xvii.

43. Self, *Robert Altman's Subliminal Reality*, 76.

44. Bordwell, Staiger, and Thompson, *Classical Hollywood Cinema*, 373.

45. Bordwell, Staiger, and Thompson, *Classical Hollywood Cinema*, 374–376.

46. More recently, Todd Berliner has provided a provocative and valuable reappraisal of storytelling practices in the Hollywood Renaissance and New Hollywood that is usefully complementary to my own work on Altman. Berliner's focus, though, is on genre and narrative form per se, avoiding the kind of detailed consideration of visual and sound style I employ here, and his discussion of Altman both lacks the systematicity of my approach and repeats many of the canards this book calls into question. Significantly, Berliner's claim that Hollywood Renaissance filmmakers find what he terms a "middle way" between Hollywood and art cinema, grounded in classical Hollywood narrative structure, resembles my own findings in relation to Altman. That said, I am skeptical about his tethering of this approach to "incoherence," both because it is a too-narrow characterization of the expansive range of elaborations Altman and other Hollywood Renaissance filmmakers aimed for and because it indirectly extends an oppositional framing. Altman's own films sometimes aim for incoherence and sometimes merely risk incoherence, at least according to the terms of Hollywood's standard-bearers (or standard-enforcers), in service of a variety of aims. See Todd Berliner, *Hollywood Incoherent: Narration in Seventies Cinema* (Austin: University of Texas Press, 2011).

47. David Bordwell, *On the History of Film Style* (Cambridge, MA: Harvard University Press, 1997), 268.

48. Bordwell, "Poetics of Cinema," 25.

49. Bordwell, Staiger, and Thompson, *Classical Hollywood Cinema*, 6–7.

50. Bordwell, Staiger, and Thompson, *Classical Hollywood Cinema*, 12.

51. Rick Altman, "Dickens, Griffith, and Film Theory Today," in *Classical Hollywood Cinema: The Paradigm Wars*, ed. Jane Gaines (Durham, NC: Duke University Press, 1992), 28–29.

52. Graham Fuller, "Altman on Altman," in *Robert Altman Interviews*, ed. David Sterritt (Jackson: University Press of Mississippi, 2000), 189.

53. David Bordwell, borrowing from Boris Tomashevsky, has described the biographical legend as a sort of authorial profile, or persona, consisting of a standard account of key attributes, practices, and intentions, "created by the filmmaker and other forces (the press, cinephiles [here, I would add scholars])," and helping to "determine how we 'should' read the films and the career." See David Bordwell, *The Films of Carl-Theodor Dreyer* (Berkeley: University of California Press, 1981), 9.

54. David Thompson, ed., *Altman on Altman* (London: Faber and Faber, 2005), xix.

55. John Belton and Lyle Tector, "The Bionic Eye: The Aesthetics of the Zoom," *Film Comment* 16, no. 5 (September/October 1980), 13.

56. Andrew Sarris, "Films in Focus," *Village Voice*, December 24, 1970, 47, and Self, *Altman's Subliminal Reality*, 37, 38.

57. Rick Altman, "24 Track Narrative? Robert Altman's *Nashville*," *Cinémas: Revue d'études cinématographiques* 1, no. 3 (1991), 102–125.

58. "Show Business: Creation in Chaos," *Time*, July 13, 1970, 62.

59. This use of "transposition" is inspired by Wagner's use of the term in relation to cinematic adaptations of novels, though it does not precisely replicate Wagner's meaning. See Geoffrey Wagner, *The Novel and the Cinema* (Rutherford, NJ: Fairleigh Dickinson University Press, 1975).

60. See, for instance, Thompson, *Altman on Altman*, 176.

## Chapter 1

1. Aljean Harmetz, "The 15th Man Who Was Asked to Direct *M\*A\*S\*H* (And Did) Makes a Peculiar Western," *New York Times Magazine*, June 20, 1971, 47.

2. David Bordwell, "Three Dimensions of Film Narrative," in *Poetics of Cinema* (New York: Routledge, 2008), 85–133.

3. Bordwell, "Three Dimensions," 92–93.

4. I say "some forms of art cinema" in part to push back against the position implicit in the arguments of Self and others that all or most art cinema is narrative-less or necessarily oppositional to classical narrative form. In fact, not enough work has been done on international art cinema norms to support this stance, which seems to present a slippage between "art cinema" per se and more straightforwardly modernist filmmaking. Recent scholarship, such as András Bálint Kovács, *Screening Modernism: European Art Cinema, 1950–1980* (Chicago: University of Chicago Press, 2007) builds on Bordwell's foundational work in ways that make useful distinctions between and within art cinema (or "art-film") and modernist filmmaking.

5. David Bordwell and Janet Staiger, "Historical Implications of the Classical Hollywood Cinema," in *The Classical Hollywood Cinema: Film Style and Mode of Production to 1960*, by David Bordwell, Janet Staiger, and Kristin Thompson (New York: Columbia University Press, 1985), 373–375.

6. Perversity, in this sense, differs from the way Todd Berliner defines the term, as "a counterproductive turn away from a narrative's linear course," and the addition of "something incongruous to an artwork." Berliner, *Hollywood Incoherent*, 10. Instead, perversity as I define it here involves using unconventional means for conventional ends or conventional means for unconventional ends.

7. Self, *Altman's Subliminal Reality*, 8.

8. Self, *Altman's Subliminal Reality*, 53.

9. Self, *Altman's Subliminal Reality*, 53.

10. Self, *Altman's Subliminal Reality*, 53.

11. Pauline Kael, "Spawn of the Movies," *New Yorker*, January 9, 1971, 64.

12. Arthur D. Murphy, "*McCabe and Mrs. Miller* (review)," *Variety* June 30, 1971, 22.

13. "*McCabe and Mrs. Miller* (review)," *Media and Methods*, October 1971, 10.

14. Pauline Kael, "Round Up the Usual Suspects," *New Yorker*, December 23, 1972, 56.

15. John Coleman, "Marlowe and His Society," *New Statesman*, November 2, 1973, 660.

16. John Coleman, "C*H*I*P*S," *New Statesman*, January 17, 1975, 88.

17. Arthur D. Murphy, "Review of *California Split*," *Variety*, August 7, 1974, 18.

18. Paul D. Zimmerman, "Return of Philip Marlowe," *Newsweek*, October 29, 1973, 107.

19. Paul D. Zimmerman, "Lovers and Phantoms," *Newsweek*, January 15, 1973, 65.

20. Zimmerman, "Return of Philip Marlowe," 108.

21. Paul D. Zimmerman, "Bowie and Keechie," *Newsweek*, February 18, 1974, 101.

22. Harmetz, "15th Man," 47.

23. Zimmerman, "Return of Philip Marlowe," 107.

24. Fuller, "Altman on Altman," 199.

25. Fuller, "Altman on Altman," 196.

26. Kristin Thompson, *Storytelling in the New Hollywood* (Cambridge, MA: Harvard University Press, 1999).

27. Thomas Elsaesser, "The Pathos of Failure: American Films in the 1970s: Notes on the Unmotivated Hero [1975]," in *The Last Great American Picture Show*, ed. Thomas Elsaesser, Alexander Horwath, and Noel King (Amsterdam University Press, 2004), 281, 283.

28. Elsaesser, "The Pathos of Failure," 285.

29. Self, *Altman's Subliminal Reality*, 56.

30. Thompson, *Storytelling*, 28.

31. Fuller, "Altman on Altman" 194.

32. Thompson, *Storytelling*, 37.

33. David Bordwell, "Mutual Friends and Chronologies of Chance," in *Poetics of Cinema* (New York: Routledge, 2008), 221–227.

34. Buckland, *Directed by Steven Spielberg*, 33–34.

35. Thompson, *Storytelling*, 29.

36. Bordwell, "Mutual Friends," 225.

37. Thompson, *Storytelling*, 47–48, 248–282.

38. David Bordwell, *Narration in the Fiction Film* (Madison: University of Wisconsin Press, 1985), 160.

39. American Film Institute, "Robert Altman Seminar," *Dialogue on Film* 4, no. 5 (February 1975), 6.

40. On concentrated exposition in classical narration, see Bordwell, Staiger, and Thompson, *Classical Hollywood Cinema*, 28–29. As a norm of popular storytelling in popular fiction and film, see Bordwell, *Narration*, 56.

41. Bordwell, *Narration*, 54.

42. Donald Crafton, "Pie and Chase: Gag, Spectacle, and Narrative in Slapstick Comedy," in *The Cinema of Attractions Reloaded*," ed. Wanda Strauven (Amsterdam: Amsterdam University Press, 2006), 355–364.

43. Daniel Barratt, "Twist Blindness," in *Puzzle Films: Complex Storytelling in Contemporary Cinema*, ed. Warren Buckland (Malden, MA: Wiley-Blackwell, 2009), 67.

44. Kristin Thompson, *Breaking the Glass Armor: Neoformalist Film Analysis* (Princeton, Princeton University Press, 1986), 259–260.

45. Bordwell, *Narration*, 210.

46. Bordwell, *Narration*, 61.

47. See, for instance, Self, *Altman's Subliminal Reality*, xxvii.

48. Thompson, *Storytelling*, 45–46.

49. Thompson, *Storytelling*, 47.

50. Bordwell, Staiger, and Thompson, *Classical Hollywood Cinema*, 30.

51. This description of the essential features of art cinema narration is based on Bordwell's chapter, "Art-Cinema Narration," in *Narration*, 205–233.

52. On the role of the monologue in cinema, see Sarah Kozloff, *Overhearing Film Dialogue* (Berkeley: University of California Press, 2000), 70–71. Kozloff similarly recognizes Altman's innovation of the monologue in *McCabe & Mrs. Miller* and *The Long Goodbye*, though she overlooks or omits its extension into *Popeye* and proposes its use is meant to suggest that the characters possess the traits of "isolation, frailty, and perhaps impotence."

53. See Bordwell, Thompson, and Staiger, *Classical Hollywood Cinema*, 25–29.

54. Fuller, "Altman on Altman," 198.

55. Gavin Smith and Richard T. Jameson, "The Movie You Saw Is the Movie We're Going to Make," in *Robert Altman Interviews*, ed. David Sterritt (Jackson: University Press of Mississippi, 2000), 165.

56. Thompson, *Altman on Altman*, 57.

57. See, for instance, Noël Carroll, *The Philosophy of Horror* (New York: Routledge, 1990), 130–137.

58. Thompson, *Altman on Altman*, 75.

59. Berliner, *Hollywood Incoherent*, 94.

## Chapter 2

1. Kolker, *A Cinema of Loneliness*, 337, 343.

2. Yuri Tsivian, "Movie Measurement and Study Tool Database," Cinemetrics, November 27, 2019. http://www.cinemetrics.lv/index.php. The Cinemetrics website provides an invaluable hub for those interested in the statistical analysis of moving image style—linking to the websites of other scholars in the tradition and providing a database with shot duration data for thousands of films as well as data and analysis from important scholars such as Barry Salt, whose *Film Style and Technology: History and Analysis* (London: Starword, 1983) and *Moving into Pictures* (London: Starword, 2006) are foundational works. In addition to Tsivian and Salt, a partial list of Cinemetrics' key figures would include: Bordwell and Thompson (davidbordwell.net); James Cutting (http://people.psych.cornell.edu/~jec7/curresearch.htm); Nick Redfern (nickredfern. wordpress.com); M. J. Baxter (mikemetrics.com); Jeremy Butler, who concentrates on television style (shotlogger.com); and Warren Buckland, who employs a Cinemetrics approach in *Directed by Steven Spielberg*.

3. Michael Dempsey, "Altman: The Empty Staircase and the Chinese Princess," *Film Comment*, September/October 1974, 10.
4. Bordwell, *On the History*, 249.
5. David Bordwell, *The Way Hollywood Tells It: Story and Style in Modern Movies* (Berkeley: University of California Press, 2006), 152.
6. Belton and Tector, "The Bionic Eye," 13.
7. Belton and Tector, "The Bionic Eye," 13.
8. Belton and Tector, "The Bionic Eye," 14.
9. Harmetz, "15th Man," 54.
10. Jonah Horwitz, "The Zoom in the American Cinema, 1958-1969," (unpublished article, 2009), 5-14.
11. Horwitz, "The Zoom in," 29-44.
12. Jonah Horwitz, "The Zoom Lens in Hollywood, from the Pages of *The American Cinematographer*," (unpublished article, 2008), 15.
13. Horwitz, "The Zoom Lens," 27.
14. Hall, *The Zoom*, 108-109.
15. Hall, *The Zoom*, 123.
16. Hall, *The Zoom*, 139-141.
17. Hall, *The Zoom*, 113.
18. Bordwell, Staiger, and Thompson, *Classical Hollywood Cinema*, chapter 3.
19. Peter Krämer, *The New Hollywood: From Bonnie and Clyde to Star Wars* (New York: Wallflower Press, 2005), 81-87.
20. Jacobs, *Hollywood Renaissance*.
21. See Appendix for the list of films selected.
22. John W. Tukey, *Exploratory Data Analysis* (Reading, MA: Addison-Wesley, 1977).
23. This should not be understood as implying those interested in ASLs do not recognize these limitations. Indeed, scholars such as Salt, in "The Numbers Speak," in *Moving into Pictures*, 389-397, use quite sophisticated statistical methods to contextualize and interpret ASLs. There, is, though, debate within the realm of Cinemetrics about the appropriateness of the use of means. Nick Redfern, for instance, also prefers to rely on medians and boxplots, and has argued against Salt's use of means. See Nick Redfern, "Some Notes on Cinemetrics IV," *Research into Film*, November 5, 2010. https://nickredfern.wordpress.com/2010/11/25/some-notes-on-cinemetrics-iv/.
24. R. Lyman Ott and Michael Longnecker, *An Introduction to Statistical Methods and Data Analysis*, 7th ed. (Boston, MA: Cengage Learning, 2010), 106-107.
25. Ott and Longnecker, *An Introduction*, 108.
26. Bernardoni, *The New Hollywood*, 16.
27. See, for instance, Bordwell, *Figures Traced in Light*.
28. Arguably, there is also a mimetic aspect to the use of the zoom for POV shots since, unlike mobile framing, it can enlarge centers of attention without giving the impression of movement provided by parallax. Of course, since objects don't actually grow larger in our field of vision when we stare at them, this characterization seems somewhat inapt.
29. Bordwell, Staiger, and Thompson, *Classical Hollywood Cinema*, 63.
30. Robert Altman, "Cat and Mouse" Commentary Track, *Combat!—Season 1, Campaign 1*, DVD (Chatsworth, CA: Selmur Productions/Image Entertainment, 2004).
31. Bordwell, *The Way Hollywood Tells It*, 134-138.

32. To avoid double-counting, this ratio was calculated by subtracting the aperture zoom types from the aesthetic zoom type category.

33. Helen Keyssar, *Robert Altman's America* (New York: Oxford University Press), 32.

34. Refer to the Introduction's rebuttal of Hall's account of an attentional zoom in *McCabe & Mrs. Miller* for one example of how even the best scholarship might be subject to this tendency.

35. Richard T. Jameson, "'Writin' it down kinda makes me feel better': Robert Altman's *Nashville*," *Movietone News* 43 (September 1975).

36. Bordwell, *The Way Hollywood Tells It*, 120.

37. Bordwell, *The Way Hollywood Tells It*, 152.

38. Michael Wilmington, "Robert Altman and *The Long Goodbye*," in *Robert Altman Interviews*, ed. David Sterritt (Jackson: University Press of Mississippi, 2000), 146.

39. Smith and Jameson, "The Movie You Saw," 164.

40. Smith and Jameson, "The Movie You Saw," 172.

41. "AMC Backstory: *M\*A\*S\*H*," supplementary material on DVD release of *M\*A\*S\*H* (Twentieth Century Fox Home Entertainment, 2001).

42. Bordwell, *On the History*, 248.

43. C. Kirk McClelland, *On Making a Movie: Brewster McCloud* (New York: Signet, 1971).

44. Horwitz, "The Zoom in," 35.

45. Horwitz, "The Zoom Lens," 20.

46. Horwitz, "The Zoom in," 29–34.

47. Thompson, *Altman on Altman*, 77.

48. Mitchell Zuckoff, *Robert Altman: The Oral Biography* (New York: Knopf, 2009), 253.

49. Harry Klomen and Lloyd Michaels with Virginia Wright Wexman, "A Foolish Optimist," in *Robert Altman: Interviews*, ed. David Sterritt (Jackson: University Press of Mississippi, 2000), 113.

50. Connie Byrne and William O. Lopez, "*Nashville*," in *Robert Altman Interviews*, ed. David Sterritt (Jackson: University Press of Mississippi, 2000), 20.

51. Byrne and Lopez, "*Nashville*," 23.

52. American Film Institute, "Robert Altman Seminar," 10.

## Chapter 3

1. Vincent Canby, "Blood, Blasphemy, and Laughs," *New York Times*, February 1, 1970, sec. D.

2. David Denby, "Breakthrough," *Atlantic Monthly*, September 1971, 129. Joseph Morgenstern, "Bloody Funny," *Newsweek*, February 2, 1970, 83. Jan Dawson, "Film Reviews: *M\*A\*S\*H*," *Sight and Sound*, June 1970, 161. Robert Hatch, "Films," *Nation*, February 9, 1970, 158. William Pechter, "M\*A\*S\*H-22," *Commentary*, September 1970, 26. Edward Grossman, "Bloody Popcorn," *Harper's*, December 1970, 34. Sarris, "Films in Focus," 47.

3. Pauline Kael, "Blessed Profanity," *New Yorker*, January 24, 1970, 74.

4. Morgenstern, "Bloody Funny," 83.

5. Hatch, "Films," 158.

6. Sarris, "Films in Focus," 47.

7. Jay Beck, "The Democratic Voice: Altman's Sound Aesthetics in the 1970s," in *A Companion to Robert Altman*, ed. Adrian Danks (John Wiley & Sons, 2015), 184.

8. Rick Altman also employs "deep focus" as a way of describing complex, overlapping sound design in his article, "Deep-Focus Sound: *Citizen Kane* and the Radio Aesthetic," *Quarterly Review of Film and Television* 15, (no. 3) 1994: 1–33. Likewise, Magee, citing Keyssar and Kolker, has suggested that Altman's "complex sound field[s] may be analogous to the deep focus and depth of field characteristic of one of Altman's acknowledged heroes, Jean Renoir." Magee, *Robert Altman's Soundtracks*, 54.

9. André Bazin, *What Is Cinema?*, trans. and ed. Hugh Gray (Berkeley: University of California Press, 2005), 1:35–36.

10. Alan Williams's assessment of Altman's overall approach to sound design, compared to Godard's, as "pseudo-Bazinian" stands out here for its recognition of Altman's negotiation of the oppositional potential of his innovations. At the same time, though, this implies an underestimation of the degree to which the sound design in Altman's films is additive and not wholly assimilable to classical Hollywood's standard aims and practices. Alan Williams, "Godard's Use of Sound," in *Film Sound: Theory and Practice*, ed. Elisabeth Weis and John Belton (New York: Columbia University Press, 1985), 337–338.

11. Jeff Jaeckle, "Introduction: A Brief Primer for Film Dialogue Study," in *Film Dialogue*, ed. Jeff Jaeckle (New York: Columbia University Press, 2013), 1–16. For a complementary approach to the transcription and analysis of overlapping dialogue, developed concurrently with, though independently from, my own, see Francois Thomas, "Orson Welles' Trademark: Overlapping Film Dialogue," trans. Leah Anderst, in *Film Dialogue*, ed. Jeff Jaeckle (New York: Columbia University Press, 2013), 126–139.

12. Michel Chion, *Audio-Vision: Sound on Screen*, ed. and trans. Claudia Gorbman (New York: Columbia University Press, 1994), xxvi.

13. Kozloff, *Overhearing Film Dialogue*.

14. Self, *Altman's Subliminal Reality*, 37, 38.

15. Self, *Altman's Subliminal Reality*, 37.

16. Kozloff, *Overhearing Film Dialogue*, 33.

17. Kozloff, *Overhearing Film Dialogue*, 36.

18. Kozloff, *Overhearing Film Dialogue*, 41.

19. Self, *Altman's Subliminal Reality*, 32.

20. Tomlinson Holman, *Sound for Film and Television*, 2nd ed. (New York: Focal Press, 2001), 107.

21. See, for instance, Michel Chion, "Wasted Words," in *Sound Theory, Sound Practice*, ed. Rick Altman (New York: Routledge, 1992), 110. Chion suggests that Altman makes use of such an approach in *Nashville*.

22. Kozloff, *Overhearing Film Dialogue*, 44.

23. Kozloff, *Overhearing Film Dialogue*, 33.

24. Thomas notes at least one instance in Welles's *Magnificent Ambersons* in which obscured mouths provide the filmmakers with liberty in their handling of overlapping dialogue. Thomas, "Orson Welles' Trademark," 130.

25. Kozloff, *Overhearing Film Dialogue*, 76.

26. Kozloff, *Overhearing Film Dialogue*, 189.

27. Self, *Altman's Subliminal Reality*, 39.

28. McClelland, *On Making a Movie*, 22.

29. McClelland, *On Making a Movie*, 108.

30. McClelland, *On Making a Movie*, 22.

31. McClelland, *On Making a Movie*, 90.
32. McClelland, *On Making a Movie*, 53.
33. C. Kirk McClelland, *On Making a Movie: Brewster McCloud* manuscript, "Eighth Week": 11–12, 1970, Box 23, Robert Altman Archive, University of Michigan.
34. Indeed, by the end of the late 1930s close-miking was the norm in Hollywood sound practice. See James Lastra, *Sound Technology and the American Cinema: Perception, Representation, Modernity* (New York: Columbia, 2000), 142.
35. Holman, *Sound for Film*, 38.
36. Holman, *Sound for Film*, 88.
37. Holman, *Sound for Film*, 91.
38. James E. Webb Jr., "Multi-Channel Dialogue and Effects Recording during Film Production," *American Cinematographer*, April 1979, 368.
39. Bazin, *What Is Cinema?*, 2:26.
40. Patrick McGilligan, *Robert Altman: Jumping off the Cliff: A Biography of the Great American Director* (New York: St. Martin's Press, 1989), 344.
41. Holman, *Sound for Film*, 88.
42. Beck, "Democratic Voice," 192.
43. Bruce Williamson, "Robert Altman," in *Robert Altman Interviews*, ed. David Sterritt (Jackson: University of Mississippi Press, 2000), 56.
44. Zuckoff, *Robert Altman*, 225–230.
45. Klomen and Michaels with Wexman, "A Foolish Optimist," 114.
46. Chion, for instance, places Altman alongside Ophuls, Tati, Fellini, and Godard as directors who want "speech *not* to be clearly understood, but to be perceived as murmuring, chattering, or noise." Michel Chion, *The Voice in Cinema*, ed. and trans. Claudia Gorbman (New York: Columbia University Press, 1999), 81. But as my discussion as well as the accounts of Lombardo and Webb indicate, Altman's attitude toward intelligibility and his mobilization of unintelligible dialogue is much more sophisticated than a desire for incomprehensibility.
47. Beck, "Democratic Voice," 192.
48. Beck, "Democratic Voice," 192.
49. Additionally, the mother's initial dialogue, "I would have beat their ass," delivered to her bottomless daughter, provides the sort of punning humor that Altman's dialogue displays elsewhere. Here, the pun operates on a kind of delay since the duo, and the ass, are not revealed until thirty seconds after the line is delivered. What we have here is Altman and company making a non-narrative function of the sound design only effortfully available, providing a kind of aesthetically motivated virtuosic stroke of vulgarity.
50. Altman, "24 Track Narrative," 104.
51. Sid Levin, "The Art of the Editor: *Nashville*," *Filmmakers Newsletter* 8, no. 10 (1975): 29.
52. Levin, "The Art of the Editor," 30.
53. Jan Stuart, *The Nashville Chronicles: The Making of Robert Altman's Masterpiece* (New York: Simon and Schuster, 2000), 144.
54. Altman, "24 Track Narrative," 113–114.
55. Altman, "24 Track Narrative," 114–115.
56. Altman, "24 Track Narrative," 116.
57. Altman, "24 Track Narrative," 118.
58. Stuart, *The Nashville Chronicles*, 143.

59. Stuart, *The Nashville Chronicles*, 144.
60. Altman, "24 Track Narrative," 119.
61. Altman, "24 Track Narrative," 120.
62. Altman, "24 Track Narrative," 120.
63. Magee interestingly claims that the sound design in the Parthenon sequence is best under-
    stood as "reproducing standard concert documentary sound design, in which a monolithic
    soundtrack suppresses and dominates individual voices . . . leaving the crowd voiceless
    and powerless" and thereby "illustrating the theme of *Nashville*: that . . . popular culture
    controls the American populace." This may or may not be the case, but even if it is it seems
    clear that the sound design in the Parthenon sequence should at the very least be under-
    stood as more or less continuous with previous musical moments rather than as the kind of
    dramatic shift she seems to characterize it as. Magee, *Robert Altman's Soundtracks*, 127.
64. Altman, "24 Track Narrative," 123–124.

## Chapter 4

1. Bordwell, Thompson, and Staiger, *Classical Hollywood Cinema*, 94, 138. For another, invaluable, account of the role and forms of the screenplay in Hollywood cinema see Steven
   Price, *A History of the Screenplay* (London: Palgrave Macmillan, 2013).
2. Billington, "Monarch after M.A.S.H."
3. Denby, "Breakthrough," 128–129.
4. "Show Business," 62.
5. For treatments of improvisation in European cinema and American independent cinema
   that provide useful contextualization with which to better understand the framing
   of Altman's early 1970s improvisations as counter-Hollywood, see Gilles Mouëllic,
   *Improvising Cinema* (Amsterdam University Press, 2014) and J. J. Murphy, *Rewriting Indie
   Cinema: Improvisation, Psychodrama, and the Screenplay* (New York: Columbia University
   Press, 2019).
6. Murphy, *Rewriting Indie Cinema*, 12–13.
7. Steven Maras, *Screenwriting: History, Theory, and Practice* (London: Wallflower Press,
   2009), 21–22.
8. Ian W. Macdonald, *Screenwriting Poetics and the Screen Idea* (New York: Palgrave
   Macmillan, 2013), 219.
9. Virginia Wright Wexman, "The Rhetoric of Cinematic Improvisation," Special issue,
   *Cinema Journal* 20, no. 1 (Fall 1980), 29. For further discussion of the complexity and
   forms of cinematic improvisation and the difficulty of identifying, on the basis of the finished film, what aspects were improvised (and when) as opposed to pre-scripted (and pre-
   scripted through what particular process), see Murphy, *Rewriting Indie Cinema*, 8–13 and
   Berliner, *Hollywood Incoherent*, 181–215.
10. Billington, "Monarch after M.A.S.H."
11. Harmetz, "15th Man," 47, 49.
12. McGilligan, *Robert Altman*, 346.
13. Steven Price, *The Screenplay: Authorship, Theory, and Criticism* (New York: Palgrave
    Macmillan, 2010), 71–72.
14. Harmetz, "15th Man," 49.

15. Harmetz, "15th Man," 52.

16. McGilligan, *Robert Altman*, 340–341.

17. Harmetz, "15th Man," 47.

18. Harmetz, "15th Man," 47.

19. Brian McKay and Robert Altman, "The Presbyterian Church Wager," First Draft, December 7, 1969, pg. 29, Box 1, Folder 9, Robert Altman Papers, 1969–1972, Wisconsin Center for Film and Theater Research.

20. McKay and Altman, "The Presbyterian Church Wager," 100.

21. "McCabe & Mrs. Miller," Revised Final Version, January 19, 1971, pg. 106, Box 48, Robert Altman Archive, University of Michigan.

22. McGilligan, *Robert Altman*, 340.

23. Warren Beatty, interview by Mike Wilmington and Gerald Peary for *The Daily Cardinal* and *The Velvet Light Trap* (Winter 1972/73), 34–35, quoted in Julie Levinson, "The Auteur Renaissance, 1969–1980," in *Acting*, ed. Claudia Springer and Julie R Levinson (London: I.B. Tauris, 2015), 102.

24. McKay and Altman, "The Presbyterian Church Wager," 138.

25. Zuckoff, *Robert Altman*, 211.

26. McKay and Altman, "The Presbyterian Church Wager," 138.

27. Kozloff, *Overhearing Film Dialogue*, 58.

28. Fuller, "Altman on Altman," 199.

29. Is it a coincidence that Roger Wade also dresses like an early twentieth-century working-class Irishman in the film?

30. Leigh Brackett, "The Long Goodbye," Revised Script, June 21, 1972, pgs. 66–74, Box 3, Folder 1, Robert Altman Papers, 1969–1972, Wisconsin Center for Film and Theater Research.

31. Wilmington, "Robert Altman," 137.

32. Elliott Gould interview by Danny Peary, *Bijou* 1, no. 3 (August 1977), 31, quoted in Julie Levinson, "The Auteur Renaissance, 1969–1980," in *Acting*, ed. Claudia Springer and Julie R Levinson (London: I.B. Tauris, 2015), 110.

33. Zuckoff, *Robert Altman*, 285.

34. Zuckoff, *Robert Altman*, 284.

35. Thompson, *Altman on Altman*, 53.

36. Brackett, "The Long Goodbye," 67.

37. McGilligan, *Robert Altman*, 364.

38. Brackett, "The Long Goodbye," 30-A.

39. McGilligan, *Robert Altman*, 364.

40. McGilligan, *Robert Altman*, 363.

41. Wilmington, "Robert Altman," 136.

42. Brackett, "The Long Goodbye," 2.

43. Brackett, "The Long Goodbye," 24-B.

44. Brackett, "The Long Goodbye," 25–26.

45. Del Harvey, "Elliott Gould: Seventies Everyman," *Film Monthly*, June 15, 2000, http://www.filmmonthly.com/Profiles/Articles/EGould/Elliott%20Gould.html (accessed August 6, 2013).

46. Elliott Gould, "Rip Van Marlowe," *The Long Goodbye*, DVD, directed by Robert Altman (Santa Monica, CA: MGM/UA Home Video, 2002).

47. Brackett, "The Long Goodbye," 9.
48. Thompson, *Storytelling*, 20.
49. McClelland, *On Making a Movie*, 1.
50. Zuckoff, *Robert Altman*, 204.
51. Cannon, "Brewster McCloud," 3.
52. McClelland, *On Making a Movie*, 113.
53. Cannon, "Brewster McCloud," 11.
54. Cannon, "Brewster McCloud," 11.
55. Cannon, "Brewster McCloud," 46.
56. Zuckoff, *Robert Altman*, 173.
57. Zuckoff, *Robert Altman*, 174–175.
58. Fuller, "Altman on Altman," 193.
59. Ring Lardner to Ingo Preminger, March 4, 1969, Box 1, Folder 2, Robert Altman Papers, 1969–1972, Wisconsin Center for Film and Theater Research.
60. McGilligan, *Robert Altman*, 319–322.
61. Ring Lardner, Jr., "M*A*S*H," Final Screenplay, February 26, 1969, pgs. 59–60, Box 1, Folder 3, Robert Altman Papers, 1969–1972, Wisconsin Center for Film and Theater Research.
62. McKay and Altman, "The Presbyterian Church Wager," 118–123.
63. Brackett, "The Long Goodbye," 60–62.
64. Lardner, "M*A*S*H," 15–18.
65. Price, *A History*, 188–189.
66. Joan Tewkesbury and Robert Altman. "Thieves Like Us," Script—1st Draft, February 1, 1973, pg. 125, Box 72, Robert Altman Archive, University of Michigan.
67. Tewkesbury and Altman, "Thieves Like Us," 126.
68. Tewkesbury and Altman, "Thieves Like Us," 117–120.
69. Tewkesbury and Altman, "Thieves Like Us," 135–137.
70. See, for instance, Tewkesbury and Altman, "Thieves Like Us," 88–89.
71. McGilligan, *Robert Altman*, 376.
72. Joseph Walsh, "California Split," Script—Edited First Draft, December 18, 1973, pgs. 11A–14E, Box 33, Robert Altman Archive, University of Michigan.
73. Joseph Walsh, "Director and Cast Commentary," *California Split*, DVD, directed by Robert Altman (Culver City, CA: Columbia TriStar Home Entertainment, 2004).
74. Walsh, "California Split," 44A.
75. Walsh, "California Split," 66.
76. Walsh, "California Split," 57.
77. Walsh, "California Split," 73–75.
78. Joan Tewkesbury, "Nashville," Original Screenplay, June 6, 1974, pgs. 10–13, Box 54, Robert Altman Archive, University of Michigan.
79. Tewkesbury, "Nashville," 38.
80. Tewkesbury, "Nashville," 87.
81. Tewkesbury, "Nashville," 88.
82. Macdonald, *Screenwriting Poetics*, 221. Here, Macdonald is paraphrasing J. J. Murphy, "No Room for the Fun Stuff: The Question of the Screenplay in American Indie Cinema," *Journal of Screenwriting* 1, no. 1 (2010), 25–42.

## Chapter 5

1. In the last several years, several media scholars have offered valuable contributions to the account of Altman's earlier career. See, for instance, Magee, *Robert Altman's Soundtracks* and "Part One" of *A Companion to Robert Altman*, ed. Adrian Danks (New York: John Wiley & Sons, 2015).
2. Self, *Altman's Subliminal Reality*, 25.
3. On "zero degree style," see John Thornton Caldwell, *Televisuality: Style, Crisis, and Authority* (New Brunswick, NJ: Rutgers University Press, 1995). On "attenuated continuity," see Jeremy G. Butler, *Television Style* (New York: Routledge, 2010).
4. John Cutts, "M*A*S*H, McCloud, & McCabe: An Interview with Robert Altman," *Films and Filming*, November 1971, 40.
5. McGilligan, *Robert Altman*, 69.
6. Cutts, "M*A*S*H, McCloud, & McCabe," 40.
7. Richard Corliss, "I Admit It, I Didn't Like M*A*S*H," *New York Times*, March 22, 1970.
8. Jan Dawson, "Altman's *Images*," *Sight and Sound*, March 1972, 68.
9. Pauline Kael, "Coming: *Nashville*," *New Yorker*, March 3, 1975, 79.
10. Rick Prelinger, *The Field Guide to Sponsored Films* (San Francisco: National Film Preservation Foundation, 2006), viii.
11. Frank Barhydt, interview with Patrick McGilligan, Patrick McGilligan Papers, Wisconsin Center for Film and Theater Research, Madison, Wisconsin.
12. "That's a Good Question!," *Aperture*, May 1949, 4.
13. Barhydt, interview.
14. Thompson, *Altman on Altman*, 9.
15. Bordwell, Staiger, and Thompson, *Classical Hollywood Cinema*, 117–118.
16. Bordwell, Staiger, and Thompson, *Classical Hollywood Cinema*, 121.
17. Barhydt, interview.
18. "Some Workshop Notes Concerning the Producer and the Customer," *Aperture*, May 1955, 8.
19. "Some Preliminary Thoughts on The Production of Industrial Motion Pictures," *Aperture*, May 1954, 4–5.
20. C. T. Smith, *Measuring the Effectiveness of Your Business Films* (San Francisco: National Film Preservation Foundation, 1962), 13.
21. McGilligan, *Robert Altman*, 72–73.
22. Bordwell, Staiger, and Thompson, *Classical Hollywood Cinema*, Chapter 16.
23. Bordwell, Staiger, and Thompson, *Classical Hollywood Cinema*, 231–233.
24. Bordwell, Staiger, and Thompson, *Classical Hollywood Cinema*, 128.
25. "The Same Old Mistakes," *Aperture*, April 1956, 4.
26. Bordwell, Staiger, and Thompson, *Classical Hollywood Cinema*, chapter 2.
27. Calvin Company, *Ninth Annual 16mm Motion Picture Production Workshop* (Kansas City, MO: The Calvin Company, 1955), 55–57, Box 2, Robert Altman Archive, University of Michigan.
28. Calvin, *Ninth Annual*, 56.
29. Calvin, *Ninth Annual*, 55.
30. Calvin, *Ninth Annual*, 57.
31. McGilligan, *Robert Altman*, 85.

32. Robert Altman, "Director Commentary," *3 Women*, DVD, directed by Robert Altman (Criterion Collection, 2004).

33. Charley Paddock, interview with Patrick McGilligan, Patrick McGilligan Papers, Wisconsin Center for Film and Theater Research, Madison, Wisconsin.

34. Thompson, *Altman on Altman*, 12.

35. Zuckoff, *Robert Altman*, 65.

36. McGilligan, *Robert Altman*, 84.

37. McGilligan, *Robert Altman*, 79.

38. Thompson, *Altman on Altman*, 154.

39. Calvin, *Ninth Annual*, 22.

40. Calvin, *Ninth Annual*, 21.

41. Calvin, *Ninth Annual*, 18.

42. Harmetz, "15th Man," 47.

43. Thompson, *Altman on Altman*, 17.

44. Zuckoff, *Robert Altman*, 166.

45. Smith and Jameson, "The Movie You Saw," 165.

46. "The Master Script," *Aperture*, February 1949, 2.

47. Tony Williams, "From *Alfred Hitchcock Presents* to *Tanner on Tanner*," in *A Companion to Robert Altman*, ed. Adrian Danks (New York: John Wiley & Sons, 2015), 44–67. Nick Hall, "Just a Station on His Way? Altman's Transition from Television to Film," in *A Companion to Robert Altman*, ed. Adrian Danks (New York: John Wiley & Sons, 2015), 68–91.

48. Hall, "Just a Station," 71.

49. Kolker, *A Cinema of Loneliness*, 333–334.

50. Thompson, *Altman on Altman*, xix.

51. Christopher Anderson, *Hollywood TV: The Studio System in the Fifties* (Austin: University of Texas Press, 1994), 251.

52. Anderson, *Hollywood TV*, 251.

53. Horace Newcomb and Robert S. Alley, *The Producer's Medium: Conversations with Creators of American TV* (New York: Oxford University Press, 1983).

54. Newcomb and Alley, *Producer's Medium*, xiv.

55. John W. Ravage, *Television: The Director's Viewpoint* (Boulder, CO: Westview Press, 1978), 7–8.

56. Ravage, *Television: The Director's Viewpoint*, 10.

57. Tino Balio, *United Artists: The Company That Changed the Film Industry* (Madison: University of Wisconsin Press, 1987), 107.

58. "Television," *New York Times*, September 11, 1959.

59. Don Page, "Troubleshooters Premiere," *New York Times* September 6, 1959.

60. McGilligan, *Robert Altman*, 153–154.

61. Fuller, "Altman on Altman," 190.

62. McGilligan, *Robert Altman*, 153.

63. McGilligan, *Robert Altman*, 154.

64. Fuller, "Altman on Altman," 192.

65. Janet Staiger, in her discussion of Hollywood's mode of production, draws on the work of a variety of management scholars to suggest a largely complementary model of three "levels of work"—"strategic management, tactical or technical management, and execution." Bordwell, Staiger, and Thompson, *Classical Hollywood Cinema*, 94.

66. Military Show Proposal by Selig J. Seligman, Undated, box 3, folder 5, Coll. 03405, Selig J. Seligman Collection, American Heritage Center, University of Wyoming.

67. Kay Gardella, "War Is Hell? Not to ABC's Ratings," *Los Angeles Times*, August 21, 1962.

68. Letter of Agreement from American Broadcasting Company to Selmur Productions, Inc., March 23, 1962, box 3, folder 5, Coll. 03405, Selig J. Seligman Collection, American Heritage Center, University of Wyoming.

69. ABC Interdepartment Correspondence from Myrna Dressler to Mr. Thomas Moore, February 29, 1962, box 3, folder 5, Coll. 03405, Selig J. Seligman Collection, American Heritage Center, University of Wyoming.

70. Robert Blees, interview with Patrick McGilligan, Patrick McGilligan Papers, Wisconsin Center for Film and Theater Research, Madison, Wisconsin.

71. Robert Altman, "Cat and Mouse."

72. Robert Altman, "Cat and Mouse."

73. Script Status Reports, April 30, 1962 through November 5, 1962, Combat! folder script status reports, box 9, Coll. MSC0124, Robert Blees Papers, University of Iowa Special Collections.

74. McGilligan, *Robert Altman*, 199.

75. Rick Jason, interview with Patrick McGilligan, Patrick McGilligan Papers, Wisconsin Center for Film and Theater Research, Madison, Wisconsin.

76. Newcomb and Alley, *Producer's Medium*, 15–16.

77. Letter from Robert Blees to Dan Melnick, November 6, 1962, Combat! Selig Seligman folder, box 11, Coll. MSC0124, Robert Blees Papers, University of Iowa Special Collections.

78. Letter from Selig J. Seligman to Mike Foster, June 8, 1962, Combat! Selig Seligman folder, box 11, Coll. MSC0124, Robert Blees Papers, University of Iowa Special Collections.

79. American Film Institute, "Robert Altman Seminar," 11–12.

80. Harmetz, "15th Man," 53.

81. Robert Altman, "Cat and Mouse."

82. McGilligan, *Robert Altman*, 212.

83. Robert Blees, interview with Patrick McGilligan, Patrick McGilligan Papers, Wisconsin Center for Film and Theater Research, Madison, Wisconsin.

84. McGilligan, *Robert Altman*, 206–207.

85. Department of Defense Directive, February 14, 1956, box 3, folder 5, Coll. 03405, Selig J. Seligman Collection, American Heritage Center, University of Wyoming.

86. Robert Blees, interview with Patrick McGilligan, Patrick McGilligan Papers, Wisconsin Center for Film and Theater Research, Madison, Wisconsin.

87. Letter from C. G. Dodge to Selig J. Seligman, August 6, 1962, Combat! Selig Seligman folder, box 11, Coll. MSC0124, Robert Blees Papers, University of Iowa Special Collections.

88. Blees, interview.

89. This is based on a comparison between Final Draft of "Just for the Record," August 7, 1962, Combat! Just for the Record final draft folder, box 11, Coll. MSC0124, Robert Blees Papers, University of Iowa Special Collections and Revised Final Script of "The Celebrity," September 17, 1962, Combat! The Celebrity revised final folder, box 11, Coll. MSC0124, Robert Blees Papers, University of Iowa Special Collections.

90. Tise Vahimagi, "Robert Altman," in *Encyclopedia of Television*, ed. Horace Newcomb (New York: Routledge, 2004), 81.

91. For more, excellent, discussion of *Combat!*'s sound design, see Magee, *Robert Altman's Soundtracks*, 32 and 41.
92. Robert Altman, "Cat and Mouse."
93. Bordwell, Staiger, and Thompson, *Classical Hollywood Cinema*, 373.
94. Thompson, *Altman on Altman*, 27.
95. Zuckoff, *Robert Altman*, 120.
96. McGilligan, *Robert Altman*, 203.
97. Williams, "From *Alfred Hitchcock Presents*," 57 and 59.
98. Thompson, *Altman on Altman*, 34.
99. Williams, "From *Alfred Hitchcock Presents*," 59.
100. Jo Davidsmeyer, *Combat!: A Viewer's Companion to the World War II Series*, Rev. ed. (Tallevast, FL: Strange New Worlds, 2002), 30.
101. Davidsmeyer, *Combat!*, 30.

## Conclusion

1. For an overarching account of Altman's career in light of shifting distribution strategies in the film industry, see Wyatt, "Economic Constraints/Economic Opportunities," 51–67.
2. Zuckoff, *Robert Altman*, 488.
3. As one particularly relevant example, scholarly accounts of American filmmaking in the early 1970s have emphasized that era's exceptionally tumultuous fluctuations in cinematic form, pointing to directors like Hellman and Hopper, whose experimentation seems much stronger and stranger than Altman's. In doing so, though, they consistently struggle to describe the relationship between this cinema and Hollywood. Elsaesser, for instance, frames it as a "push-pull model" where "the question . . . is whether the non-classical, romantic, European, baroque aesthetics, as well as the antagonistic, critical, and countercultural energies manifested in the first New Hollywood were a genuine, if short-lived and aborted alternative, or whether the misfits, rebels and outsiders were necessary for the 'system' to first adjust and then renew itself." He acknowledges that this model might be "too neat—or cynical—an opposition," and I tend to agree, if by "system" he intends to indicate the same formulation of principles. One advantage of the elaborative account is that it acknowledges and works with the possibility that this formulation is always in flux. See Elsaesser, "American Auteur Cinema," 44.

# Bibliography

Academy of Motion Picture Arts and Sciences. "Academy Awards Database—AMPAS." http://awardsdatabase.oscars.org/ampas_awards/DisplayMain.jsp?curTime=1262832683008 (accessed January 7, 2009).

Altman, Rick. "24 Track Narrative? Robert Altman's *Nashville*." *Cinémas: Revue d'études cinématographiques* 1, no. 3 (1991): 102–125.

Altman, Rick. "Deep-Focus Sound: *Citizen Kane* and the Radio Aesthetic." *Quarterly Review of Film and Television* 15, no. 3 (1994): 1–33.

Altman, Rick. "Dickens, Griffith, and Film Theory Today." In *Classical Hollywood Cinema: The Paradigm Wars*, edited by Jane Gaines, 9–47. Durham, NC: Duke University Press, 2002.

Altman, Robert, dir. *Brewster McCloud*. 1970. Warner Bros., 2010. DVD.

Altman, Robert, dir. *California Split*. 1974. Columbia TriStar Home Entertainment, 2004. DVD.

Altman, Robert. "Cat and Mouse Commentary." Supplementary material on DVD release of *Combat!—Season 1, Campaign 1*. Selmur Productions/Image Entertainment, 2004.

Altman, Robert. "Director Commentary." Supplementary material on DVD release of *3 Women*. Criterion Collection, 2004.

Altman, Robert, dir. *Images*. 1972. MGM, 2003. DVD.

Altman, Robert, dir. *The Long Goodbye*. 1973. MGM, 2002. DVD.

Altman, Robert, dir. *M\*A\*S\*H*. 1970; 20th Century Fox, 2004. DVD.

Altman, Robert, dir. *McCabe & Mrs. Miller*. 1971; Warner Bros., 2002. DVD.

Altman, Robert, dir. *Nashville*. 1975. Paramount, 2000. DVD.

Altman, Robert, dir. *Thieves Like Us*. 1974. MGM, 2007. DVD.

"AMC Backstory: *M\*A\*S\*H*." Supplementary material on DVD release of *M\*A\*S\*H*. Twentieth Century Fox Home Entertainment, 2001.

American Film Institute. "Robert Altman Seminar." *Dialogue on Film*, February 1975.

Anderson, Christopher. *Hollywood TV: The Studio System in the Fifties*. Austin: University of Texas Press, 1994.

Ashby, Hal, dir. *Harold and Maude*. 1971. Paramount, 2000. DVD.

Balio, Tino. *United Artists: The Company That Changed the Film Industry*. Madison: University of Wisconsin Press, 1987.

Barratt, Daniel. "Twist Blindness." In *Puzzle Films: Complex Storytelling in Contemporary Cinema*, edited by Warren Buckland, 62–86. Malden, MA: Wiley-Blackwell, 2009.

Bazin, André. *What Is Cinema?* Vol. 1. Translated and edited by Hugh Gray. Berkeley: University of California Press, 2005.

Bazin, André. *What Is Cinema?* Vol. 2. Translated and edited by Hugh Gray. Berkeley: University of California Press, 2005.

Beck, Jay. "The Democratic Voice: Altman's Sound Aesthetics in the 1970s." In *A Companion to Robert Altman*, edited by Adrian Danks, 184–209. John Wiley & Sons, 2015.

Belton, John, and Lyle Tector. "The Bionic Eye: The Aesthetics of the Zoom." *Film Comment*, September/October 1980.

Berliner, Todd. *Hollywood Incoherent: Narration in Seventies Cinema*. Austin: University of Texas Press, 2010.

Bernardoni, James. *The New Hollywood: What the Movies Did with the New Freedoms of the Seventies*. Jefferson, NC: McFarland and Company, 1991.

Billington, Michael. "The Monarch after M.A.S.H." *The Times of London*, February 4, 1971.

Bordwell, David. *Figures Traced in Light: On Cinematic Staging*. Berkeley: University of California Press, 2005.

Bordwell, David. *The Films of Carl-Theodor Dreyer*. Berkeley: University of California Press, 1981.

Bordwell, David. *Narration in the Fiction Film*. Madison: University of Wisconsin Press, 1985.

Bordwell, David. "Neo-Structuralist Narratology and the Functions of Filmic Storytelling." In *Narrative across Media: The Languages of Storytelling*, edited by Marie-Laure Ryan, 203–219. Lincoln: University of Nebraska Press, 2004.

Bordwell, David. *On the History of Film Style*. Cambridge, MA: Harvard University Press, 1997.

Bordwell, David. *Poetics of Cinema*. New York: Routledge, 2008.

Bordwell, David. *The Way Hollywood Tells It: Story and Style in Modern Movies*. Berkeley: University of California Press, 2006.

Bordwell, David, Janet Staiger, and Kristin Thompson. *The Classical Hollywood Cinema: Film Style and Mode of Production to 1960*. New York: Columbia University Press, 1985.

Buckland, Warren. *Directed by Steven Spielberg: Poetics of the Contemporary Blockbuster*. New York: Continuum, 2006.

Butler, Jeremy G. *Television Style*. New York: Routledge, 2010.

Byrne, Connie, and William O. Lopez. "*Nashville*." In *Robert Altman Interviews*, edited by David Sterritt, 19–33. Jackson: University Press of Mississippi, 2000.

Caldwell, John Thornton. *Televisuality: Style, Crisis, and Authority in American Television*. New Brunswick, NJ: Rutgers University Press, 1995.

Canby, Vincent. "Blood, Blasphemy, and Laughs." *New York Times*, February 1, 1970, sec. D.

Carroll, Noël. *The Philosophy of Horror*. New York: Routledge, 1990.

Chion, Michel. *Audio-Vision: Sound on Screen*. Edited and Translated by Claudia Gorbman. New York: Columbia University Press, 1994.

Chion, Michel. *The Voice in Cinema*. Edited and Translated by Claudia Gorbman. New York: Columbia University Press, 1999.

Chion, Michel. "Wasted Words." In *Sound Theory, Sound Practice*, edited by Rick Altman, 104–112. New York: Routledge, 1992.

Coleman, John. "C*H*I*P*S." *New Statesman*, January 17, 1975.

Coleman, John. "Marlowe and His Society." *New Statesman*, November 2, 1973.

*Combat!—Season 1*. Selmur Productions/Image Entertainment, 2004. DVD.

Cook, David A. *Lost Illusions: American Cinema in the Shadow of Watergate and Vietnam, 1970–1979*. Berkeley: University of California Press, 2000.

Corliss, Richard. "I Admit It, I Didn't Like *M*A*S*H*." *New York Times*, March 22, 1970.

Crafton, Donald. "Pie and Chase: Gag, Spectacle, and Narrative in Slapstick Comedy." In *The Cinema of Attractions Reloaded*, edited by Wanda Strauven, 355–364. Amsterdam: Amsterdam University Press, 2006.

Crofts, Stephen. "Authorship and Hollywood." In *The Oxford Guide to Film Studies*, edited by John Hill and Pamela Church Gibson, 310–324. New York: Oxford University Press, 1998.

Cutts, John. "M*A*S*H, McCloud & McCabe: An Interview with Robert Altman." *Films and Filming*, November 1971.

Danks, Adrian, ed. *A Companion to Robert Altman*. New York: John Wiley & Sons, 2015.

Davidsmeyer, Jo. *Combat! A Viewer's Companion to the World War II Series*. Rev. ed. Tallevast, FL: Strange New Worlds, 2002.

Dawson, Jan. "Altman's Images." *Sight and Sound*, March 1972.

Dawson, Jan. "Film Reviews: *M*A*S*H*." *Sight and Sound*, June 1970.

Dempsey, Michael. "Altman: The Empty Staircase and the Chinese Princess." *Film Comment*, September/October 1974.

Denby, David. "Breakthrough." *Atlantic Monthly*, September 1971.

Elsaesser, Thomas. "American Auteur Cinema: The Last—or First—Picture Show?" In *The Last Great American Picture Show*, edited by Thomas Elsaesser, Alexander Horwath, and Noel King, 37–69. Amsterdam: Amsterdam University Press, 2004.

Elsaesser, Thomas. "The Pathos of Failure: American Film in the 1970s: Notes on the Unmotivated Hero [1975]." In *The Last Great American Picture Show*, edited by Thomas Elsaesser, Alexander Horwath, and Noel King, 279–292. Amsterdam: Amsterdam University Press, 2004.

Fuller, Graham. "Altman on Altman." In *Robert Altman Interviews*, edited by David Sterritt, 188–210. Jackson: University Press of Mississippi, 2000.

Gardella, Kay. "War Is Hell? Not to ABC's Ratings." *Los Angeles Times*, August 21, 1962.

Gaut, Berys. *A Philosophy of Cinematic Art*. Cambridge: Cambridge University Press, 2010.

Gibson, James J. *The Ecological Approach to Visual Perception*. Boston, MA: Houghton Mifflin, 1979.

Gould, Elliott. "Rip Van Marlowe." Supplementary material on DVD release of *The Long Goodbye*. Santa Monica, CA: MGM/UA Home Video, 2002.

Grossman, Edward. "Bloody Popcorn." *Harper's*, December 1970.

Hall, Nick. "Just a Station on His Way? Altman's Transition from Television to Film." In *A Companion to Robert Altman*, edited by Adrian Danks, 68–91. John Wiley & Sons, 2015.

Hall, Nick. *The Zoom: Drama at the Touch of a Lever*. New Brunswick, NJ: Rutgers University Press, 2018.

Harmetz, Aljean. "The 15th Man Who Was Asked to Direct *M\*A\*S\*H* (and Did) Makes a Peculiar Western." *New York Times Magazine*, June 20, 1971.

Harvey, Del. "Elliott Gould: Seventies Everyman." *Film Monthly*, June 15, 2000. http://www.filmmonthly.com/Profiles/Articles/EGould/Elliott%20Gould.html (accessed August 6, 2013).

Hatch, Robert. "Films." *Nation*, February 9, 1970.

Holman, Tomlinson. *Sound for Film and Television*. 2nd ed. New York: Focal Press, 2001.

Horwitz, Jonah. "The Zoom in the American Cinema, 1958–1969." Unpublished article, 2009.

Horwitz, Jonah. "The Zoom Lens in Hollywood, from the Pages of the *American Cinematographer*." Unpublished article, 2008.

Jacobs, Diane. *Hollywood Renaissance*. New York: Dell, 1980.

Jaeckle, Jeff. "Introduction: A Brief Primer for Film Dialogue Study." In *Film Dialogue*, edited by Jeff Jaeckle, 1–16. New York: Columbia University Press, 2013.

Jameson, Richard T. "'Writin' it down kinda makes me feel better': Robert Altman's *Nashville*." *Movietone News*, September 1975.

Kael, Pauline. "Blessed Profanity." *New Yorker*, January 24, 1970.

Kael, Pauline. "Coming: *Nashville*." *New Yorker*, March 3, 1975.

Kael, Pauline. "Round Up the Usual Suspects." *New Yorker*, December 23, 1972.

Kael, Pauline. "Spawn of the Movies." *New Yorker*, January 9, 1971.

Keyssar, Helen. *Robert Altman's America*. New York: Oxford University Press, 1991.

Klomen, Harry, and Lloyd Michaels with Virginia Wright Wexman. "A Foolish Optimist." In *Robert Altman Interviews*, edited by David Sterritt, 107–116. Jackson: University Press of Mississippi, 2000.

Kolker, Robert. *A Cinema of Loneliness*. 3rd ed. New York: Oxford University Press, 2000.

Kovács, András Bálint. *Screening Modernism: European Art Cinema, 1950–1980*. University of Chicago Press, 2007.

Kozloff, Sarah. *Overhearing Film Dialogue*. Berkeley: University of California Press, 2000.

Krämer, Peter. *The New Hollywood: From Bonnie and Clyde to Star Wars*. New York: Wallflower, 2005.

Lastra, James. *Sound Technology and the American Cinema: Perception, Representation, Modernity*. New York: Columbia, 2000.

Levin, Sid. "The Art of the Editor: *Nashville*." *Filmmakers Newsletter* 8, no. 10 (1975): 29–33.

Levinson, Julie R. "The Auteur Renaissance." In *Acting*, edited by Claudia Springer and Julie R. Levinson, 95–119. London: I.B. Tauris, 2015.

Lewis, Jon. *Whom God Wishes to Destroy . . . : Francis Coppola and the New Hollywood*. Durham, NC: Duke University Press, 1995.

Macdonald, Ian W. *Screenwriting Poetics and the Screen Idea*. New York: Palgrave Macmillan, 2013.

Magee, Gayle Sherwood. *Robert Altman's Soundtracks: Film, Music, and Sound from M\*A\*S\*H to a Prairie Home Companion*. New York: Oxford University Press, 2000.

Maras, Steven. *Screenwriting: History, Theory, and Practice*. London: Wallflower Press, 2009.

"The Master Script." *Aperture*, February 1949.

"*McCabe and Mrs. Miller* (review)." *Media and Methods*, October 1971.

McClelland, C. Kirk. *On Making a Movie: Brewster McCloud*. New York: Signet, 1971.

McGilligan, Patrick. *Robert Altman: Jumping off the Cliff: A Biography of the Great American Director*. New York: St. Martin's Press, 1989.

Morgenstern, Joseph. "Bloody Funny." *Newsweek*, February 2, 1970.

Mouëllic, Gilles. *Improvising Cinema*. Amsterdam: Amsterdam University Press, 2014.

Murphy, Arthur D. "*McCabe and Mrs. Miller* (review)." *Variety*, June 30, 1971.

Murphy, Arthur D. "Review of *California Split*." *Variety*, August 7, 1974.

Murphy, J. J. "No Room for the Fun Stuff: The Question of the Screenplay in American Indie Cinema." *Journal of Screenwriting* 1, no. 1 (2010): 25–42.

Murphy, J. J. *Rewriting Indie Cinema: Improvisation, Psychodrama, and the Screenplay*. New York: Columbia University Press, 2019.

Neale, Steve. "'The Last Good Time We Ever Had?': Revising the Hollywood Renaissance." In *Contemporary American Cinema*, edited by Linda Ruth Williams and Michael Hammond, 90–92. London: McGraw Hill, 2006.

Newcomb, Horace, and Robert S. Alley. *The Producer's Medium: Conversations with Creators of American TV*. New York: Oxford University Press, 1983.

Ott, R. Lyman, and Michael Longnecker. *An Introduction to Statistical Methods and Data Analysis*. 7th ed. Boston, MA: Cengage Learning, 2010.

Page, Don. "Troubleshooters Premiere." *New York Times*, September 6, 1959.

Patrick McGilligan Papers. Wisconsin Center for Film and Theater Research, Madison.

Peary, Danny. "Danny Peary Interviews Elliott Gould on Barbra, Brooklyn, Ingmar Bergman, Bert Lahl; M\*A\*S\*H and . . . " *Bijou* 1, no. 3 (August 1977): 31.

Pechter, William. "M\*A\*S\*H-22." *Commentary*, September 1970.

Prelinger, Rick. *The Field Guide to Sponsored Films*. San Francisco: National Film Preservation Foundation, 2006.

Price, Steven. *A History of the Screenplay*. London: Palgrave Macmillan, 2013.

Price, Steven. *The Screenplay: Authorship, Theory, and Criticism*. New York: Palgrave Macmillan, 2010.

Ramaeker, Paul. "A New Kind of Movie: Style and Form in Hollywood Cinema 1965—1988." PhD diss., University of Wisconsin-Madison, 2002.

Ravage, John W. *Television: The Director's Viewpoint*. Boulder, CO: Westview Press, 1978.

Redfern, Nick. "Some Notes on Cinemetrics IV." Research into Film. November 5, 2010. https://nickredfern.wordpress.com/2010/11/25/some-notes-on-cinemetrics-iv/.

Robert Altman Archive. University of Michigan Special Collections.

Robert Altman Papers. Wisconsin Center for Film and Theater Research, Madison.

Robert Blees Papers. University of Iowa Special Collections.

Ryan, Marie-Laure. "Introduction." In *Narrative across Media: The Languages of Storytelling*, edited by Marie-Laure Ryan, 1–40. Lincoln: University of Nebraska Press, 2004.

Salt, Barry. *Film Style and Technology: History and Analysis*. London: Starword, 1983.

Salt, Barry. *Moving into Pictures*. London: Starword, 2006.

"The Same Old Mistakes." *Aperture*, April 1965.

Sarris, Andrew. "Films in Focus." *Village Voice*, December 24, 1970.

Schatz, Thomas. *Old Hollywood/New Hollywood: Ritual, Art, and Industry*. Ann Arbor: University of Michigan Research Press, 1983.

Self, Robert T. *Robert Altman's Subliminal Reality*. Minneapolis: University of Minnesota Press, 2002.

Selig, J. Seligman Collection. American Heritage Center, University of Wyoming.

Shiel, Mark. "American Cinema 1965–1970." In *Contemporary American Cinema*, edited by Linda Ruth Williams and Michael Hammond, 12–13. London: McGraw Hill, 2006.

"Show Business: Creation in Chaos." *Time*, July 13, 1970.

Smith, C. T. *Measuring the Effectiveness of Your Business Films*. San Francisco: National Film Preservation Foundation, 1962.

Smith, Gavin, and Richard T. Jameson. "The Movie You Saw Is the Movie We're Going to Make." In *Robert Altman Interviews*, edited by David Sterritt, 163–181. Jackson: University Press of Mississippi, 2000.

Smith, Murray. "Theses on the Philosophy of Hollywood History." In *Contemporary Hollywood Cinema*, edited by Steve Neale and Murray Smith, 3–20. London: Routledge, 1998.

"Some Preliminary Thoughts on The Production of Industrial Motion Pictures." *Aperture*, May 1954.

"Some Workshop Notes Concerning the Producer and the Customer." *Aperture*, May 1955.

Sternberg, Meir. "Reconceptualizing Narratology. Arguments for a Functionalist and Constructivist Approach to Narrative." *Enthymema* 4 (2011): 35–50.

Stuart, Jan. *The Nashville Chronicles: The Making of Robert Altman's Masterpiece*. New York: Simon and Schuster, 2000.

"Television." *New York Times*, September 11, 1959.

"That's a Good Question!" *Aperture*, May 1949.

Thomas, Francois. "Orson Welles' Trademark: Overlapping Film Dialogue." Translated by Leah Anderst. In *Film Dialogue*, edited by Jeff Jaeckle, 126–139. New York: Columbia University Press, 2013.

Thompson, David. *Altman on Altman*. London: Faber and Faber Limited, 2006.

Thompson, Kristin. *Breaking the Glass Armor: Neoformalist Film Analysis*. Princeton, NJ: Princeton University Press, 1986.

Thompson, Kristin. *Storytelling in the New Hollywood*. Cambridge, MA: Harvard University Press, 2009.

Tsivian, Yuri. "Movie Measurement and Study Tool Database." Cinemetrics. November 27, 2019. http://www.cinemetrics.lv/index.php.

Tukey, John W. *Exploratory Data Analysis*. Reading, MA: Addison-Wesley, 1977.

Vahimagi, Tise. "Robert Altman." In *Encyclopedia of Television*, edited by Horace Newcomb, 80–83. New York: Fitzroy Dearborn, 2004.

Wagner, Geoffrey. *The Novel and the Cinema*. Rutherford, NJ: Fairleigh Dickinson University Press, 1975.

Walsh, Joseph. "Director and Cast Commentary." Supplementary material on DVD release of *California Split*. Columbia TriStar Home Entertainment, 2004.

Webb, James E., Jr. "Multi-Channel Dialogue and Effects Recording during Film Production." *American Cinematographer*, April 1979.

Wexman, Virginia Wright. "The Rhetoric of Cinematic Improvisation." *Cinema Journal* 20, no. 1 (Fall 1980): 29–41.

Wexman, Virginia Wright, and Gretchen Bisplinghoff. *Robert Altman: A Guide to References and Resources*. Boston, MA: G.K. Hall, 1984.

Williams, Alan. "Godard's Use of Sound." In *Film Sound: Theory and Practice*, edited by Elisabeth Weis and John Belton, 332–345. New York: Columbia University Press, 1985.

Williams, Tony. "From *Alfred Hitchcock Presents* to *Tanner on Tanner*." In *A Companion to Robert Altman*, edited by Adrian Danks, 44–67. New York: John Wiley & Sons, 2015.

Williamson, Bruce. "Robert Altman." In *Robert Altman Interviews*, edited by David Sterritt, 34–62. Jackson: University Press of Mississippi.

Wilmington, Michael. "Robert Altman and *The Long Goodbye*." In *Robert Altman Interviews*, edited by David Sterritt, 131–151. Jackson: University Press of Mississippi, 2000.

Wilmington, Michael, and Gerald Peary. "Interview with Warren Beatty." *The Velvet Light Trap* (Winter 1972/1973): 32–36.

Wyatt, Justin. "Economic Constraints/Economic Opportunities: Robert Altman as Auteur." *Velvet Light Trap* (Fall 1996): 51–67.

Zimmerman, Paul D. "Bowie and Keechie." *Newsweek*, February 18, 1974.

Zimmerman, Paul D. "Lovers and Phantoms." *Newsweek*, January 15, 1973.

Zimmerman, Paul D. "Return of Philip Marlowe." *Newsweek*, October 29, 1973.

Zuckoff, Mitchell. *Robert Altman: The Oral Biography*. New York: Knopf, 2009.

# Index